OF ANGELS, BEASTS, AND PLAGUES

OF ANGELS, BEASTS, AND PLAGUES

The Message of Revelation for a New Millennium

Kenneth H. Maahs

With a Foreword by Tony Campolo

Judson Press

Valley Forge

Library of Congress Cataloging-in-Publication Data
Maahs, Kenneth H.
    Of angels, beasts, and plagues : the message of Revelation for a new millennium / Kenneth H. Maahs.
        p. cm.
    Includes bibliographical references (p.).
    ISBN 0-8170-1299-0 (alk. paper)
    1. Bible. N.T. Revelation – Commentaries.   I. Title.
BS2825.3.M22 1999
228'.07 — dc21   98-32059

Printed in the U.S.A.
06   05   04   03   02   01   00   99
10   9   8   7   6   5   4   3   2   1

To
those churches that patiently and lovingly allowed me
to develop these thoughts as we jointly
sought the Revelation of Jesus Christ for our own lives
and
my wife, Vivian, and our beloved children,
without whose understanding and gentle indulgence
this work would not have been possible.

CONTENTS

FOREWORD

When I was a teenager, the Revelation of Saint John the Divine provided me with endless fascination. I believed the book to be a coded message that, for those who understood it, could explain current events and even predict the future. For me it was a kind of Christian version of the prophecies of Nostradamus. I thought that if I just could make sense of the beasts, broken seals, candlesticks, and other oddities that pervade the book, I would be able to play one-upmanship with those lesser types who were not able to discern "the signs of the times."

Whenever the minister of my church wanted to build up attendance at the Sunday evening services, all he had to do was announce that he would be doing a series on the book of Revelation. I was not the only one who wanted guided excursions into that exotic world of the seven churches of Asia, the whore of Babylon, and the awesome Antichrist. These Sunday evening services held the promise for everyone that our pastor would let us in on an array of "deep secrets," not the least of which would be a good reading about when to expect the second coming of Christ. After we heard our pastor's sermons, it seemed so obviously clear that we were living in the last days and that the Antichrist was already among us. The colorful charts that he used as he showed us "God's Plan for the Ages" left us deeply impressed with how fortunate we were to have a minister who was able to discern "the signs of the times."

At first we were informed that the Antichrist was Hitler and that the German army was the terrible "Army of the North" that God's people would have to battle at Armageddon. But then Hitler failed to turn out as expected, and my minister and others had to come up with another Antichrist...and another...and then another. There always seemed to be a new Antichrist when an earlier designation no longer measured up.

Now at my ripe old age of sixty-one, I have lived long enough and listened to enough prophecy preaching on the Antichrist to have seen Hitler replaced by Stalin, who in turn was replaced by Khrushchev, who in turn was replaced by Kissinger, who in turn was replaced by

Gorbachev. For certain Religious Right types who are into Antichrist "spotting," President Clinton has, of late, come to fit the bill. When in doubt, these prophecy preachers can always be counted on to fall back on "old reliable" and reannounce the pope as the designated heavy hitter for this evil role.

After a while even a slow learner like me began to be suspicious as to whether or not these prophecy preachers really knew what they were talking about. Like Martin Luther, I became just plain cynical about all this kind of prophecy preaching from the book of Revelation; I decided that this last book of the Bible really was not worth my time and energy. I came to the conclusion that if, according to the Bible, Jesus himself did not know the date of the second coming (Mark 13:32), then it was not likely that Hal Lindsey and his company of would-be followers and imitators had any better insights on the matter. Eventually, I gave up on the book of Revelation and considered it irrelevant to anything that is meaningful for Christians in our contemporary society. And that was my loss!

Things are different now. In the not-too-distant past, some fellow Christians taught me a whole new way of reading the book of Revelation. They introduced me to the idea that this book was written in a very specialized genre common in the ancient world, called *apocalyptic literature*. According to this approach to understanding the book, there is still a need for decoding. But rather than understanding Revelation as a collection of prophecies of futuristic events, I came to see that this book could be a useful instrument for understanding what God wants to tell his people in *every* age, including our own. In coming to read the book of Revelation as apocalyptic literature, I found that I could learn from it crucial lessons about how to live, what to guard against in my everyday life, and how to understand what it means to live out Christianity as a countercultural lifestyle. Also, I have come to see that this book has a great deal to say to the church.

What John said about the seven churches of Asia back there and then can be used as a typology to evaluate and understand churches at any time or place over the last two thousand years of church history and especially our own. For instance, his description of the backslidden church at Ephesus gives insights and warning to every backslidden church throughout the history of Christendom. And what Revelation says about the church at Thyatira reminds us that an attempt to be tolerant of other forms of religion can easily compromise the essence of the gospel. The description and prescriptions that John gave to the church at Smyrna were not only relevant to a persecuted church in ancient Asia but are relevant to persecuted churches in our own time, whether they be in Nepal or Burma or China. It does not take much imagination to realize that when John addressed the church at Laodicea, he was saying things that lukewarm churches in our own affluent society ought to heed. And when he told about what was happening to the church at Sardis, he also was describing what is wrong with all too many of our own churches here in America. (So often the rest of the world thinks that our big-time American churches are energized by the dynamism of the Holy Spirit, when in reality many of them are simply hyperactive, efficiently programmed organizations devoid of spiritual aliveness.) The church at Philadelphia, as described in the book of Revelation, is like all of those churches throughout history that have heeded the call of Christ and lived up to the missionary opportunities that God has laid before them, while the church at Pergamum represents all of those churches located in seats of political power that have yielded to the heresies that come with being in places where "cultural religion" is common and encouraged.

Kenneth Maahs is also one who views the book of Revelation as apocalyptic literature. In doing so, he finds in the dramatic imagery of John a host of messages that are brilliantly relevant to contemporary Christianity. In this commentary, Maahs explains how the book of Revelation sets forth a countercultural lifestyle that raises serious questions about the nature of our discipleship. This radical lifestyle assumes that we view the societal system in which we presently live as being in need of radical transformation and that those who would be Christians in this world are called to commit themselves to living out the values of a countervailing "kingdom." This is particularly true, as Maahs explains, in the last few chapters of John's writings.

The last part of the book of Revelation is about two cities. One city is Jerusalem, which, for those who see this book as apocalyptic literature, represents the kingdom of God. The other city is Babylon, which stands for the dominant culture in which the people of God, who are ambassadors of God's kingdom, must live. At the time John wrote all this, the dominant culture was the Roman Empire. Thus, the early Christians were able to figure out from reading the book of Revelation a great deal about the problems and the struggles that John saw waiting for them in their world. For those of us living in America at the end of the second millennium, Babylon obviously refers to our own societal system. For us, America is the Babylon that John describes, and to be Christian is to live in opposition to what our own Babylon is trying to do to us as it calls us to embrace its values and way of life.

We learn from Revelation that Babylon, both then and now, is a societal system that calls all people to worship it. What this means for us is that when jingoistic nationalism plays itself out in America, we may, at times, be called upon to render a kind of worship of what our nation is all about. When we observe the chauvinism that is commonly a part of the American psyche, we may have to face the fact that the cult of nationalism can become for us, as it did for those in the early church, a form of idolatry. Distorted patriotism can lead us away from giving Christ the priority due him.

Babylon is also revealed in the book of Revelation as a society that self-destructs through overconsumption, both of its own resources and the resources that it takes from other nations. It is seen as a city that overindulges in luxuries while lesser nations suffer privation. When we as Americans read this account of Babylon, we are apt to have an eerie sensation that what we are being given is a picture of ourselves. It is easy to make a correlation between the ways of Babylon and our own affluent lifestyles. It does not take much imagination to figure out that our wasteful exploitation of the world's resources is already affecting us and the rest of those who share this planet with us. We realize from John's words that the Roman Empire is not the only Babylon, but America is Babylon too.

Finally, we are told in the book of Revelation that Babylon will one day fall. To the ancient Christians who first read this prediction, the words must have seemed unbelievable. It must have been hard for them to believe that *their* Babylon, the Roman Empire, would ever collapse. To them, Rome must have seemed invincible and destined to be everlasting. But fall it did, even as all Babylons must eventually fall.

This, of course, should be ample warning to us Americans. We may sometimes find it inconceivable that the America we love and enjoy has been sealed with the same destiny that has awaited all the Babylons of this world. But we ought to deduce from John's writings that America is only the latest and the greatest of the Babylons of history and, as he predicts, it too will pass away.

In the book of Revelation, we are allowed to view what will happen when our American Babylon falls. John tells us that there will be two reactions. One reaction will be that of the merchants who have made their wealth in their dealings with Babylon. The merchants weep as they view the fall of the great city. They weep because everything into which they had invested their lives has gone up in smoke. Everything they had worked for disappears.

The other reaction is that of the angels. They rejoice and shout

"Hallelujah" when they see the fall of Babylon. They celebrate because they know that the "whore," who had seduced so many into its luxuries and away from faithfulness to God, is no more. They realize that the hypnotic power that Babylon once exercised over people has been broken. The angels are thrilled because the people of God are at last freed from the tyranny of Babylon and are now free to live out joyful lives as citizens of a new kingdom — the New Jerusalem. Jerusalem is the kingdom of God that John sees coming down from heaven and breaking loose in history.

The apocalyptic message of the book of Revelation forces us to ask an array of existential questions. First and foremost is the question about our own personal future. When the fall of our Babylon comes, with whom will we stand? Will we stand with the merchants who weep because we likewise have invested our lives in the dominant society that is being abolished? Are we a people who have been so seduced by the affluence of the American Babylon that when this great whore comes to an end, everything that has been precious to us will also end? Are we a people who have allowed our national loyalties to be transformed into a patriotic idolatry that confuses America with the kingdom of God?

The hope of the writer of the book of Revelation is that on the awesome day when Babylon falls, we will not have lost what is important to us; our treasures will have been laid up in another kingdom. In light of John's apocalyptic message, all of us should be seriously evaluating our lives to see whether or not this will be true. We should be asking if we have truly established citizenship in that countercultural society called Jerusalem or if we still belong to that doomed city called Babylon. We should all be asking ourselves if the lifestyle to which we are committed is one that will warrant our Lord's saying to us in that hour of judgment of which John speaks, "Well done, thou good and faithful servants."

Reading the book of Revelation can be tough going, but we should read it because it raises the ultimate challenges of our lives. We should read Kenneth Maahs's book on Revelation because it equips us with invaluable interpretive tools that will take much of the tough out of the going and will leave us better able to meet the challenges we face in trying to live godly lives in American Babylon.

TONY CAMPOLO

PREFACE

This volume was conceived in both a labor of love and a return to my own roots. I had been a Christian for less than two years when I was first captivated by the message of the wonderful book of Revelation. From that youthful point in my life to the present, the Revelation has never been far from my studies, interests, or teaching ministry. Always it has been near to disturb, challenge, and probe my very Christian identity.

When I was just sixteen and yet a new Christian living in Tucson, Arizona, a noted Bible teacher came to a local high school and held evening classes on the book of Revelation. Charles Woodbridge held me absolutely spellbound for months, until finally the Revelation was etched indelibly into my consciousness as an essential, formative element of my youthful faith. For this I will always be grateful, even though later studies gradually led me in directions divergent from his interpretation of the Revelation.

Subsequently, my educational pursuits allowed me to further this study with many other scholars who have each added depth and girth to my understanding of the Revelation. I would be remiss, however, were I not to mention specifically the name of Dr. George Ladd, with whom I studied at Fuller Seminary; he first challenged my understanding of Revelation from the perspective of the ancient, historic Christian interpretation of the book. Nor can I forget the course taken with Dr. Bruce Metzger at Princeton Seminary; it was he who first triggered insights that would eventually lead me to my present understanding of this book. Finally, Dr. J. Massyngberde Ford of the University of Notre Dame encouraged both a deeper sense of mystery and daring creativity in my study of the Revelation, as well as a keener appreciation of its kinship to the apocalyptic genre of literature. I gladly confess my deep sense of appreciation and debt to each of these, my mentors, who have contributed more to this volume than I can ever truly acknowledge. I can only hope that I will be able to pass on the enthusiasm and sheer joy they have bequeathed.

In light of the myriad volumes recently written on the Revelation, one might well ask, "Why another?" Here I can only plead what every writer hopes and imagines, namely, "There is something different here!" I believe this to be true in the sense that this volume makes no pretense to being a technical commentary. I will not try to comment on every verse or to address all the standard issues that so intrigue critical scholars. The very structure of the book suggests a more discursive style of study. Moreover, *Of Angels, Beasts, and Plagues* is aimed, not at the critical scholar, but at the faithful Bible teacher who seeks to make God's Word known within the church today; perhaps this means the Sunday school teacher, youth minister, adult leader, or the pastor. I have endeavored to pay most attention to details and issues that will plague, or perhaps bless, the average lay and student discussion of the book's contents, not necessarily those favored by technical specialists, though happily overlap does occur. The emphasis at all points will be as much on insights of a devotional and instructional nature as those of more critical interest.

My goal for this work is to present a practical program for introducing the basic message of Revelation to any group seeking its enlightenment. At the same time, I hope to indicate at many points how technical information gleaned from more detailed commentaries can be integrated into that agenda. I myself have used this material for two and a half decades to teach John's message. The generations of students at Eastern College and Eastern Baptist Theological Seminary whose counsel, questions, and encouragement have shared in the construction of this book also participate in its ministry to the church. And if this work leads others to study and incarnate the message of Revelation in the new millennium, then some of God's purposes for my life will have borne fruit.

Each of the chapters in this volume is meant to comprise one teaching session, though several (most notably chap. 15) could profitably be divided into two or even three units. Hopefully, each chapter will provide more information than will be needed for a lesson; judicious pruning with an eye to the needs of the particular audience involved will be prudent. Furthermore, each chapter of this book may be taken and transformed into the lecture notes for that lesson. That is, the reader may freely use this book as the basis of his or her teaching without fear of infringing on the author's literary rights. This book is, in the fullest and most direct sense, a teaching manual.

Lastly, I need to thank those who have helped and encouraged me in the production of this manuscript. To my former students, Jeane Higgins and Marianne Finlan (early proofreaders), the Reverend Thomas Beers (a great promoter), and my secretary, Caroline

Wall. My colleague at Eastern College, Dr. "Tony" Campolo, agreed most graciously to write a foreword for the book and did so with dispatch, for which I thank him. Those at Judson Press, however, require my special gratitude for all the many ways they have aided in bringing this book to publication. Randy Frame, Victoria McGoey, Mary Nicol, and Rebecca Irwin Diehl have all walked the second mile with me. Finally, Ruthann C. Dwyer undertook the copyediting of the final text and made many invaluable suggestions. Each of these, my friends and associates, have entered into the very DNA of this volume and share in its future ministry (Matt. 10:41–42). For what remains to disturb either the reader's aesthetic or theological sensitivities, though, I take full responsibility.

Christmas 1998

Introduction

MILLENNIUM MANIA
VERSUS THE REVELATION

At the dawn of the third Christian millennium, the world stands poised at the gateway of a new and uncharted era, a momentous crossroads of *history* and *hope*. One age is passing — "For a thousand years in your sight / are like a day that has just gone by" (Ps. 90:4) — and another is beginning. In the past, such millennial transitions were rarely acknowledged and, therefore, were not celebrated by many of the world's peoples. Few have pegged them to the advent of Jesus Christ, nor have they shared with the Christian world any sense of mutual destiny. In fact, this is the first and only time in recorded history that the whole family of humankind has recognized and shared the arrival of such a millennial divide *together*.

The significance of the moment is further highlighted by the hawking and hyping of its every conceivable by-product. Note the continuing proliferation of millennium conferences and websites, the *Millennium* television series, the Millenia automobile, England's Millennium Dome, and even Millennia perfume and wine. And, of course, there is the millennium bug that threatens to infest and destroy our cultural databases in a time-warp meltdown. Some are predicting that the Y2K bug alone will create a financial Armageddon leading anywhere from a 20 percent decline on Wall Street to a mild or strong recession, perhaps even to political and social disruptions (Levy, 62). Clearly, the boom in futurism is on!

Unhappily, the book of Revelation will also play a role in the frenzy to come. As the big triple zero arrives, we can count on the mystery mongers, puzzle addicts, and doomsday cults to abuse its message shamelessly. All will contribute their bit to the mania about to descend upon us. For its part, the Revelation has eternally fascinated those who have tried to use it as a soothsayer's manual to the future. Many a modern reader treads its corridors seeking nothing more than those doorways that will lead into the imminent and

uncharted landscapes of what is yet to be. And now, once again, the
end times are bubbling to the surface all around us.

Prophetic Voyeurism

In 1555, Nostradamus, the French physician and astrologer, published
his most famous work, entitled *Centuries*. In rhyming verses known
as quatrains, he predicted many events he thought would occur from
the mid-1500s to the end of time. His interest in gleaning and exploiting tidbits from the Revelation is clearly evident. Observe two of his
many quatrains:

Century X, #72

> In the year of 1999 and seven months
> Shall come a great and horrible king
> To revive the great King of the Barbarians
> Before and after, Mars rules by whim.
>
> (Sternau and Greenberg, 257)

Century X, #74

> At the end of the year of the great seventh number
> it will appear at the time of the games of sacrifice
> Not far from the great age of the Millennium
> When the buried shall come forth from their tombs.
>
> (Sternau and Greenberg, 289)

Quite certainly, the current millennial moment will produce many
new sensationalistic predictions concerning end-time events, that is,
future schlock, because Christians and others as well have a long and
unhappy history of falling prey to such theological chicanery. Indeed,
there seems to be a universal *spiritual lust* that leads us all into an unbridled prophetic voyeurism (a deep and unquenchable need to peek
into the future and master its secrets). Unfortunately, the typical dis-
illusionment that always results is the price we pay for our illusions.
But in this case, many of the illusions are founded on cultic and even
our own illegitimate uses of Scripture.

Biblical prophecy was never meant to satisfy these sinful, voyeuris-
tic tendencies, for it was never designed to be tomorrow's news
written today. Surely this is why the Jewish people did not adequately
discern the presence of their Messiah in Jesus of Nazareth. Yes, of
course, he is portrayed throughout the Hebrew Scriptures but always in a stained-glass window. That is, there are various and often

divergent facets or panes of his portraiture depicted in a variety of books and passages. Sometimes he is the conquering Davidic king to come, a general who will elevate Israel to a preeminent position of political power on earth (e.g., Ps. 2; Isa. 9:6–7). On the other hand, he is also a suffering servant who dies on behalf of those he is redeeming (Isa. 53). And what of the son of man who appears as a supernatural, transcendent, and heavenly personage (Dan. 7:13) — how does his program enter into the picture? Is the Messiah a *human* descendant of King David leading the nation from victory to victory or a supernatural and *divine* resident of heaven? Does he inflict judgment and death on the enemies of Israel, or does he himself die for his people? I suggest that such issues in prophecy were ultimately irresolvable until the life of Jesus had revealed their inner logic and coherence.

The prophetic literature of the Bible is always clear enough to give hope and a general sense of what is to come, but rarely is it digitally enhanced to the point of yielding precise pictures of that future. Generally, it is only when a biblical prophecy has come to pass, thus interpreting itself, that we know for sure what the prediction truly concerned (Kaiser, 22). The nature of predictive prophecy, then, suggests that *biblical predictions are meant to be understood as programs for the present.* They are a call to action in the here and now. Thus, if we know the general direction God's future is taking, we need to buy our ticket and jump aboard, for once our destiny is revealed, we have certainly been told how to shape our lives presently. That is the issue: not who can best print up tomorrow's headlines or juggle dates, but who will begin the work that leads to God's tomorrow. God has shown us, perhaps in a glass darkly, enough to reveal the path to be trod in the present if we wish to share his future.

Yet, we seem to be slow learners of these important lessons. The sport of "who can play the prophecy game best" began very early in Christian history. Already in the second century, many early fathers of the church (Ignatius, Polycarp, Justin, and Irenaeus) believed that they lived in the last days and that the end was near at hand. In the third century, Hippolytus predicted that the end would arrive within five hundred years of Christ's birth, and Lactantius, in the fourth, taught that the last judgment was imminent. Many others were convinced that the end of the first Christian millennium would precipitate the end of history. For example, the great learned scholar Augustine (A.D. 354–430) predicted that the end would come at this auspicious, millennial juncture. The Italian mystic, theologian, and biblical commentator Joachim of Floris pointed to the year 1260 as the date that would initiate the final chapter of history, the age of the spirit. Militz of Kromeriz thought the years 1365–67 would produce the end times. In the Reformation period, Melchior Hoffman set the date of 1533. And even Martin Luther allowed himself to indulge in the lust to predict; with equal futility, he programmed 1558 as destiny's final year. Later, the German Calvinist Johann Alsted argued that the second Advent would take place in 1694.

More recent attempts to play this "goosebump game" have yielded similar results. In 1831, an early Adventist by the name of William Miller prepared his people (fifty to one hundred thousand was his estimate) for the second coming of the Lord in 1843; their hopes were soon to be dashed but only after a decade of squandered expectations and activity. Charles Taze Russell, founder of the Jehovah's Witnesses, proclaimed 1914 as the year of the final Advent. Henry G. Guinness, a celebrated Christian evangelist, proposed 1930; Leonard Sale-Harrison, a famous Bible teacher with interdenominational connections and many prophetic conferences to his credit, espoused 1940 or 1941 (Amerding and Gasque, 27–39). And in one of the most famous recent debacles, the Jehovah's Witnesses spent considerable time and effort in preparing their faithful for Armageddon in 1976. This memorable failure led to substantial reversals of fortune for their movement at large.

Nor do contemporary orthodox traditions fare much better. Those that hold to a futurist interpretation of the Revelation (i.e., the events of the book mainly forecast what is to come) have rather frequently engaged in the predicting game. Most notably, the dispensationalist movement has often stumbled rather embarrassingly in this fantasy world. Their most famous recent foray into this swampland of disappointed hopes was presented by Hal Lindsey. In his well-known book *The Late Great Planet Earth* (1970), Lindsey suggested to his many adoring readers that the end of history would begin within forty years (one biblical generation) of Israel's national rebirth, that is, May 14, 1948 (Lindsey, 43). Not content, however, with just one such prediction — what if it (May 1988) should fail? — Lindsey later supplemented his scheme with two backup dates, both based on the one generation scheme he erroneously derived from Matthew 24:34. Now his followers are directed to look forward to either A.D. 2007, forty years after the recapture of Old Jerusalem by Israel, or 2022, forty years subsequent to the formation of a ten-member European Common Market (Walters, 839–40). One down, two to go! Or as the man falling off a ten-story building was overheard saying, as he passed the fifth floor, "So far so good." The date-setting trap has sprung once again!

One must wonder how the simple words of Jesus have been so frequently and conveniently forgotten. When asked about the signs of his coming (Matt. 24:3), Jesus responded by assessing some general conditions of the end times. Then he concluded, "No one knows about that day or hour, not even the angels in heaven, nor the Son, but only the Father" (Matt. 24:36). Thus, those who do know have an edge on Jesus himself! Later, during his final moments with the apostles, Jesus again addressed their interest in future events. Whether the kingdom was about to arrive — their concern — is answered by this powerful rejoinder: "It is not for you to know the times or dates that the Father has set by his own authority" (Acts 1:7). On the contrary, rather than speculating on the timing of final events, they were to be his witnesses (Acts 1:8; cf. Rev. 12:11; 19:10); this was his last word on the subject. Our task is to change lives not juggle dates.

As any historical review will amply demonstrate, the lust of prophetic voyeurism is a powerful temptation, and the railway timetable approach to prophecy has been predominant. We can only speculate at the damage unwittingly done by the mistaken hopes often raised by well-meaning Christians. Historically, it seems that the Bible's friends have often done about as much damage to its reputation as its enemies. And the Revelation, the most widely and seriously misunderstood book in the Bible, is certainly going to be victimized by a new wave of manic millennialism, for, sadly, no book has proven itself more vulnerable to the manipulations and distortions of the misinformed than has the Revelation. John would surely have been deeply saddened by the ghastly perversions that have afflicted his precious work. Almost every new doomsday prediction or emerging cult has distorted the book into its own grotesque image (in America alone, nearly 1,500 new cults have appeared since 1965). This very day, there are those sifting its contents seeking the identity of the new triggerman who will instigate the Armageddon event. One of the last candidate's for Antichrist was Saddam Hussein. Who is next?

The shadow of a new millennium hanging over us is itself a significant threat. A popular cultic and literalist understanding of history suggests that Adam was created at about 4000 B.C. That would mean that the next thousand years (the third in the Christian era) will give birth to history's seventh millennium. And if a day is as a thousand years to the Lord (Ps. 90:4; 2 Pet. 3:8), then this one about to begin is the seventh, the sabbath rest of the universe (on the model of a seven-day creation week found in Gen. 1). Many cults will seize upon this creation-millennial time theme to suggest that the day of the Lord is at hand. The damage that this will do may be very serious, indeed.

This is a time for those who care for Scripture and its integrity to come to the aid of its last word, the omega point that is John's Revelation. We must not abandon its truths to the "squirrels" so often found scampering through its boughs. For if we do, our children and our children's children will be their new victims. A fresh wave of cultic predictions is probably about to emerge. They will involve the arrival of new prophets, founders of new cults, emerging antichrists, and so on. Here the guidance of Scripture will be helpful.

The classic guidelines for true and false prophecy are found in Deuteronomy 18:18–22. What is prophesied can be legitimate only if it is consistent and coherent with previous revelation and its commitment to the one true God (Deut. 18:20). Does any new prophecy continue a developing theme within already established Scripture, or is it new and novel, that is, alien to the expectations of previous revelation from God? If so, even if what the prophet foretells comes to pass, that one must be judged false (cf. Deut. 13:1–4). Thus, the Hebrew Scriptures look forward to the arrival of the Messiah, and the Gospels fulfill that anticipation by describing his arrival (Christianity, therefore, confirms and conforms to biblical expectations).

On the other hand, does either testament raise hopes of yet another messiah or prophet beyond the expected Davidic one? Could such a new and contemporary figure be consistent with biblical expectations? No! Hence, cults like Mormonism and Moonism (and others soon to arrive) are dealing with unanticipated events, of which Scripture knows nothing. Moses, Isaiah, and many others speak of one to come, but does Jesus or any other New Testament passage speak of his successor, another great figure, such as Muhammad, Joseph Smith, or Sun Myung Moon? If not, their claims must be judged as false and unbiblical. There is no further revelation, prophet, or messiah expected or possible after God has revealed himself through his Son, who is the very radiance and image of his own glory (Heb. 1:1–3).

The second great criterion Deuteronomy speaks of is fulfillment (Deut. 18:22; Ezek. 33:30–33). Does the predicted event actually take place? This means that every prediction must be treated cautiously until proven true. Thus, the word from Amos about the eventual downfall of the northern nation of Israel was not fully accepted by the ancient Israelites, though it was consistent with previous threats contained in the covenant. But when 721 B.C. brought the destruction of the ten northern tribes, Amos was finally accredited as a true prophet, and his book was enshrined in the canon.

Scripture clearly warns against novel departures from the traditions of established biblical faith. Nor are we to accept too quickly any prediction about the future. The first criterion (spiritual validation) is primary, obviously, since the latter (fulfillment validation) will require time and even hindsight to fully establish. The testimony of prophecy, therefore, is not so much about some*thing* to come as some*one* (Rev. 19:10). Hence, the prophet John conveys to us the Revelation of *Jesus Christ.*

Keys to Revelation's Message

How then shall we find our way through the Revelation and avoid the pitfalls of the apocalypse mongers? Do we simply ask what our parents and grandparents thought of the book? Do we look to Nostradamus and seek the wisdom of his insights into the future, imagining all the while that Revelation must surely fall into lockstep with so famous a prognosticator? Do we permit some other tradition or leader to dictate what is currently fashionable, or do we allow Revelation, and Revelation alone, to help us find its message for our day? As we begin our pilgrimage into the heart of the book, let us keep in mind three main keys that unlock the corridors of its message: (1) We must work on understanding John's symbol world and at dampening our natural tendency toward rigid literalism. (2) We must be aware of the original historical setting of the book and be very wary not to insert our own hobbyhorses and agendas into Revelation's message. (3) Finally, we must seek to understand the difference between an apocalypse and other types of biblical literature.

Recognizing Symbolism

Anyone who has ever read Hal Lindsey's *Late Great Planet Earth* will well remember his tedious and tiresome emphasis on literalism. For some, literalism is a spiritual mantra that seemingly opens all doors. But, we must frankly say, not everything in Scripture yields to this approach. For instance, did the Israelites really number in the trillions ("as the stars") on that day when Moses began his great Deuteronomic sermon (Deut. 1:10; 28:62)? Moreover, is the mustard seed the smallest of seeds (Matt. 13:31–32), or were there really Chinese, Mayan, and even German "Jews" in Jerusalem on the day of Pentecost (Acts

2:5)? And where are the four corners of the earth (Rev. 7:1)? Further-more, how is one to read the poetry of Scripture literally (Song 4:1–5; 5:10–16)? No fewer than seven passages in Psalms speak of God's "wings" (e.g., Ps. 91:4). Is this literally true?

Naturally, a variety of explanations can quite properly be used to deal with each of these issues, but each reinforces the obvious — that no one takes everything in Scripture with wooden literalism. In-deed, the *literal* interpretation of a figure of speech remains a figure of speech; the *literal* meaning of poetry requires one to understand the difference between poetic and scientific expression. And the *literal* interpretation of a symbol is a decoding of that for which the sym-bol stands. In short, symbols are not real, though they stand for real things. Uncle Sam may well be a symbolic representative of America, but he doesn't exist literally. Nowhere in Scripture is the distinction between what is literal and nonliteral more decisive than for those who hope to understand the Revelation.

Recognizing the Historical Setting

Another concern for the modern reader, living at a great distance from the original period in which Revelation was written, is the issue of historical setting, for "God's word is rarely, if ever, disasso-ciated from the historical sphere in which it was first communicated" (Kaiser, 84). As first-century Christians faced a *System*[1] that was threatening to compromise their spiritual commitment by the ac-cretion of a thousand concessions, John was writing to encourage them to continue struggling against Rome. If only, Rome said, they were civilized enough to accommodate to the culture of the day, the way the Laodicean church had, there would be no need for them to be poor and persecuted, as were the Smyrnan Christians. If only they were sophisticated enough to engage in caesar worship, with-out necessarily giving up their attachment to Christ, then unpleasant executions like Antipas's (Rev. 2:13) could be avoided.

John was not writing about or predicting events that were irrel-evant to the everyday realities facing his churches. In fact, just the opposite is the case, for the Revelation speaks of dangers and realities that are a part of their day and time. And the book offers spiritual truths that would help the churches weather the storm of imperial state religion and internal decay, thus having the potential to change their lives and their world. Simply, what John wrote had relevance to his beloved congregations.

Futurist interpreters do not seem to grasp the relationship between the Revelation and its historical setting, glibly arguing that John did not know what he was predicting, nor did his readers, for his predictions point to realities (such as microchips and bar codes) unknown to their world. For them, the Revelation is about understanding the intriguing history of Russia or China, the history of military science with its fascinating story of nuclear and space weaponry, or the identification of the "mark of the beast" with a modern leader or some new technology. However, futurists would do well to hear the sage counsel of Walter Kaiser. He observes that revelations about realities of which the original readers could have known nothing would, in fact, be quite *non*revealing. After all, how could a biblical writer communicate or his reader understand what neither of them had ever experienced (Kaiser, 51)? Quite obviously, "a revelation must be intelligible, or it is no revelation at all" (128), for "when God addressed humanity, he did so in order to instruct, to reprove, to comfort, and not to mystify and to confuse" (135).

Those who would find B-1 bombers, tanks, and biological warfare skillfully hidden in John's visions are secretly suggesting that the book was disclosing and unveiling a truth that was totally unintelligible to its readers. They suggest that for two thousand years this book has revealed nothing that could be accurately understood, until, that is, their day. Here is the proverbial inch — the required contemporary, inspired "Papa Doc" who knows what even John did not understand — from which the cults stretch their mile! To the contrary, we must conclude that the Revelation is written to and for the seven churches; this is the book's first (Rev. 1:4) and last (22:16) understanding of itself. But it does this in such a fashion as to throw light on the whole future of the church, in all times and places, where the prevailing world System continues its onslaught against God's people.

Recognizing the Genre

Understanding the *genre* (type of literature or communication) with which we are dealing is also critical to unlocking the message of the Revelation. For example, those passing by one of my classes at Eastern College, hearing a few comments about Scripture, and deciding to enter thinking they were about to enjoy a sermon, would quickly discover they had made a serious mistake, that is, misunderstanding the genre of discourse taking place in that room. The genre might be a lengthy, intellectual discussion of some biblical passage but most certainly would not be a brief, entertaining sermon with a moral challenge and altar call at the end. So it is with Scripture. It is very important that we understand the differences between a book of history (Joshua), poetry (Psalms), wisdom (Ecclesiastes), or prophecy (Amos) and an apocalypse (Daniel or Revelation). The differences between these types of Scripture and the ways in which we must interpret them are diverse and numerous.

As we begin our work in Revelation, it will make all the difference in the world if we recognize it as *apocalyptic,* with some special characteristics. Here the themes, theology, and even symbols must be placed in a special frame of reference. They are part and parcel of a type of literature and world-view that became very popular in the centuries before Jesus' birth and remained so for some time after his death. Therefore, we cannot read Revelation the way we read Romans, though both do contain Christian theology. Nor can we read it as if it were a Gospel, though it does portray Christ's ministry from birth to resurrection. Still less is it to be approached as we would the book of Acts, though the Revelation often discusses first-century church history. Revelation is an apocalyptic book and can be truly appreciated only as such. I can almost hear John echoing that clever comment that is so utterly apropos of Revelation's message: "I know you believe you understand what you think I said. But I am not sure you realize that what you heard is not what I meant."

By using these three simple keys to gain a proper entrée through the forbidding doorways of misunderstanding and into the innermost precincts of Revelation's message for the new millennium, we may enable ourselves and others to hear as John meant us to hear and to understand what he was actually saying. To that end, we will seek next to grapple more seriously with the issues posed by such a special and even unique work, John's Revelation, the only New Testament book that is truly an apocalypse.

Note

1. The term *System* shall be capitalized and used throughout this book to refer to the dominant social, religious, and political context in which any generation of Christians must live their lives.

Chapter 1

WHAT KIND OF BEAST IS APOCALYPTIC?

Grappling with the Beast

The word *apocalypse* has been used to designate many similar works in the Judeo-Christian heritage. Most of these books were written between 200 B.C. and A.D. 200, and all are now called "apocalyptic literature."[1] The roughly seventy Jewish and Christian apocalypses (some are whole books; others are only sections or even fragments of other works) that have been discovered provide much background information for our understanding of this unique type of literature. However, only two of the group were ever recognized as inspired and incorporated into Scripture — Daniel and Revelation. Unfortunately, the latter holds the unenviable distinction of being the most misunderstood book in the Bible.[2]

How, then, are we to enter the dark landscapes of the Revelation and yet allow common sense to prevail? Given the special complexities of a book, or more accurately a "letter" written largely in symbolic language, containing both prophetic and apocalyptic elements and emerging out of a historical period now 1,900 years removed from us, it is not difficult to understand why readers of all ages have found the Revelation exasperatingly difficult to understand and integrate into their Christian lives. "When turning to the book of Revelation from the rest of the New Testament," comments a noted modern writer, "one feels as if he or she were entering a foreign country" (Fee and Stuart, 231). Occasionally, Christian people have even told me they purposely avoid reading or studying this book, out of respect and outright fear for its puzzling intricacies.

This is not just our problem. Even the earliest Christians found the Revelation a tough nut to crack. The great church father Jerome, who translated the Latin Vulgate version of the Bible, commented that the Revelation either found one mad or would certainly leave one so. He also observed, however, something that is very close to the truth, namely, that there is a riddle hidden in nearly every verse of the book. But this latter feature he praised as indicative of its great depth as the Word of God.

It seems clear that the keys for interpreting the Revelation were lost pretty quickly in the early church. Within a hundred years of its production, Christian authors were already beginning to *guess* at its meaning. Apparently, the context of Christian experience that John presumes he shares with his readers (he gives little hint of any overt difficulty they should have in understanding his words) was soon lost. Evidently, the church's Judaic background and first-century environment quickly faded, and new eras and cultural milieus emerged that did not understand John's language.

To take one extreme example from a later time period, Martin Luther, the great reformer and biblical scholar, read the Revelation in the sixteenth century and promptly declared that the Holy Spirit had little to do with its composition. Furthermore, he asserted, it was neither prophetic nor apostolic. Luther felt Revelation lacked the requisite credentials of a New Testament book, for Christ was "neither sought nor known in it" (Wainwright, 100). Happily, these harsh, though memorable, comments made in the preface of the original edition (1522) of his German New Testament were omitted in the later edition of 1530. He also complained, however, that while the Revelation promises great blessings to those who keep its precepts and pronounces curses on those who do not, it was so obscure that no one could figure out what they were commanded to keep or to shun (Kiddle, xx). Even such unrestrained criticism, however, did not keep Luther from using the book to advantage. His antipapal interpretations of its message will be noted below.

Luther's problem with the Revelation came about in part because he interpreted it the same way he did his beloved Romans. Now Romans requires a rather straightforward, logical, and literal interpretive technique. But if you use that approach with the Revelation, as Luther did, you will end up with utter nonsense. In his day, most of the other apocalyptic works had not yet been discovered or analyzed. Consequently, no one understood the unique nature of apocalyptic literature or had the necessary clues for interpreting its symbolism. Alas, Luther's problem was inevitable and shared by other great reformers (and sadly by many modern Christians). Ulrich Zwingli refused to use the book as a foundation of Christian doctrine, and John Calvin, who wrote commentaries on all the other New Testament books, also condemned it to death by silence.

Nor has the modern world been any less confused and divided in its evaluation of the Revelation. R. H. Charles, a turn-of-the-century biblical scholar who spent twenty-five years of his life studying this book, argued that after John's original work, Revelation had later been edited by a "shallow-brained fanatic and celibate," an "unintelligent" and "monkish interpolator" (1:lv, lix; 2:9). Charles was particularly offended by Revelation 14:4, which he took to elevate male celibates (women were inherently excluded) to the highest rank of Christian experience. The influential English novelist and poet D. H. Lawrence attacked the Revelation as the manifestation of spiteful envy on the part of the have-nots against all the pleasures and achievements of civilization that were not theirs. Thus, he declared it "the work of a second-rate mind. It appeals intensely to second-rate minds in every country and every century"; he finally dismissed it as the "Judas" of the New Testament canon (Lawrence, 14, 17–18). Moreover, even one of the greatest New Testament scholars of the twentieth century, C. H. Dodd, had severe doubts about the book's presentation of God and the Messiah.[3]

However, others who have devoted themselves to the Revelation have discovered one of the most exciting and sublime summaries of biblical faith to be found in all the Scriptures. Immeasurable are the comfort and hope this book has brought through the ages to those who have genuinely opened their hearts to its spirit. For them, Philip Carrington speaks most eloquently:

> But in the case of the *Revelation* we are dealing with an artist greater than Stevenson or Coleridge or Bach. St. John has a better sense of the right word than Stevenson; he has a greater command of unearthly supernatural loveliness than Coleridge; he has a richer sense of melody and rhythm and composition than Bach. . . . It is the only masterpiece of pure art in the New Testament. (Carrington, xvii)[4]

If we wish to share Carrington's appreciation of the book, we must recognize that Revelation's genre, apocalyptic, is a distinct type of literature — as different from others as science fiction is from poetry or as the Pauline epistles are from the Psalms. As a unique kind of literature, it possesses characteristics that define a world-view all its own. Often described as the follow-on tradition or child of biblical prophecy, it differs from its parent in significant ways. Apocalyptic books manifest the following key ingredients, though these are only a few of their more distinctive features: cosmic dualism, pessimism, and symbolism. We will go on to discover that the Revelation possesses a unique feature of its own as well.

Cosmic Dualism

Apocalyptic books viewed the universe as a gigantic battlefield (*cosmic*), behind which supernatural forces of good and evil (*dualism*) were struggling and locked in perpetual warfare over the souls of humanity (see Dan. 10:12–13,20–21). The point is that the forces arrayed against God and God's people are not merely historical; they are principalities and powers (Eph. 6:10–12) not of this world (Rev. 12:7–9). But while the conflict is sharp, the outcome is not in doubt. Individual human beings may be the allies of angels, often mirroring their heavenly struggles on earth, but humans are not the prime actors or powers on the stage. This aspect of apocalyptic might best be understood as "decision dualism," for its practical effect is to demand a spiritual commitment on the part of its readers. Where, it inquires, do we stand in this great conflict?

In contrast, biblical prophecy focused most typically on human history and social conflict, not the universe. Amos, for instance, has a quite different texture when compared to Revelation, for Amos is an earthly story of confrontation between the good and evil that people do. For the prophets, humanity is the problem (Amos 5:11–15; 8:4–6), a problem that must be dealt with and transformed here, on this earth. And so, the prophets called upon people to repent and thereby change history. This was the way that God's kingdom was to come upon the earth (cf. Isa. 2:2–4; 9:6–7; 11:1–5; Amos 4:6–12).

With a different view, the apocalypses tended to focus on "the deep" (cf. Gen. 1:2, Rev. 13:1), that is, the unseen spiritual reservoirs and wellsprings of cosmic evil. From their perspective, people can do little to influence the outcome of this battle. Our role is to trust, to suffer if need be, and faithfully to await God's ultimate vindication (Dan. 3:17–18; Rev. 12:11), for only this final cataclysmic inbreaking of the Almighty will announce and enforce the ultimate shape of the future.

Are prophecy and apocalyptic incompatible or even contradictory truths? Certainly not! Taken together, each of the messages yields its prismatic share of truth to the substance of the Revelation. Jointly they say, God's people are always called upon to fight the good and godly fight here and now (so said the prophets), but we must always remember, in moments of difficulty, that only God will ultimately gain the victory over forces far beyond our grasp (as the apocalyptists argue). Our efforts are at best only tributaries to the final divine triumph.

Pessimism

It is natural, then, that the apocalyptists stressed a negative view (*pessimism*) of everyday life in this world. For them, earth's history is one dominated by sinister forces of radical evil (Rev. 13:5–8; 18:4). They held out little hope for life here but rather emphasized the glorious prospects of eternity. They would agree with the book of Ecclesiastes and its verdict of "vanity" on everything "under the sun." Thus, most apocalypses incorporate detailed, topographical depictions of heaven and the afterlife (see Rev. 4–5; 22). While the prophets may envision a future of splendor for a renewed earth whose every environmental blemish is healed (Isa. 11:6–9; Ezek. 47:1–12), the apocalyptists generally see hope only in a coming celestial domain that will bring history as we know it to an end.

Such apocalyptic pessimism, however, has at least two positive purposes. First, it intends to force people into a decision-making lifestyle. To which environment or lifestyle is one committed — to the present, which is dominated by evil, or to the one marked by faith and anticipation that is yet to come (Heb. 11:1)? Second, from this perspective history does not end with a whimper in a blind alley; rather, a bright and purposeful future dominates the horizon (Rev. 21). We might say, therefore, that for the apocalypses, "There is power in a positive eschatology."[5] The way you believe things will end up definitely influences the way you play the game of life. If you know that your team will finally overcome and win the game, you will play more confidently and joyously, even when the coming victory is not visible and defeat might seem imminent. The rough-and-tumble tactics of the opponent will be dealt with through patience and hope. This is why apocalyptic books always tended to concentrate on the moment of divine victory — the end of history.

Symbolism

As noted in the Introduction (see pp. 7–8), symbolism is the most well-known and most dreaded hallmark of apocalyptic literature. Apocalyptic seems to have been written primarily in the stressful climate of political and religious uncertainty or even outright persecution. This may be one reason why these books are written in virtual code. Should a Roman imperial soldier, for instance, have come across someone writing or even reading an apocalypse, it would not have been at all obvious that treasonous sedition was afoot. What he would have found (presuming the soldier could read) was a maze of symbols, ciphers "full of sound and fury but (apparently) signifying nothing."

More precisely, the language of apocalyptic is *symbolic,* not pure code. Whereas code is meant to be decoded so that it can be understood in a known language, symbolic language resists being translated into simple literal truths. It is artistic and multifaceted, exhibiting the logic of the kaleidoscope, with its ever-changing perspectives and landscapes. Thus, symbolism communicates through pictures; it is the language of the artist and poet, speaking to those realities for which we do not have an adequate vocabulary. Such books are never meant to be reduced to simple logic, like the book of Romans, but to remain ever radiant with a translucent spirituality.

Furthermore, such "visionary rhetoric" (Fiorenza, *Book of Revelation,* 187) allows the reader to apply the teaching of such a book not just to one era, to which it is uniquely linked, but to each of history's succeeding crises, for which it also retains a message. The characteristic genius of apocalyptic literature, according to David Aune, is that it takes the painful realities of a single historical moment and transposes them into a universal key (1301). By this key, then, we are able to see the linkages between many similar historical eras and their true inner spiritual dimensions. The symbols used in Revelation were meant, not to conceal, but to inspire the church in a desperate moment (Boring, *Revelation,* 51–59).

One reason for the level of difficulty we encounter in attempting to understand these symbols is that some of them are drawn from the most ancient folklore of the Near East. Perhaps this is because in times of trouble people wish for the reassurance of tradition, that what is, is what has been — in other words, that their experiences are only part of a pattern running through all history. In Revelation, for instance, old and popular stories concerning the "monsters of chaos" (vaguely reverberated in Ps. 74:12–17; Isa. 51:9–10; etc.) now stand again in the shadows behind the new situation that John relates. When the beast of imperial Roman power confronts the church, old foes are alive again and at work. They are merely the latest reincarnations of those ancient forces (part of "that ancient serpent"; Rev. 12:9; cf. 13:1).[6]

Another major reason many find Revelation so "unrevealing" is its main source of symbolism — the Hebrew Scriptures. By all accounts, the prime backdrop to Revelation's symbolic world-view is the Bible of Jesus, the only Scriptures he ever read. Tragically, modern Christians know and care little about the bulk of the Bible. We dismissively call it "old" partly, I am convinced, to disguise our utter lack of enthusiasm to study its truth. But hidden within the 404 verses of Revelation are over five hundred allusions (hints and echoes falling short of quotations) to the Old Testament. Revelation is virtually a distillation of the whole biblical message — the Bible in a nutshell — now focused on Jesus and his church. One could also say, then, that there is not so much that is utterly new in Revelation as there is a new and delightfully fresh way of reviewing the old. Naturally, unfamiliarity with the Scriptures severely complicates the attempt to unravel John's message.

Furthermore, there are many other images in Revelation drawn from the political background of the first-century Roman world. Many have suggested, in fact, that some symbols in Revelation are virtually political cartoons drawn from known aspects of Rome's imperial history. But again, these are matters that the modern reader usually knows little about.[7] Here, however, we are actually on common ground, for similar political symbolism is still used even in our own day. When we speak of a contest between the donkey and elephant, we sense the presence of a political battle. Or if we noted the historic confrontation between the rapacious bear and the spread eagle, the reference to international affairs is obvious. And if someone suggested that the "spirit of '76" just manifested itself, no one would turn to see a ghost. We instantly sense a reference to the spirit of freedom and do not look for eerie apparitions. Thus, the Revelation frequently analyzes political, social, and religious issues through the use of a code grounded in ancient symbols, the Hebrew Scriptures, and first-century politics.[8]

Unfortunately, the remarkable complexity of apocalyptic and of the Revelation, in particular, has left such works vulnerable to continuous exploitation by a coven of cults. The many difficulties related to Revelation's historically conditioned context constantly allow the unscrupulous or uninformed to misconstrue and misrepresent its true message. I believe, however, that we can forge a bulwark against the contrived interpretations of the non-Christian cults by implementing this basic guideline: *"A text cannot mean what it never meant"* (Fee and Stuart, 26).

By that simple truism, we are reminded that we must seek the meaning of any text, including symbolic ones, in the intent of the passage when it was first written or read. How would first-century Christians, with both Jewish and Greek cultural roots (not contemporary Baptists, Methodists, or dispensationalists), have understood a given symbol? Gordon Fee and Douglas Stuart further suggest that "the Holy Spirit cannot be called in [to the interpretive process] to contradict himself" (26), meaning that the interpretation we give a text today must be in line with what God's Spirit *first* intended and inspired (i.e., what would have been understood originally). This safely rules out our finding atomic bombers, tanks, intercontinental missiles, or modern politicians within Revelation's pages.[9]

Prophetic-Apocalyptic

Cosmic dualism, pessimism, and symbolism do not represent the whole story, however; still more complexity awaits. If Revelation is apocalyptic, it *is* a prophetic book as well. (For a review of the nature of biblical prophecy, see Introduction, pp. 2–7.) This is clear from its designation as "prophecy" in the beginning and ending of the volume (cf. Rev. 1:3; 22:7,10,18–19). Such headlining of a subject at the opening and closing of a passage or book is called an "inclusio" and means that the whole of the text in between is meant to be seen from these twin peaks of perspective. Hence, John is told that he must "prophesy" (10:11) and that he is brother to "the prophets" (22:9). To the extent that the book is prophetic, then, it will deal with themes dear to the biblical prophets, for example, politics, economics, justice, power and pride, false religion, and the coming of God's kingdom.[10] Or as Paul put it so aptly,

> Those who prophesy speak to other people for their upbuilding and encouragement and consolation...but those who prophesy build up the church...an unbeliever or outsider who enters is reproved by all and called to account by all. After the secrets of the unbeliever's heart are disclosed, that person will bow down before God and worship him, declaring, "God is really among you." (1 Cor. 14:3–4,24–25, NRSV)

Thus, I prefer to call Revelation by the term that George Ladd coined, namely, *prophetic-apocalyptic* (Ladd, "Why Not Prophetic-Apocalyptic?" 192–200). This means, of course, that the book is doubly complex, with the characteristics of two types of biblical literature. The prophetic aspect points to the present and analyzes what is going on in John's day, while the apocalyptic focuses on history's future. Moreover, if the prophetic side of this analysis is a sort of spiritual x-ray of the seven churches, then it also represents a commentary on the continuing or contemporary church as well. The apocalyptic side of the book, on the other hand, remains a symbolic preview of history's terminus. Revelation represents, then, a truly bifocal perspective on the life of the seven churches and their future destiny.

Four Historic Routes through Revelation

The historic church tradition has used four main road maps to enter the uncharted territory of Revelation. And since they are still with us, we need to understand them, for they will determine not only our approach to but also our *appropriation* of Revelation's message. Certainly it is the composite character of Revelation as prophetic-apocalyptic that has led to such divergent interpretations of its contents. Some have emphasized the antique pastness of John's own day; others, its contemporary, prophetic application to our present day, while even more have sadly seen the book primarily as a sooth-sayer's syllabus to the future, in which date-fixing puzzle addicts identify the modern actors on Revelation's stage. In the long history of its interpretation, Revelation has had to survive many a strange sideshow set up to hawk its wares. Ruefully, G. K. Chesterton, commenting on this history, once observed that "though St. John the Evangelist saw many strange monsters in his vision, he saw no creature so wild as one of his own commentators" (29).

In light of the problems this book and its symbolism have given interpreters over the centuries, perhaps it is not unusual that four prominent paths to its interpretation have evolved: the preterite, historicist, futurist, and apocalyptic. This variety of trails into the interior of Revelation's coded landscape is symptomatic of a book that affirms two biblical traditions — the prophetic outlook (what's really going on in history?) and the apocalyptic (what is the final outcome?). A book that is genuinely prophetic-apocalyptic in character will be more than challenging; it is a cryptographer's dream and an artist's paradise. Christian interpreters, therefore, have followed four different road maps, seeking the lost world of Revelation's roots.

The four routes we shall survey struggle for answers to the questions arising from the opening words of the book. There John assures the reader that he is speaking of "what must soon take place" (1:1), and this he reconfirms in the later observation that "the time is near" (1:3). That this is genuinely the perspective of the book is guaranteed by the inclusio at the end of the Revelation (22:6,10). Just what is it that "must soon take place"? What "time is near"? Was John correct in this assessment? Did something happen that fulfilled his words? A blessing is promised to those who know the answers to these questions.

The Preterite Path

The word *preterite* describes one of the main roadways into the message of the Revelation. If you have ever studied Latin or Spanish, you will know that the *preterite tense* of verbs is the *past tense,* which is the key to this view of the Revelation. It suggests that if you were to plot the position of the book's author with regard to the history and materials in the book, he would stand near its end, meaning that the majority of Revelation's contents represents, from his perspective, what is already in his "past."

Let's try to sketch this viewpoint graphically. Revelation 1 is understood, by all four approaches, to be a description of the book's first-century background. Here John describes his own imprisonment on the island of Patmos, where he was granted an extraordinary vision that became the basis of the Revelation. Chapters 2 and 3 are understood as cover letters written as introductions to the larger document. Throughout the entire book, then, all seven churches are constantly being addressed, with every scene engaging their individual lives (see Fig. 1a).

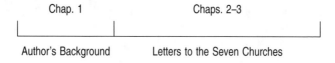

Chap. 1   Chaps. 2–3

Author's Background   Letters to the Seven Churches

Fig. 1a. Preterite View of Rev. 1–3

Now to skip to the end of our developing sketch, chapters 18–22 represent the end of world history, that is, the second coming (the *Parousia*) of Jesus Christ, the general resurrection, the final judgment, and the establishment of the Eternal City. Here are events that clearly are part of the future and that no generation of Christians has yet seen (see Fig. 1b).

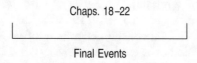

Chaps. 18–22

Final Events

Fig. 1b. Preterite View of Rev. 18–22

This brings us to the really important question that divides the major theories of interpretation: To what time zone, or era, do chapters

4–17 refer? In other words, what is it that "must soon take place"? What "time is near"? Every assessment of Revelation must address the question of the time frame presented in these chapters.[11] Here is precisely where the preterite interpretation distinguishes itself from the others, for it holds that the time period is already *past* for the author and the churches noted. Therefore, the author, representing John's perspective, is placed at the end of these chapters, indicating that he is looking back on events that have already transpired (see Fig. 1c).

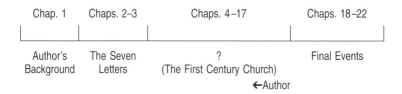

Fig. 1c. Preterite View of Rev. 1–22

Why would John and the Revelation move in this direction? What could such knowledge of the past possibly do for his readers or for us? The preterite path to understanding the Revelation suggests that John is describing something immensely important and historic — *the church's first confrontation with the World System.* Thus, this time zone represents a fundamental pattern or model for the church's life. Revelation 4–17 indicates the tactics with which the church battled the forces of Rome that were threatening to contaminate or even destroy its unique identity. These chapters, then, reveal the spiritual guidelines that piloted the seven churches through the darkness of this "suffering" (1:9; "tribulation" in KJV, RSV) and how the Jesus of Revelation intended John's Christian brothers and sisters to continue the struggle.

What is it that "must soon take place"? What "time is near"? For John, the second coming of Christ was the next great event on the church's calendar; already chapter 18 was on the horizon of history and the day of redemption imminent. It was this momentous hope that constantly undergirded and comforted the church as it faced the Roman beast. Until that day arrived, however, John counseled his churches to continue their spiritual warfare along the lines already established. This is the preterite path through John's Revelation.[12]

The Historicist Path

This view, originating in the twelfth century A.D. with Joachim of Floris, became a contributive factor to the Crusades (due to its identification of the Islamic leader Saladin with one of the heads of the beast) and later was very fashionable during the Middle Ages. It was refined and developed in the early 1300s by the Parisian theologian Nicolas of Lyra (Mounce, *Book of Revelation*, 40; Wainwright, 49–51). Generally it agreed with the preterite interpretation of chapters 1, 2–3, and 18–22. But it too distinguishes itself by a special understanding of chapters 4–17. The preterite view tended to see the Revelation as prophecy, but prophecy understood as a sociospiritual analysis of society (where prophets are God's sociologists, as in the Hebrew Scriptures; cf. 1 Cor. 14:3,24–25). In contrast, the historicist school sees these chapters as prophecy, but prophecy that is *predictive* in nature.

In the historicist view, the heart of the book (chaps. 4–17) is an extended prediction of all major events throughout the church age, that is, a complete history of the church from beginning to end, sketched through symbols. From the perspective of this approach, various significant moments in church history (e.g., the advent of Islam, the Reformation, significant revivals, etc.) are first singled out for attention, then symbols for these events are discovered in the Revelation. Depending on who is guiding the procedure and what his or her tradition's view of church history is, very different events would be significant, and sometimes very different symbols in Revelation would be found to represent them. Obviously this procedure has been excessively subjective, more based on one's own background than on Scripture (see Fig. 2).

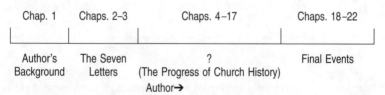

Fig. 2. Historicist View of Rev. 1–22

Martin Luther, who held the historicist view, was certain that the Roman Catholic Church, his great adversary, would be symbolized in Revelation's sweeping portrayal of the church's story. But what symbol would he seize upon as representative of that organization? If the figure of the beast in chapter 13 comes to your mind, you're think-ing as Luther did. The beast, whose symbolic signature is the number 666, was taken to be the Roman primate, a correspondence achieved by totaling the value of the letters (which were taken as Roman nu-merals) in the official Latin title of the pope.[13] Intriguingly, at least to Luther, they could be tallied to that dismal result — 666. And so he identified the beast, through its number, as the Roman pontiff and, therefore, as the Catholic Church.

Now if that seems rather arbitrary and subjective on the great re-former's part, note the response. Not to be outdone in ingenuity, Catholic scholars noticed that the name *Martin Luther* could also be calculated and reduced to the dreaded 666.[14] Unsurprisingly, they be-lieved that the Protestant Reformation was the major beastly event in church history. But while Catholics sometimes used the same analysis of Revelation to turn the tables against Protestant antipapalism, their more innovative reaction was to create a new approach to the book called *futurism.* Clearly, if Revelation's story was primarily about fu-ture events, the medieval popes could not possibly be identified with the beast or Antichrist. Hence, a new approach to the book was born, one that would become very influential in Protestant circles as well.[15]

As one might guess, the historicist path to the book has been grad-ually discredited, having been found to be so highly biased and almost totally subjective that today few hold it. But among those who still cling to this approach, the views of Luther are usually still dominant. Thus, Revelation is sadly misdirected and turned into a specific as-sault on Roman Catholicism. Accordingly, historicism identifies what "must soon take place," the next events on the horizon, as the de-struction of the System (papal Rome) and the return of Christ (Rev. 18–19).

The Futurist Path

This method of interpreting the Revelation is similar to the historicist approach in its view that much of the book represents the predicted future. As in the three other approaches, chapter 1 remains as the *who, how,* and *when* of John's involvement in the reception of the Revelation. Beginning in chapters 2–3, however, certain forks in the pathway appear.

Many evangelical biblical scholars adopting the futurist stance view the seven letters in chapters 2–3, as do the preterite and historicist approaches, as simply John's attempt to communicate with cher-ished congregations.[16] On the other hand, a different approach is taken by dispensationalists, whose views are linked to J. N. Darby (a mid-nineteenth-century Englishman associated with the Plymouth Brethren movement), C. I. Scofield (whose notes appended to the King James Version have become virtually the fifth Gospel for many of his followers), and, more recently, Hal Lindsey (who authored the hugely popular *Late Great Planet Earth* and has coincidentally predicted three separate dates for the second coming of Christ and the "rapture" of the church; Walters, 839–40).[17]

Dispensationalism is founded on an interpretive principle that its adherents believe to be decisively important to understanding the Revelation. This fundamental tenet is the alleged distinction between God's will and prophetic programs for Jews (i.e., Israel) as opposed to those for Gentiles (i.e., the church). Accordingly, they attempt to define what portions of Revelation are addressed to each group (see the comment on Rev. 4:1).[18] Dispensationalists understand the seven letters (chaps. 2–3) to be predictive of seven stages or eras of church history, from the early and dedicated church of Ephesus to the final, degenerate phase of Laodicea. Since seven periods must be passed through before the tribulation period arrives (i.e., chaps. 4–17), adherents of this view have always believed they were in the Laodicean era and that the rapture (Latin, "to be snatched away") of the church was, therefore, genuinely imminent.

Once again, the utterly subjective nature of such an outline for church history has severely undermined its credibility. Those who have adopted this approach have regularly disagreed over the correspondence between the churches and the time periods of church history. This has led, in turn, to many fantastic attempts to bring the various schemes into harmony with each other, but these attempts have been made without credible success. Furthermore, attempting to judge the spiritual life of the whole, broad church throughout the ages and to fix time segments reflecting those judgments surely reveals more about the spiritual arrogance and prejudices of the one judging than about the church of Jesus Christ. Most deem this project completely unjustifiable and thoroughly unbiblical![19]

From the dispensationalist perspective, the author of the book of Revelation stands in the time frame of the church at Ephesus with the entire subsequent contents of the book *future* to his day (see Fig. 3a).

On the more important issue of chapters 4–17, all futurists hold to a common view. This section of the book is thought to represent the final period of earth's history, which is popularly called "the tribulation period." This era is usually defined as a seven-year interval of intense tribulation or persecution for God's people. However, such a

Chaps. 2–3

Ephesus	Smyrna	Pergamum	Thyatira	Sardis	Philadelphia	Laodicea
John's Day	To A.D. 316	Following A.D. 316	The Papacy	Protestant Reformation	The True Church	The Final Apostasy

Author→

The Seven Letters = The Seven Church Ages[20]

Fig. 3a. Dispensationalist View of Rev. 2–3

period is not explicitly described in biblical prophecy or elsewhere, and to many it seems largely an imaginary theological construct. It is derived by means of a very debatable, and to this author unlikely, interpretation of Daniel's "seventy weeks" (Dan. 9). That a period of intense persecution awaits the church in the final days of history is certainly true. But that it is seven years in duration and specifically defined in ways dispensationalists are so fond of describing is clearly never stated in Scripture. Futurists view the concluding chapters of Revelation as do the preterists and historicists (see Fig. 3b).

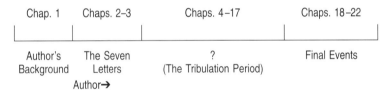

Chap. 1	Chaps. 2–3	Chaps. 4–17	Chaps. 18–22
Author's Background	The Seven Letters	? (The Tribulation Period)	Final Events

Author→

Fig. 3b. Futurist View of Rev. 1–22

As in the historicist view, the bulk of the book is *future* to the author, with the key section devoted to a uniquely dramatic period of history. What is it, then, that "must soon take place"? What "time is near"? Here it is the tribulation period, often defined as a seven-year span of unparalleled horror for the people of God. It is the next juncture in church history but affects only earth's final generation. Dispensationalists argue that Christians do not experience this time period because they have been "raptured," or evacuated, before it begins (to be precise at Rev. 4:1). For the church, then, it is its departure that is near and soon. Other evangelical futurists see no reference to such an event in 4:1 and maintain that the final generation of Christians does go through the tribulation period, experiencing its appalling persecution.[21] Actually, it is this period for which they are being encouraged to prepare.

The Apocalyptic Path

Notice that the preterite view (chaps. 4–17 are about the *first* generation) and the futurist view (chaps. 4–17 are about the *last* generation) are diametric opposites. Even so, both are consistent interpretations, and each yields a powerful message for the church of any era. But how can both be possible? Can a book of the Bible mean two different things at the same time? The apocalyptic approach seeks to explain this impasse and why two opposing views seem equally feasible.[22] They are, in fact, the two sides of one apocalyptic coin. This approach to Revelation seeks to take into account the many other apocalypses and their special features, for this type of literature has a literary technique all its own and may supply keys to the interpretation of our Apocalypse.[23]

According to this more recent approach, the central chapters represent "the omnipresent," the always-contemporary situation of the church as it faces the perennial battle with the World System. Such was the church's first battle with the world (preterite view), and such will be the last battle of church history (futurist view), but — and here is the bombshell — this is also how it is *now!* These are the spiritual dynamics of the church's omnipresent clash with the System (i.e., the beast) in every age (see Fig. 4).[24]

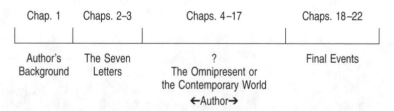

Fig. 4. Apocalyptic View of Rev. 1–22

Thus, the preterite approach is correct on an important issue. John did use the symbols of his first-century background — the only world he and his readers had experienced — to communicate the Revelation to us. Further, these symbols stand for the early church's original battle with the world. He was saying, "Keep on keeping on! This is how you have been effectively resisting the beast; remember the end is coming." However, the futurist path also has commendable insights because it tells us that the final generation of Christians will face the same struggle and that the spiritual dynamics of their appointment with the beast will remain essentially the same. It also reminds us that we might be that end-time generation. Nevertheless, what we need most for the living of our days and nights is, not yesterday's or tomorrow's headlines, but spiritual wisdom and encouragement today.

Where the apocalyptic approach makes its real impact is the insight that Revelation reveals the way in which *every* generation of Christians engages the enemy — the System. What is about to begin is our own involvement in the story of this book. Yes, the first and last generations encounter the System through these spiritual dynamics, but, most importantly, this is how it always is when the church faces the beast faithfully, without compromise. The apocalyptic approach also recognizes Revelation as a manual for contemporary holy war. Here is how the church is meant to deal with the overwhelming forces arrayed against it. Revelation is not just a description of the first century — which would say little to us — nor is it merely a sketch of the final generation — which may not involve us either; rather, it is a portrayal of life here and now, as we are living it. Its first-century context is a transparency, a looking glass, through which we are to see our own world, which might already be in its final phase. Thus, there are symbols in the book that stand for *us!* We must start to live them!

> Blessed is the one who reads the words of this prophecy, and blessed are those who hear it and take to heart what is written in it, because the time is near. (Rev. 1:3)

This book will pursue the apocalyptic path through the Revelation, perceiving it as x-raying our day and our lives through the reality-symbol-codes of the first century and offering a special blessing to those who live its message. We will now forge our path into this revealing volume, looking for symbols in the book that are *us and now.*

Notes

1. For a thorough introduction to the specific characteristics of this type of literature, see the writings of John J. Collins.

2. "The simplest reader," comments J. W. C. Wand, "can, without too much difficulty, understand the Gospels and Acts; the most learned cannot,

without some special training in Jewish literature, understand the Revelation of St. John" (in Preston and Hanson, 15 n. 1).

3. "The God of the Apocalypse can hardly be recognized as the Father of our Lord Jesus Christ, nor has the fierce Messiah, whose warriors ride in blood up to their horses' bridles, many traits that could recall Him....[who] went about doing good and healing all who were oppressed by the devil" (Dodd, 41).

4. Concerning the artistic nature of the Revelation, we need to remember the variety of ways in which it has influenced the history of art, music, and literature. It has influenced Albrecht Dürer's woodcuts of the *Four Horsemen of the Apocalypse* and *Saint Michael Fighting the Dragon;* Michelangelo's portrayals of the prophet John and Christ in the *Last Judgment* in the Sistine Chapel; Hubert and Jan van Eyck's *Adoration of the Lamb* in the altarpiece of Ghent; Handel's *Messiah;* Matthew Bridges's "Crown Him with Many Crowns"; Edmund Spenser's *Faerie Queene;* D. H. Lawrence's *Apocalypse;* Dante's *Divine Comedy;* John Milton's *Paradise Lost;* Daniel Berrigan's *Beside the Sea of Glass;* and Martin Luther King Jr.'s "We Shall Overcome." For more, see Boring, *Revelation,* 61.

5. The term *eschatology* simply means "the study of final events." In Christian theology, it usually denotes topics related to Christ's second coming, the general resurrection, the Last Judgment, the arrival of heaven, and so on.

6. Even such a conservative scholar as Gordon Fee recognizes that "the images of apocalyptic are often forms of fantasy, rather than of reality" (Fee and Stuart, 233). Bruce Metzger sagely reminds that "the descriptions [in Revelation] are not descriptions of real occurrences, but of symbols of the real occurrences" (66).

7. When good and well-meaning Christians try to interpret Revelation's symbols but are unfamiliar with their various backgrounds, frequently the most egregious errors result. Those related to the gematric (number code) puzzle "666" have often been hilariously absurd. For that reason, according to E. F. Scott, "more than any other writing in the Bible, it [the Revelation] has attracted the fanatical and curious-minded, and the Church has been too willing to abandon it to them as their natural prey" (in Preston and Hanson, 11). With great frequency, the many cults springing up in our day (in America alone, more than fifteen hundred have materialized since 1965) have used and abused Revelation for their own slanted purposes. For this reason, the church must be about the business of reclaiming this powerful component of its heritage, lest it be lost to future generations of Christians.

8. The ever-relevant and perennial nature of the Revelation's symbol world is evident in its reapplication throughout the centuries to the ever-changing religious and political scene. Holy Roman Emperor Frederick II (1194–1250), having led a crusade to the Holy Land and crowned himself king of Jerusalem, was once expected to return as the rider on a white horse (Rev. 19:11) and to reign a thousand years. Oliver Cromwell was

seen as triumphant over those who sang hosannas to the Whore, for he had chased the beast to its Roman lair, thus hastening the final days. Boston was hailed as the New Jerusalem of human freedom, while France was denounced as Babylon (an honor soon inherited by England) in the early American colonial period. On the other hand, American Israelism later proclaimed Queen Victoria the restorer of Israel, an accomplishment that would eventually usher in the millennium. The Jew has been identified with the Antichrist, as has almost everyone of note. The United Nations has been seen to be prefigured in the countless multitude who give glory to God (Rev. 7:9–17) and to inaugurate the end times. For a brief and fascinating history of the imaginative political use of Revelation's symbols, see Wainwright, 161–76.

9. I could not agree more with Fee when he argues that *"any keys to interpreting the Revelation must be intrinsic to the text of the Revelation itself or otherwise available to the original recipients from their own historical context"* (Fee and Stuart, 236). If we try to fit this book into our own preconceived notions of what it ought to refer to, we will do little but twist and distort that through which the Holy Spirit seeks to bless us.

10. One must be careful to avoid the common error of imagining that Israel's prophets did nothing but predict the future. In fact, the themes they dealt with were very broad and covered the whole of life. Do "consider in this connection the following statistics: Less than 2 percent of Old Testament prophecy is messianic. Less than 5 percent specifically describes the New Covenant age. Less than 1 percent concerns events yet to come" (Fee and Stuart, 166). For the sake of convenience and clarity, try thinking of the Hebrew prophets as "God's sociologists."

11. For a stimulating and useful treatment of these issues, see M. Rissi.

12. An excellent commentary that takes this view, with many helpful insights, and demonstrates its defensibility is *The Revelation of St. John* by Martin Kiddle.

13. This sort of procedure is called *gematria,* which refers to number games that were popular in the early centuries before the appearance of Arabic numbers. Previously letters of the alphabet also represented numbers (A = 1, B = 2, etc.). What we call *Roman numerals* (actually they are letters of the Latin alphabet) are relics of this era and still convey this function to us. This meant, of course, that every word, name, or even phrase contained a numerical equivalent of itself, that is, the sum total of all its letters understood as numbers. A charming example of this is found at Pompeii. When it was uncovered from the volcanic ash that had buried it, an inscription etched on a wall read, "I love her whose number is 545" (Ford, 225).

14. Since that time, nearly everyone who is anyone's bad boy has been skewered by the stigma of 666, for example, Napoleon, Adolf Hitler, Franklin Roosevelt, Henry Kissinger, and, more recently, even Ronald (6 letters) Wilson (6 letters) Reagan (6 letters) and Bill Gates.

15. This new mode of interpretation apparently originated with Francisco

Ribera (1537–91), a Spanish Jesuit priest residing in Salamanca. Coincidentally, preterism was formulated in 1547 by John Hentennius, and further refined by the Spanish Jesuit Alcasar (d. 1614), as a Catholic response to Protestant antipapalism (Mounce, *Book of Revelation,* 40; Wainwright, 61–66, 81).

16. For one of the most important commentaries from this evangelical and nondispensationalist approach, see Ladd.

17. The dates are (1) forty years (one biblical generation) after the establishment of the modern state of Israel, that is, 1988; (2) forty years after the recapture of Old Jerusalem, that is, 2007; and (3) in the event of the failure of the first two, forty years after the establishment of a ten-member Common Market, that is, 2022.

18. For the definitive dispensationalist-futurist commentary on Revelation, see *The Revelation of Jesus Christ* by John F. Walvoord, the former president of Dallas Theological Seminary.

19. Mounce's cogent rejoinder to this approach is insightful: "It would be little comfort for a first-century believer facing persecution to learn that after seven long church ages Christ would return and punish the enemy" (Mounce, *Book of Revelation,* 42–43).

20. These dates and characterizations of the seven churches are found and deemed to be "most conclusively" the exact "*spiritual* history of the church, and in this precise order" in the *Scofield Reference Bible* (1331–32 n. 3; cf. 1332–34). Some softening of tone can be found in the more recent and revised edition of this work.

21. Ladd, among others, is such an evangelical futurist who holds this most ancient view of early Christian tradition. His commentary focuses a critical eye on what he considers the unwarranted and unbiblical novelties of the dispensational position. Another such volume is R. Gundry's *The Church and the Tribulation.* A dispensationalist, Gundry has rejected that position's "pretribulation rapture" tenet.

22. Others have also used this term *apocalyptic* to indicate an approach to the book of Revelation (cf. Love, 48). It attempts to recognize the genius of this genre of literature, for apocalyptic will not allow us to concretize its message in an exact or precise historical location. The use of symbolic language is partially an attempt to allow the message of a given apocalyptic book to remain current and applicable in a variety of ages and eras. Its message, then, is not exhausted in any single period of need, for its symbols remain perennially relevant. The goal of apocalyptic literature is to reveal the presence, in any age, of those cosmic and eternal forces that are always and everywhere at work. In every moment and day of history, there is a great Babylon seeking to expand its dominion in direct competition with the Holy City. Only the names change; the underlying realities do not!

23. For additional insights into this special kind of biblical literature and its noncanonical counterparts, the work of the following authors will be helpful: John J. Collins (*Apocalyptic Imagination*); Paul D. Hanson; Klaus Koch; and D. S. Russell (*Jewish Apocalyptic*).

24. J. P. Love's capsule analysis of the apocalyptic approach to the book's message follows:

> [This is] how things always turn out in this world where evil seems to be in power but where God is actually the unseen Ruler. Given such and such causes, this is the series of results that will follow. Given such and such types of sin, here are the inevitable judgments. Given such and such faithful uses of the "means of grace," here are the triumphs that will ensue. (48)

Chapter 2

UNVEILING THE REVELATION

Who, What, and Why?

Rev. 1:1–11

Many people who refer to this book will misname it in a significant way by calling it the "Revelations." What this plural title commonly — and almost subconsciously — means is that the book seems to be a confusing jumble of incoherent, undigested visions without any strong sense of direction or central theme. One of my relatives once observed that to him these were not John's visions but his nightmares. And many would agree! However, there is no going back now that you have joined the ranks of those who seriously study the Revelation. Let's begin by examining how the text itself identifies the words that follow.

1:1–3 • The title of the book comes from the opening word in the original Greek text. Something is to be learned by noticing that the title is the "Revelation." It is a singular word, not plural, because the message of the book is singular, focused on one fundamental theme. Look again at the book's opening words. They proclaim it to be "the revelation of Jesus Christ." This book belongs to and is revealed by a singular person who is also its subject — Jesus Christ. This is his book, communicated for the edification of his body, the seven churches. Here we have the core theme of the entire book. Thus with wry wit, Eugene Peterson observes that "people who do not take these opening words at their full value will very likely end up using the Revelation as a Rorschach [inkblot] test rather than a religious text, reading more into the ink than they read out of it" (27).

Revelation is not a jumble of confusing visions but centers on the significance of Jesus Christ for times of trial, including the hope that his return is near at hand. Not only does the book begin with this expectation — "Look, he is coming with the clouds, and every eye will see him" (Rev. 1:7), but so it also concludes — "Behold, I am coming soon! My reward is with me, and I will give to everyone according to what he has done" (22:12; cf. 22:20–21). H. H. Rowley insightfully and wisely called the Revelation "first and foremost a vision of the glory of Christ" (134). Agreeing, G. R. Beasley-Murray once described the book's core theme as "one great exposition of what the coming of Christ means" (in George, 44). Neglect this insight and one risks missing the path to the book's central message.

Thus, we will refer to the book as the "Revelation." But if you wish to identify yourself as a devoted student, you may call it by the opening words of the Greek text, the "Apocalypse." This will identify you, among the initiated, as a true aficionado! Once again, we meet this intriguing term *apocalypse*. Quite simply, it means "to remove the veil," that is, to uncover something previously concealed or unseen. This is what Jesus has done for his people (cf. Heb. 10:19–20); he has torn the curtain back so that they might see the hidden, spiritual realities of the present that lead inevitably to God's mysterious future. For John, the word particularly means a revealing of truths that had been veiled or unappreciated in the life of the church, spiritual truths that were vital to its ongoing battle with the world of the beast. Furthermore, it is this word *apocalypse* in the opening verse of the Revelation that subsequently has been used to designate many similar works in the Judeo-Christian heritage, about seventy in all (for characteristics of apocalyptic literature, see Chapter 1).

Moreover, this first verse, speaking of the process by which the unveiled message is to be brought to God's people, says that Jesus has "made it known." Here John has used a most interesting verb that suggests much about the book from the outset. This verb, *sēmainō*, means "to signify," that is, to convey a message through signs. John has used the word elsewhere in his writings also, to indicate that which is hinted at but not plainly stated (cf. John 12:33; 18:32; 21:19). Thus does John tell us from the beginning that what the Revelation is shortly to reveal is not a videotaped presentation but something more akin to symbolic truth, not photographic but impressionistic art.

For good reason, then, does the Apocalypse, the book of Revelation, pronounce a special blessing upon those who study and communicate its message (1:3). In fact, this is just the first of seven blessings, or beatitudes, to occur in the book (cf. 14:13; 16:15; 19:9; 20:6; 22:7,14).[1] The Holy Spirit always knew that this was to be one of the Bible's most difficult books. But also, it would seem that from the very beginning Revelation was meant to be heard, to have an *audible* impact upon listeners just as surely as it has a *visual* effect. Perhaps we ought to spend more time, therefore, simply reading it

aloud to each other as we seek its inner meaning; we may hear reverberations of the Spirit that the eye knows not of. Here is a volume
that seeks our ears (cf. 2:7; 3:20; 22:18) as well as our eyes (cf. 1:7;
3:18; 22:4,7,12).

From the beginnings of the Christian church, Revelation was
widely circulated and debated. In fact, it was nearly barred from the
New Testament canon in the Eastern Church. This happened for
a variety of reasons, but partly because it was not as easily understood as other biblical books. Be assured, however, that our time
and commitment to it will be amply rewarded, not only in wonderful blessings for ourselves but also for those whom we will teach,
for this book is not merely about the past or future; it is meant to
help God's people live in the present. Philip Edgcumbe Hughes force-
fully affirms this, observing that "the prophetic teaching of the New
Testament is...intended, not as pabulum for mystery-mongers and
puzzle-solvers, but as an incentive to godly living" (30). To hear is
not enough; to hear properly is to keep, or obey, its message (Luke
11:28).

John is quite clear that the message he is conveying is not for a
dim and distant time or some future generation, for what is revealed
is "what must soon take place" (v. 1) "because the time is near" (v. 3).
This sense of dramatic immediacy stands both at the beginning and
ending of the book (cf. 22:6,10). And the oft-repeated refrain "Let
anyone who has an ear listen to [i.e., keep] what the Spirit is saying
to the churches" (2:7,11,17,29; 3:6,13,22, NRSV)[2] is its main challenge. This is no volume for the escapist or date juggler who lives
in a neurotic fantasy world. John is speaking to people who are trying to find meaning and commitment in a world filled with chaos and
overwhelmed by entrenched evil. Michael Wilcock is right, I believe,
about John's intent: "As soon as his letter reaches its destination in
the churches of Asia, they will be able to say, 'These things are happening *now*'" (33). We need to be careful lest we allow our lust for
prediction to become mere procrastination, a putting off (into the
future) of those agendas God has for us today. It is we the readers
and hearers of this message who are meant to keep (do!) what is revealed, for these things are happening (cf. Mulholland, 67–69)! The
apocalypse is *now!*

Our situation is actually quite comparable to the times in which
the book was written. The blessing in verse 3 on those who read Revelation aloud indicates that few in the early church could read. If one
who had that ability did not exercise it for others, not many would
ever have the opportunity to hear and obey Revelation's message.

And in the modern church, most Christians still consider the book closed because they have few clues as to how it should be understood or applied. Thus, today, the church again needs those who can share this great revelation with others who need to know its message and experience the transforming power of its unique blessing. So, blessed are those who read and study this book today with a view to communicating its many blessings to others, for to see *Jesus* here — not a date puzzle — is to begin to *know* him, then to *love* and *serve* him.

1:4–5 • Who is this "John" who commands a hearing and asserts an authority over the seven churches by merely mentioning his name four times (1:1, 4, 9; 22:8)? Surely the name carried a reputation that must have been well known, a name that automatically held authority among a certain group of people, namely, the seven churches. Christian scholars have debated long and inconclusively over this issue. The earliest Christian tradition, from the early second century, incontestably affirms apostolic authorship, i.e., John the apostle. Later periods in early church history, however, saw much debate over the identity of the "John" in this book, some believing there was another Elder or church leader of the same name in the area of Ephesus. They cite the great dissimilarity between the language and style of Revelation and those revealed in the Fourth Gospel and epistles that more certainly come from the apostle John. They also note that the author of Revelation does not overtly associate himself with the apostles, though they are mentioned in 21:14, nor does he ever claim that title for himself, preferring the appellations "servant" (1:1), "brother and companion" (1:9), and "prophet" (22:9). This hypothetical and non-apostolic "John" has been identified by various authors as (a) a member of the apostle's inner group of disciples, though not he himself, speaking in his master's name (virtually the same as having the apostle write it himself); (b) a mysterious "John the Elder," a shadowy figure mentioned by an early bishop named Papias as possibly living in Ephesus, but about whom almost nothing is certainly known, not even that he was understood as someone other than the apostle; (c) an unknown and uncelebrated man known as "John the Prophet" (cf. 10:11; 22:9), i.e., an author who is recognized locally as a Christian holding that important but non-apostolic office; (d) John Mark, author of the second Gospel, though there are few similarities between the two books; (e) John the Baptist (Ford 28–46, 50–56), though this suggestion brings a highly complex theory of composition to bear, failing to explain both the lack of any attempt to distinguish the two "Johns" from each other and the origin of the presumed authority that is being exercised by the author.

The problems that such non-apostolic solutions pose, however, are difficult and numerous. Why was the earliest tradition unanimous in affirming apostolic authorship? How was this other "John" and his role in Revelation's origin initially and generally forgotten? Would any, otherwise unknown elder or prophet have the authority to address all seven Asian churches as our author did? Who besides a superintendent of all could possibly have such intimate knowledge of the inner workings of so many different churches? Why are there so many notable similarities between the thought and terminology of the other Johannine writings and the Revelation?[3] It is the combination of strong external testimony (early church fathers who so affirm) with internal evidence that is not contradictory (terminology, concepts and knowledge associated with John the apostle) that continues to lead many to maintain the traditional answer that Revelation comes from the hand of John, the apostle and beloved disciple.

Early church tradition held that late in his life John had moved to Ephesus, where there was a major church originally built by Paul. There John became the regional bishop, exercising control over several local churches, and eventually he was exiled on Patmos, where he wrote the Revelation. While this traditional view of the authorship of the book cannot be decisively proved, neither should it easily be set aside. There are genuine questions and difficulties associated with this position (Mounce, *Book of Revelation*, 30), though fewer and less serious, in my judgment, than those raised by other options. Who could simply drop the name *John*, without claiming the prerogatives of other administrative titles associated with organizational leadership, and expect a hearing and obedience? No elder or prophet held such an office, so far as we know, over an entire province, over seven churches. The absence of such a claim to apostleship in Revelation need indicate nothing further than the fact that such a title was obviously acknowledged and that modesty was therefore being exercised. Probably, tradition has given us the best lead; our author is the apostle John himself, writing while on Patmos and without the aid of a secretary, hence a different style than that exhibited by other Johannine documents.[4]

In verses 4–5, note the presence of the whole Godhead — God on the throne, God the Son, and God the (sevenfold) Spirit! This suggests a rather clear-cut component in Revelation that we can watch for as we read this book, which, as we shall discover, is probably the most Trinitarian book in the New Testament. This emphasis on the community and complete equality of persons within the triune

Godhead will be found at many points throughout its pages, right to the end (22:16–17,19).

For John, the crucified Messiah who is also God, this Jesus, must constantly be remembered as one who models true and "faithful witness," the willingness to give one's whole life as a testimony to faith (cf. 2:13; 12:11; 13:7). This is the lifestyle that ultimately leads to life "from the dead" and incorporates one into the community of the eternal future (cf. 20:6), for in that life there is fellowship with the one who holds the "keys of death" (1:18) and who promises that eventually death will be no more, when the "old order of things has passed away" (21:4). It is this member of the triune Godhead, Jesus the Christ, who is truly "the ruler of the kings of the earth" (cf. 6:15–16; 11:15; 19:11–16). But just as important as any of these attributes is the echo of John 3:16 heard in the words "who loves us" (v. 5b). This is the love the churches will need to weather the storms ahead. It is a love that promises to free them from their sins and give eventual victory over opponents (3:9), but it is also a compassion that leads to victory over their own, inner faults as well (3:19). Here is a deep, compassionate love that seeks to consummate itself in the intimacy of an eternal, face-to-face communion (22:4).

There is one final consideration to which we must pay attention. Verses 4 and 5, which follow the conventional letter form so often seen in Pauline letters, and verse 11 make it absolutely clear that this book is essentially a communication addressed to the seven churches noted.[5] Yes, John's work is prophetic-apocalyptic, but it is also a letter. Such is confirmed by the conclusion found in 22:21 (cf. 1 Cor. 16:23; Gal. 6:18). This important insight will help us steer clear of the misunderstanding that this book was meant chiefly for future generations. It is a genuine letter directed to seven congregations in John's day; hence, the seven church letters are seven cover letters to the remainder of the book.

1:6 • God's wonderful liberation (v. 5b) of the people of God from every physical oppression of the past and God's emancipation of them from all forms of present spiritual bondage represent central themes in this book. Thus, from the very outset, the people of God are viewed through the mirror image of the Exodus. Just as the Passover lamb freed the people of Israel from the plague of the death angel, so now the blood of the true Lamb redeems God's people from eternal and everlasting death, the second death (Rev. 20:14). That such freed people become "a priestly kingdom" (Exod. 19:6, NRSV; cf. 1 Pet. 2:5,9) also derives from the original Exodus event. This passage is but the first of many in Revelation in which the redeemed are viewed as the spiritual counterparts of ancient Israel, now continuing the Exodus pilgrimage. It was a commonplace in Judaism that as they participated in the Passover meal, all Jews were to consider that they were actually present in the Exodus events being commemorated. Now, John sees the church of the Messiah as a continuing participant in that story, for the events of Exodus-eve pointed toward the ultimate and final exodus from every bondage, namely, the redemption of the cross and the resurrection.

1:7 • If John's "revelation of Jesus Christ" reveals a character not unlike the Passover lamb, then it also portrays a continuing hope among his people for a glorious reunion with him. As the Old Testament people of God (i.e., the Jews) continue even now to await the Messiah's arrival, so the new people of God (i.e., the Christian church) also await the coming of their Lord. Throughout the book, this anticipation of his coming is the unfolding dynamic propelling the plot (2:25; 3:11; 6:16–17; 14:14; 16:15) to that final manifestation (19:11–21). This is not only the ultimate promise of the book — "Yes, I am coming soon" (22:20), but also the defining hope and prayer of the messianic community — "Amen. Come, Lord Jesus" (22:20). Clearly, this book is about "the revelation of Jesus Christ." It is he who reveals the past, the present, and the future, and it is he who ultimately will be revealed.

1:8 • The God who is both the beginning and ending of all reality (*alpha* and *omega* are the first and last letters of the Greek alphabet) is Israel's God (Isa. 41:4; 44:6; 48:12; cf. 43:10), "who is, and who was, and who is to come." Later, John will describe this God as "the One who is and who was" (11:17). Don't miss the omission of the third element of time: "is to come"! This alteration takes place because, in 11:15–18, God has already come and "begun to reign" (v. 17).

God the Father speaks on only two occasions in this book (1:8; 21:5–8). In both places God says: "I am the Alpha and the Omega" (1:8), adding "the Beginning and the End" in 21:6. Interestingly, in these contexts, Jesus defines himself also as "the First and the Last" (1:17) and as "the Alpha and the Omega, the First and the Last, the Beginning and the End" (22:13). Clearly, the desire to assign and transfer the characteristics of God Almighty to Jesus the Lamb is unmistakable and thoroughgoing. In Revelation, the divine Godhead is both "fashioner" and "finisher" of the cosmic story. John is perhaps reminding his faithful friends on the mainland that no matter how bad things might ever appear, they must remember that their Lord will always have the last word. Their lives are always being lived "in the center," midway between creation and providence. Their God will never lead them into places where grace cannot sustain them.

1:9 • From the outset, we learn that John was a Christian who had led a life so divergent from the dominant culture that the System had cast him out (cf. by contrast 3:16). He calls himself our "brother," for as "children of God" (John 1:12; 1 John 3:1) we are all "brothers and sisters" (1 John 3:10, NRSV) and share together in the adventure of spiritual warfare against the world (cf. Eph. 6:10–18). But as we patiently endure our pilgrimage, including its sufferings, John reminds us, we are also enjoying the blessings of the kingdom of God.

The only time this kingdom and its blessings are clearly defined in the New Testament is when Paul counsels consideration for brothers and sisters in matters of personal conviction: "For the kingdom of God is not a matter of eating and drinking, but of righteousness, peace and joy in the Holy Spirit" (Rom. 14:17; cf. Gal. 5:22–23). R. H. Charles was right in his assessment that John, even in exile, and despite all that was happening to him, possessed "a faith immeasurable, an optimism inexpungible, a joy inextinguishable" (1:xiv), and so may we if we do not allow our circumstances to confine our spirits or to destroy our God-given dreams. We too may live in the midst of our own Patmos, but we dare not let it define who we are, for we are the citizens of the kingdom of God. From Patmos, John saw and nourished his spirit by the vision of the heavenly city; it, not Patmos, is our destiny and sustaining hope. That destiny is the destination of the book and is finally achieved in chapters 21–22.

The imprisonment of John must be one of the early fulfillments of Jesus' words concerning future persecution of his followers (Mark 13:9–13; John 15:18–21). To merit exile to Patmos (modern Patino), an island used by Rome to isolate those deemed politically disruptive, John must have been an unusually powerful spokesman for the gospel. Patmos, a Roman Alcatraz, is a rocky island, five by eight miles in size and just off the southwestern coast of Asia Minor (modern Turkey). In John's day, it was used for troublemakers whom Rome wished to quarantine from society (Hemer, 27–29.).

Perhaps it is no accident that other New Testament books were also written from a prison. We call four of Paul's letters "Prison Epistles." They are Ephesians, Philippians, Colossians, and Philemon; each gives evidence that Paul was under arrest, the prisoner of Rome while he was writing. The richness of that prison cell reminds one of the old adage that "no sailor ever distinguished himself on calm seas." And those like Paul (2 Cor. 11:23–28) and John (Rev. 1:9) who have suffered for Christ and, in the heat of the day, have born the burdens of the kingdom of God are those best equipped to share the divine truth with others. The best theologians and pastors have always made their stand where the people are, in the midst of their needs. Hence, John is more than just a prophetic theologian; he is also a concerned pastor, speaking from his great heart to the hearts of those he loved about the beasts and plagues they were battling.

1:10–11 • The New Testament has spoken on other occasions of "the first day of the week" (Acts 20:7; cf. 1 Cor. 16:2), but this is the first time we find it being designated as "the Lord's Day." It is the day when the Lord rose from the grave, making a mockery of death and proclaiming, "I hold the keys of death and Hades" (1:18). As with so much else in the Revelation, this is probably a protest against "the emperor's feast, also called *hēmera kuriakē* [day of the Lord]" (Ford, 382). Perhaps John is hinting at the issue of the two lords who seek preeminence in this world and in the lives of God's people.

As John, the prisoner, is in prayer on "the Lord's Day," something absolutely stunning took place. Though he was literally *"en ... Patmō"* (v. 9, "on ... Patmos") suddenly he is also *"en pneumati"* (v. 10, "in the Spirit"). *En Patmō* may well be where he lives and is imprisoned but *en pneumati* defines the vision by which John lives. Through the "Spirit,"[6] he was suddenly engaged by a trumpetlike voice[7] and charged with the writing of a circular letter to seven specific churches. It is this letter that was to be known as the book of Revelation. And it is these churches who are the intended readers and recipients of the wonderful counsel that is John's Revelation. Quite simply, then, and it must not be forgotten throughout, this book from beginning to end is *for the seven churches* (cf. 22:16).

The seven cities mentioned, Ephesus, Smyrna, Pergamum, Thyatira, Sardis, Philadelphia, and Laodicea, represent the normal routing of a great postal circuit that connected these important cities in the Roman province of Asia Minor, or Western Turkey as we know it. The cities ranged from thirty to nearly forty-five miles distant from each other. They are seven, although John could have included other churches, because in their symbolic "sevenness," they represent all the people of God in all places and all times. As such, they portray a wide-ranging catalog of vices and virtues that so often characterize the church's existence. In reality, they are meant to be a counterculture at loggerheads with the System that surrounds them, and the analysis of their spiritual condition is a mirror in which we perceive our life, truth, and reality. There is a prophetic word for each of God's people here and an understanding of holy living that will touch all those who take time to enter into Revelation's special blessings.

Notes

1. An interesting way to study and perhaps present this group of texts would be in comparison with the Beatitudes of Matthew 5:3–12 and Luke 6:20–21.

2. Perhaps it is no accident that the word *prophecy* also occurs exactly seven times in the book (1:3; 11:6; 19:10; 22:7,10,18,19). The "prophecy" of this book (1:3) is the message to which the churches are to listen.

3. Everett F. Harrison list twelve distinctive words, phrases, and concepts that occur infrequently or not at all outside the acknowledged Johannine (written by John) literature and Revelation (441–442).

4. Discussions of date and authorship are the very substance of volumes generically designated as an *Introduction to the New Testament*. Reliable evangelical contributions to the field are those by E. F. Harrison (*Introduction to the New Testament* [Grand Rapids: Eerdmans, 1964) and Donald Guthrie (*New Testament Introduction: Hebrews to Revelation* [Chicago: InterVarsity Press, 1962]).

5. In verse 4 is John's first of fifty-four uses of the number *seven*. Its general symbolic function is to indicate that a subject is being observed in its "totality" or "completeness."

6. Reference to the Holy "Spirit" is made fourteen times in the Revelation. There are seven such references in chapters 2–3, "listen to what the Spirit is saying to the churches" (2:7,11,17,29; 3:6,13,22, NRSV) and seven more outside the context of the church letters ("in the spirit," 1:10; 4:2; 17:3; 21:10; comments of the Spirit, 14:13; 22:17; and the definition, "the spirit of prophecy," 19:10). In addition, the phrase "the seven spirits" also occurs a total of four times (see the note at 3:1). (Bauckham, 109–10)

7. Interesting in this regard is an eight-foot-long broken stone found at the base of the southwestern corner of the temple mount in Jerusalem. At one time it had rested atop that corner of the temple wall. What remains legible of an inscription reads: "To the house of trumpeting." According to Jack Finegan, "The reference is understood to be to the place on top of the Temple enclosure wall where a priest would stand to blow a trumpet to announce the beginning and the end of the Sabbath day" (212). In the Revelation also, the voice of the trumpet and the "Lord's Day" are linked.

Chapter 3

JOHN'S INAUGURAL VISION

Scripture's Final Word

Rev. 1:12–20

Since John's work is identified in Revelation 1:1 as "the revelation of Jesus Christ," it is fitting that we should be given a portrait of this revealer who becomes the revealed, for he is the one disclosing the message of this book. Here the great "I AM WHO I AM"[1] is unveiled through the incarnation of the Son of Man, inviting humanity to know and enter into relationship with Almighty God. And surely, this is the eternal truth about our God, namely, that we would never have known or discovered God if the Lord had not revealed himself to us. But graciously God has been self-disclosed in the Son (Heb. 1:1–2), and the staggering reality of the revelatory incarnation is this: "Anyone who has seen me," said Jesus, "has seen the Father" (John 14:9). Hence, in Revelation 1:12–20, John turns to see the one who has come to address him. But turning to see the voice "like a trumpet" (v. 10),[2] John finds the utterly unexpected.

1:12–13 • The first sight to greet John's astonished eyes is a group of "seven golden lampstands." *Lampstands* are supports holding small vessels containing oil with wicks that could be lighted. We must remember there are seven; it is important.

Standing among the lampstands is the one whose voice John had turned to behold. This is a most important image for the remainder of the book, for it reminds us of what we all know but often forget: "Jesus Christ is not dead, absent, hidden, or silent; he is present among his churches and speaks through his prophet to the distress and crisis of their particular situations" (Boring, *Revelation*, 63). He is the ultimate light that shines through all the work of the church: "the Lamb is its lamp" (Rev. 21:23). Any church that is not true to his central presence will not long enjoy its position among the churches.

Then John describes this one who stands among the lampstands

42

and in so doing discloses much of the inner essence of what is yet to be revealed concerning Jesus throughout the remainder of the Revelation. The description begins with the words "someone 'like a son of man.'" Here Revelation is building on its New Testament background. Do you remember Jesus' favorite title for himself? In the Gospels, he is the only one to ever speak of himself as "the Son of Man." More than eighty times, this is his unique term of self-disclosure to his disciples (see Matt. 16:13–16). It is a descriptive title that Jesus apparently took from Daniel 7:13, where a heavenly vista is viewed by Daniel and "one like a son of man" suddenly and boldly approaches "the Ancient of Days." Later in this chapter, Daniel guides us to understand that the one he has beheld in heavenly splendor is none other than the representative embodiment (or incarnation?) of the "people of the Most High" (cf. Dan. 7:14,27).

One is tempted here to think of Paul's favorite metaphor for the church, that is, the body of Christ. If for Daniel the son of man is the symbol or personification of God's people (a little like our "Uncle Sam"), for Paul the church can be understood as the manifestation of that body or person known as Jesus Christ. The only other place in Revelation where the title "Son of Man" will appear is in 14:14, at which point the final fate of humanity is achieved. He is truly "the First and the Last" (1:17).

Next, this one who embodies the people of God is portrayed as a priest. The Greek words used here to denote the long robe are found six times in the Septuagint (the Greek version of the Hebrew Scriptures, which is known by the symbol LXX) for the garment belonging to the high priest (e.g., Exod. 28:4; 29:5; Lev. 16:4). Similarly, the girdle, or "golden sash," which was worn around the breast distinguishes the wearer as one of royal majesty, not a commoner.

Clearly, John is now describing a great high priest, such as is mentioned in Hebrews 6:19–20: "We have this as a sure and steadfast anchor of the soul, a hope that enters into the inner shrine behind the curtain, where Jesus has gone as a forerunner on our behalf, having become a high priest for ever after the order of Melchizedek" (RSV). As Revelation has already noted, Jesus "freed us from our sins by his blood" (1:5), and so too affirms the author of Hebrews! He has offered himself up, once, for our sins and ever lives to make continual intercession for his people (Heb. 7:23–27). He is ever the Lamb "slain" (Rev. 5:6), for this priest offers himself as his only sacrifice.

1:14 • The white head and hair of verse 14 continues this thought.[3] Christ's priesthood is final and utterly efficacious because he is himself divine. John has turned again to Daniel 7:9, where

God is similarly described. And this is only the first of a long chain of passages in Revelation in which John explicitly clothes Jesus in phraseology previously reserved for the Almighty alone.

For John, Jesus is clearly not just divine, but more precisely he is co-equal with the God of the Hebrew Scriptures. Hence, the divine seat of power will be "the throne of God and of the Lamb" (Rev. 22:3); it is the throne Jesus has ascended because he has conquered, and so must we if we wish to share his future. Thus, Revelation 12:11 is a summary of the whole book and its message:

> They [our sisters and brothers] overcame him [Satan]
>   by the blood of the Lamb
>   and by the word of their testimony;
> they did not love their lives so much
>   as to shrink from death.

To "overcome," in Revelation, is to maintain a consistent testimony that reveals the presence of Jesus Christ in history, "for the testimony of Jesus is the spirit of prophecy" (19:10). This is, of course, a testimony for life and one maintained to the extremity of death itself. Those who preserve such a witness, for example, Antipas of Pergamum (2:13), share the title of "faithful witness" with Jesus (1:5).

The mention of "his eyes," which appear like fire, recalls Daniel 10:6 and suggests the penetrating vision of one who fathoms all truth and all reality. This, John's practical way of describing "omniscience," reminds us of Jesus' own words and the sovereignty of the one from whom nothing can be hidden (Mark 4:22; Luke 8:17). No amount of sham or hypocrisy can shield us from that holy gaze, for the holiness of God is a "consuming fire" (Heb. 12:29; cf. Isa. 10:17). All is open and transparent before him who returns to tread the winepress of God's wrath (14:19), for "his eyes are like blazing fire" (19:12).[4]

1:15 • Strength and stability, sureness of foot, a fixed foundation, these are the implications of the one who stands above time and nature, whose feet are like bronze. The background of this description is reminiscent of Daniel 10:6 and Ezekiel 1:4–7, but given the Danielic context, there is most likely a contrast being established between the Son of Man, who stands like a cornerstone of truth, and the clay and iron-footed statue, which symbolizes the flawed and fleeting kingdoms of human dominion (Dan. 2:32–35,41–45). The Son of Man stands when all else crumbles and disintegrates into chaos; he is the foundation of Christian life (1 Cor. 3:11).

His "voice," which is like "rushing waters," once again reveals John's dictionary of symbols as the Hebrew Scriptures. We already know that this voice is "like a trumpet" (1:10), which may be a reference to the trumpet sounds accompanying the divine appearance at Sinai (Exod. 19:16,19).[5] But how does the "sound of rushing waters" modify the sound of the trumpet? John may be thinking of the passage found in Ezekiel 43:2: "And I saw the glory of the God of Israel coming from the east. His voice was like the roar of rushing waters, and the land was radiant with his glory." Clearly, John wishes us to hear the overwhelming majesty of the voice of God, that which drowns out all else by its exclusionary dominance. And once again, a lofty Christology is being asserted.

1:16 • Moreover, this divine mouth contains a "sharp double-edged sword." I will never forget the day Dr. Bruce Metzger walked into a class on the Revelation and dismayed some of us: "Young men," he said, "you must never make the Bible *mean* what it *says*." Then, having caught us with minds in gear, he continued: "All you can do is to allow the Bible to *mean* what it *means*." He was, in fact, commenting on this very passage.

Metzger's words were sage counsel, for words and phrases often mean much more than they seem to say on the surface.[6] This perspective on symbolic language is fundamental and never more needed for proper biblical exposition than in the Revelation. The book simply demands that we ask what is *meant* by a passage, for what is *said* is often inexplicable at a purely literal level. Apocalyptic literature is built on a rich world of symbolism, a world that must be examined and studied to be understood, not merely repeated by rote.

The "sword" in this verse is a precise example of Revelation's pictorial and nonobjectifying language. To imagine a sword protruding from the delicate tissues of the mouth is literally gruesome, invoking the image of torture more than disclosure. But what does this image really *mean*? Let's not forget that long before John wrote the Revelation, the figure of a sword had already achieved a clear symbolic meaning.

In the Hebrew Scriptures, the mouth of God's suffering servant had been likened to a "sharpened sword" in its incisive mission to arouse Israel (Isa. 49:2). The New Testament finds Paul speaking of "the sword of the Spirit, which is the word of God" (Eph. 6:17). Similarly, the author of Hebrews compares the word of God and its ability to pierce the spirit and discern the thoughts or intentions of the heart to a sharp "double-edged sword" (Heb. 4:12). Moreover, the apostle John had already seen a direct connection between the word of God and Jesus Christ (John 1:1; cf. Rev. 19:13). In light of this background of Scripture, what is meant by "the sword" that emanates from the Son of Man's mouth? The sword simply suggests that when this one speaks, nothing less than the very voice of God is heard, and the result is divine revelation. That is, to confront this Son of Man is to encounter God (19:15).

Verse 16 goes on to describe the Son of Man's face as shining like the sun. Perhaps John had seen that sunlit face once before on the Mount of Transfiguration when Jesus' face "shone like the sun" (Matt. 17:2). Moses' face shone because of his encounter with God (Exod. 34:29), and so will all the righteous shine in the final day of redemption (Matt. 13:43). But for now, John has beheld the source of that light and life, which began to make itself known in the very beginning of creation (Gen. 1:3; John 1:4) and is, in fact, "the glory of God" (2 Cor. 4:6).

1:17–18 • The vision sends John to his knees, the only position appropriate for those who behold the divine glory (Isa. 6:5; Ezek. 1:28; Dan. 8:17–18; 10:8–10). However, Jesus extends a gracious hand to John and bids him "not be afraid"; this echoes the manner in which Jesus spoke to his disciples in a previous moment of panic (Matt. 14:27; John 6:20). Immediately thereafter Jesus' reassurance takes the form of a stupendous self-identification, "I am the First and the Last," the very title designating the one and only God of the Old Testament:

> "This is what the LORD says—
> Israel's King and Redeemer, the LORD Almighty:
> I am the first and I am the last;
>   apart from me there is no God."

> —Isaiah 44:6 (see also 48:12)

John has a perfectly clear understanding of the Son of Man, the one who stands in the midst of the lampstands (1:13). Where he is, there is God!

If there is any doubt whatsoever concerning the one John is encountering, it is dispelled by the continuing identification in verse 18. This description of one who was dead but now is alive forevermore can indicate no one other than Jesus of Nazareth. By virtue of that very death and resurrection, he now possesses "the keys of death and Hades." He is the Lord of the resurrection and promises this victory over death to all his faithful (20:4–6). Even those who pass into that realm are blessed, for they are at rest and await their certain reward (14:13), freed from their enslavement to the power of death (cf. Heb. 2:14–15). In other words, the future has a welcoming face, that of Jesus, the Son of Man.

1:19 • Concluding John's inaugural vision, which calls him to prophetic ministry (cf. Isa. 6; Ezek. 1), is this fundamental charge: "Write, therefore, what you have seen, what is now and what will take place later." Previously, this assignment had been voiced as "Write on a scroll what you see" (1:11); now that is expanded and explained in two concluding clauses. What John has seen, the substance of this book, is those realities that constitute "what is now" and will lead to "what will take place later." Quite naturally the two are always linked, for if you understand the present, you know something of the future since one seamless garment clothes the church's story. Not to be forgotten in this connection is the description of the Almighty "who is, and who was, and who is to come" (1:8). To know who this one *is,* is to know the past and future as well, for the process of history affecting the churches is also reflected in God's own eternal nature.

Verse 19 has long been recognized as one of the most difficult and most critical verses in all the Revelation. Three main interpretations have emerged:

1. John is told to write concerning *three* different eras covered in the Revelation. These are the past that he had "seen" (the vision of the Son of Man; Rev. 1), the present that "is" (the churches and their day; Rev. 2–3), and the future that will "take place later" (usually defined as the tribulation period and the culmination of history; Rev. 4–22).

2. What John had *seen* is equivalent to *two* different realms of time, the present and the future as it leads to the final consummation. That is, what he had "seen" was in essence the entire book (1:11), now understood to encompass "what is" (we might call it "the church age"; Rev. 1–17) and "what will take place" (that is, the final goal of history; Rev. 18–22).

3. The contents of John's vision represent the perpetual and persistent present; that is, what John has *seen* is "what is now" going on in his day and what "will [continue to] take place later," after his day, in all the church's history (Rev. 1–17). This mixture of eras underlies the whole of the Revelation because it is about the omnipresent that has but one outcome (Rev. 18–22).

"It accords more with the actual contents of the prophecy," concluded G. R. Beasley-Murray, "to recognize that *what is and what is to take place hereafter* applies to the entire book, for there is a perpetual movement between past, present, and future in the visions" (Beasley-Murray, *Book of Revelation,* 68). Perhaps we should also say that while both eras interpenetrate all sectors of the book, the early chapters deal with the future as the inevitable consequence of our present actions (2:7,11), and the later chapters deal with the present as causative factors in God's future (22:11–12). We could paraphrase 1:19, then, by saying that John is commanded to write about those things he has been allowed to see, namely, the dynamics of confrontation with the beast (the System of his day), which are and always will be until the final Day of Judgment.[7]

J. Ramsey Michaels investigated this verse by inquiring into the narrative structure of a variety of passages in Revelation. He too comes to the conclusion that three interpenetrating eras are discussed. The first is the vision(s) that John is allowed to see — technically a part of his past. The second is the meaning or interpretation of this vision for the present, that is, how it applies to his contemporary scene and what reality is deeply about. The third is the issue of what such current realities prophesy for the future, that is, where and in what ways they come to termination. Thus, in agreement with Beasley-Murray, Michaels suggests that 1:19 is a key, not to the structural outline of the book, but rather to its narrative technique. Through a variety of narrative voices — sometimes divine or angels, even John's own — there is a perpetual shift from past (the original vision), to present (his day) and future (the last day), as the book engages in a process of continuous self-interpretation (Michaels, "Narrative Voices," 604–20). In this regard, the comment of Paul Minear is most helpful: "[H]is commission to write covered three things: what he had seen and heard, 'what is,' 'what is about to happen' (1:19). Each vision in the book is structured to include all three" (179). John was allowed, by the heavenly vision, to see so deeply into what now is that what is about to be was also perceived as the only possible outcome.

Dogmatism ill behooves the informed student of the Revelation, especially given the great proliferation of views on the book's structure, which are often based upon 1:19. Nevertheless, and with humility, I opt for the third interpretation. Not only is it an acceptable reading of the text, but experience indicates that it is most fruitful in challenging the lives of Christian people and their churches. I believe it to hold the best key to unlock the rich insights of this marvelous book. Accordingly, look at the juxtaposition of the charge in verse 19 and the multifaceted description of the Son of Man standing at the threshold of the Revelation. He is the one who ultimately "is," and he is determinative for "what will take place later." Hence, he is the ultimate high priest of creation, lifting and offering it back to God, its Creator. He is also the manifestation of God Almighty, capable of executing God's will in history. That his word is the final word, concluding the story of biblical revelation, is one of the important messages of the book and is highlighted in this symbolic, personal sketch of Jesus. All revelation is aimed at Jesus; he is the alpha and omega of redemptive history.

Hence, the Revelation is "the revelation of Jesus Christ" as the apex of Scripture. He is the culminating word of all divine words. To understand him is to grasp the key to all Scripture. He is its last word, for "God spoke to our forefathers through the prophets at many times and in various ways, but in these last days he has spoken to us by his Son, whom he appointed heir of all things, and through whom he made the universe" (Heb. 1:1–2). To write this revelation concerning God's last word, an author was required who was deeply steeped in the Hebrew Scriptures and who knew all its words. He was so saturated with biblical lore that he could draw pictures and theological landscapes with echoes, hints, and shadows of biblical data. Never forget that within this book of 404 verses, there are no fewer than 518 allusions to the Old Testament (Preston and Hanson, 26) and 104 more to the New Testament (Ford, 42–43), though no direct quotes are found, only allusions.

These ties between the testaments and the Revelation lead to another important principle of interpretation: In the Revelation is not so much that is completely new as that which restates the whole biblical message, now focused on Jesus. Carl Auberlen (1824–64) once observed that "in this book all the other biblical books end and meet" (in Wainwright, 114).[8] The Revelation might even be called "the Bible in a nutshell." Here is the essence of the agelong battle between the kingdoms of man and the kingdom of God. What this means is that we ought not to be looking to the modern world for the codes that decipher this book (e.g., tanks, submarines, atomic bombs, the Common Market, or UN), for the cipher we seek is found largely within previous revelation.

1:20 • Finally, the Lord of the symbols reveals the nature of the Revelation by decoding two symbols that are of special import: "The seven stars are the angels of the seven churches, and the seven lampstands are the seven churches." We will discuss the meaning of the "angels" in the next chapter but turn our attention now to the lampstands. To a first-century Jewish author, only one frame of reference is possible for the lampstands, namely, Israel's national symbol, the seven-branched golden lampstand known as the "menorah" that stood in the temple.[9] In the aftermath of Jerusalem's downfall, in A.D. 70, the menorah had become the national symbol of the Jewish people (Reznick, 130).

What does it mean that John now describes the church as a menorah? True, the "lampstands" are here described in the plural rather than singular, but that is probably because Revelation plainly means to individualize and treat each lamp (or church) separately. Tangentially, the churches (seven lamps) are being represented as that place where the light and life of God shine outward into a darkened world where the beast roams free. As that monster represents a sevenfold team of darkness, so the church is the sevenfold team of light. Who will win the battle, securing the allegiance and fate of humanity?

When the Revelation defines the church as a menorah, it is continuing an Old Testament theme found in Isaiah. In the words of the prophet, then, the church is "a light for the Gentiles" (Isa. 49:6), even as the suffering servant of Israel was meant to be. And the following letters to these churches represent John's attempt to trim their wicks, for the church is nothing less than the eschatological fulfillment of the light that first glowed in the tabernacle; it is the embodiment of Christ (cf. Rev. 21:23). As such, it is the *messianic menorah* and the continuing story of Israel (see the illustration on the facing page).

Does the structure of a menorah tell us anything about the seven churches — Ephesus, Smyrna, Pergamum, Thyatira, Sardis, Philadelphia, and Laodicea?[10] Given the configuration, how do they relate to each other? The configuration links various churches together. Ephesus and Laodicea are joined by the same branch of the lampstand, as are Smyrna and Philadelphia. Then, Pergamum, Thyatira, and Sardis stand in the middle, bracketed by the others. This represents a classic "envelope pattern," of which Jewish writers were so very fond. Note the relationships: a b c [d] c′ b′ a′. Technically, this is called a "chiasm."

It is no accident that the *outsiders,* Ephesus and Laodicea, are the only two that are threatened with expulsion from the church (Rev. 2:5; 3:16); they share the same branch of the lampstand. Smyrna and Philadelphia, apparently ideal models, have no censures lodged against them; they also share a branch. The three middle churches are sad and varied manifestations of compromised congregations. Perhaps their central position suggests that they are more numerous or typical. They even seem to be placed on a continuum of imperfection. See if you can discover the progression towards decadence suggested among the three by the comments made at 2:14 and 3:4.[11]

The number *seven* (as in "seven lampstands") as a symbolic figure bears a few different connotations. Usually, it means something like "totality," "completeness," or "fullness" but often includes the idea of "essence." The menorah's seven-ness is likely to be significant in all

these ways, representing the essence of the sevenfold church of all times, in all places. It is the church in all its splendor and affliction.[12]

John's outlook for the future of these churches is clearly very optimistic because of the one who stands "among" them in their triumphs and trials (1:13). He is the all-sufficient one, "the light of the world...the light of life" (John 8:12; cf. Rev. 21:23). And, if they live in that light, they too will be "the light of the world" (Matt. 5:14). The menorah is a wonderful symbol of both the unity and vocation of Christ and his body, the church.

Notes

1. "I AM WHO I AM" is the English translation of the name of God — Yahweh — in the Hebrew Scriptures, also known as the Tetragrammaton (i.e., the four letters YHWH; Exod. 3:13–15; cf. John 8:58, "I tell you the truth...before Abraham was born, I am!").

2. The Greek word *hōs*, meaning "like" or "as," is used no fewer than fifty-six times in Revelation, an occurrence that indicates one of the essential truths about apocalyptic literature. That is, there are realities that inadequate human language is incapable of expressing. Therefore, much is

conveyed through the use of similes, metaphors, and symbols, which become the mirrors of divine truth.

3. Eugene Peterson suggests that the description of the Son of Man as wearing the vestments of a priest begins with "his head" (v. 14) and chiastically (a b c d c' b' a') ends at the same point with "his face" (v. 16), thus producing a seven-point sketch. Given the pervasive use of the symbol *seven* in Revelation, he is likely correct (Peterson, 39).

4. Indeed, this is a core theme of Scripture (Ps. 65:5; Eccles. 12:14; Jer. 16:17; Dan. 2:22; Hos. 5:3; Luke 8:17; 12:2–3; 1 Cor. 4:5; Heb. 4:13).

5. Also note that a trumpet invokes the Day of Atonement (Lev. 25:9), is used by the watchman to warn of imminent destruction (Ezek. 33:6), and, therefore, symbolizes the approach of the eschatological Day of Judgment (1 Cor. 15:52; 1 Thess. 4:16).

6. Commenting on this concept, Herschel Hobbs reminisces: "Dr. A. T. Robertson used to say, 'Let the Bible say what it says.' I think Dr. W. T. Conner was more to the point when he used to say, 'Let the Bible say what it means.' Sometimes the Bible doesn't mean what it *says*" (in George, 138).

7. For helpful discussions of this problem, see Beale, 360–87; A. Collins, *The Apocalypse,* 32–33; Gundry, *Church and the Tribulation,* 64–66; Mounce, *Book of Revelation,* 81–82; Mulholland, 35, 88–89; Wall, 63–65.

8. Cf. Peterson: "I do not read the Revelation to get additional information about the life of faith in Christ. I have read it all before in law and prophet, in gospel and epistle. Everything in the Revelation can be found in the previous sixty-five books of the Bible. The Revelation adds nothing of substance to what we already know. The truth of the gospel is already complete, revealed in Jesus Christ. There is nothing new to say on the subject. But there is a new way to say it" (Peterson, xi).

9. In Exodus 25:31–37, the original design of the menorah is set forth. John's seven lampstands are probably a combined reinterpretation of this original lampstand with the seven lamps of Zechariah 4:2,10, where the seven stand for God's presence in all the world. Elisabeth Fiorenza notes "the seven-branched candelabra reminds one of the golden temple Menorah which was a symbol of the Jewish people in the first century. Rev 1:20 identifies this candelabra with the Christian community to whom the book is addressed" (Fiorenza, *Revelation,* 52); David Aune agrees (1305). And John W. Bowman argues that as John stood on the isle of Patmos viewing the mainland, the positional pattern of these churches on the mainland would have approximated the contours of a menorah ("Revelation, Book of," 4:69); similarly, Philip Carrington (87).

10. Can you remember the names of the seven churches? It's easy! All you have to do is remember two simple abbreviations: ESP and TSP (the first stands for "extrasensory perception," and the second is the abbreviation for "teaspoon"). If you can simply remember those clues and that the *L* in the *last* church is for Laodicea, you will never forget the seven: Ephesus, Smyrna, Pergamum, Thyatira, Sardis, Philadelphia, and Laodicea.

11. Did you notice that while the church at Pergamum is criticized for only "a few things" that the Spirit has against it, Sardis, on the other hand, has only "a few people" (i.e., real, live Christians) remaining who have not defiled themselves. The central threesome progress from slightly to profoundly compromised manifestations of church life, failing in various degrees to produce a Christian "countercommunity."

12. This is the oldest interpretation of the "seven churches" we have. The Muratorian Canon, drawn up toward the end of the second century, was the church's first attempt to establish an authoritative list of the books to be included in the New Testament. It incorporates the comment that John wrote to "seven" churches as a way of addressing all churches throughout the world; it further notes the parallel of Paul's "seven" letters to churches (Michaels, *Interpreting the Book of Revelation*, 36, n. 2).

Chapter 4

EPHESUS AND THYATIRA

That Which Must Never Pass Away

Rev. 2:1–7,18–29

In chapter 1, John has introduced himself and the circumstances under which he received the Revelation. He has spoken of seven churches to which he was directed to convey this message, and he has recounted the inaugural vision through which he was introduced to the essential themes that now must be shared with these brothers and sisters. The cover letters to follow, in chapters 2–3, are among the most frequently taught passages of the book. And, happily, a wide range of agreement, or at least minimal disagreement, exists among commentators on their interpretation. These two chapters also remind us that this book is not just a "prophecy" or an "apocalypse" but is truly a "letter" sent to the people of God—the seven churches.[1] As did the Hebrew prophets before him, John takes his stance firmly in his own day and among his own people. He speaks to strengthen, encourage, and console (1 Cor. 14:3) these churches as they face the maelstrom of the Roman world. Even in the last chapter of the Revelation, the entire book can be summarized as "this testimony for the churches" (22:16). Do not lose sight of this fact as you read through Revelation; it is always and everywhere *for the seven churches*.

Let us begin by noting one of John's most pervasive literary techniques, his constant use of *comparison* and *contrast*. Beyond the physical linkages that branches of the menorah build among these churches (a b c [d] c′ b′ a′) is another conceptual level of relationship that John uses to develop the spiritual x-rays found in these letters. Between Ephesus and Thyatira there is just such a conceptual theme that links the destiny of these two churches. An indispensable aspect of any vigorous church's life is *love*. They have each experienced and manifested it in contrasting ways, which have come to define the essential character of their congregations.

54

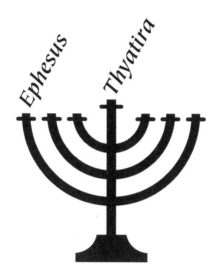

Ephesus (Rev. 2:1–7)

Historical Background

Ephesus was a highly significant city in the Roman province of Asia, what we know as western Turkey. Three important trade routes converged on this seaport, producing one of the greatest shipping facilities in all the ancient world. Ephesus was, in fact, the third largest city in the empire, with a population somewhere between a quarter and a half million. A treasured accolade to its political importance was its title "Supreme Metropolis of Asia." Though not the provincial capital — an honor reserved for Pergamum — Ephesus was the residence of the Roman proconsul.

Culturally a sophisticated and cosmopolitan city, Ephesus boasted one of the greatest theaters in the known world. Its physical structure and splendid staging possibly influenced John's method of presenting Revelation.[2] Another of the crown jewels of Ephesian culture was the magnificent temple of Diana. One of the seven wonders of the world, it was 425 feet long, 220 feet wide, and 60 feet tall. Its 127 pillars were gifts from various kings, and 36 were encrusted with gold and precious gems. Pictures of it graced Greek coins, and a contemporary slogan suggested, "The sun sees nothing finer in his course than Diana's Temple" (Barclay, *Letters to the Seven Churches*, 15).

Ephesus was also a center for the practice of magic, a magician's mecca. Available for sale were formulas that reputedly could affect almost any change deemed desirable. No area of life was left out, with formulas for physical health, sporting events, romantic ventures, and many other facets of life. Often the formula was a single mystical word, which was chanted over and over in slightly different form. Perhaps their intrigue with magic and other similar interests stand behind and help explain the strange way in which the gospel came to Ephesus and the sacrifices required there of those wishing to become Christians (Acts 19:11–19).

All of this — the bustling busyness of a seaport, the sizable population, the culture, the pagan cult, and the practice of magic — helps to form the backdrop to the church addressed in Revelation. Now, let us look at the letter John sends to the still fledgling church, which is trying to survive and influence the swirling currents of Ephesian life.

The Letter

2:1 • Debate over the identity of the "angel" to whom this letter is addressed and who seems to be in some way responsible for the nature and destiny of the congregation continues. Three main possibilities, however, have most frequently been suggested. First, the Greek word used here for "angel" means, as it also does in Hebrew, either a supernatural being or an earthly, human messenger. If this symbol is meant to convey the latter, the "messenger" would probably be the pastor of the Ephesian congregation. Second, the angel might be a "collective figure" (not unlike John Bull or Uncle Sam), a symbol for "the spirit of the church" or its composite religious personality (Beasley-Murray, *Book of Revelation,* 69–70; Hemer, 32–33). Third, John may be addressing heavenly beings, literal "angels."

Consider the third possibility. Here the chain of communication is quite strange, for this information has originally been brought to John by an angel (1:1). What would it mean for an angelic courier to bring John a message in order that he could return that message heavenward to angels again? Probably, the first and second suggestions are more in keeping with the symbolic and multiple meanings often found in John's coded language. They would also best explain why these "angels" seem to represent or share responsibility for the direction and destiny of these churches.

John communicates to the angel of Ephesus the words of the one "who holds the seven stars in his right hand." These stars represent yet another level of symbolism being added to the angels, for Revelation 1:20 clearly says, "The seven stars are the angels of the seven

churches." Hence, whatever we make of the angels — pastors or embodied corporate manifestations of a church's spiritual life — John
assures us they are held secure in the hand of divine sovereignty, the
right hand. They cannot slip or be snatched away; they are grasped
and wielded by God's eternal purposes.

In the ancient world, the seven known planets were considered
moving "stars," heavenly manifestations of the gods. As such, they
often exercised a terrible power over the lives of people who believed
in them. And since the ancients did not distinguish stars from planets, stars were often incorporated into the design of Roman coins so
as to depict the empire's *divine* might and supernatural connections.
By exhibiting these seven stars in Christ's right hand, John is clearly
saying something about the one who holds the destiny of the universe. By overlapping the meaning of the stars with that of the angels,
John is further proclaiming a very important truth about the church.
Ultimate authority resides, not in Rome, but in the body of Christ,
the church — more precisely, in that church where the Son of Man
walks and speaks. The church in Ephesus is warned, then, that it is in
the grip of one who comprehends its life, who has walked among its
people, and who holds its destiny at his discretion.

2:2–3 • Much is to be commended in Ephesus! But in this passage is the first use of a word, or theme, that gradually unfolds
throughout the book. Ephesian spiritual defenses have identified and
rejected "apostles" who are described as "false." Elsewhere in the Revelation, the word *false* (*pseudeis*, literally "liars") or a related word is
used where someone is deemed to be fraudulent.

There are Jews, in Smyrna and Philadelphia, who "are not" (2:9);
in fact, they are "liars" (*pseudontai;* 3:9). At Thyatira is a woman
who "calls herself a prophetess" (2:20), and John implies that this
claim constitutes a fraud. Later in the book, one of the church's
most fearsome foes, a beast from the earth (13:11–18) who demands
that all worship his companion from the sea (13:1), is specifically
called "the false prophet" (*ho pseudoprophētēs;* 16:13; 19:20; 20:10).
Finally, among those who are ultimately excluded from the Holy
City and are destined for the lake of fire, which is the second death,
are "all liars" (*pasin tois pseudesin;* 21:8; cf. 21:27 and 22:15). On the
other hand, ideal, or messianic, Israel, the 144,000 who stand with
Christ on Mount Zion and "follow the Lamb wherever he goes"
(14:4), are described as those in whose mouths is found "no lie"
(*pseudos;* 14:5).

Who are the false (lying) apostles unmasked by the Ephesians (2:2),
and what is the nature of their falsehood? In fact, why is there such a

pronounced concern over falsity, lies, and lying in this book? J. Ramsey Michaels compares and contrasts this negative aspect of life (i.e., living under false colors) to the doing of "what is true" in John 3:21 (NRSV). In the light of this Johannine context, he concludes, "What is condemned is not simply telling lies, but living a lie in the sense of living contrary to the values of the author and his community [i.e., the churches] while pretending to uphold the truth. The meaning of *liars* and *lying* is consistent throughout the book" (Michaels, *Interpreting the Book of Revelation*, 42–43). Lying prophets at Ephesus and pseudo-Christians today share one thing in common; they do not truly follow him who is "the way and the truth and the life" (John 14:6; cf. John 1:14; 8:32; 16:13), nor do they practice the lifestyle he modeled. This is always the fundamental nature of sin; its very essence is a sham and a suppression of truth (Rom. 1:18).

The Ephesian Christians had examined many and found some to be false; masquerading apostles have been unmasked and probably for good reason. Moreover, true Christian brothers and sisters have not grown weary in the battle for truth. More than thirty years earlier, Paul had warned this congregation about the coming encroachments of spiritual wolves (e.g., false apostles):

> I know that after I leave, savage wolves will come in among you and will not spare the flock. Even from your own number men will arise and distort the truth in order to draw away disciples after them. So be on your guard! Remember that for three years I never stopped warning each of you night and day with tears. (Acts 20:29–31)

Apparently they had taken this prediction to heart.

2:4 • Unfortunately, what also seems to have developed among the Ephesian Christians was a rather testy spirit of suspicion. This warding off of predators had finally produced a highly judgmental atmosphere, a straining of gnats while swallowing camels whole (Matt. 23:24). For this reason they are indicted; they have taken a good insight too far and turned it to evil (cf. 2 John 10–11).

Every strength is a two-edged sword, every coin has a flip side, and every human virtue embraces the seed of its own undoing. The very commitment that had allowed the Ephesian Christians to weed out those of unsound doctrine and lifestyle had slowly curdled into a distorted and distasteful spirit unsuitable to the nature and nurture of the church. Something had been lost, something critical and of prime importance; John calls it "your first love." "I remember the devotion of your youth, your love" (Jer. 2:2, NRSV) is a similar comment on the life of God's earlier people. And they too were to be judged, by a great exile, for their betrayal of this relationship.

The Ephesians were world famous for their fertility goddess, Diana. In contrast, the church is created and commanded by one who bids us to love as he loves (John 15:12). How does the contemporary church fare? Have we, like the Ephesian church, lost something? Do we too suffer the defects of our best qualities?

"God is love" (1 John 4:8), and the fellowship God creates is known by its power to bring that love to life and reveal the divine nature (John 13:35). It is not possible for a church to continue when organizational rigidity has replaced compassionate concern. Ephesus has become the First Church of the Frigidaire, very straight laced, very orthodox, but lacking the fundamental rudiment of the church — Christlike love. Wesley Baker suggests that Ephesus has fallen victim to the age-old malady of institutionalism (39–40). Sadly, when self-preservation becomes the ultimate imperative, the words of Jesus are fulfilled, for those who would save themselves succeed only in losing all (Mark 8:35).

2:5 • To such a church, one dire warning alone can be issued: they must "remember" and "repent." This declaration depicts Ephesus as a church that has *backslid*. Amazingly, this has happened to the very church in which Paul had most plainly taught the relation of faith and its expression through loving works: "For by grace you have been saved through faith...[and] created in Christ Jesus for good works" (Eph. 2:8,10, NRSV; see also Titus 2:14). Nevertheless, the Ephesian Christians had lost "the offensive of love and adopted the defensive of orthodoxy" (Mulholland, 95). Thus shriveled, Ephesus had withdrawn from the life of love it once knew, and only repentance could redeem its future.

Further, if this warning is not heeded, the ultimate penalty will be inflicted: removal of its lampstand from the life of the church. Only Ephesus and Laodicea, which share a common branching of the church's lampstands, are so threatened with divine nullification or excommunication, the most extreme judgment made against any of the churches.

2:6 • Despite the serious straits this church is in, there are aspects of Ephesus's life that can still be commended. Beyond those previously noted, this church resists the "Nicolaitans," a group that must have been rendered recognizable by this symbolic, or perhaps literal, title. They are mentioned again in the letter to Pergamum (2:14–15), where a direct relationship is drawn between them and the Baalamites, who also manifest aspects similar to problems observed at Thyatira (2:20).

Though it is not so specified here, certainly practical issues relative to dietary laws and sexual morality were involved in the Nicolaitans' challenge to church life (see p. 101 for more about this group).

2:7 • That the message to the church in Ephesus is meant for the whole church of every age is clearly stated: "He who has an ear, let him hear what the Spirit says to the churches." Don't miss the plural! The whole church is to take in and live out what is said to each of the seven "churches." There is significance in this letter for every Christian, for it is a comment on that which must never pass away. Churches may have a variety of ministries and personality traits, but love, "the greatest of these" (1 Cor. 13:13), is that without which no church can truly continue to participate in the Kingdom's work.

To that one who not only hears but keeps what he hears (Rev. 1:3), there is a special promise and unique privilege. For John, "overcoming" is sharing the suffering (tribulation) and the patient endurance that characterize those who walk with Jesus (1:9). The nearest John ever comes to defining "overcoming" is in 2:26, where he parallels or defines it by keeping faith with Jesus until the end, whatever that end might be. Those who live in the seven cities are strangers and aliens here (cf. Phil. 3:20; Heb. 11:9–10; 1 Pet. 1:1,17; 2:11) and must remember to maintain their allegiance to the New Jerusalem (Rev. 21–22), their true home. Here they are exiles, living in a foreign land, yet living victoriously as "conquerors" if they live faithfully as Jesus did.

The "tree of life" recalls the past and promises things to come, for that tree, first recognized in Genesis 2:9 and barred to human exploitation in Genesis 3:22-24, is not finally enjoyed by humankind until God's future is achieved (Rev. 22:2,14). And it is no coincidence that this promise is made to the church living in Ephesus. Frequently, Ephesian coins featured the sacred tree in conjunction with Diana (her Roman name), or Artemis (as she was known in Greek culture), the mother goddess. Let us not forget that this tree is the biblical symbol for "eternal life," which proceeds only from God (1 Tim. 6:16) and which only those in loving fellowship with God will ever know.[3]

Thyatira (Rev. 2:18–29)

Historical Background

This letter, the longest of the group, is written to the congregation in the smallest and least significant of the seven cities, but that does not mean Thyatira had no distinguishing features. It became a Roman city in 190 B.C., partly due to its strategic site. Located in the kingdom of Lydia, Thyatira was situated on the main highway from Pergamum to Sardis, and other important trade routes also ran through the city's commercial districts. Accordingly, many crucial commodities and trades were centered here.

Thyatira was known for its weaving industry, leather goods, bronze implements, and pottery, among others. Perhaps even purple, one of the most costly commodities in the whole ancient world, was part of its commercial life, for Lydia, a woman dealing in purple fabrics and Paul's first European convert, came from this town (Acts 16:14).

Syncretism, the tendency to intermingle and blend unrelated religious traditions, seems to have been one of the perennial problems faced by both Jewish and Christian congregations in Thyatira. Thus, J. Massyngberde Ford suggests that the many trade guilds entrenched in this city may have led Christians in the direction of cultural compromise. Indeed, Thyatira may have possessed more of these guilds than any other city its size in Asia. In that day, such groups "combined the legal and organizational power of today's labor unions with the economic power of trade associations, the social influence of clubs and voluntary associations, and the political power of special interest groups" (Linthicum, 303). One of the dominant characteristics of these guilds was their promotion of emperor worship, which was the evidence of a worker's loyalty to society and the empire. This meant, of course, that the routine workaday world was also a profoundly theological arena of life (Ford, 405; Hemer, 128).

The Letter

2:18 • The reference to "bronze" feet naturally relates to one of the main enterprises of Thyatira's business district, that is, the making of bronze implements. Here is the Christ, the one who knows their trade and who has eyes that pierce all cloaking devices. There is nothing secret from him, not even the bedroom of Jezebel (v. 22). Indeed, there is nothing secret that will not eventually be revealed (Matt. 10:22; Mark 4:22; Luke 8:17).

2:19 • "I know your deeds," proclaims the all-knowing Lord. Then the nature of these works is explained further. They have love, faith, service, and perseverance. These are works that are uniquely the hallmarks of Christian life. Do not miss, however, which of these is first, particularly because it is in such notable contrast with Ephesus. Can John have failed to note that while one city, Ephesus, had backslid in its expression of love, another was "doing more than...at first." Here is one of those pervasive contrasts of which Revelation is so exceedingly fond.

Baker finds the crisis of this church to be the issue of "theology" (56–57). Thyatira is facing the practical issue of that boundary where Christian doctrine defines its relationship to secular society, even as Ephesus defined itself over against aberrant Christianity. This church is surely progressing in its ability to manifest loving relationships, but it has also paid a price for doing so. It has become too lenient in situations that ought to scandalize any true church.

2:20 • This church is clearly too *tolerant!* If to make progress we have to lower our voice, if to get along we have to go along, if to sail smoothly we have to refrain from rocking the boat, if to beat the beast we become a beast, then the beast has won.

We cannot be entirely certain what immoral practices are being censured, but the connected issue of eating what is inappropriate may be telling. Jezebel, who is certainly not called by that symbolic nickname in the church where her true identity is known, is probably sponsoring participation in local trade guilds, where such practices are a part of their meetings. After all, many members of this church must have been associated with these unions before becoming Christians. Now, they face the issue of either continuing in practices that are repugnant to Christian faith in order to maintain their professional livelihoods or to repudiate these affiliations and lose social standing.

The adoration of heathen gods and the eating of foods offered to them in worshipful sacrifice, as well as a variety of sexual adventures, were all elements intrinsic to the trade guild's social life. Attendance at professional banquets where business pertinent to the guild was conducted was a normal obligation of membership. Apparently, Jezebel argued, one must do whatever one must to maintain the façade of normal life.

William Barclay astutely draws attention to a time slightly later, in the second century, when Tertullian, the great North African bishop, had written a treatise entitled *On Idolatry*. There he dealt with the issue of Christians defending their occupations — the making, decorating, and selling of idols — on the grounds that this was all they knew how to do. If they could not maintain these trades, it seemed to them, life itself would be at hazard. To this argument, Tertullian retorted that they should have considered the consequences before entering such vocations. In any event, he replied, the real issue was, "Must you live?" Elsewhere, he added, "There are no musts where faith is concerned" (in Barclay, *Letters to the Seven Churches,* 70).

Obviously, the same question faces every Christian, every day. Whether compromise can be rationalized as essential and the failure of faith be justified as inconsequential is the daily dilemma of spiritual life. As in Ephesus, collision with the System has provoked a response, here an easygoing tolerant compromise, there an unyielding orthodox rigidity. As with Ephesus, the greatest danger was from within.

2:21–22 • The Christ of Thyatira will grant time for repentance, both to Jezebel and to those who follow her (i.e., "her children"). But if this grace meets continuing defiance, then severe judgment will follow. Their "adultery" is their betrayal of union with Christ, a union that had brought them into his very body. They had been made new creatures, reborn from the death that is life in Babylon (Revelation's symbol for the world System; Rev. 18); now they will be returned to it.

2:23–25 • Jezebel, claiming to be a prophetess, was usurping a position of leadership in a congregation too tolerant by half. She had led her coterie into what she might have termed "the deep things of God," for so Paul spoke of "God's secret wisdom" that the world did not comprehend (1 Cor. 2:7,10). Thus, she had argued that they could remain pure in participating in heathen society, for what contaminated the body touched only it and not the spirit. However, says the living Christ, what she imagines to be deep insights are really "Satan's... deep secrets."

Jezebel's teaching may reflect certain known trends in *gnosticism,* an early Christian heresy that combined Greek philosophy and religion with Christian theology. But it might also be possible that Jezebel literally taught "Satan's... deep secrets," meaning that because of her insights, she and her clique were free to move among and ravage the satanic world. Loosed from the bonds of timidity that restrict the less insightful, they were liberated to join in activities, most notably the guild banquets, by which the "weak" were offended. This foray into the precincts of hell, unsullied by its defilement, was not only a great adventure but also a way of maintaining status among the enemy.

2:26–29 • On the other hand, the contrasting response to the usurped authority of Jezebel is the promise of genuine clout. Here John alludes to Psalm 2:8–9, which by John's time had already been interpreted messianically to refer to the future king's ultimate domination. When the Hebrew text is understood in context, to "rule ...with an iron scepter" probably has the same meaning as "shepherding with a shepherd's staff" (Mounce, *Book of Revelation,* 106). Hence, the Spirit's promise is of a joint dominion with the great Shepherd of the sheep, the Messiah himself (cf. Rev. 7:17). Such a sharing in his future rule had already been promised by Jesus (Matt. 19:28) as well as presumed by Paul (1 Cor. 6:3) and is promulgated in Revelation (5:10).

Once again, we must note that information about the future is not restricted to the latter chapters of Revelation alone, for the first three chapters also offer such insight. This is fully expected because there is power in a positive eschatology. That is, if you know where you are going and that your destiny is the victor's, then you will live differently; you will experience the rough and smooth of life from the vantage point of ultimate triumph.

Contrasting Evaluations

The Revelation has linked Ephesus and Thyatira by their contrasting expressions of love, each exhibiting the faults of its virtue. Ephesus, surrounded by the pomp of the ancient world, sought to guard itself against intruding wolves and doctrinal error. In the process, apparently legalistic in nature, it lost its very soul and the ability to express God's loving presence in its church life. Thyatira, less threatened perhaps, responded by tolerant concessionism. It continued to love and gained much but also experienced significant loss. The accepting love it radiated could not compassionately say no. The two churches thus pose for us this disquieting question: Which strength is the greater (orthodoxy or love), and which weakness is the more disastrous (coldness and the loss of love or undisciplined toleration)? The ideal, of course, is to combine the strengths of each, eliminating their associated weaknesses.

These two contrasting churches bring to our attention an essential element of Christian faith and life. The Christian world-view recognizes a love that is often encountered as "tough love" (see Rev. 3:19) and a love that is our total response to the divine initiative (12:11). Love is that which must never pass away and, therefore, must ever be guarded attentively and vigilantly. It is the fruit of the Spirit (Gal. 5:22) without which no church can serve the God who is love. Let love be boundless but not blind, and let anyone who has an ear remember this:

If I have the gift of prophecy and can fathom all mysteries and all knowledge, and if I have a faith that can move mountains, *but have not love, I am nothing.* If I give all I possess to the poor and surrender my body to the flames, *but have not love, I gain nothing.* (1 Cor. 13:2–3, emphasis added)

Ephesus, despite notable strengths, was little more than *nothing,* while Thyatira, despite serious weaknesses, was *something.*

Notes

1. That these two chapters are a central and integral part of the book's message is evident from the manner in which John links the opening lines of each letter (2:1,8,12,18; 3:1,7,14) to the inaugural vision, while the closing challenges (2:7,11,17,26–28; 3:5,12,21) are linked to Revelation's final chapters, where they are brought to closure.

2. James Blevins (*Revelation as Drama*) believes that the architecture of this famous theater, with its seven windows, is a fundamental backdrop to the outline of the Revelation, which may have been written to be performed on its stage. His book is very readable and helps stimulate an artistic approach to the book.

3. Colin Hemer suggests that to the original readers the "tree of life" may have brought to mind the "cross of Christ" (41–44, 55).

Chapter 5

SMYRNA AND LAODICEA

Success and the Church

Rev. 2:8–11; 3:14–22

Since the time of the prophet Amos, wealth and its attendant spiritual dangers have often occupied the center of Scripture's attention, so it is no accident that the most obvious contrast joining Smyrna and Laodicea is the theme of success and its related issues of security and social standing. Both cities were centers of commercial enterprise and financial power, but these two congregations responded to their cultural environment in utterly different ways. One of the two produced a counterculture, subversive and dangerous to its social setting, while the other simply acculturated, adapted, and adjusted to fit into the scene as harmoniously as possible.

One of the main issues these churches raise for all others is the age-old question regarding how we are to evaluate the nature and quality of success in the Christian church. Is church growth and expansion at the heart of all we are attempting, or are there more central issues that determine whether a church is being faithful to the commitment it has to Christ? The Revelation presents two churches of very divergent natures to discuss the issue of *wealth,* or perhaps *success,* as it affects the life of a church and the way in which that church is to gauge its own level of success. Smyrna may have considered itself to be of little consequence in the kingdom of God because it had a very limited budget and had been socially ostracized to the extreme of overt persecution. Laodicea, on the other hand, imagined that it had achieved a very high level of success, particularly because of its social and economic accomplishments. It was a very fashionable church, exclusive in membership to the point that Jesus himself had to stand outside seeking admittance. To each church, the voice of the Spirit has quite special insights to share.

Smyrna (Rev. 2:8–11)

Historical Background

Claiming to be the birthplace of the great epic poet Homer, whose works were the standard educational textbooks of the day, Smyrna occupied a place of great honor in the ancient world. One of the truly impressive Asian cities in John's day, it vied with Ephesus and Pergamum for political and mercantile leadership. However, for one very long period of its history, about 600 to 290 B.C., this proud city was destroyed and lay "dead," due to a Lydian invasion. Then it arose from the ashes, and the city that was "dead...came to life" (Rev. 2:8, NRSV) when it was rebuilt by King Lysimachus.

Laid out along straight, spacious streets, Smyrna's urban development had proceeded along orderly lines. Its leading boulevard was called the "Golden Street" (Barclay, *Letters to the Seven Churches,* 30). Fortunately, the city lay astride a major trade corridor that ran to the East. Possessing an enviable harbor, Smyrna boasted port facilities that were second only to those of Ephesus in volume of exports to the Mediterranean world.

Religion was also a thriving enterprise in this bustling metropolis, as evidenced by its temples of Aphrodite, Apollo, Asclepius, Dea Roma (the first shrine in the empire dedicated to this Roman goddess), and Zeus. A temple in honor of Emperor Tiberius and the Senate was built in A.D. 26. Indeed, grandeur once characterized

Smyrna, and one wonders what such a city thought of the struggling, little congregation nestled humbly in its midst.[1]

Currently known as Izmir, Smyrna has survived into the modern period. It is still a sizable municipality — the second largest in Asiatic Turkey — and is now nearly half Christian.

The Letter

2:8 • The Son of Man continues to build bridges of kinship with these congregations. Smyrna had continuously vied with Pergamum and Ephesus for the title "First in Asia." Indeed, the city's coins were sometimes stamped with "First of Asia in beauty and size" (Mounce, *Book of Revelation*, 91). Now the little church is addressed here by one who is all this town had ever hoped to be — the first Word in power and glory. And if Smyrna had known what it meant to lie dead for some centuries, then here is the one who knows how to resurrect a future out of the dust of history.

2:9 • Here is a real contrast! The Revelation loves to take double exposures of life to reveal to God's people the truth hidden in the tragedy. No big budget, no growing membership roll, but it is sumptuous. Something here is remarkably right!

The Smyrnan church faces "afflictions" (RSV: "tribulation") and faces them triumphantly because it has never forgotten what its Lord once said: "In this world you will have trouble [RSV: "tribulation"]. But take heart! I have overcome the world" (John 16:33). This is how the people of God will forever purify themselves, that is, by overcoming the tribulation that represents the distress and travail inflicted by a hostile world. Leon Morris calls it "the burden that crushes" (Morris, 63). Yet it is this very process that produces the ultimate victory (Rev. 7:14). Does the Lord select his most loyal servants to receive ever more radical testing? John himself is presently undergoing such "suffering" (1:9; RSV: "tribulation"). Often such testing is the ultimate compliment, as it was with Job (Job 1:8: "Have you considered my servant Job? There is no one on earth like him").

As in Smyrna, so it was also among the churches of Paul; the testing of their souls had produced "extreme poverty" and, as a side effect, "their overflowing joy" (2 Cor. 8:2). There is a spiritual pattern here that is based on the model of Jesus himself: "For you know the grace of our Lord Jesus Christ, that though he was rich, yet for your sakes he became poor, so that you through his poverty might become rich" (2 Cor. 8:9). The church at Smyrna was a persecuted church, and it was a desperately poor church. The Greek word *ptōcheia* indicates not mere poverty (*penia*) but utter destitution. Yet in the hand of him who holds the seven stars, they were *rich* (note John's love of contrast), for they served shoulder to shoulder with the one who had also suffered poverty that riches might result. In other words, things are not always the way they seem. No cross, no crown!

Thus, Smyrna is the church of the great reversal. Here is a richness of spirit that is totally unrelated to the wealth the world counts as gain. Living in the midst of earthly opulence, this little church was wealthy as the future counts spiritual wealth (v. 11). But this city, Smyrna, was only another passing manifestation of "Babylon the Great" — the beast, the System — which will be judged, will be laid waste, and will lose all its wealth "in one hour" (18:10,17,19).

Despite its spiritual riches, the Smyrnan congregation did face serious problems, and none was worse than religious strife. One of its greatest enemies was the local population of Jews, now greatly expanded since the destruction of Jerusalem in A.D. 70. "I know the slander of those who say they are Jews and are not, but are a synagogue of Satan" is probably the harshest comment on Judaism in the New Testament. If the phrase "a synagogue of Satan" was uttered today, it would surely represent an anti-Semitic attitude repugnant to Christian people. In fact, the phrase can be understood responsibly only within its original context.

First-century Judaism struggled with the issue of how best to deal with its latest "cult" — Christianity — which threatened to swamp the parent tradition. Part of the Jewish response took place in the mid-to-late 80s with the creation of what was known as the *birkat-ha-minim* (the blessing/prayer against the heretics). This element of liturgical ritual, the twelfth of the eighteen benedictions,[2] was introduced into synagogue worship and represented an actual curse against a variety of heretics, including the early Christians. Thus did orthodox Judaism serve God, by denouncing and excluding deviants from worship services (John 9:22; 12:42; 16:2). In fact, Jewish Christians could no longer enter synagogues freely and participate with a view to sharing the gospel message, for an element of those ceremonies now invoked a curse on what they understood to be the messianic community — or *faithful* Judaism (Hemer, 4, 9).

Polycarp, the elderly bishop of Smyrna, had become one of the most famous Christians of the second-century church. He was the "twelfth martyr in Smyrna" in A.D. 156. The story of his death, certainly the most well-known martyrdom of the century, is contained in the *Martyrdom of Polycarp*. It documents the story of Jewish crowds stirring up Roman officials to put the local Christian leader to death. Finally apprehended and having openly admitted that he was a follower of Christ, Polycarp was granted the choice of recanting his faith and worshiping the divinity of Caesar or immediate death. His reply is renowned:

> Eighty and six years have I served Christ, and He has never done me wrong. How can I blaspheme my King who saved me? . . . I fear not the fire that burns for a season, and after a while is quenched. Why do you delay? Come, do your will. (Barclay, *Letters to the Seven Churches*, 36)

And though it was then the sabbath day, the Jews of Smyrna, righteously inflamed against those who would destroy Judaism, or so they believed of the Christians, led the mobs in the gathering of wood to feed the flames (Hemer, 67). As he died, Polycarp prayed, grateful that he had been found worthy to surrender his life for Christ. Possibly his last thoughts were of the opening words of this letter written to his church.

John will eventually call Satan "the accuser of our brothers" (12:10), and that is exactly what the Jewish population of Smyrna became sixty years later. These Jews, "who . . . are not," are being faulted, not for their ethnicity (which would be anti-Semitism), but for their "slander." In this regard, it is equally important to recognize that this was also an intra-Jewish dispute. This phrase, "they . . . are a synagogue of Satan," isn't Gentile anti-Semitism, for many of these early Christian churches had Jewish leaders (John is a case in point himself).

The beloved disciple is writing in a critical time of strife and controversy. As a matter of fact, he has already depicted the followers of Jesus as the fulfilling continuation of historic Israel; the church is that "kingdom, priests to his God" (1:6, RSV) that is first founded in Exodus 19:6 (cf. 1 Pet. 2:9). John would surely have thought the "true" Jew to be one who had come to faith in the Messiah of Israel,[3] whereas the pseudo-Jew persecuted this messianic community. Those who did such things were not of father Abraham's heritage but another (John 8:33,44). Austin Farrer comments wryly that while Ephesus is troubled by "self-styled apostles," Smyrna is troubled by "self-styled Israelites" (72).

No, this is not modern anti-Semitism but a reflection of a disastrous, however temporary, period during which the synagogue and church were dramatically pitted one against the other.[4] As such, it was not essentially different from the dispute the Jews of Qumran (the Essenes?) had with their fellow Jews whom they denounced as " 'an assembly of deceit and a congregation of Belial [i.e., Satan]' (1 QH 2:22)" (in Bauckham, 124).

2:10 • Smyrna's suffering is not a new thing for the early Christians. Already the author of Hebrews had noted that his readers have "endured a hard struggle with sufferings" and that this had even involved "the plundering of your property"; however, this can all be endured, "joyfully" even, when we remember that we have "a better possession and an abiding one" (Heb. 10:32–34, RSV). Almost certainly, such suffering was largely responsible for the profound poverty of this congregation. W. R. Maltby once observed that "Christ promised His people three things — that they would be in constant trouble; that they would be completely fearless; and that they would be absurdly happy" (in Barclay, *Letters to the Seven Churches*, 44).

As the Smyrnan Christians are promised a persecution lasting ten days, so Daniel also faced a ten-day testing period (Dan. 1:12). If John was thinking of Daniel's experience, then he is hopeful about the outcome, for Daniel was vindicated by a faithfulness to God that resisted an alien lifestyle. "Ten days" is usually taken to mean a fairly short period of time. On the other hand, sometimes it stands for completeness and thoroughness — not unlike the number *seven* — probably because it is the total number of one's fingers. Illuminating examples of this latter symbolic value are found in Genesis 31:7,41; Numbers 14:22; Nehemiah 4:12; Job 19:3; and Daniel 1:20. In these passages, the phrase "ten times" connotes "to the uttermost" or "as far as you can go." If this is the symbolic background to the "ten days," then the congregation in Smyrna is going to be tested dreadfully. But also, it clearly suggests a limitation and leash placed on Satan's power.

The awful seriousness of the challenge to be faithful to death would seem to confirm the gravest connotation of the "ten days." Testing, of course, can be a productive process in which one's mettle is confirmed. It can even clarify what is of most value in one's life. In any event, death is certainly not seen as the ultimate tragedy of life in Scripture; there are worse things. And the death spoken of here can even generate a crown — not a royal diadem, but the *stephanos,* which was the laurel crown, a trophy for athletic victory. It was often worn on festal occasions and was also the garland awarded for exceptional civic service. Whichever was meant, it produces a death that is victorious and purposeful (cf. 12:11; 14:13).

Verse 10 makes a point that is repeated on many occasions in the Revelation. To live in fallen Babylon — the System — can be dangerous to those whose true citizenship is in the New Jerusalem. John will eventually tell us just how dangerous (18:24). But for the moment, the faithful at Smyrna will need to remember that they follow one "who was dead" (v. 8, NRSV) and that to be true to him means, as Paul reminds, "completing what is lacking in Christ's afflictions for the sake of his body, that is, the church" (Col. 1:24, NRSV).

2:11 • Yes, there is something worse than mere death. Henry Alford has articulated the point well, "As there is a second and higher life, so there is also a second and deeper death. And as after that life there is no more death (ch. xxi.4), so after that death there is no more life" (in Mounce, *Book of Revelation*, 367). In the midst of opulence, the church in Smyrna endured, choosing "to be mistreated...rather than to enjoy the pleasures of sin for a short time" (Heb. 11:25). This they did looking to "him who is invisible" (Heb. 11:27).

Laodicea (Rev. 3:14–22)

Historical Background

Comparatively speaking, Laodicea was "the new kid on the block." It was built in 250 B.C. by Antiochus II Seleucid in honor of his wife, whose name it was given. The city was situated in a most favorable location at the center of three major commercial highways. Here the main trade route that ran from Ephesus to the east crossed another commercial artery stretching from Pergamum, the capital of Asia, south through Thyatira, Sardis, Philadelphia, and Laodicea toward Colossae and the Mediterranean. The result, at the heart of this strategic intersection, was one of the richest centers of commerce in the world, a hub famed for its banking and mercantile enterprises (cf. 3:18a).

Some hint at the wealth present here is suggested by the amount of gold Flaccus, governor of Asia in A.D. 62, seized from the Jewish community alone. He took 22.5 pounds of the precious metal (nearly $150,000) from Jews who had collected it for a contribution to the temple in Jerusalem (Ford, 420; Hemer, 182).

With regard to manufactured goods, Laodicea was widely recognized for its woolen carpets and clothing; no fewer than four standard types of garments were shipped throughout the Mediterranean world (cf. 3:18b). Their success was largely due to a celebrated breed of sheep, featuring rich black wool, which was indigenous to the area.

Laodicea also possessed the leading medical facility in Asia. Indeed, this renowned medical school, prominent in the treatment of eye and ear diseases, was widely known throughout the Roman world. It exported a famous eye medication called *Tephra Phrygia* (i.e., Phrygian powder), which was mixed with oil to yield a therapeutic ointment (cf. 3:18c). Laodicea's great temple of Asclepius, the Greek god of healing, fit conveniently into this environment.

Few cities could hold their heads higher. In A.D. 60, Laodicea suffered a devastating earthquake, along with other local towns. And though Roman aid was offered, it was refused by this proud center of wealth and power. In fact, the city rebuilt itself back into a splendor that exceeded past glories.

The Letter

3:14 • This is the one church whose letter does not include in the address a descriptive element from the vision of the Son of Man in chapter 1. He seems more distant from this church than the others (v. 20). However, the titles "the Amen, the faithful and true witness," stress the absolute authenticity of what is about to be expressed.

In the Gospels, Jesus frequently prefaces important comments with the phrase, "Amen, amen, I say to you." Modern versions usually translate the "Amen, amen" as "Truly, truly" or "Verily, verily." However, no Jewish rabbi in recorded literature ever used this word in that manner because it asserts the absolute, unswerving truthfulness of what is stated. Only Jesus claims to know and to teach, as none other does, that which is categorically and unequivocally true (Matt. 7:28–29; Mark 1:22). Perhaps the suggestion in Revelation 3:14 is that there is little truth available in this church, so squalid is its lack of genuine Christian experience.

The titles "the Amen, the faithful and true witness" probably derive from Isaiah 65:16, where Israel's God is defined as "the God of truth [the Hebrew is literally 'amen']." If so, then John has once again transferred a divine title to Jesus. The additional emphasis on his faithfulness in witnessing further highlights what is woefully missing in this church.

The remainder of the address, noting the origin of creation, hints obliquely and ominously at a horrendous possibility — *de* creation. He is "the Alpha and the Omega, the First and the Last, the Beginning and the End" (Rev. 22:13). He who was the instrument of creation, the Word, can also disgorge or *de* create, by the same process (3:16). Without this one, nothing that was created can continue (John 1:3); in him and him alone, creation is continuously renewed and given a future as it becomes part of his will (2 Cor. 5:17).

3:15 • Generations of Christians have taken these words to mean that faith in Laodicea was neither feigned nor fervent but fragmentary. This certainly is the general import; Laodicea was not defunct or deep. Still there may be a more specific backdrop to these contemporary connotations of the English text (where "cold" connotes "dead" and "hot" connotes "alive").

It is well known that one of the greatest problems Laodicea faced was the absence of any convenient water supply. Water had to be transported either from the Lycus River itself or from two nearby tributaries. Additionally, some water was transmitted through stone pipes from hot springs near Denizli (Mounce, *Book of Revelation,* 125, n. 36). This water, lukewarm by the time it arrived, was neither refreshing nor particularly potable. Often it was used for medicinal purposes, that is, to cause vomiting or a bowel movement. The Laodiceans, then, were like this lime-laden, tepid water, neither cold and exhilarating like the waters at Colossae nor hot and healing as were the springs at Hierapolis. They were sickening, ineffective, and good for nothing.[5]

This explanation taken from the context of the city's water supply has the advantage of explaining the next sentence: "I wish you were either one or the other!" Yes, the Son of Man would prefer that they were "cold," not meaning "dead" — he would not wish that — but "spiritually zesty." Alternately, "hot," that is, "healthy and healing," would also be acceptable, but not lukewarm. To be "lukewarm" is nauseating, good for only one thing — purging. If, however, the more traditional approach to "neither cold nor hot" is correct, then Martin Kiddle's comment is appropriate: "Far better to be completely untouched by the flame of religion than to have only smoldering embers, half choked in ashes" (58).

3:16 • In John's Gospel, Jesus makes a similar and equally dire comment to those who do not bear the fruit of the kingdom of God. It is possible for such a one to be "thrown away . . . into the fire and burned" (John 15:6). Nevertheless, this church is loved. And this very rebuke is the proof, for those whom he loves he chastens to bring them back to repentance (Rev. 3:19). Nothing is commended in this church. Its condemnation is absolute, and the reason for this is found in the boast of verse 17.

3:17 • Among the most outrageous claims in the book, this church's bravado implies its complicity with those who will ultimately cower before the "wrath of the Lamb," for among them will be "the rich" (6:15–16). The comment also suggests the nature of Laodicea's accommodation to the System of Babylon the Great;

apparently, the Laodicean Christians are among those who will one day lament the fall of the great city (cf. 18:2,15,19). This is a most corrosive spiritual environment. That they are well-off is not in itself the problem, but their wealth has become a central feature of this church's ethos — a boast (cf. Rom. 3:27). Jesus had frequently commented on the negative link between prosperity and spirituality (Matt. 13:22; Luke 16:19,25; 18:24). Here is a church imbibing deeply from the value system of its culture and confusing social standing with spiritual vitality. Nicolas Berdyaev's indictment of his own generation (and ours) applies equally to Laodicea: "Historical Christianity has grown cold and intolerably prosaic; its activity consists mainly in adapting itself to the commonplace, to the bourgeois patterns and habits of life. But Christ came to send heavenly fire on earth" (297). Wesley Baker characterizes this church's situation as the "crisis of provincialism" (75). Laodicea has simply become the incarnation of the ambitions and ideals of its own social parochialism. This congregation is not simply at home in Babylon; it is part and parcel of Babylon's System. This is the cause of Laodicea's lukewarmness.

Surveying Laodicea's spiritual landscape, M. Robert Mulholland suggests that it had embraced "the promises of the preachers of the 'prosperity gospel'! It has wealth, plenty, and prosperity, surely the sign of God's blessing. It has 'named it and claimed it' and now rejoices in the blessings God has showered upon it. It is, however, the sickest of all the churches" (133–34). Whereas John was calling his churches to share "in the suffering and [as a result the] kingdom" (1:9), Laodicea had lost its way and was treading a very different path toward ostentatious self-sufficiency. The church had confused social status with spiritual vitality and was now dying of complacency and pride. So comfortable was Laodicea in its self-chosen destiny, that it does "not realize" and is now totally uncaring of its master's true verdict.

This is the spiritual x-ray of Laodicea's affluent congregation. Here is the ultimate hypocrisy, not conscious falsehood, but ignorance of one's true condition coupled with an aversion to diagnosis. The irony was that this church, dwelling in a town that prided itself on the ability to treat physical myopia, was unaware of its own spiritual blindness. Jacques Ellul suggests that the opposite of and antidote to their kind of hypocrisy is Christian "hope" and that "from the moment there is nothing to hope for, there is no longer anything to receive" (141). Laodicea has lost its vision of holiness and is, therefore, just as hopeless as it is complacent. In the realm of the spiritual, self-delusion is ever the flip side of self-satisfaction.

3:18 • There follows a range of needs wherein this church is deficient but had thought itself well provisioned. The backdrop to the discussion is directly related to the well-known reputation of Laodicea, the city of great wealth (gold), famous for its textile industry (white clothes), the city of world-famous medicines (salve). It is no accident that this catalog of self-sufficiency is reminiscent of life in the "great city," which is "Babylon" (18:10; note the list of goods in vv. 11–13).

If one accepts the offer of "the Amen" to obtain from him what is needful, it also means that one has heard the voice of the Spirit calling to the "great city": "Come out of her, my people, so that you will not share in her sins, so that you will not receive any of her plagues" (18:4). The spiritual climate in that city is much like the attitude of Laodicean Christianity. When Babylon the Great boasts, "I sit as queen; I am not a widow, and I will never mourn" (18:7), she is modeling the words, "I am rich; I...do not need a thing" (3:17).

3:19 • There is always a blessing intended by the approach of God, even when it is disciplinary in nature (cf. Heb. 12:6–8). On the other hand, his simple withdrawal, "God gave them over" (Rom. 1:24,26,28), is the most fearsome judgment any creature will ever experience, for God's greatest wrath, observed Jerome, is when God withdraws his anger and simply allows us to seek and desire our own level. Indeed, writes the author of Hebrews, "Today, if you hear his voice, do not harden your hearts" as those in the past who missed the blessing of God and found only destruction (Heb. 3:7; 4:7; cf. Deut. 4:36; Ps. 95:7). This is a touching reminder of a Lord who constantly walks among the lampstands and seeks the healing of even the most apathetic churches. In the words "those whom I love" is a reminder that we dare not give up on any but love even as the Lord does. In Laodicea, too, there is hope!

3:20 • This church has certainly been successful at developing an exclusive membership. Jesus, himself, is required to knock and seek special admittance to this congregation. And given the credentials he used to introduce himself elsewhere (Luke 9:57–58), even Jesus might not gain access to the social register of this church. The invitation to hear the voice of the Lord is similar to the command in each of the letters to "hear what the Spirit says to the churches," for only those who are guided by (hear) the Spirit can claim relationship to Jesus (Rom. 8:14).

Christ's willingness to partake of table fellowship with the one who hears his voice (John 10:4–5) is also an invitation to the

Communion table,[6] where the repentant spirit will always find forgiveness and renewal. This offer of fellowship includes and anticipates the banquet spoken of in 19:9, namely, the wedding feast foreshadowed in the Lord's Supper, one of the oldest symbols of the future joy awaiting God's people (Isa. 25:6–9).

3:21 • An important detail is added here to the significance of "overcoming." It is now described as a replication of what Christ also did: "just as I overcame." That, of course, can mean one thing only — his path to the cross. This will not seem a happy prospect, especially at Laodicea, where people seem to have so much to live for. But do not forget that this apparent defeat was Christ's ultimate victory (cf. 5:5,6,9; 12:11), an act of divine wisdom that even the hidden forces of evil had not understood (1 Cor. 2:8).

As wonderful a promise as it is, to reign with Christ (cf. Matt. 19:28–30; Luke 22:30; 1 Cor. 6:2; 2 Tim. 2:11–13), it is not obtained by those who lose their first love (Ephesus), who teach false doctrine (Pergamum), who tolerate immorality (Thyatira), who fail to propagate the faith (Sardis), or, like those at Laodicea, who are lukewarm. This is a pledge made to conquerors who have endured the "pain" to obtain the "gain." The fulfillment of this promise to those who not only "talk the talk" but "walk the walk" is found in the millennial passage, Revelation 20:4–6, and also in John's description of the eternal future: "they will reign for ever and ever" (22:5). This is the final and perhaps the all-inclusive promise made to any who can still hear.

3:22 • Again we hear the Gospel voice of Jesus (Matt. 11:15; 13:9,43). There is a particular kind of hearing that is the very essence of what it means to enter the Kingdom (Mark 4:9,14,16,18,20,23–24); it is to hear, accept, and bear fruit. One final time, midway through the book, Revelation will issue the call to hear: "He who has an ear, let him hear.... This calls for patient endurance and faithfulness on the part of the saints" (13:9–10). Revelation and its message for the church is not to be taken lightly. On the contrary, it is for every church and every generation.

Contrasting Evaluations

Surely, John has purposefully contrasted these two churches. One is rich in all that this transient world does not value, and the other is poor in all that belongs to the eternal world. One has developed the characteristics of a counterculture shaped by its Lord; the other has been shaped by the acculturation process. They represent the perennial questions, What is the measure of spiritual success? Can it be gauged by wealth and power? Seemingly, it is possible to be impoverished by the very things we value most.[7]

Instructively, Smyrna lives on as a contemporary city, but Laodicea seems to have passed from the scene rather quickly, at least as a viable church. We know that Paul was acquainted with this congregation (Col. 4:13–15). And Ignatius, bishop of Antioch, being transported to Rome where martyrdom awaited, passed through the area about A.D. 107. As he did so, he wrote letters to Colossae and Hierapolis but without any reference to a church at Laodicea. Apparently, this congregation did not withstand the spiritual storms John foresaw. Let all who can, *hear!*

Notes

1. This is the point of departure for Wesley Baker, who sees this letter as a modern warning to the church surrounded and tempted by the splendors of *technology*, that is, the contemporary siren of wealth (Baker, 45–51).

2. Its text reads as follows: "May the Nazarenes and the Minim suddenly perish, and may they be blotted out of the book of Life [*sic*] and not enrolled along with the righteous" (in Hemer, 149). "Minim" refers to heretics in general.

3. Paul had long since pioneered the way for such thought in the following important passages: Romans 2:28–29; Galatians 3:28–29; 6:16; Ephesians 2:14; Philippians 3:3.

4. In similar fashion, the early editions of the Westminster Confession called its adherents to understand the papacy as anti-Christian. That comment has since been expunged, and few modern adherents of that confession would seek its restitution.

5. This interpretation of cold and hot was first argued by M. J. S. Rudwick and E. M. B. Green in their article "The Laodicean Lukewarmness" (176–78). This alternative approach has been appreciated by many modern interpreters, such as Hemer, 186–91; Mounce, *Book of Revelation*, 125–26; and Morris, 81–82.

6. This Greek word for "eat" (the verb) or "supper" (the noun) is used frequently in special conjunction with the institution of the Lord's Supper (Luke 22:20; John 13:2,4; 21:20; 1 Cor. 11:20,25). It is also found in Revelation 19:9,17, where the "marriage supper" prepared for the faithful is distinguished from the "great supper of God" at which the ungodly themselves represent the menu and are consumed.

7. Adela Collins suggests that the contrasting comments made about these two churches, based on their relation to power and wealth, have a

rationale: "It is striking that the economically rich have nothing to fear from the authorities, whereas the poor are threatened with persecution. The underlying reason seems to be that it was possible to get and to maintain wealth only by accommodation to the polytheistic culture" (*Crisis and Catharsis*, 133).

Chapter 6

SARDIS AND PHILADELPHIA

The Church's Vocation

Rev. 3:1–13

The duo of Sardis and Philadelphia, Revelation's third pairing of churches, also concentrates on a key issue that determines a church's ability to withstand the pressures of the beast's System. What do these two churches, or any for that matter, have to live for? Is there a central calling that is meant to give meaning and purpose to their very existence? What is the revelation to Sardis and Philadelphia?

The comparison that most clearly draws Sardis and Philadelphia together is the theme of the church's primary vocation, an issue that must have been of paramount importance to John, locked away as he was and writing to cherished congregations. We have learned that despite the presence of other commendable features, there is no church without love (Ephesus and Thyatira). Further, making the proper distinction between spiritual wealth and material success is definitive of a church's quality (Smyrna and Laodicea). Now we discover that Christian love and vibrant spirituality are essential because of the church's strategic objective, a mission regularly articulated in the remainder of the book (cf. Rev. 6:9–11; 11:1–13; 12:11; 19:10).

If the beast is a sevenfold force of darkness and misguided spirituality that is constantly attempting to place its brand even on the household of faith, in what way should the church manifest its essential nature in this evil world? Just what is the church meant to accomplish? What is its assignment in the kingdom of God? From as far back as the ministry of Jesus, the church has been called to a great pilgrimage into the world. In Luke 9:51, Jesus launches a crusade that is spearheaded by the "seventy" (Luke 10:1, NRSV), who were to go before him on the way to his final destiny in Jerusalem. In the Jewish system of symbols, the number *seventy* always stands for the whole world of nations because of the enumeration of peoples listed

80

in Genesis 10, where all the nations mentioned as the outgrowth of Shem, Ham, and Japheth come to that symbolic number. Hence, the Revelation also calls the church to a mission to every tongue, tribe, nation, and people before the end arrives.

Sardis (Rev. 3:1–6)

Historical Background

If, as it is said, geography is the mother of history, then Sardis's location at the center of five converging trade routes defined its destiny. Fifty miles east of Ephesus and thirty miles southeast of Thyatira, it too was a commercial vortex of Asia Minor. Sardis had once been the first capital of the Lydian Empire and reached the zenith of its influence during the reign of the fabled King Croesus. In 560 B.C., Croesus, whose very name is synonymous with wealth, minted the first coinage the world had ever seen; that is, money as we know it today was born in Sardis. Once again, geography or nature had dictated destiny, for Herodotus, the Greek historian, informs us that a gold-bearing river ran directly through the central marketplace of the city (Barclay, *Letters to the Seven Churches*, 83). The Pactolus literally

ran with gold and seemingly had conspired to make Sardis a city of
unrivaled opportunity.

Sardis was also a center of the textile industry, an outcome no
doubt related to its claim of being the first city of the ancient world
to learn the secret of dyeing wool. Also the presence of a large Phrygian sheep business marketed in Sardis helped establish the city as
the greatest center for wool distribution in Asia Minor. It surely was
rich in the material fabric of life but much poorer in the spiritual
vestments of the soul (Rev. 3:4).

Sardis was as active religiously as any other city. Devotion to the
goddess Cybele, a nature deity usually identified with the Greek goddess Artemis, was greatly in vogue, involving an orgiastic and frenzied
style of worship. Cybele's priests were all eunuchs. One of her special
claims to fame was her reputed ability to restore life to the dead (cf.
3:1). Many other religions also flourished in Sardis. In the city was
an unauthorized temple to Tiberius, whose generosity Sardis had enjoyed following the disastrous earthquake of A.D. 17. Nevertheless,
Sardis was not a main center of caesar worship. Therefore, the local
danger to Christians was somewhat diminished. During the Roman
period, its population varied from sixty thousand to one hundred
thousand. However, recent archaeological explorations have revealed
one of the largest synagogues yet uncovered, with the capacity to hold
about one thousand worshipers. Sardis must have possessed a large
and influential community of Jews.

Just behind the city and high above on Mount Tmolus lay the
site of Sardis's nearly impregnable citadel. Jutting out from a northern spur of the mount was a massive solid-rock pier, 1,500 feet above
the plain; on it the Sardians had built an all but inaccessible mountain fortress for use in time of war. There it stood, towering over the
plain, mute testimony to the power and safety Sardis had built for
itself.

Tragically, on two memorable occasions, Sardis dreamed away the
untroubled sleep of the self-assured and suffered total loss. Cyrus, in
549 B.C., and then Antiochus the Great, in 216 B.C., crept into the
unsuspecting sanctuary, left unguarded because it was considered invulnerable. In each case, by morning, Sardis had lost all (Mounce,
Book of Revelation, 110–11). The biting allusion found in verse 2,
"Wake up," is a not-so-subtle reminder that on one occasion one man
had cost the city all it possessed and that on a second fifteen men
had repeated the deed (Barclay, *Letters to the Seven Churches*, 81–82).
A third is now threatened (v. 3).

The Letter

3:1 • It is a dubious honor to share part of its greeting (the seven stars) with Ephesus, a church on the brink of excommunication (note other similarities in 2:5 and 3:3). In both cases, the one who possesses the "seven stars" controls the destiny of the church's "angel" (1:20), that is, the pastor or, better, the spiritual life of this congregation. The fate of this church is being determined, and as at Ephesus, the future is clouded. As possessor of the "seven spirits of God," indicating the fullness of the Holy Spirit (notice the Trinitarian structure of 1:4–5), the Lord knows all there is to know about this church, despite the façade they project. Indeed, from the piercing gaze of God's Spirit (4:5; 5:6), nothing can be hidden. No amount of sham can shield one from the shame of having what is hidden revealed and shouted from the rooftops. These passages associated with the seven-fold Spirit are based on Zechariah 4:2–10, where seven lamps (v. 2) and seven eyes (v. 10) are related to the activity of the Lord's Spirit (v. 6) in all the earth.[1]

Yes! God knows their deeds and reputation! This church cannot bear vital witness to the power of the gospel, cannot project the light of life into the dark world of the beast; hence, there is no word of appreciation, no compliment, paid this congregation. It receives one of the sharpest denunciations of any of the seven churches. Unlike the prodigal son, who was dead but came to life (Luke 15:24), this congregation has reversed the gospel process. G. R. Beasley-Murray suggests its "appearance is that of a beautifully adorned corpse in a funeral parlor, and the Lord is not deceived," for Sardis is "the incarnation of mediocrity" (*Book of Revelation*, 95). Others, however, may be misled; even sister churches and the surrounding world of Babylon may perceive this church as a commendable example of what effective organizations ought to be. But, in fact, it is all form and no power (2 Tim. 3:5) or, as someone has said, a morgue with a steeple.

The Christians of the church at Sardis have a reputation, a name for liveliness. No society page is without mention of activities being programmed through its facilities. Sardis is the "live wire" church, totally plugged into the contemporary scene. No doubt, their buildings were constantly being refurbished and expanded. Here is clearly a church on the go; here is animated Christianity. The church has a club for every age group, a program for every conceivable constituency. Nevertheless, all this was no more than a titillating form of failure, revealing the truth about nominal, acculturated faith. "This is a church which everyone speaks well of," writes G. B. Caird, "the perfect model of inoffensive Christianity, unable to distinguish between the peace of well-being and the peace of death" (48).

No claim to life can place a corpse on its feet. And just as surely, Sardis was dead. Spiritual mediocrity had taken root in such a way as to slay genuine Christian life. It is the decadent congregation, the most compliant of the three churches (in the center of the menorah) marked by "compromise" with the Roman System. Yet, it is not immediately threatened with excommunication, as are Ephesus and Laodicea. Why?

3:2 • Sardis needs to rouse itself, to sound a clear cry of alarm, for just as in its past, a terrible debacle is in the process of unfolding, almost unnoticed. In spite of the frenetic furor that surrounds this church, much is already dead because the Lord has found none of its works "complete," that is, mature, perfected, and accomplishing the true mission of the church. This church had majored in a minor, the superficial and flashy works that do not regenerate people or societies, and only minored in the intended major of spiritual renewal. The vital quality in any church was rapidly slipping and nearing total extinction, even as success was to all appearances blessing its efforts. Sardis was the precise model of inoffensive Christianity that Søren Kierkegaard once called "a toothless twaddle." Still, there is something here that is "about to die," though it is not yet extinct.

God knows the works of this church and also knows how to appraise its members. Inappropriate in motivation, unspiritual in execution, defunct in purpose, its works did not measure up to standard (cf. 2:19). They were, with generous allowance, incomplete and fatally flawed. "When we remember what 'complete' fulfillment of the Christian life meant to the Christians of Smyrna," comments Martin Kiddle, "we shall better understand what John demanded of the church at Sardis" (45). Why is there no persecution from Rome or the Jews here? Kiddle continues his indictment by defining the mission this community had evidently assigned itself: "the church at Sardis set herself the task of avoiding hardship, by pursuing a policy based on convenience and circumspection, rather than wholehearted zeal" (45). Secure, complacent and thoroughly acculturated, like the city of its birth, Sardis was untroubled. This is its final wake-up call!

3:3 • Sardis's Lord will return one day, and he himself proclaims this coming to be a threat to this church. Later in the book, nearer the second Advent, the Lord of the church repeats his warning: "Behold, I come like a thief! Blessed is he who stays awake and keeps his clothes with him, so that he may not go naked and be shamefully exposed" (16:15). John probably alludes to a contemporary judgment, some surprisingly calamitous event in the near future that will also be echoed in the final day of the Lord.

Most in this church have already "soiled their clothes" (v. 4); that is the problem. The remedy for the situation is expressed in just three razor-sharp words: "Remember…obey…repent." Here are three words for every Christian at every stage of his or her journey.

3:4 • Here is the phrase that is one basis for the underlying structure of Revelation's menorah of light (i.e., the church). Among the three central lampstands, representing the compromised churches, Pergamum has only "a few things" lodged against it (2:14). Thyatira's prophetess, "Jezebel," and her children constitute *many* defections, while in Sardis the majority have wavered and departed, so only "a few people" remain faithful. Indeed, a majority in this church needs to hear the challenge to repent. And those who do will have washed their robes in the blood of the Lamb and made them "white" (7:14; cf. 7:9); they will accomplish the "righteous acts" Sardis must perfect (19:8); they will have resisted the System of Babylon to the death (6:11), if need be; and they will join the heavenly army of God, as part of their march into the future (19:14).

3:5 – 6 • The concept of a book in which the names of God's true people are written is first found in Exodus 32:32-33, where Moses speaks of "the book you [God] have written." From this beginning, the idea progresses through Scripture that such a heavenly register holds the destiny of God's people (Ps. 69:28; Dan. 7:10; 12:1; Mal. 3:16–18; Luke 10:20; Phil. 4:3; Heb. 12:23). Revelation extends this tradition through several additional comments on the "book of life" (13:8; 17:8; 20:12,15; 21:27). Notice how each reference adds a new insight to the significance of the book. Revelation's prime innovation, however, is the unequivocal comment that it is uniquely the property of "the Lamb" (13:8; 21:27). It belongs to him because he has purchased its contents by his own blood (5:8–9). Therefore, it is his prerogative to add to or blot names out of this book (3:5), for it is written in his life's blood. It is the registry of citizenship in the New Jerusalem (21:27).

Given the frequency of its appearance in Revelation, the signal importance of this book can hardly be denied. However, the existence of another book (the same word, *biblos*, is there translated "scroll"), whose contents the Lamb alone may exercise control over (5:1-5), leads to the interesting question of their relationship. Does John long to have this scroll (literally "book") opened because he wonders, as we all would, "Is my name written there?" We shall discuss this possibility later. (See discussion of Rev. 5:1 in Chapter 10, pp. 131–33.)

The additional promise to confess the name of the conqueror before the court of heaven is nothing more than the fulfilling echo of the very words of Jesus and another hint at what had been deficient at Sardis. Jesus had said that he would acknowledge before the father all who faithfully witnessed to him, but he would disavow in heaven those who denied him before men (Matt. 10:32–33; Luke 12:8–9). The believer who confesses openly a relationship to Jesus can know at that very moment that his or her own name is on the lips of the Master: "That one belongs to me! Well done, good and faithful servant!"

Certainly, Sardis, though wired for a high activity level, must have been missing one of the essential ingredients; that is, there was neither a genuine, penetrating witness nor any evangelistic zeal. Hence, its lively reputation is dismissed, "You are dead, and virtually blotted out!"[2] Let all churches hear what the Spirit says.

Philadelphia (Rev. 3:7–13)

Historical Background

"Gateway to the East" was the title Philadelphia proudly bore; moreover, it characterizes the nature of the small congregation there, struggling to do its master's work. Less than thirty miles southeast of Sardis, Philadelphia shared many of that city's historical and geographical advantages.

Originating in the second century B.C., Philadelphia gained its name from its probable founder, Attalus II, whose fraternal affection for his older brother, Eumenes II (king of Pergamum at the time), earned for him the epithet *Philadelphus,* "brother lover." Philadelphia was built as an outpost to disseminate Greek culture, a sort of "cultural mission station" to the East.

Unfortunately, the city had been built on a continental fault, not unlike the famous San Andreas fault in California; consequently, it was frequently subject to very destructive earthquakes. In A.D. 17, some seventy-five years prior to John's writing of the Revelation, Philadelphia had experienced one of its most devastating quakes, which in one night leveled twelve local cities. Writers at the time considered it the worst earthquake in human history. This milieu probably accounts for quake-related images found in the letter (an immovable pillar in 3:12) and the remainder of the book (6:12; 8:5; 11:13,19; 16:18). Apparently, seismic destruction is also the projected fate of the world System, Babylon. Note the connection between 16:18–19 and the fall of the great city "thrown down" (18:21) "in one hour" (18:10,17,19). The churches of Asia Minor were traumatically sensitized to earthquakes.

The city took a new name (cf. 3:12) after the disaster of A.D. 17. In appreciation for extensive help received from Rome, Philadelphia called itself Neocaesarea, "Caesar's New City." Though caesar worship was not rampant here, dedication to Rome was devout. So popular were the Flavian emperors that Philadelphia's coins bear the title *Flavia* (seemingly another new name for the city) during their reign (A.D. 69–96). Finally, in the early third century an imperial temple was built in Philadelphia, and the city was granted the civic honor of being designated Neocoros, "warden to the temple of Caesar." But by far the main pagan religion was the cult of Dionysus, the god of wine, an expected occurrence since Philadelphia was famous for its wine production.

The power of Philadelphia, such as it was, rested on three commercial mainstays: agriculture and viniculture in the plains to the north, textile and leather industries within the city, and the all-important trade routes, which allowed unlimited export to the eastern frontiers. Philadelphia was a crucial link on Rome's imperial post road in John's day. This highway originated in Rome, eventually reached Troas, and then through Pergamum and Sardis accessed Philadelphia and the East. For good reason, the church at Philadelphia had before it "an open door" (v. 8).

The Letter

3:7 • The descriptive elements "holy" and "true" are used in 6:10 for God; their presence here can only continue that process by which Revelation is bidding us to see in Jesus, the Son of Man, the presence of the eternal God of Israel.

In 1:18, the Son of Man possesses "the keys of death and Hades." Here they are further described as "the key of David," a phrase probably referring to Isaiah 22:15–22. There an oracle pronounced against Shebna, David's household steward, replaces him in office with Eliakim. The latter is described as one possessing "the key to the house of David," the one who will have authority to open or close the king's palace and presence to those seeking an audience. Moreover, he (Eliakim) will also be "a father to those who live in Jerusalem," exactly what the members of this church are already — citizens of the New Jerusalem (21:1–3,27). Thus, the Jesus who has invaded the realm of death and plundered its power is also the messianic door to the New Jerusalem (John 10:7); no one gains access to it except by him.

3:8 • Not a single word of correction or criticism is offered in this letter, for like Smyrna, and unlike Sardis, Philadelphia has succeeded in the church's assignment suggested by an "open door." Don't forget we have already heard of the Lord who has "the key of David" (3:7). The door that he opens and that none other can shut can only be the Kingdom's door, that is, the entrance into the heavenly city, the New Jerusalem.

Sometimes John photographs double exposures of his symbols, and here, I believe, is one. Given the strategic location of this city, sitting at the juncture of access routes to Mysia, Phrygia, and Lydia, a secondary background to the "open door" symbol is probably found in Acts 14:27; 1 Corinthians 16:9; 2 Corinthians 2:12; and Colossians 4:3. In these texts, it stands for outstanding opportunities in evangelistic and missionary enterprises. And, as we are shortly to learn, this congregation has been confessing the name of Jesus and not hesitantly.

In Revelation 4:1, John uses the phrase "open door" to indicate access to a far different world, the heavenly scene. In this letter to the church in Philadelphia, it stands more clearly for entry into the kingdom of God. John, however, no doubt saw a connection between those who invite others into the kingdom and those who enter it themselves. In any case, the purpose of the initial greeting of this letter is to remind the Philadelphian Christians that the ultimate key of success is held by the one whose will cannot be thwarted.

Now we see John's insightful contrast to the preceding church. The Christians of Sardis, the "live wire" church, do have a reputation for stamina and vigor; Philadelphia, on the other hand, has "little strength." Sardis has not engaged in the fundamental labor of the Kingdom (probably thought of as genuine gospel witness), but Philadelphia has kept his word of command because they have not denied his name. By bringing into the light those who live all their lives in the darkness of the System called "Babylon," this congregation has accomplished what every true church and Christian hopes to achieve.

3:9 • Jesus himself had once spoken of Jews who were of their father, the devil, whose lying and murdering nature they incarnated. This was his analysis of their rejection of him and the counterclaim that he, Jesus, was in league with the demons (John 8:39–48).

Interestingly, only two letters speak of the Jews who "are not," Smyrna and Philadelphia. And just as clearly, these two churches, sharing a common branch of the menorah, are portrayed as those who *truly are* the conquering people of God. Paul would say that these have been circumcised by Christ himself (Rom. 2:28–29; Phil. 3:3; Col. 2:11–13) and are, therefore, "the Israel of God" (Gal. 6:16). However, the fundamental concept that more than simple circumcision of the flesh was necessary began with Moses (Deut. 10:16; 30:6) and was reiterated by the prophet Jeremiah, who was the first to prioritize an internal state of being (Jer. 4:4) over the mere externality of the flesh (Jer. 9:25–26). These are ideas to which Christians in Asia Minor had been exposed for decades, ever since the labors of Paul in the same region and to some of the same churches.

In these descriptions of true and false Jews, John was probably invoking what had already become conventional wisdom, namely, that the church of the Messiah was the continuation of the true Israel, complete with its own set of twelve founding fathers (Rev. 21:14). For their trouble in sharing this word of witness, Jewish Christians in John's day would probably have been excommunicated from local synagogues (John 9:22; 12:42; 16:2). Nevertheless, here (2:9 and 3:9) they are the real "Jews" (Collins, *Crisis and Catharsis*, 125).

However, what is often missed but complements the interpretation suggested above is the allusion to Isaiah 43:4 and 60:14 in this very passage. In Isaiah, the Lord claims the people of Israel to be uniquely precious in God's sight; they are told that one day their Gentile enemies who had oppressed them will come and bow at their feet. Furthermore, those so beloved of God are described as "the City of the LORD, Zion of the Holy One of Israel."

Here, Revelation endorses a most startling role reversal. We are now told that those lying about their Jewish status (presumably ethnic Jews) will one day come and bow down to Christians (Gentiles) whom they have been persecuting. In other words, John seems to understand contemporary Jews as Isaiah once thought of pagans. The obeisance Jews were longing to receive from Gentiles was actually going to be experienced by the church, for it had become the true messianic community. Moreover, Revelation, as Isaiah before it, also takes this community (i.e., the church) to be the true Holy City (20:2,9–10), the dwelling place of "the Lord God Almighty and the Lamb" (20:22; cf. 21:3). The thought even closes this letter (v. 12), where conquerors are the citizens of the New Jerusalem.

Does John mean that through this acknowledgment of God's love for the church, the "Jews" too will find faith in their Messiah? Does he mean that this bending of the knee, that is, falling at the feet of the saints, is tantamount to entrance into the Kingdom? Though it cannot be certain from this text alone, some take this passage to mean just that (Caird, 51–53; Ladd, *Commentary on the Revelation*, 60). Notice the "if" of Romans 11:23!

3:10 • "Patient endurance" (NRSV) is a virtue demonstrated by John (1:9), commended among the churches (2:2,19), required of those who do battle with the System (13:10), and imperative if one is to obey God's commandments and maintain faith in Jesus (14:12). Perhaps its basic meaning is something like "steadfast allegiance"; William Barclay defines it as "triumphant fortitude...not simply the patience which accepts and submits" but "which can transmute suffering into glory" (*Letters to the Seven Churches*, 22–23). This virtue of resolute loyalty is indispensable for the facing of what John is sure will come — "the hour of trial."

John is being persecuted (1:9), Smyrna suffers (2:10), Antipas has been martyred at Pergamum (2:13), and great distress is looming over Thyatira (2:22). The problems of this congregation and the others foreshadow an ominous future. And while the Christian church of Asia Minor could never have imagined that life in Christ was to be idyllic, a trial of even greater proportions is now announced. This hour of trial coming over "the whole world" and subjecting all of humanity to a test will never harm those who have already passed the primary examination of faithfulness to God's Word. Because they have already endured, future endurance is assured. But most importantly, they have come out of Babylon and, therefore, will not partake of her plagues (18:4), plagues that afflict the whole world, except Christians.

Whether John was thinking of deliverance from that trial or protection through it is a difficult question. John Walvoord speaks immediately of a pretribulation rapture that would produce deliverance away "from" that event (87). Robert Mounce's reply, however, is telling and persuasive. The text says their past faithfulness is the foundation and prerequisite of their future victory. Jesus' own high priestly prayer is very similar: "My prayer is not that you take them out of the world but that you protect them from the evil one" (John 17:15). Nor is there any hint of physical deliverance "out of" the world when the martyrs of the fifth seal are told that they must be patient until their brothers and sisters who are to be killed for their testimony have joined them (Rev. 6:9–11). The issue is spiritual perseverance and faithful endurance, not physical survival (Mounce, *Book of Revelation*, 119).

The great trial that is to come on all the earth is pictured variously throughout the book. It is that awful period at the end of time concluding with the revealing of the "wrath of the Lamb" (6:12–17), when the destroyers of the earth are destroyed (11:15–18), the judgment of God consumes the earth (14:7), and blood flows "as high as the horses' bridles" (14:20). Philadelphia is already experiencing a foreshadowing of this coming conflagration, the already and not-yet where the present and the future coalesce. In that final day, the System, Babylon the Great, will be "Fallen! Fallen," wept over only by the desperate denizens of its final degradation (chap. 18).

But not so the people of God! In Revelation, the "perseverance" of the saints, that is, the certainty their faithfulness will produce ultimate victory, is a key theme. Though characterized under a variety of symbols — the sealing of the saints (7:1–3), the measuring of the temple and its worshipers (11:1), the nourishing of the woman in the wilderness (12:6,14), and the inscribing of names in the book of life (13:8) — it always asserts that the saints are freed to act courageously and boldly now, for they have no reason to fear the future.[3]

3:11 • The focus of the Revelation, from beginning (1:7) to end (22:20), is this long-anticipated reunion of the Lord with his people. However, that which represents a frightening ordeal to "those who live on the earth" (3:10) is what Paul called "the blessed hope" of the church, a hope that challenges us to be "eager to do what is good" (Titus 2:12–14). But not every church, like Philadelphia, will find this promise a godsend. Those less zealous — "I know your works" — will find that his coming also contains a threat to them as well. Ephesus (as well as Laodicea) may lose its church standing (2:5), Pergamum may be dismembered by his blade (2:16), and Sardis may be unexpectedly plundered (3:3). Hence, the urgency of the call to all who have ears.

The crown promised by the Savior is also mentioned in 2:10, where the Smyrnans are called to faithful endurance in the face of dreadful persecution, knowing that steadfastness will result in the "crown of life." But remember the arrogance of Shebna, a previous holder of the key to the king's door (Isa. 22:15–19), for his fate was to lose his position and authority to another more worthy of that distinction.

3:12–13 • Those who persevere will become bulwarks of the church and Kingdom. John hints that many will have the honor of joining himself and Peter and James, who also were accounted as "pillars" (Gal. 2:9). It should not be forgotten that in Solomon's temple two columns bore personal names — Jachin and Boaz (1 Kings

7:21). But here the more immediate reference is to that trustworthy stability and permanence that characterize the church and that Philadelphia, with its seismic history, so lacked. The tremors that frequently caused panicked citizens to retreat to the countryside would never touch one of these whose dwelling was in the New Jerusalem; they would never be forced to flee. And he promises to inscribe upon these faithful the names of God, the city of God, and Christ's own new name.

For John, the earthly Jerusalem with its temple in ruins is not of much importance; now the eternal Jerusalem and the temple above are the only true reality or concern for Christians.[4] In the ancient world, a name was not simply *who* one was but more precisely *what* one was. One's name represented a virtual genetic code of being, even a destiny. By receiving these names, the Christians of Philadelphia were in process of being recreated and "conformed to the image of his Son" (Rom. 8:29, NRSV). These names represent a triple confirmation of the Pauline truth that the Christian's "citizenship is in heaven" (Phil. 3:20).

Though not specifically mentioned, Revelation plainly envisages these names as written on the forehead. They are first received in 7:3 when the servants of God are marked with "a seal on the foreheads." And finally this seal is ultimately revealed to be the Lamb's "name and his Father's name written on their foreheads" (14:1; cf. 22:4). However, the sharing of Christ's own new name will not be perfectly experienced until his promised coming (19:12), for it celebrates a level of intimacy that awaits this reunion. The name "new Jerusalem" may well include the concept of "mother" (Gal. 4:26; cf. Isa. 66:7–13; Heb. 12:22) and is probably to be equated, at one level of symbolism, with the wondrous woman later revealed as the womb of the messianic community (Rev. 12:1–2). Those who bear this new name are her true children (12:17). In retrospect, because they had not denied Jesus' name (v. 8), they will now receive all three of these precious designations.

Contrasting Evaluations

John has compared the activities of two churches located in towns originally established as vehicles to spread the Greek culture into the hinterland of Asia Minor. But as churches, their assignment was to be lighthouses, shining as "lights in the world" (Phil. 2:15, RSV). One was very lively, though a failure in its assigned task; the other had little strength but, nevertheless, had used it skillfully. About the one, nothing good is said (except "you have a few people"); about the other, nothing unfavorable. But why is Sardis not threatened with excommunication, as were Ephesus and Laodicea? Perhaps it is because Sardis's fault was to be misguided in its efforts but did not represent a fatal loss of love (Ephesus) or egoistic self-sufficiency (Laodicea). To be misguided is often preferable to being self-enthralled.

Knowing itself to be ultimately safe, assured in its future destiny, the church should be free to act with abandon, to live dangerously for the Kingdom, even when strength is marginal. Perhaps it is true, as Jacques Ellul observes, that "those who have power, of whatever kind, always turn away from God" (138). If so, Philadelphia's "little strength" is related inversely to its keeping of God's Word. The church at Philadelphia has not based its claim to ministry on some spurious form of worldly clout but on having entered the doorway of service. Surely, there is still something to be said for a boasting in that "weakness" wherein Paul found Christ's sustaining power "made perfect" (2 Cor. 12:9).

"Anyone who has an ear, let him learn from what the Spirit is counseling the churches."

Notes

1. The phrase "seven spirits" is unique to the Revelation; it is found four times (1:4; 3:1; 4:5; 5:6). Richard Bauckham observes, "The four references to the sevenfold Spirit [4 x 7 = 28] correspond to the seven occurrences of the fourfold phrase which designates all the peoples of the earth (5:9; 7:9; 10:11; 11:9; 13:7; 14:6; 17:15). They also correspond to the 28 (7 x 4) references to the Lamb, which,... indicate the worldwide scope of the Lamb's complete victory" (109).

2. William Barclay offers four symptoms of a church that is dying, of a church in great danger of becoming "Sardis": (1) it begins to worship its own history and heritage more than to serve its hopes, and tradition supersedes vision; (2) the forms of ritual assume an importance superior to the needs of people, and the "how" of worship becomes more consequential than the "why"; (3) systems of ecclesiastical polity or theological purity are served more than Jesus; and (4) material realities become the focus at the expense of the spiritual goal of bringing Jesus to people (*Letters to the Seven Churches*, 87–88).

3. Of the seven churches addressed by John, all are in ruins today except Smyrna and Philadelphia. Moreover, the latter still holds the Christian banner high: "Over the centuries as Islam spread across Asia Minor, the church

in Philadelphia stood firm. The city remained the last bastion of Asian Christianity, not falling before the Mohammedans until the fourteenth century. The church continues today and has a bishop and about a thousand believers" (Linthicum, 308).

4. See the chapter "A New City, Revelation" in the volume by Walker, 235–65.

Chapter 7

PERGAMUM

Where Satan Has His Throne

Rev. 2:12–17

Pergamum is the final congregation (actually the third in the order of the lampstands) with which John communicates in the Revelation. As such, there is no contrasting church over against which he portrays its reality. Still there is a special quality to this letter. In it John discusses what must have been one of the most disturbing issues facing all the churches, an issue encapsulated in the puzzling comment that this church lives "where Satan has his throne" (Rev. 2:12). Only by investigating the social, political, and religious background of this important city can we have any hope of understanding this reference.

However, the mysterious and intriguing reference to Satan's throne is important for all the churches, for if this throne is in the capital, Pergamum, its dominion must extend to all the other neighboring churches as well. Moreover, we must constantly remind ourselves that the entire book following these letters is "to the seven churches" and "for the churches" (cf. Rev. 1:4; 22:16). The issues raised by John in the seven letters only open discussions that will be continued and refined again and again throughout the remainder of the book.

Pergamum (Rev. 2:12–17)

Historical Background

With a long-standing reputation as the seat of power in Asia Minor, Pergamum could clearly claim fame in John's day as the Roman provincial capital. For over three hundred years, this city had been a capital, earlier of the Pergamene Empire and later in the Roman province of Asia Minor. The Roman author Pliny reports that it

95

Pergamum

was "by far the most distinguished city in Asia" (in Mounce, *Book of Revelation*, 95).

Pergamum lay just ten miles from the seacoast and eighty-five miles north of Ephesus. The city's nearest neighbors among the seven were Thyatira and Smyrna, the latter being forty-five miles directly south. It occupied a prominence overlooking the Caikus Valley. On its thousand-foot bluff, a great acropolis stood with many other major buildings. Proudly it stood, virtually invulnerable to attack. Power flowed out of this great city from a variety of sources but not least its vaunted library, second in the world only to the Egyptian library at Alexandria. Its holdings of two hundred thousand volumes made it an intellectual mecca of the ancient world.

Zeal for religious expression ran rampant throughout this Roman citadel. Temples dedicated to a variety of gods and religious monuments of all kinds dotted the conical hill that stood behind the city. Indeed, this hill was virtually a throne of darkness on which numerous deities played "king of the mountain," and the city of Pergamum was a veritable microcosm of Roman paganism. The three most famous of these shrines honored Asclepius, Zeus, and the emperor.

In Pergamum, the shrine of Asclepius, the god of health and healing, was one of the leading temples dedicated to him and drew pilgrims from all over the Roman world. The presence of this hospital-temple led R. H. Charles to call Pergamum "the Lourdes of the Province of Asia" (Charles, 1:60). Serpents were the symbol of this god (cf. Rev. 12:9), and his favored title was *Soter,* meaning "savior." The temple priests were the custodians of the most treasured secrets of contemporary medical science; naturally, therefore, Pergamum boasted one of the most famous medical schools in the ancient world. In fact, Galen, the extraordinary Greek physician, was born and studied medical science in Pergamum. Could the temple and worship of this god qualify to be "the throne of Satan"?

The father of humanity, the Greek god Zeus, was also worshiped in Pergamum, and appropriately so, for in Greek mythology Zeus called Pergamum "home." Allegedly, he was born within this city. Situated high up on the prominence, his ninety-foot-square altar was one of the most famous sites of Greek worship in the world. Around the altar's huge base stretched a massive, engraved frieze that depicted the battle of the Greek gods against earth's giants (civilization vs. barbarism). Moreover, at twenty feet tall, it was one of the largest sacrificial altars the world has ever known; the smoke of ceaseless offerings ascended continuously. Is this seat of Zeus worship the background to the throne of Satan?

The third prominent feature of Pergamum's religious life was caesar worship. In John's day, the imperial cult in Asia had long been focused on Pergamum, where for the first time in history an Asian city was authorized to erect a temple for the worship of a living caesar. Caesar Augustus bestowed this privilege in 29 B.C. Overlooking all the lesser temples from its thronelike position, the Augustan temple occupied the highest and noblest site on the hill of divinities. This was certainly one of the most dangerous cities in the empire for dedicated Christians.

Pergamum was granted the prized title "Neocoros of Caesar." The civic honor represented in this quaint title, "temple sweeper," was the undertaking of provision and maintenance of an official shrine of Caesar. Thus, the citizens of Pergamum had dedicated themselves, as a matter of public policy, to the continual glorifying of Caesar's reign. Such glorification often included public worship of his bust, and on stated occasions throughout the year, all loyal inhabitants were called upon to make a small sacrifice to the genius of Caesar. This sacrifice would normally entail the offering of incense and wine before Caesar's image and those of other Roman gods.

These small acts of emperor worship, of glorification and sacrifice, were understood in much the same way as pledging allegiance to the flag is today. They were a simple demonstration of one's faithfulness and loyalty to the empire, an acknowledgment of gratitude for its many benefits. And since most Roman citizens were polytheists, they had no problem with such a modest expression of devotion to Caesar. Moreover, they would be utterly unable to comprehend any Christian hesitation in this regard. However, according to one tradition, those engaging in emperor worship were also required to make the simple two-word confession "Kurios Kaisaros," that is, "Caesar is Lord," an acknowledgment of absolute Roman sovereignty. Such a confession would be, of course, repugnant and unacceptable to Christians, for whom the phrase "Jesus is Lord" (Rom. 10:9; 1 Cor. 12:3) was fundamental.

In other cities the obligations of emperor worship might arise less frequently, but in Pergamum, where the whole weight of Roman administrative bureaucracy rested, the danger was unceasing. Martin Kiddle rightly observes, "Pergamum was a stronger fortress of pagan life than any other of the seven cities" (30). It is assuredly "where Satan has his throne," for its vitality is directly supplied by "the dragon" (Rev. 13:4). Here the fundamental battle with fallen Babylon and the struggle with "civil religion" are most plainly revealed. This is "where Satan lives" (2:13) and where his power is most clearly revealed.

Pergamum had it all! The city could boast all that a Roman power center might have: the seat of government, academic and literary resources, a Roman mint, baths, gymnasiums, an amphitheater, and the stage. These were the accoutrements of clout that made Pergamum a miniature of all that John sought to safeguard his churches against — fallen Babylon. Pergamum represented and revealed the apex of Roman culture!

The Letter

2:12 • A prismatic facet of the cosmic Christ now revealed to this church in Pergamum is that of the messianic warrior-king, a most typical portrayal of the first-century Jewish hope for the Messiah. The word used for his messianic sword is *rhomphaia*. Though it occurs about 230 times in the LXX, the Greek Old Testament,[1] six of only seven occurrences in the New Testament are in Revelation (the only exception is Luke 2:34–35). The background for this warrior-king's sword that proceeds from his mouth (Rev. 1:16; 19:15) is Isaiah 11:4; Hosea 6:5; and Amos 9:4, all of which use divine pronouncements, that is, the "word," as a weapon of destruction. The Lord who now confronts this congregation endangered by its naked proximity to Roman domination is the eschatological judge whose mouth will pronounce the final verdict over existence and nonexistence.

"The sharp, double-edged sword" would also have reminded John's readers of a Roman sword. *Ius gladii*, the "right of the sword," was granted the Roman proconsul, allowing him the indiscriminate and ultimate power of execution. Any who dared to challenge the Roman government would be liable to his sword (cf. Rom. 13:4). From this perspective, who ought the Christians of Pergamum to fear? Rome can only kill the body, and nothing more, but there is one who can both kill and then condemn the whole being to hell (Luke 12:4–5; cf. Matt. 10:28). This church lives in a dangerous place, indeed, but there are greater hazards to be feared in this universe. Death is not the ultimate danger!

This sword is to serve a grim purpose (2:16); its razor edge will distinguish and divide the false (Nicolaitans; v. 15) from the faithful (Antipas and his comrades; v. 13) in this and other churches. It is the sword of truth that will also descend upon all the unfaithful on the Day of Judgment:

> From his mouth comes a sharp sword with which to strike down the nations, and he will rule them with a rod of iron; he will tread the wine press of the fury of the wrath of God the Almighty. On his robe and on his thigh he has a name inscribed. "King of kings and Lord of lords." (Rev. 19:15–16, NRSV; note v. 21)

2:13 • If Satan's throne is in Pergamum, then so is the beast's. Revelation 13:4 notes that the dragon (i.e., Satan) has given his power to this monster. Thus, when people give allegiance to the beast, they are actually worshiping the dragon. It is almost beyond question that John is referring to the Roman imperial power that resides in and emanates from Pergamum, namely, the proconsul's seat (Satan's throne) of government. John's only other mention of this throne is found in 13:2, where it is shared by the beast. On this throne, the beast enjoys the dragon's power and authority.

If we understand "the beast" as the personification of "the System,"[2] the engulfing force that holds individuals in thrall to the power and authority of its vitality (in John's day "Rome"), then we can see more easily the role of Satan or the dragon as that threatening presence standing behind the System's throne. Paul has defined this reality memorably in a remarkable passage:

> As for you, you were dead in your transgressions and sins, in which you used to live, when you followed *the ways of this world* and of the ruler of the kingdom of the air, *the spirit who is now at work* in those who are disobedient.... Like the rest, we were by nature objects of wrath. (Eph. 2:1–3, emphasis added)

The beast is this "spirit" incarnated and at work in the System, or "this world." In keeping with this line of interpretation, M. Robert Mulholland suggests that "the Beast is the pervasive and controlling posture of life or perceptual framework that captures human beings and holds them in bondage as citizens of Fallen Babylon" (106). It is Satan, says the Revelation, who inspires and energizes the Roman beast, who stands behind the forces opposing the church; even synagogues can be seats of his power (2:9; 3:9).

The bad news is that this congregation must struggle under the very shadow of Satan's dominating presence. To maintain consistent and faithful witness here will be difficult, indeed.³ In Pergamum, the pressures of fallen Babylon will be most dazzling and most deadly. The good news is that the warrior-king is standing with his people and is aware of their spiritual condition and danger.

The Christians at Pergamum had not yielded to the temptation of simply burning a little incense and proclaiming, "Caesar is Lord." That name — Lord — was too precious. What might have seemed a slight sacrifice to pay for the privilege of living in the Roman world was a great sacrilege to them. However, the Roman proconsul did not bear the sword in vain. Already this church has suffered the persecution (RSV: "tribulation") Jesus predicted (John 16:33); martyrdom has come to live at Pergamum, but having developed a consistent Christian counterculture, this congregation will not suffer defeat (cf. Mark 4:17).

We do not know who Antipas was, but obviously Jesus has never forgotten him, for Antipas lived the kind of life that is an irritant to the System. Jesus knows him by name because good shepherds and caring pastors always know the names of their sheep (John 10:3). One day Antipas was led into a Roman government building and did not emerge alive. Legend has it that during Domitian's reign he was roasted in a brazen bull until slowly death ended his torture. On the day of his death, his Lord was there, never to forget and never to leave him. Antipas has experienced and knows the meaning of "hidden manna" (v. 17). He was probably executed for his audacious witness and failure to acknowledge Caesar. Yet the church at Pergamum did not "renounce" its faith during this outbreak of persecution (the aorist tense of the Greek verb suggests a specific and intense outburst of oppression that had been successfully withstood).

The title Antipas bears — "faithful witness" — is shared with his Lord (1:5) and may be related to the new name promised to conquerors (2:17). Perhaps by this common title, Revelation means to relate Antipas's death to Jesus' own, suggesting that it too will count in the balance and truly make a difference. Just as we discovered hope through the suffering of Jesus, others may find that same life and hope through our faithful sufferings (Ewing, 74). For better or worse, each person changes the world.

2:14 • Surely no group in this church actually called themselves "Balaamites." This was a detested name out of Hebrew history that could only have functioned as a symbolic reference to a way of life similar to that of Balaam, a Gentile prophet. Balaam's story is found in Numbers 22–24. He was remembered as a great menace to the success of the Exodus pilgrimage to the Promised Land.

Hired by Balak, the king of Moab, to cast a curse on Israel, Balaam was initially unable to accomplish this commission. Finally, through evil advice given to Balak by Balaam, the prophet succeeded in leading the Israelites into immoral and obscene idolatry (cf. Num. 25:1–3; 31:16). The result was a devastating judgment. Thus, in biblical history Balaam became the prototype of false prophets who lead the people of God into ruinous compromise. Some group within the church of Pergamum advocated a program that threatened the same result. Perhaps they held an antinomian (i.e., antilaw or libertine) perversion of the gospel, similar or identical to the Nicolaitans.

2:15 • It is these Nicolaitans who are carrying out a project reminiscent of Balaam, yet this time from within the church. Little if anything is known about this group, except that in Ephesus their blandishments had also been faced and withstood (2:6). They almost certainly seemed very sane and even sage in John's day. Perhaps they advocated a form of Christianity that could coexist with Rome and include the best of both.[4]

After all, the cost of penetrating and using the System probably seemed quite small. Participation in banquets where religious practices could be rationalized as harmless, attendance at Roman ceremonies complete with the adoration of their gods, failing to defend Antipas and his unseemly zeal, compliance with political programs beneficial to the rich and powerful, winking at "that's human nature" laxity in the church, yielding to the reverie of Babylon the Great (18:3) — all of these were a small price for the full participation in society that the Nicolaitans relished. Theirs was a progressive, accommodating, and pale vision of Christian faith that cleverly avoided persecution and friction with the System, despite the cost. This is not the group to produce a "faithful witness" (v. 13). In their midst, even Satan might be comfortable enough to take a seat.

2:16 • Yes, this is a church where much is right; that is abundantly clear. Still, John must deal with "them." They apparently do not "remain true to my name" (v. 13); rather, they are at peace with themselves and the Roman world. Many Christians find such a peace, but, says Revelation, it is a peace that produces war with Christ. They need to repent, for the power of life and death (the sword of truth) belongs to Christ (2:12), not Caesar. Peace must be achieved but in the proper way and by the proper authority. "We must obey God," Peter once pointed out, "rather than men" (Acts 5:29)!

Yet the words "Repent then" (NRSV) seem addressed to all, for when a church is in trouble, all are involved. Does this command also suggest that there might be a third group in the church? Some are holding fast; others are Nicolaitans. Are there also some who are being swayed by the success and advancing prospects of the concessionists? Such would be true to reality as we know it. Therefore, the whole church needs to repent of a disposition that has fostered the situation; the Nicolaitans need to see themselves as God does, for a state of war exists, and the hard of (spiritual) hearing need their ears to be opened.

The "coming soon" noted in the verse is probably the same one mentioned in chapter 19, where again the "sword" is conspicuously present (19:15,21). Through this warning to a long-ago church of an event that has yet to happen, we learn once more that every generation has the right to expect this blessed hope. And given the brevity of life, we all will meet the Lord sooner than we imagine. This anticipated "coming" represents a hope that purifies those who await its arrival (1 John 3:2-3); it is a hope that is the very basis of the Revelation (1:7; 3:11; 22:7,12,20).

2:17 • The seven messages to the churches are intended to be heard and implemented in more than seven local communities. They are addressed to the whole church of all times and in all places. That is, of course, exactly who the seven churches stand for in Revelation's symbolic or visionary world — "anyone who has an ear" (NRSV).

The promises made to the overcomers or conquerors in Pergamum are, as usual, pertinent to their dire situation. "Hidden manna" calls to our mind's eye the day on which Jesus revealed to his disciples, "I have food to eat that you know nothing about" (John 4:32); the food he referred to is defined two verses later: "My food is to do the will of him who sent me and to finish his work" (v. 34). The witness Jesus had just borne to the Samaritan woman represented the divine call upon his life. And in the pursuit of that call, there is always nourishment of spirit and the sustenance of divine fellowship.

Another background to the "hidden manna" is a well-known Jewish legend, which states that Jeremiah had taken the jar of manna from the ark of the covenant (Exod. 16:32–34) and deposited it in a cave on Mount Nebo (in present-day Jordan) at the time of the temple's destruction in 586 B.C. (2 Macc. 2:4–8). The tradition promises that at the time of the end the manna would be recovered and revealed, representing a promise of a future and eternal nurture, a manna that is "the bread of angels" (Ps. 78:25).

While the Nicolaitans indulge in the fellowship and food of dead idols (v. 14), the faithful are sustained by the living Lord. Only he is "the bread that comes down from heaven, so that one may eat of it and not die" (John 6:50, NRSV). This hidden source of spiritual nourishment was just what a church that lives "where Satan has his throne" needed most.

Among several possible explanations for Christ's gift of a "white stone," only two carry conviction. White stones would have been instantly recognized in John's day as the tokens a jury used to vote for acquittal in legal proceedings. It was the opposite of the dark stone, which, if dropped in the ballot box, signified (as in Antipas's case?) condemnation. But white stones (pieces of wood or metal too) were also commonly used as coupons or tickets in a variety of situations, for example, for admission to public banquets, rations of bread or corn, and even manumission for victorious gladiators from the arena. In 2:17, acquittal from the "few things" (v. 14) held against this church would be important and might mean the acquittal from divine judgment that is redemption itself. Moreover, admittance to the final messianic banquet (19:9) would then be the final result of this vote of confidence. So, perhaps both ideas are part of the promise of the "white stone."

Along with the white stone comes a "new name." As noted in 19:12, Christ also has a "new name," one connected to his victory over all forces resisting the kingdom of God and the dawning of the eternal future. Hence, it is like Paul's description of heaven (1 Cor. 2:9), specifically that which has never yet been imagined in the heart or mind. Remember, a "name" is not *who* but *what* one is. The new name stands for our mysterious destiny commencing at the resurrection as the perishable becomes imperishable, the mortal achieves immortality, and death is swallowed up in victory (1 Cor. 15:51–54). Our new name is that unique reality to which we have been predestined to be conformed — the very eternal image of Jesus Christ (Rom. 8:29). No one else will know (experience) it but the one to whom the Son grants that "new name."

Finally, if Pergamum is the church that lives "where Satan has his throne" and if that throne is virtually the equivalent of the beast (the subject to which we turn in the next chapter), then it is the archetypal church that is addressed in the Revelation. The church surrounded by Babylon the Great, immersed in the System of the beast and compromised from within, this is the church that represents all churches. Pergamum is a key representative of the seven, to which John is commissioned to reveal the victorious Christ, who holds the ultimate sword.

The Seven Letters — A Postscript

We have seen Revelation's delight in provoking dialogue and insight by comparing and contrasting the spiritual life manifested in a variety of churches. These seven, carefully chosen as illustrations of the church universal, portray a wide range of responses the church makes to the System seeking to co-opt it. In some, the light is nearly extinguished (Ephesus and Laodicea); they have forgotten what is essential and what stands at the heart of church life. Others are models of committed witness (Smyrna and Philadelphia). As the church in mission, they have taken up the cross and followed the Lamb. More the norm, however, are those threatened by slow and disastrous accommodation and retreat (Pergamum, Thyatira, Sardis). They are engaged in various degrees of compromise with the fallen order, and Babylon is seeping into their midst.[5]

If these seven cover letters had been meant merely to chastise or simply to confront these churches with issues specific to each, the book could have ended here. But it continues! The ongoing story of the struggle between God and Satan for the soul of society, revealing the dynamics of the city of Satan and the city of God, also discloses the calling of the church. The vision of the New Jerusalem, the city of God in chapters 21–22, is a reality Christ calls all of his people to begin implementing in the cities where they are called to live:

> It was that vision which answered the question for all the churches, "Why should we be faithful?" It was not just to make God happy. It was not so they might somehow be doing what was right. They were to be faithful as an integral part of God's plan to bring about God's kingdom. (Linthicum, 311)

True, only God can ultimately bring that kingdom, but each church is to work as if that future depended upon its faithfulness. In short, once we know where God is going, we have been given our marching orders, indeed, a battle plan for the present. "He who has an ear, let him hear what the Spirit says to the churches."

As John writes to his beloved congregations, he is communicating a vision that seeks to train them in Christlike love (Ephesus), the value of genuine suffering (Smyrna), courageous truth speaking (Pergamum), an unpopular holiness (Thyatira), authentic service (Sardis), assertive mission (Philadelphia), and humble repentance (Laodicea). And clearly, these continue to be the major challenges for all churches.[6] Sadly, there just isn't much evidence that the church has ever been significantly better or more spiritual than it is today. Hence, there is no golden age to which we might retreat, only a continuing battle with the beast. And to that reality we turn next.

Notes

1. The first use of the word in the LXX is in Genesis 3:24, where it signifies the sword that guards the entrance to Eden.

2. "Uncle Sam" as the representative of the American system of government and history might be a contemporary example of this type of political symbol. Perhaps Luther, the Roman pontiff, Calvin, Wesley, or Lenin, who stand as representatives of massive traditions and varietal interpretations of reality, have analogous functions.

3. M. Eugene Boring catalogs the various options Christians could utilize in the struggle with the System and its demands on their loyalty: (1) quit (the pressures of church membership were unexpectedly high), (2) lie (truth is not owed to a beastly System, and true faith is a matter of the heart not public formalities; John calls such people "liars" and reserves places in the fiery lake for them; 21:8), (3) fight (theoretically possible but clearly rejected by Revelation; cf. 12:11), (4) change the "law" (not a genuine possibility in a totalitarian state, especially for a minority such as the Christians), (5) adjust (acculturate and adjust Christian faith so it could embrace "civil religion," even the emperor cult; tolerance and inclusiveness must be developed — this is the crisis so frequently addressed in the Revelation), and (6) die (by sharing the testimony of Jesus, the faithful Christian shares the fate and triumph of his or her Lord; 12:11; 13:5,7). Only the latter is advocated by John (*Revelation*, 21–23).

4. After an extensive study of what is known of this group, Colin Hemer concludes "that Nicolaitanism was an antinomian movement whose antecedents can be traced in the misrepresentation of Pauline liberty, and whose incidence may be connected with the special pressures of emperor worship and pagan society" (94).

5. For a different analysis of the interrelations among the churches that integrates their letters into the structure of the whole book, see Farrer, 83–86; and Bauckham, 122–23.

6. Elisabeth Fiorenza summarizes the positive message of these letters as follows: "The strength of the Christian community in Asia Minor consists: in mutual love, in service to others, in fidelity and steadfastness, in the keeping of God's word and the rejecting of false teachers, in the confession of its faith even during persecution, and in consistent resistance" (*Revelation*, 53).

Chapter 8

THAT BEASTLY BEAUTY

The Prostituted Society

Rev. 17:1–18

Failing to grasp a key theme from the beginning can ruin much of the punch, not to mention the basic message, of any book. This is especially important in the case of John's Revelation. In chapter 17, John decodes the identity of the beast, the churches' prime enemy. Since the beast is a figure of major importance to the intent of the whole book, it is exceedingly crucial that we now grasp the nature of this archantagonist. Lest we lose our way as we move through the Revelation, we shall proceed to chapter 17 and then will return to the intervening chapters.

The Beauty

17:1–2 • Once again, John is invited to view another vision that will further clarify the Revelation of Jesus Christ. This scene will reveal the prostituted flip side of all that the Lamb seeks to build, namely, the kingdom of God. Here, and in chapter 18, is the "prostitute," the polar opposite of that Kingdom, truly an illegitimate vision of the destiny of humanity, a reality that transforms God's creation into a besotted, meaningless orgy. The city discussed in this chapter reveals the depths and profound ugliness of human sin. It is a prostituted city because it has failed to live up to the grand design of God; it has failed to be what might have been!

The prostitute is "great" because she will soon be equated with the *great* city, that is, "Babylon the Great" (cf. 17:5,18; 18:2,10). No ordinary lady, or courtesan, is this! She is one who commands great power and immense prestige. The power structures of earth (the kings) are in bed with her. Positioned upon the earth's economic arteries, its waterways, she commands the commercial might of her world (cf. 17:15). Yes, it is appropriate to remember that this is where the seven churches dwell, an arena dominated by Roman commercial enterprise. As this whore quaffs moral atrocities from the goblet in her hand, a stupor seeps into the business and social dynamics of her world. Moreover, spiritual inebriation has proved as real a malady as physical intoxication.

Beauty is her game, but "prostitute" is her name! Later in the chapter, we will learn that forces from within the beast's own realm eventually destroy her (v. 16). The indication is, therefore, that while the beast is a continuing reality, she has a more limited, contemporary, and transitory life expectancy. Her beauty is, indeed, fleeting. And not every future manifestation of beastly power will reflect her degree of comeliness. She is the alluring and enchanting beauty that was Rome (the System) but also something more.

It is always a mistake to imagine that a title or any descriptive term in Revelation is simply accidental. Is there a deeper reason why John has called her a prostitute? In this case, we need to be aware that the Hebrew Scriptures contain "five principle texts which refer to Jerusalem or Israel as a harlot and only two which refer to non-Israelite cities with the same image" (Ford, 283).[1] And while J. Massyngberde Ford probably goes too far in suggesting that this prostitute is Jerusalem, there is, perhaps, at least some hint of collusion between the prostitute and that seat of Jewish tradition. This term is not inadvertent, and we should be remembering just now that among the seven letters there are two external sources of enmity opposed to the church: Satan's throne (2:13) and the "synagogue of Satan" (2:9; 3:9). John does not indulge slips of the tongue!

17:3 • "Great," perhaps, but she is also hideously repulsive! When one does a double take on this scene, suddenly one notices something that doesn't come into focus immediately. There, just beneath the charming woman who has captivated your eye, is a monstrosity. Prostitutes usually entice by packaging and presenting their charms in the most attractive light. This one, however, has failed to mask the presence of her dark side. Just beneath her glamour lurks a brutish monstrosity.

No ordinary beast is this one. Surely we are meant to notice that these descriptive details are also the description of someone else, "an enormous red dragon," who has "seven heads and ten horns" (12:3; cf. 17:9). This beast is virtually the alter ego, a mirror image on earth, of a far greater power dwelling in transcendent realms.

17:4 • Possessing all the seductive accoutrements of her profession, the prostitute exudes a form of beauty that often beguiles and just as often betrays. She is lovely as the world counts loveliness, adorning herself in the goods typical of the debauched city she personifies (cf. 18:11–12). Nevertheless, this is the flame that has attracted the "rich" Laodicean church, and hers is the judgment they will likewise share.

We will eventually discover that Revelation has once again engaged in a program of startling comparison and contrast. Prior to the appearance of this woman in chapter 17, John has already seen a magnificent lady, whom he describes in 12:1–2. Clothed with the beauty of creation and filled with its life (cf. 19:8), she is the very antithesis of everything that is the prostitute. Each represents a community of the committed; each represents a fate awaiting her children. One is the bride of Christ; the other, the bride of Satan.

17:5 – 6 • The prostitute also is a mother to those who draw nourishment from her ideals and designs on life.[2] Drunkenness signifies that one has indulged an appetite to excess. And this mysterious woman seems to have one main craving, the lives of the people of God. She has presently persecuted and imprisoned John just because he was a powerful witness (1:9) and has afflicted the Smyrnan church (2:9); Antipas of Pergamum has been martyred (2:13). Moreover, many additional victims are clearly anticipated (6:9–11).

One of the most revealing texts concerning this symbol of the great prostitute/great city/Babylon the Great is Revelation 18:24: "In her was found the blood of prophets and of the saints, / and of *all* who have been killed on the earth" (emphasis added). The implication is clear. Whatever she stands for, it includes *all* the carnage, torture, and violence ever committed on planet Earth. No one city could possibly account for the massive evil chronicled here, although Jerusalem is similarly described by Jesus (Matt. 23:34–35). And John would agree: Jerusalem is part of this city (11:8), but those who live in it include all the inhabitants of the world (11:9–10). Therefore, the great prostitute, that is, the great city of Babylon, is the *World System*, a composite of all the cities and all the peoples who make up a fallen creation in rebellion against the Creator.

Even as it must have astounded John, such monstrous and inhuman cruelty astonishes all who behold it. And so, with Daniel in the Old Testament apocalypse, we desire to understand but also need help (Dan. 7:15,17,19). How are we to interpret this unpleasant scene and its relation to us?

17:7 • The approach of a heavenly interpreter to aid the reader is a common feature among all the apocalyptic books. The offer of this sort of help points to the reader's need for the guidance of "a God in heaven who reveals mysteries" (Dan. 2:28), for only God can reveal the hidden depths of reality to us. However, what we are about to hear produces almost as many problems as insights.

And the Beast

17:8 • Puzzling, indeed, in the verse is the twice-repeated parody of a divine title: " 'I am the Alpha and the Omega,' says the Lord God, 'who is, and who was, and who is to come, the Almighty' " (1:8). Yet each of the elements of the beast's title is a twisted mockery of the order ("was, . . . is not" instead of "is, . . . was") and significance ("come up . . . and go to his destruction" instead of "to come") of the divine attributes. This beast dares to counterfeit the deific identity. And the only group not to be overawed with the pluck and pomp of this brute will be those whose names (destinies) have been bought and paid for by the Lamb and inscribed in the register of New Jerusalem.

17:9 • Now we are told to exercise our insight (i.e., put your thinking cap on), for the decoding game begins in earnest. Suddenly, John reveals that the lumbering beast on which the woman is seated has seven heads that are actually seven hills or "mountains" (NRSV). Surely, that is clear! No one in John's day could possibly have read or heard this without recognizing the fabled "seven hills of Rome," one of the world's most widely known geographical markers. Rome's characteristic seven hills, on which the city literally was built, had already been rendered famous by poets, historians, and playwrights. Legend has it that Rome was first founded on one of these hills in 753 B.C. In time, each of the seven was named and remembered as a specific district of the city. Domitian himself had built the Flavian Palace on the Palatine Hill. This woman's address — she lives on the "seven hills" — is unmistakably the empire's capital, the greatest and most extravagant city in the Roman world.

17:10–11 • Then a singularly important double exposure is revealed. Yes, the seven represent a place, but these heads also represent something even more consequential — a presence. Seven monarchs stand at the heart of this reality. But are they meant to be understood as *seven specific kings* whose personages are identifiable or *seven kings* who stand for the totality and agelong duration of human empires?

If viewed as a listing of specific rulers — the first approach — then the most popular outline begins with the Roman emperor reigning at the time of Jesus' birth, when his battle with the System began (cf. 12:4). This approach usually deletes the names of three interregnum emperors who reigned so briefly as to be largely unknown or insignificant and concludes with the emperor in John's day, Domitian (Harrington, 211; Rissi, 81):

1. Augustus, 27 B.C.–A.D. 14 (Jesus is born 7–4 B.C.)

2. Tiberius, A.D. 14–37

3. Caligula, A.D. 37–41

4. Claudius, A.D. 41–54

5. Nero, A.D. 54–68

   [Interregnum emperors: Galba, A.D. 68–69; Otho, 69; Vitellius, 69]

6. Vespasian, A.D. 69–79

7. Titus, A.D. 79–81

8. Domitian, A.D. 81–96 (John imprisoned on Patmos)

This simple and persuasive lineup concludes with the beast, the eighth, as the deranged Domitian. There is, however, one important problem. The text continues: "Five have fallen, one is, the other has not yet come; but when he does come, he must remain for a little while." If we take the approach noted above, that would mean then that the fifth emperor who has fallen is Nero, and if we omit the interregnum emperors, the one presently living (reigning) would be Vespasian. Unfortunately, A.D. 69–79 is not the era in which most commentators believe the book of Revelation was written. Most feel John wrote in the early 90s, during the reign of Domitian.

Possible responses to this difficulty do exist. For instance, perhaps John predicted this turn of events earlier in his prophetic career, when Vespasian was emperor, and then subsequently incorporated that prediction into his later book to publicly demonstrate the accuracy and fulfillment of his earlier prophecy (Charles, 2:69). Had he not predicted that the eighth emperor from Christ's birth, Domitian, would turn out to be a beast?[3] His had been a true prophecy, as demonstrated by subsequent history.

Another possibility is that this exceptionally tidy sequence is the product of *vaticinia ex eventu*, or as John Goldingay refers to it, "quasi-prophecy" (*Daniel*, Word Biblical Commentary, xxxix, xl, 282–86). This phrase names the ancient practice of stating already existing fact or known history as though it were being predicted from some vantage point in the past. It was a recognized literary technique used as far back as 2000 B.C. in ancient Egypt (Gammie, 105). The most famous passage in the Bible evidencing this technique may be Daniel 11, where a very long historical era is seemingly *predicted* in immense detail, such as is not found in any other prophetic passage in Scripture.[4] In addition, prediction here would be all the more surprising since Daniel 11 is not even a messianic passage, where one might expect the most detailed degree of prediction.

If John is penning quasi-prophecy, then he is writing out of his experience with Domitian (the eighth) but writing *as though* he had predicted this at a much earlier date ("Five have fallen, one is [Vespasian]"). This process wherein recent history is treated *as if* it were being predicted in an earlier day may seem, to the modern mind, a fraudulent procedure, and in our day it certainly would be. But clearly, to first-century Jews, it was not. About seventy apocalyptic books were written before and after John's era. Their authors frequently utilized *vaticinia ex eventu,* that is, wrote as if they lived in an earlier time in order to record and interpret known history as though it were prophecy. One of the more famous of these books is called Enoch. In this Jewish apocalyptic book, written in the first and second centuries B.C., the author writes as though he were biblical Enoch (Gen. 5:21–24). He tells us then of knowledge gained after his ascension into heaven. Thus, vast expanses of biblical history subsequent to Enoch's day are recounted in this apocalypse as if the original Enoch had *predicted* them. Of course, the book is actually much later in origin. This process should be understood as an "apocalyptic convention," for it was a typical and expected element of such literature in John's day (Laws, 51 n. 14).

Thus, it is totally inappropriate to call such a conventional style "fraud." Modern authors who hold that *vaticinia ex eventu* may occasionally be found in Scripture are not denying the reality of predictive prophecy, which they also often hold. They simply believe that in a few passages something else is happening. This technique had become conventional, an accepted practice of the day. By this quasi-prophecy, apocalyptic authors stated their conviction that God is always in control of the details and is never surprised by any development in history. That is, God "could have" predicted every known detail of history in advance had he wished. Hence, God has always known about the beast and planned appropriately. God is always in control, and God's people can be at ease.

Is it possible for God to employ such a literary convention to good and holy effect? Some will say this is not acceptable divine behavior. However, if God is free to use whatever approach he wishes, even the conventions of contemporary apocalyptic, then this staple of the genre may also be at home in the Apocalypse (Barclay, *Revelation of John,* 2:190; Hayes, 459; Swete, 218). Moreover, we ought not be in the business of dictating on what grounds God's Word is acceptable and what God may or may not do.

Given all the uncertainties of the first approach, many scholars suggest a second. They argue it is the symbol *seven* that is significant, for with this number John is trying to interpret the durability of human power. From this perspective, the "seven kings" represent the totality of human sovereignty within history and not a definable list of known emperors (Aune, 1315; Caird, 218–19; Kiddle, 350; Ladd, *Commentary on the Revelation,* 229–31). Hence, if five have fallen, the sixth is ruling; a seventh will have power briefly, concluding with the grand finale — the eighth; then humanity is near the end of its tether. The eschatological day, with all attendant horrors, is approaching rapidly (Mounce, *Book of Revelation,* 316). Clearly, that is a prime message of the book that both approaches emphasize correctly.

Are we led nearer an understanding by any of the other details John has supplied? We are told emphatically, for example, that this beast "was," presently "is not," yet "will come up" as he "is going to his destruction" (17:8,11). If we believe that seven specific emperors are in view here, then we can take two approaches to these phrases. (1) If these comments had originally been written during Vespasian's reign, then used in Revelation later in the century, they would mean that the malevolent spirit evidenced in some previous entity is currently absent (during Vespasian's day) but will reemerge in an eighth emperor still to come. (2) The *vaticinia ex eventu* approach observes that if current history (events of the 90s) had been written as a prediction made in an earlier time, Domitian, the reigning emperor, would have been treated as if he were a future ruler not yet on the scene (hence, "is not"). Then, given this quasi-earlier perspective, apparently from Vespasian's reign, the eighth emperor would be the current one, Domitian.[5] What "was" would have been the Roman persecution of Christians, which, begun by Nero, was absent ("is not") since his reign but is now resurgent in Domitian's demented cruelty. Both Christian and Roman writers commented on the similarities between Nero and Domitian.

In the case of the second approach (where the symbolic number *seven* is the key), a different problem presents itself. What "will come up out of the Abyss" is clear (the beast), but what "was" and now "is not" is less clear. In what sense "was" this beast if now (in John's day) it "is not"? It is evident that the coming king is a monster before whom all others will pale. Nevertheless, how "was" relates to a present "is not" is difficult. Is "evil" currently nonexistent? Has the satanic temporarily taken leave? Are Christians not under attack? Perhaps it would be best, from this perspective, to say that some evil, manifested in infamous moments of past history, for example, the pharaoh of the Exodus and Antiochus IV, is presently not as evident but will reemerge in its final, most vicious form at the end of history.

An additional detail must also be noted. Despite its definition as an "eighth," the beast "belongs to the seven," which makes the status of "is not" even more difficult. Can a relationship to the seven be both operative in the past ("was") and currently inoperative ("is not")? Fortunately, here there is an interpretation that is widely held. Revelation seems to base part of the beast's character (a past, present, and future aspect) on a Roman legend concerning Nero. When Nero died by his own hand in A.D. 68, the scene was sufficiently private and secluded that a myth grew up to the effect that he was not truly dead.[6] He had secretly fled to Parthia, Rome's great superpower enemy to the east, or so the story purported. And from that frightening power base, he was supposedly plotting a vengeful return. So seriously was this legend taken by the empire that on different occasions pretenders sought the imperial throne claiming to be "Nero returned," thus the name of the legend, *Nero Redivivus* (Beasley-Murray, *Book of Revelation*, 254; Caird, 215–19; Charles, 2:67–72).

Therefore, whatever is to be made of the eighth king, whether an identifiable emperor or the final machination of cosmic evil, it is someone or something that reanimates the spirit of Nero, the first emperor to persecute Christians. He was in fact a great archenemy of the early church; both Peter and Paul were martyred in Rome during his reign. This, no doubt, is why he became a foreshadowing prototype of the beast. Their linkage is further clarified in Revelation 13; we shall speak more about Nero and his legend in our discussion of that chapter.

17:12 • The number *ten* may, once again, represent the concept of perpetuity or "as far as you can go" (cf. 2:10).[7] If so, the beast betters the cat's record of nine lives by one. "Kings . . . not yet" seems to indicate future phases (cf. v. 17) of whatever reality the other seven kings stand for,[8] whereas "along with" implies that these future editions of evil are also manifestations of the beast's continuing historical power and that the *ten* share a unity of purpose with their grim puppet master. Still, a dominion of merely "one hour" emphatically downplays the significance of their challenge to the Lamb. They too will be overcome in their own time, which also will be brief. How different their reality is from the one who commands all time (cf. 2 Pet. 3:8).

There is a most important implication here. The eighth king is not the very last or final manifestation of evil, for there are ten more who continue the disastrous dominion and spirit of the beast. Again, John would say that "many antichrists" (1 John 2:18) are yet to go forth into history. No single generation will exhaust the horror of the beast's assault on humanity. The eighth will represent a horrendous chapter in the history of the beast's power, but it will also continue to reincarnate itself ten more times, until the end.

17:13 – 14 • The eighth king might indicate a temporal perspective with regard to the seven, but this eighth, the beast, continues in spirit to the very end. Then it and its diabolical extensions will endure a total and eternal defeat. Nevertheless, there is a phrase here that defines all that is associated with the beast throughout the whole of its existence — "war on the Lamb" (NRSV). That is truly what makes the beast so beastly: it is unalterably opposed to all that is represented by the kingdom of God. The book of Revelation, then, is about a continuing war and the role the seven churches play in that warfare. They must never forget that it is the beast's very business to "make war" not only against Christ but also "against the saints" (13:7) because they are "with him."

17:15 • A well-established symbol from the Hebrew Scriptures, "waters" often represented the surrounding nations and especially the enemies of the people of Israel. It is so used most clearly and frequently in the Psalms: 18:16–17; 69:1–4,14; 124:2–6; 144:7–8. The prostitute has seduced the world with her alluring charms. Then, however, and totally without warning a stunning reversal is announced.

17:16 • She and her lush beauty are to be stripped, consumed, and burned. Since we are immediately told that the prostitute is "the great city that rules over the kings of the earth" (v. 18), we need to think of her as "the beauty that was Rome." But this utterly unexpected about-face is an ironically insightful symbol for the self-consuming nature of evil. Uncreative and unproductive, evil can ultimately do nothing but destroy itself and those deluded by it. In another similar vision, the demonic locusts from the bottomless pit are capable of harming none but those who are already under the sway of the fallen one (9:1,4). Evil always carries the seed of its own destruction.

Glorious Rome was unmatched in her absolute control of John's world. Political and commercial mistress of a civilization in awe of her majesty, she was a beauty but one founded on the misery and suffering of the unfortunate who bore her burdensome yoke. The prophets spoke of cities built on foundations of "blood" (Jer. 19:4; Mic. 3:10), and Revelation predicts that such prostituted, beastly beauty cannot survive. A time will always come "for destroying those who destroy the earth" (11:18). And there will surely be future forces that will destroy Rome, producing a shudder that will be heard around the world when her light goes out.

17:17 • Still it is odd that forces allied with the beast eventually destroy the prostitute, who rides the same whirlwind. However, John quickly supplies a reason for this seemingly irrational behavior. Against their own best interests, they end up destroying an ally because it is the purpose of God. The one who uses even the wrath of humanity to bring praise to God's own self (Ps. 76:10) will also use the beast against its own. The ten kings to come will also serve the King of kings, and this they will continue to do "until the words of God will be fulfilled" (NRSV). Revelation is saying that their story represents the remainder of history, for the Almighty's purposes will not be complete until God's word has accomplished all it was sent to achieve. That is why the prostitute will be devoured and the ten share a like fate.

17:18 • John concludes the chapter by equating the "great prostitute" (v. 1) with "the great city," which has already been decoded as "BABYLON THE GREAT, / THE MOTHER OF PROSTITUTES / AND OF THE ABOMINATIONS OF THE EARTH" (v. 5). And with this identification, the reader has been prepared for chapter 18. It will further analyze the reality and discuss the future of "the great city," even as chapters 21–22 define the future of "the eternal city."[9]

For the present, however, the great prostitute is the city "that rules over the kings of the earth." She is the beauty and grandeur that was Rome! Thus, Pergamum is "where Satan's throne is" (2:13, NRSV) because it was the seat of Roman authority and power in Asia Minor. Here, her rule over the forces of the earth is meant to remind us of the present scope of her reach. She controls the politics, the social life, and commerce in the world of the seven churches. It is she that they must face and resist! The temptations to dally with her, to prostitute the churches' true identity, and to indulge in her abominations, these are the challenges of serving the living Lord, the warnings Revelation thunders.

Notes

1. These texts are found in Hosea (2:5; 3:3; 4:15), Isaiah (1:4,9,21), Jeremiah (2:20; 5:7), Micah (1:7), and Ezekiel (chap. 23). The only texts to apply this title to non-Israelite cities are Isaiah 23:15–18 (Tyre) and Nahum 3:4 (Nineveh). Ford believes Ezekiel 23 to be the main backdrop to the description of Revelation 17.

2. Robert Linthicum observes that the rival cities of this book begin their history side by side in the early chapters of Genesis. Originally, the tower of Babel was built on the plain of Shinar, a site later to become Babylon. Ultimately, its builders are judged because of the stated goal of their enterprise, to "make a name for ourselves" (Gen. 11:4). Jerusalem also begins its history in Genesis; it is noted in Genesis 14:17–24 as the city of Melchizedek, the king-priest of Salem (the earlier name for Jerusalem). Fittingly, the final denouement or end result of these two ancient realities is found in Revelation 17–22, as Babylon the Great and the New Jerusalem (Linthicum, 24–25).

3. Is the eighth an "antichrist"? Since John is the only biblical author to use this term, he probably would have been pleased to call the beast by this title. For John, the spirit of the Antichrist (1 John 4:3; cf. 2:22; 2 John v. 7), which opposes the true work of God, was already in the world of his day. Many antichrists had in fact already gone forth into the world (1 John 2:18); this is not a term that John reserves for only one final personality.

4. That Daniel 11 relates past history veiled in the garb of predictive prophecy is held by a significant range of modern evangelicals: Robert A. Anderson (119); the late New Testament scholar F. F. Bruce (124, 133, 141 n. 1); John Goldingay, a British author in the Word Biblical Commentary/ Themes series (*Daniel*, Word Biblical Themes, 39–43); Paul M. Lederach, a Mennonite biblical scholar (226, 235); and D. S. Russell, the British Baptist famous for his studies of apocalyptic literature (204).

5. Herschel Hobbs sought a way around the *vaticinia* approach by imagining that "the angel referred to Vespasian [the sixth emperor who is living] deliberately so that if the Romans got hold of this writing they would not realize that he was actually identifying Domitian" as the beast (in George, 128).

6. Very similar legends sprang up after the Second World War. Hitler and others were supposedly alive and intriguing to return from South America. Throughout history there have been many examples of the fear of an evil so great that it cannot be accepted as over.

7. Cf. Gen. 31:7; Num. 14:22; Neh. 4:12; Job 19:3; Dan. 1:20.

8. For similar views of the "ten," see Ladd, *Commentary*, 229; Mulholland, 281.

9. Many have noted "the tale of two cities" that develops throughout the Revelation. M. Eugene Boring has even suggested an outline that utilizes this motif: "Letter Opening (1:1–8)"; I. "God Speaks to the Churches

in the Cities (1:9–3:22)"; II. "God Judges the 'Great City' (4:1–18:24)"; III. "God Redeems the Holy City (19:1–22:20a)"; "Letter Closing (22:20b–21)" (see "Revelation 19–21," 83–84). This is a helpful approach to Revelation's focus on citizenship and its call to all who have an ear for the things of God.

Chapter 9

THE COCKPIT OF HISTORY
Rev. 4:1–11

Having already read Revelation 17, we now know that John will soon bring his readers face to face with a fearsome adversary. In fact, the beast overwhelms all who face it — all, that is, except those whose names are written in the Lamb's book of life (13:3,8); they have caught and live out of the sustaining vision in chapters 4 and 5, which is addressed to the seven churches just as certainly as are the earlier ones.

Here John seeks to assure faithful Christians that despite the darkest night and the most frightful persecutions to come, their sovereign Lord possesses an unlimited arsenal of power and maintains absolute control over the universe and its future. This chapter, along with the following, is the theological center of the book — "the fulcrum of the Revelation" (Beasley-Murray, *Book of Revelation*, 108). We cannot overemphasize the importance of chapters 4 and 5. They do not contain the most famously bizarre scenes in the book, but theologically they are, nevertheless, at the essential heart of the Revelation's message to the churches. What will soon be described in gory detail, the beast, must be seen and understood against the backdrop of the heavenly throne.

Tours of heaven and especially its central throne room are somewhat typical of the apocalyptic tradition. It was a type of literature that was birthed by hard times, when the people of God were under severe cultural and religious pressure from the outside world. Thus, many Jewish and Christian apocalypses frequently feature a vision of the throne room of God to remind their hard-pressed people of who is ultimately in control. Moreover, they are being reminded of their own future destiny. This is also the function of such a vision in John's Revelation.

The beast is leading a rebellion against God and God's kingdom; thus, outlying districts may be destroyed, and faithful warriors may

119

be martyred. Chapter 4 adds to this scenario a spotlight on the role of the universe's central government, what G. B. Caird once called "the control room at Supreme Headquarters." He described it as "a room lined with maps, in which someone has placed clusters of little flags.... It is war-time, and the flags represent units of a military command" (60–61). As flags are moved from one position to another, changes have occurred on the battlefield below. Troops are expected to respond to orders and move to the high ground. Smyrna must continue to endure the frontline hardships, and Philadelphia must advance the push into enemy territory. Pergamum needs to continue its intelligence gathering where the enemy "has his throne" (2:13). As Caird explains, "The strange and complex symbols of John's vision are, like the flags in this parable, the pictorial counterpart of earthly realities; and these symbols too may be either 'determinative' or 'descriptive' " (61).

4:1 • Before John deals with the reality of the beast and the continuing history of its war against the church, he steps back and fixes his gaze heavenward. This is not the first time a prophet — what John is (19:10; 22:9) — has received an invitation from the throne of God to an interview of great consequence (cf. 1 Kings 22:19; Isa. 6; Ezek. 1:4–28). He will now experience the heavenly council and hear deliberations in which all true prophets have shared (Job 15:8; Ps. 89:7; 107:32; Jer. 23:18–22). This is not a heaven of the philosophers, splendidly isolated in infinity; it is the heaven of Scripture, brimming over with the joy of community and worship.

Dispensationalists usually take the phrase "Come up here" to represent the rapture of the church, that point in time when Christ returns for his people, delivers them from the wrath of the tribulation period, and thus initiates the final seven years of history.[1] Defined as the time of "Jacob's trouble" (Jer. 30:7, KJV), this period (the tribulation) is uniquely reserved, therefore, for Jews. The Gentile church is thus absent from the events of the greater part of the book, according to this school of thought, for they have been raptured to heaven.[2] One leading dispensationalist, however, admits the crucial detail that the rapture is not explicitly taught in this passage, though he is less helpful when he suggests that it, nevertheless, should be implied or assumed.[3] It is possible, of course, to *assume* anything one wishes; virtually any system can be supported by such procedures, but it is not an advisable maneuver for serious Bible study.[4]

Dispensationalists delight in noting that while the word *church* has been used twenty times already in the book, it is not used again until 22:17. Does this not mean, they argue, that the Gentile church is in heaven with her Lord during the events of chapters 4–21? Were such an argument to stand, it would mean also that the church is absent from the great wedding feast of the Lamb in chapter 19 since no mention is made there of the "church."[5] Surely, it would be an intolerable situation for the bride, that is, the Gentile church of Christ, to be completely absent from her own wedding (cf. Eph. 5:23–32).

"Saints" is the term John does use in the remainder of the book. While dispensationalists suggest it signifies "Jews," this title more likely refers to the "church universal." After all, this is the time-honored title Paul had already affixed to the Gentile Christians of Ephesus (Eph. 1:1; cf. 1:15; 2:11–19), as well as in many other Christian communities. At least one of the seven churches (Ephesus) would clearly have read the remainder of the book seeing themselves through that designation. What then do we make of the earlier twenty usages of the word *church?* Quite simply, they all have reference to individual churches in seven local communities, not once to the "church universal."[6]

The phrase "what must take place after this" has often been seen as the very linchpin of the book's structure, an explicit reference back to 1:19. But that is hardly a necessary conclusion; it may mean nothing more than "events from now on," namely, from this vision onward.[7] Adela Collins suggests that the phrase marks a division in the book in terms of perspective. While the seven messages to the churches described their individual involvement in God's judgment and salvation, what now comes are the same events viewed from the wider perspective of all humanity (*The Apocalypse*, 33). Thus, "what must take place after this" represents "what always is/will be as one tensive picture" (Boring, *Revelation*, 101). This is probably the best approach. Then, as John looked homeward, something marvelous took place.

4:2 • "At once," he was "in the Spirit." This is John's way of describing a visionary and mystical state that Paul said could not be distinguished as either "in the body or out of the body" (2 Cor. 12:2); it is an inexpressible spiritual experience. John had previously noted this type of spirituality in 1:10, but here he links it to the other item Paul has mentioned. Paul also "was caught up to the third heaven" (2 Cor. 12:2).[8] There, John saw a "throne," which begins a theme Revelation is profoundly interested in, one that occupies the center of its theological heartland. We will find the word mentioned in nearly every chapter of the book (exceptions are chaps. 9–10, 15, 17–18). John uses the word forty-seven times (almost a third are in this chapter alone) out of a total of sixty-two instances in all the New

Testament. Two that are exceedingly important, representing the centers of false authority, are Satan's throne (2:13) and the beast's (16:10); they are virtually one and the same (cf. 13:4).

The challenge of this scene, for the world and especially the churches, is obvious: What is worthy of worship? Who or what occupies the throne of our universe? Why do we worship? In the center of each life stands a throne "with someone sitting on it." These questions stand climactically and definitively as the crux of the entire message of Revelation. The throne John now depicts also stands at the very center of the New Jerusalem (22:1–3), is occupied by the plenitude of the Godhead (3:21; 5:6; 7:17; 12:5), and asserts dominion over the entire universe.

4:3 • Martin Kiddle suggests that in Revelation, "The technical name for God the Father . . . is *One seated on the throne*" (81). Once again, John uses the word *like* to indicate that which he is not allowed to describe, as was the case with Paul (2 Cor. 12:4), or that which is simply beyond his ability to articulate (1 Cor. 2:9–10). The analogies John uses, "jasper and carnelian," symbolize in the only way open to him what the presence of the one on the throne was "like" (cf. Ps. 104:2; 1 Tim. 6:15–16). Certainly not to be taken literally, they again indicate the greater importance of knowing what biblical language *means* and not only what it *says*.

According to John, jasper is a cool and clear stone (21:11) like quartz crystal or diamond (though sometimes also greenish in color). It probably stands for the sanctity and purity of holiness, which is always the corollary of God's wrath. On the other hand, carnelian is a dark reddish stone. Its color has often been taken to signify the furious wrath of God, whose fiery rage burns against all that offends the divine holiness. It is this offended righteousness that ignites the flames of wrath. Viewed from this perspective, our God is seen as a consuming and purifying fire (Exod. 24:17; Heb. 12:29), a holy God who first confronted Moses in a burning bush.

The iridescent nimbus around the throne, presented as a green (emerald) rainbow, seems to indicate an ambiance or context within which the other symbols exist. The rainbow is an obvious reference to the Noahic covenant of grace, wherein God promised to grant time for the history of redemption in which the earth would not again be judged by flood (Gen. 9:11–17). And green is both the color of spring's fresh foliage and an identifying hint in yet another direction. The ancient breastplate worn by the high priest, associated with the "ephod" (Exod. 28:17–21), bore twelve stones, each a symbolic memorial of one of the tribes. The last of the twelve, a remembrance of Benjamin, was jasper, and the first, a reference to Reuben, was carnelian. One of the others, the third,[9] is emerald or green; it stands for Judah (cf. Rev. 5:5; 7:5; here listed first but so specified nowhere else in Scripture). Through the green aura of this rainbow, a collage of symbolic images is seen; it seems to indicate that the one on the throne is characterized supremely by an ever fresh and forbearing grace, a grace focused most precisely through the tribe of Judah. This must not be forgotten as we continue down the darker corridors of the Revelation.

4:4 • One of the more difficult symbols to interpret, the twenty-four elders have been equated with many different realities.[10] Nevertheless, the only time the number *twenty-four* is explicitly used elsewhere in Scripture is in regard to the twenty-four shifts of priests who were to minister in the temple of God in Jerusalem (1 Chron. 24:1–19) and the twenty-four orders of Levites, whose duty was to "prophesy with lyres, with harps, and with cymbals" (1 Chron. 25:1, RSV). John is apparently experiencing heaven as a massive temple where God is continuously worshiped (by twenty-four elders) even as God had been on earth in Solomon's temple (Mounce, *Book of Revelation*, 135–36). But we must not fail to note that into this heavenly worship even the prayers of earthly saints may enter, as they join with heaven itself in praising and petitioning God Almighty (5:8; 8:4).

The "twenty-four elders," then, probably represent special members of the angelic hosts who are in charge of the heavenly liturgy. Their number could hint, however, at the idealized and combined worship/history of Israel (twelve tribes) and the church (twelve apostles).

4:5 • John then observes the same phenomena that were first experienced at Mount Sinai (Exod. 19:16) when Moses was called to the divine presence. Such language, reminiscent of a devastating thunderstorm, became traditional whenever the nearness of God was most dramatically felt (Judg. 5:4–5; Ps. 18:7–15; 29:3–10; cf. Heb. 12:18–24). John is approaching a throne before which the universe trembles with awe.

Once again the number *seven* receives special attention in "seven lamps" and "seven spirits of God." Though numbers are often used for counting, sometimes they are not; that is, they are symbolic representations. For example, when we hear that one has "sailed the seven seas," we are not meant to begin counting the specific seven involved but to realize that "all" are included in this number; in other words, seas in all their variety and "essence" have been experienced (Wilcock, 62). So it is with the seven spirits; they are the Holy Spirit, who is before the throne (1:4) and who shares in the ministry of God and the Lamb (5:6).

Why is the Spirit portrayed as "lamps...blazing" in this passage? Is it due to a causal relationship between the Holy Spirit and the spiritual vitality of the churches on earth? "The seven lights of heaven," Austin Farrer observes, "supply the spiritual fire to the seven lamps of the churches on earth" (90). For any church to truly carry out its mission, it is vital that the warmth, light, and power of the Spirit's presence be enshrined at its heart.

Symbolically represented, the being on the throne has already been encountered. Now we hear of "seven spirits," and shortly (in chapter 5) a Lamb will be announced. Taking these together, one can hardly fail to notice the strong Trinitarian presence in this throne room. In fact, the Revelation is famous for its development of this emerging doctrine. The Trinity is more frequently and clearly observed in this book than in any other New Testament document.

4:6 • Between the throne and the rest of creation is a sea. Seas can be symbols of many things, but this sea is differentiated from others in a later text: "Then I saw a new heaven and a new earth, for the first heaven and the first earth had passed away, and there was no longer any sea" (21:1). What kind of sea is eventually to be banished from creation along with the rest of the old, fallen universe? Why does Revelation define this sea in terms of its own annihilation or *de* creation?

One of the more typical meanings for seas is "separation" ("My Bonnie lies over the ocean; My Bonnie lies over the sea"). The far shore, lying over the horizon, is a natural symbol for distance, division, and detachment. Accordingly, this sea represents that which comes between God and God's creation. When we continue reading in 21:2–4, we soon discover what it is that has no place in the New Jerusalem. If God's original purposes for creation are to be achieved so that he can be at home with his people, all that is flawed must be eliminated. And let us not forget that the beast emerges "out of the sea" (13:1), along with all the baggage of evil traveling in its entourage.

In effect, John says that the people of God must find their way out of spiritual bondage, as if across threatening waters to the far side of victory, even as Moses and Israel once did in the past. Like them, we too will sing the victory song, with all those who have gone before, when we have negotiated this dangerous spiritual journey (15:2–4). This sea, then, stands for all the forces of evil separating God from creation, forces that have lifted the banner of rebellion against God's will (Ps. 74:12–14; Isa. 27:1; 51:9–10). In light of 13:1, it is not too much to designate this sea the "Supreme Headquarters of Cosmic Evil." But if the sea stands for what is separated from God, it also stands as a direct threat to all that is a part of its unredeemed nature (cf. Rev. 17:1,15), for one day the sea and all contained within it will be "no longer."

Perhaps an anecdote will give life to this idea. As a guest at Eastern College, Clarence Bass once delivered a lecture in my class on the Revelation in which he shared a charming story from his boyhood. It seems his grandfather, who was blind, had often asked the boy to read the Bible to him. On one occasion, young Clarence was reading from the latter portions of the Revelation when suddenly his grandfather said, "Clarence, it doesn't say 'the sea'; read it again." Little Clarence did, only to have his grandpa repeat his comment: "No, it doesn't say that." Exasperated, Clarence read it a final time: "Grandpa, it says, 'there ... was ... no ... longer ... any ... sea.'" This time, however, the grandfather responded, "Clarence, what it says is, 'and *blindness* was no longer' there." That is indeed the sense, the *meaning* of what John is saying through this image, applied in a personal way, and the grandpa saw that meaning more clearly than a young lad who had not yet experienced the brokenness of life.[11] One day, every imperfection, defect, and blemish that haunts God's world will be eradicated.

"Four" is the number of the earth. Just as it contains "four corners" and "four winds" (7:1; cf. Acts 10:11), so earth stands as the four-square physical stage on which the drama of creation is being played out. Few are aware that in the Bible animals are described as "souls" just as are humans.[12] This passage points to the shared relationship that all the ensouled creation shares. Beginning in Genesis 2:19, where the phrase "each living creature" (literally "every living soul") relates the animal world to Adam, who also was made a "living being" (literally "living soul") in 2:7, the fate and future of the whole animate creation are inextricably linked. The four here in Revelation 4:6 are the celestial representatives of all ensouled beings who are constantly observing and being observed by the one who "created all things" (v. 11).

This is certainly one of those scenes meant to excite one's theological imagination ("covered with eyes") but not to yield a photograph. These creatures are the omniscience, omnipresence, and very face of God represented in "nature." Elsewhere Paul has described their reality as "his eternal power and divine nature, invisible ... [yet] understood and seen through the things he has made" (Rom. 1:20, NRSV).

4:7 • The first living creature is lionlike, representing the most

majestic of *wild animals*. They codify a divine presence whose freedom, independence, and nobility are not subject to human restraints.
Indicating the multipurpose nature of biblical imagery, the lion can
symbolize both the devil (1 Pet. 5:8) and Christ (Rev. 5:5).

The second creature represents the world of *domesticated animals*.
It is like an ox, the one animal that was indispensable to the agrarian
economy of John's day. Great strength and usefulness are the keys
to its meaning. One might even be led here to think of domestic
pets, those creatures who have brought so much of God's sustaining
love into our lives. Does this passage imply that they, too, have a
permanent place, function, and future as part of the Creator's will?
Many would happily agree with such a suggestion.

The third (surprisingly not the first) creature locates *humankind*
firmly within the matrix of the natural world. Perhaps a quick reading of Psalm 104, sometimes called "The Ecologist's Psalm," would
remind us that the Creator loves and delights in all creation and not
just in its human sector. This face might stand for creative intelligence
and wisdom, but such qualities are only parts, not the whole, of the
scene's fourfold nature.

The fourth creature is like an eagle, reputedly the only animal that
can look directly into the sun. It stands for *the winged world* of swift-
ness, a world that often symbolizes hope, the eternal, the lofty (Isa.
40:31).[13] This fourth creature reminds us that Jesus once said that not
even a sparrow can fall to the ground without his Father's concern
(Matt. 10:29). God's love for all creation is manifestly evident in this
book of Revelation (cf. 11:18).

4:8 • John's vision is highly reminiscent of Isaiah's own famous
encounter with God (Isa. 6; cf. Ezek. 1), where the seraphim also
each possess six wings and intone the holiness of God. This passage
in Revelation (4:8–11) represents the first of sixteen hymns or hymnic
compositions scattered throughout the book (Aune, 1310). The worship of a holy God who basks in the melodies of the universe is also
one of those motifs that flow through the Bible (cf. Ps. 65:13–66:4;
96:12; 98:4–8). The God of Scripture is truly at home in creation.

John's four living creatures are an echo of Isaiah's vision of future
ecological harmony (Isa. 11:1–9), of that cooperative and harmonious
future, its nobility, strength, wisdom, and loftiness. It is a creation
longing for relief from human depredation and for nature to attain
the freedom and glory for which it was created (Rom. 8:19–22). Anticipating that day of redemption, the creatures chant the majesty
of God.

The essence of this vision is to make God's presence felt as the

"ALL-mighty," for John's readers are soon to experience tribulation even as he already does (1:9; "suffering" is the same word translated "tribulation" elsewhere). Jesus had told his followers that they would have to endure tribulation, but he also reminded them that it would only be temporary, for he had already overcome the foe (John 16:33). More importantly for the seven churches, however, is the protection that God affords the saints; it is spiritual and eternal (Matt. 10:28), though not necessarily physical (cf. Rev. 12:11; 13:7).

Eventually a time will arrive when the chronological/historical perspective (cf. 1:8) within the divine title will no longer apply and that future for which the four creatures long will have come (cf. 11:16; note the missing element). However, at this point John's vision anticipates a future that is yet to be. Though God is the All-mighty, there is still a turbulent "sea" that must be faced, crossed, and eventually tolerated "no longer" (21:1).

4:9 – 11 • Worship is also a central concern of this chapter, for everyone has to worship something, serve something — reality or un-reality. John reminds his distant congregations that when they engage in proper worship, they are experiencing what is taking place at the very heart of the universe. But what of those who do not spend time before heaven's throne? Eugene Peterson's conclusion is quite powerful and illuminating:

> People who do not worship live in a vast shopping mall where they go from shop to shop, expending enormous sums of energy and making endless trips to meet first this need and then that appetite, this whim and that fancy. Life lurches from one partial satisfaction to another, interrupted by ditches of disappointment. Motion is fueled by the successive illusions that purchasing this wardrobe, driving that car, eating this meal, drinking that beverage will center life and give it coherence. (60)

We are reminded of the scene at Sardis and Laodicea, full of pseudolife and wealth but signifying nothing — not so those who have encountered the living God. He is "the one who is seated on the throne" (NRSV). Can it be an accident that this exact phrase (identical in Greek except for case) is found *seven* times in Revelation (4:9; 5:1,7,13; 6:16; 7:15; 21:5)? Only once is Satan's throne mentioned (2:13), and once the beast's (16:10). This would suggest that one of the main themes of the book is God's dominion (theocracy) as opposed to Satan's domination (totalitarianism).

Revelation bids us remember that there is only one who is un-created, who alone is intrinsically immortal (1 Tim. 6:16), and who has brought into existence and sustains all derived life. To prostrate oneself originally meant to make ready to kiss the feet of the one so honored. All the elders' crowns lay at the feet of the one who is the source of their power because that was the typical oriental way of denoting profound respect (worth-ship).

Eventually, as we have already seen in part, John will speak more clearly of the terrifying beast his beloved people are facing. As he calls them to battle, he proposes that they keep this vision — the Cockpit of History — close to their hearts and, like himself, keep looking heavenward, for it is inevitable that the war of the thrones will soon engulf their lives and churches.

This chapter poses a decisive question for its readers: Do we, like the twenty-four elders (heavenly hosts) and the four living creatures (ensouled creation), worship the true and living God, or have we been seduced into worshiping the beast, his System, and values (13:4), as do the citizens of Babylon the Great? Paul had formulated the issue a bit differently but with the same topic in mind:

> For since the creation of the world God's invisible qualities — his eternal power and divine nature — have been clearly seen, being understood from what has been made, so that men are without excuse.
>
> For although they knew God, they neither glorified him as God nor gave thanks to him, but their thinking became futile and their foolish hearts were darkened. Although they claimed to be wise, they became fools and exchanged the glory of the immortal God for images made to look like mortal man and birds and animals and reptiles. (Rom. 1:20–23)

Notes

1. The great preponderance of believers through the centuries have interpreted Paul's "rapture" (from the Latin *rapere*, "to snatch up") in 1 Thessalonians 4:17 to refer to what Christian creeds call "the resurrection of the body and the life everlasting" (note v. 16: "the dead in Christ will rise first"), and this event is announced, not in Revelation 4, but in Revelation 20 ("They came to life.... This is the first resurrection"; vv. 4–5). It is also worth noting that no text in the Revelation "suggests that the tribulation is seven years in length.... Such a notion is derived from the seventy sevens, or weeks of years, in Dan. 9:24–27, on the questionable assumption that John's great tribulation is equivalent to Daniel's seventieth week" (Michaels, *Interpreting the Book of Revelation*, 141).

2. "The effect of this 'pretribulation rapture' is to dissociate Christian readers from any persecution and suffering at the hands of the Beast and to

deny the church's identity as a martyr church" (Michaels, *Interpreting the Book of Revelation,* 140).

3. Walvoord, 103. Such groundless argumentation leads Robert Gundry to observe that "the theological and exegetical grounds for pretribulationism rest on insufficient evidence, *non sequitur* reasoning, and faulty exegesis" (*Church and the Tribulation,* 10).

4. In the words of Gundry, "The book of Revelation treats final events in fuller detail than does any other portion of the NT. Yet not a single verse in Revelation straightforwardly describes a pretribulational rapture of the Church or advent of Christ" (*Church and the Tribulation,* 69). His thesis is that "direct, unquestioned statements of Scripture that Jesus Christ will return after the tribulation...with the absence of statements placing similar events before the tribulation, make it natural to place the rapture of the Church after the tribulation" (10).

5. In 19:7–8, only "saints" are invited to don white robes and attend the wedding banquet of the Lamb. And in 18:24, only two divisions of the righteous are included among "all who have been killed on the earth" — prophets and "saints." Have no Gentile Christians been martyred during whatever era is to be imagined as the context?

6. In the New Testament, the word *church* does not usually refer to its universal or generic aspect (only 15–20 times out of a total of 114). There would be no reason, then, to expect that it should have been used outside the local contexts of the first three chapters (Gundry, *Church and the Tribulation,* 78).

7. Wilcock, 67; Gundry, *Church and the Tribulation,* 65–66. On the other hand, M. Robert Mulholland translates 4:1: "I will show you the things [i.e., the larger realities] that are necessary to take place along with these things [i.e., local developments among the churches]." He argues that the churches experience their lives within the larger vistas of 4:1–22:20 and are simply contemporary manifestations of that wider reality (88–89, 140). Ray F. Robbins notes that the Greek New Testament as edited by Westcott and Hort had placed these words ("after these things") at the beginning of verse 2, that is, "after these things I was in the Spirit" (in George, 162–63).

8. Sophie Laws connects this experience with the broader description of Christian prophets/prophecy in the New Testament (80–95).

9. Since different translations place the "emerald" in a variety of positions in this Exodus text, the reader will note that various locations are attributed to this stone in differing commentaries. The RSV placed the emerald fourth; the NIV, sixth; and the NRSV, third. This indicates the difficulty translators have had in interpreting the ancient names of these twelve stones (Mounce, *Book of Revelation,* 134; Mulholland, 145–46).

10. One of the more popular interpretations is that the number stands for the union of both the old (twelve tribes) and new (twelve apostles) people of God. These two numbers are juxtaposed in 21:12–14, but they are always "twelve"/"twelve," never "twenty-four." Further, the elder's song (5:9–10)

seems to distinguish them from those redeemed by the blood of the Lamb (Mounce, *Book of Revelation,* 135). And, finally, the twenty-four are distinguished from the Christian faithful in 14:3 and 15:2–4 and from the bride of Christ in 19:4–9 (Harrington, 109).

11. For a helpful and extended discussion of "the sea," see Mulholland, 149–54. He defines it as "the realm of rebellion in the presence of the sovereignty of God" and equates it with "the lake of fire (19:20; 20:10,14–15)" as well as "Death and Hades (20:13)" (153).

12. In Genesis 1:20–21,24, the phrase "living creature(s)" is literally "living soul(s)." The Hebrew word *nephesh* (soul) was not used to distinguish humans from animals. Such an approach was more typical of the Greek philosophical tradition.

13. Exod. 19:4; 2 Sam. 1:23; Isa. 40:31; Jer. 4:13; Lam. 4:19.

Chapter 10

THE BOOK AND THE LAMB

Rev. 5:1-14

In both Revelation 4 and 5, we are surrounded by a unified theater — the heavenly throne room. But whereas chapter 4 deals more with the stage setting (i.e., the throne, gemstones, twenty-four elders, four living creatures, a sea, etc.), chapter 5 is increasingly theological in outlook and discusses the theme of redemption. So as chapter 4 ends with its theological emphasis on God the *Creator*, chapter 5 turns to God the *Redeemer*. Subtly, but throughout the book, John focuses on the relationship between the Father and Son (as in his Gospel; cf. John 1:1; 8:58; 10:30; 14:9; 20:28). In this context, finally, John will reveal to us Revelation's most prized title for Jesus, through which his relation to the church is illumined — he is the Lamb. Furthermore, he is a Lamb who has unique rights to a very special book, one John longs to investigate.

5:1 • First we must face one of the most important questions to be asked in this chapter: What is the scroll (Gk. *biblion*, "book") seen in the hand of God, and what are its contents? Much hangs on the answer to this apocalyptic puzzle. There is general agreement that this scroll/book represents the will of God in one way or another. Beyond that, however, there is little agreement.

Each of the following suggestions about the scroll has its defenders:

1. Some have felt the scroll is actually the Old Testament, waiting for and requiring the presence of Christ to be interpreted properly. As attractive as this sounds, it is not the way Old Testament texts are treated in Revelation, namely, as inscrutable, mysterious, or uniquely messianic in content.

2. Another more important view makes this book the inheritance of the saints in the sense that this scroll is a contract-deed concerning the future; its contents are a guaranteed promise that the covenantal Kingdom will come (Beasley-Murray, *Book of Revelation*, 120–23). But

131

where does any clear text, later in Revelation, show a connection between this scroll and the bestowal of the New Jerusalem? Nowhere are the physical contents of the eternal future linked to this scroll.

3. Most popular is the view that the scroll/book is a divine blueprint to judgments in the future that will terminate this age and usher in an eternal kingdom. The similarity of this volume to the one in Ezekiel 2:8–3:3 is the cornerstone of this theory. There, Ezekiel is shown a scroll, on both sides of which were written "words of lament and mourning and woe" (Mounce, *Book of Revelation,* 142). But this view presupposes that the seal judgments of chapter 6 are the *contents* of the scroll, thus representing divine wrath as in Ezekiel. It is more likely, however, that the seals represent preceding realities that must be experienced before the contents of the scroll/book can be opened or actualized. Furthermore, the content of the various scenes in chapter 6 focus on both past and present events; they do not concentrate solely on future judgments. The assumption on which this approach stands or falls, therefore, is unproved.

4. The approach we will take is that the scroll (literally *biblion,* "scroll/book") is also the "Lamb's book of life" (Corsini, 132–33; Niles, 55). This view takes an internal approach to identification. Within Revelation itself, there are many other references to a *biblion* that probably are the intended context for the scroll/book of chapter 5 (note 3:5; 13:8; 17:8; 20:12,15; 21:27).[1] It would be strange if, having specifically noted a *biblion* uniquely linked to the Lamb in chapter 5, John would then speak in the same work of a different and unrelated *biblion* that also, coincidentally and uniquely, belonged to the same Lamb (13:8; 21:27). Coincidences are not the stuff of apocalyptic literature, where just this sort of riddling process is the stock-in-trade. It must not be overlooked that on the two occasions when the book of life is described in terms of ownership, it is "the Lamb's book" (21:27), and it belongs to "the Lamb that was slain" (13:8). Both passages go a long way in identifying this book with the one found in chapter 5. Never is the Lamb portrayed as possessing "two" books. This understanding of the book is nearly demanded by the contents of the Revelation itself.

Identifying the scroll/book of chapter 5 with the Lamb's book of life is usually disputed on the grounds that "the book" of 5:1 leads to the disclosure of horrendous judgments, the participants in divine wrath, not the recipients of messianic redemption. This difficulty, however, is overcome if the following seal-judgments are understood as the content or actions of the seals themselves and not the interior contents of the scroll/book. It is just as feasible to understand the seals as the manifestations of human rebellion, that is, life in

Babylon, which must be overcome, judged, and destroyed before "the book of life" is finally opened (20:12; the only time a book is ever "opened" in Revelation). The seals, then, would be, not the *content* of the book, but those realities that must be dealt with (broken off the scroll) before its contents can be opened and viewed.

Normally scrolls were written only on their obverse side, which was composed of horizontal, pressed strips of papyrus pith. Thus, when the scroll was rolled, the inner text would be protected. But this one was also inscribed on the reverse, which was made of vertical strips of papyrus, making writing much more difficult. That this scroll was written on both sides means it was complete and filled to overflowing. And well it should be if these are the names of the redeemed, for we will later learn that they are an uncountable multitude (7:9).

The copious closure implied by "seven seals" would indicate that the contents are absolutely unalterable and inviolable. (Jesus once said of those the Father had given him: "No one can snatch them out of my hand"; John 10:28).[2] At the same time, these seven seals stand for those things that Christ's followers must also overcome in order to be inscribed within the scroll/book. If we are right in assuming that these seals are affixed to the front of the document, top to bottom, then all seven need to be broken open before the scroll is accessible.[3] Interestingly, the celebrated Israeli archaeologist Yigael Yadin once found just such a scroll in the Judean desert. Dating from Revelation's era, the scroll was complete with seven threads attached to the names of seven witnesses on its front seam (Ford, 92).

5:2–3 • Something about the contents of this scroll disqualifies all creatures from contact. In the past, however, prophets have regularly been granted access to revelations of God's future plans. Even Ezekiel, a mortal, receives a scroll that prophesies the future, accepting it, apparently, from the very hand of God (Ezek. 2:9–3:2). But John's scroll is forbidden to *all* — except one.

5:4 • There is not another single example in Scripture where a prophet or anyone else weeps because he is denied access to the future. Why is John so overcome with grief? What is really at stake here? Might it be that he knows the content of this book and is distraught over the question most important to any individual — "Is *my* name written there?" Such a scenario could explain his intensely personal response to the scroll, especially as we remember that the Lamb has power to strike names from this book and has threatened to do so (3:5). Further, it would also explain why there are more references to the book of life in Revelation than in any other book of the Bible.

It is a matter of intimate concern to one imprisoned and facing the prospect of martyrdom, namely, John himself.

5:5 • Suddenly John hears comforting words from those near the throne: one approaches who can boldly grasp the scroll and open both it and its seals. The one coming is now described through two powerful messianic images. "The Lion" is a symbol from Jacob's blessing on his sons in Genesis 49:8–12.[4] There Judah is "a lion's cub" from whom "the scepter will not depart." "The Root of David" harks back to a prophecy in Isaiah 11:1,10, where the coming messianic king is called "a shoot" and "a Branch" from Jesse's "roots" as well as "the Root of Jesse." As David's father, Jesse is often thought of as the founding and originating progenitor of the Davidic dynasty.

Still, the question lingers: Why can he, and he alone, uniquely open this scroll? Is it because this scroll is the roll call of those invited to the wedding feast of the Lamb (19:9), the registry of the New Jerusalem? With great and hopeful expectation, John turns to behold the one approaching. But note what greets his bewildered eyes.

5:6 • To John's astonishment there is no lion, only a lamb.[5] Once again the visual art of the double exposure asserts itself. The contrast between what John hears (5:5) and what he sees (5:6) suggests, perhaps, that the Messiah of expectation has come in a form utterly unanticipated. The long anticipated Lion of David is a messianic king so astonishingly unforeseen that he can only be perceived through the transparency of a lamb. By making the Lamb the victor and using this title for the Messiah twenty-eight times in Revelation,[6] John is saying, "No Lamb, no Lion! — no cross, no victory!"

The Lion of history is a lamb. Why? The Lion is a lamb because "God is love" (1 John 4:8), and love is ultimately the most powerful and creative force — the only true force — in the universe, hence, the impasse at Ephesus. And there is no greater love than that which relinquishes itself for the beloved (John 15:13). Ronald Preston and Anthony Hanson call verses 5–6

> two of the most profound verses in the whole of the Apocalypse; they relate Jewish Messianic hopes to the distinctively Christian good news of the advent of the Messiah...but a Messiah of a character so wholly unexpected by the Jews that they rejected him. (75)

In fact, only the kingdom of God dares take a lamb as its figurehead. Where political powers of this world choose to be seen through the symbols of wild, carnivorous beasts (e.g., eagles, tigers, leopards, lions, dragons, etc.), this kingdom projects its image through a humble, gentle, and submissive lamb (Morris, 94). And yet in this figure, a lamb, there is wonderful theological symbolism. For instance, can John fail to remember that a battle is brewing with the beast? How can one follow a lamb into such a conflict? It appears a mismatch from the outset, or is he saying that even the weakness of God is more powerful than the might of human beings (1 Cor. 1:25; cf. 2 Cor. 12:9; 13:4)?[7] The church must always remember that it walks the path of life with a lamb — the Lamb who is also the Lion.

As though it were not enough to pit a simple, lowly lamb against a beast, Revelation goes on to describe this lamb more precisely; its posture is that of one who has been butchered (NRSV: "slaughtered"). This is a way of saying that he is the Passover Lamb who, rather than seeking vengeance, has redeemed his people by laying down his own life (cf. John 1:29). In a moving chapter entitled "Lamb Power," Ward Ewing seeks to illustrate *a power less used* (92–110). Many illustrations are put forward, but one that well portrays the spirit of Revelation is found in the famous words of Martin Luther King Jr.:

> We must say to our white brothers . . . : We will match your capacity to inflict suffering with our capacity to endure suffering. We will meet your physical force with soul force. Do to us what you will, and we will not hate you. And yet we cannot in all good conscience obey your evil laws, because noncooperation with evil is as much a moral obligation as is cooperation with good. (in Ewing, 105)

If you are going to stand with the Lamb, remember you are standing back-to-back with one who has been brutalized. Yet in his very humiliation, there is an extraordinary strength — he has conquered by laying down his own life (3:21); this is he whom we are called to follow (12:11) — the "slaughtered" one. He is the Lion of the cosmos precisely because he was the Lamb of Calvary. Here "in one brilliant stroke," Robert Mounce observes, "John portrays the central theme of NT revelation — victory through sacrifice" (*Book of Revelation*, 144). This is "the Christological Redefinition of Winning," as M. Eugene Boring puts it (*Revelation*, 108).

As John continues his description, we learn the Lamb is far from helpless, for he possesses "seven horns and seven eyes." John's decoding of the horns and eyes reminds us not to convert his symbols into photographs. More than ever, we must observe what Scripture *says* but then, and even more importantly, discover what it *means*. Horns are often a symbol for power in the Hebrew Scriptures (Deut. 33:17; Dan. 7:7–8; 8:3–7); hence, the Lamb possesses a sevenfold inexhaustible might. To some, he is a lamb; to others, truly a lion.

Moreover, this phenomenal power is directed by one who has all knowledge of all places in all times. Eyes are obvious and universal symbols for discernment, acuity, and vigilance (cf. Prov. 15:3; see Zech. 4:2,10, where a link is drawn between seven lamps and the omniscient "eyes of the LORD"). His eyes are also the "spirits of God" and thus symbolize and project God's presence with and concern for all the beloved (Deut. 11:12; Ps. 33:18–19; Isa. 1:15). Proceeding from the Son, in this manner, the Holy Spirit completes the Trinitarian structure of the chapter.

5:7–8 • There is no false modesty here, for this is also the Lamb's throne (cf. 6:16; 7:10; 22:1). He has taken the scroll/book, and we will shortly (in vv. 9–10) be informed of the three reasons why this action is possible in the case of the Lamb but none else.

Falling down before the Lamb is a sign of worship (19:10) allowed only to God (22:9); that the Lamb is so worshiped by the twenty-four elders is another sign of his full deity in the Revelation. Now John turns again to the Hebrew Scriptures for its catalog of symbols: "May my prayer be set before you like incense," prays the psalmist, "may the lifting up of my hands be like the evening sacrifice" (Ps. 141:2). Among the elements of worship constantly being brought before the great throne of God are the prayers of the saints. A similar scene is found in Revelation 8:3, where an angel offers the prayers of all the saints upon the golden altar before God's throne. Though we ought not limit the contents of these prayers, perhaps John has special reference to that prayer all Christians have always shared: "Our Father in heaven,... your kingdom come, / your will be done / on earth [in my life] as it is in heaven" (Matt. 6:9–10).

The Revelation places an incredible valuation on the prayer life of the seven churches. And separated from fellow believers and living on a prison island, John must have deeply valued his "sweet hour(s) of prayer" that had often been shared with brothers and sisters. We too should remember that as we are pouring out our hearts before God, our prayers are conveyed before and fused with the will of a sovereign who rules the universe, yet who allows us an ongoing role in the governance of God's creation.

5:9–10 • After the Lamb takes the scroll, heaven erupts in paeans of praise. And what should be sung by the heavenly choir but the three unique qualifications that produce the Lamb's exclusive access to the scroll/book: (1) He died; (2) by that death, saints were ransomed for God from every human family;[8] (3) they were constituted a kingdom that will rule the earth. For these reasons, the Lamb is given unrivaled control over the contents of this scroll/book. That it is the roll call of the saints fits well in this context, for it is not the victory over hostile forces that has been highlighted, which could potentially have led to the unraveling of a scroll of judgment. Rather, it is the redemption of people from every background that is his unique qualification.

These three credentials constitute a "new song," not just another depiction of judgment to come, but the reality of eternal redemption for which both testaments have longed. This is also the song of the 144,000 who follow the Lamb always because they have been redeemed from humankind (14:1–4). Little wonder, then, that "the book of life" is so frequently noted throughout the Revelation.

Verse 10 extends a theme first introduced in Revelation 1. In 1:6, we had heard that Jesus has loved and cleansed "us" (the people of the seven churches), making "us to be a kingdom and priests" in service to God. The present passage continues the theme, which will be finalized in 20:6. By picking up this thread that originated in Exodus 19:6, John suggests that the quest to establish a people, peculiarly God's own, has culminated in the seven churches. As Mounce notes, "What was promised to the Israelites at Sinai...is fulfilled in the establishment of the church through the death of Christ" (*Book of Revelation*, 148). Thus, here is one further backdrop to the difficult and rather harsh language of 2:9 and 3:9. The eternal purposes of Sinai do not run aground in the synagogue but rather spread their sails among the seven churches, for it is now in the church where the purposes and future of God's kingdom are being worked out.

5:11–12 • Do not fail to notice that the benediction invoked on the Lamb is sevenfold. Such complete ascription of praise suggests that his is an equally complete divinity. Whereas the choruses of chapter 4 are directed at the Creator, these ascribe the Redeemer. In the eternal plan of redemption, the Creator and Redeemer have co-equal functions. Martin Kiddle concludes, as do many, that "nowhere else in the New Testament is Christ adored on such absolutely equal terms with the Godhead" (105).

5:13–14 • Now the whole of creation joins in the music of the spheres as every living creature adores "him who sits on the throne," who creates, upholds, and re-creates all of existence. And again, the equality of the one on the throne and the Lamb is stressed. What God has created, the Lamb has redeemed! The ascription of praise is fourfold, accenting the four realms of reality (heaven, earth, under the earth, the sea) from which it emanates. Appropriately culminating John's visit to the throne room, all the universe lifts up adoring praise to the Creator and the Lamb.

Many students of this book have come to feel that the frequent scenes of music and worship found in Revelation reflect liturgical practices current and known in Asia Minor among the seven churches (Shepherd, 77–84). If correct, then John continues to suggest that what happens on earth as the churches worship, truly originates, reflects, and enters into what is happening in heaven. Amen!

Notes

1. The "little" scroll/book of 10:2 is held open by an angel, whereas the book of 5:1 cannot be opened or looked into by anyone but the Lamb. This is clearly a different book. The only other use of the word *biblion* is in 22:7–19, where the book is plainly the text of the Revelation, not a volume found within its contents. The theory that the substance of the scroll/book is the content of the book of Revelation is not compelling because the Revelation is mediated by an angelic messenger (1:1; 22:8), whereas the scroll/ book cannot be revealed by any but the Lamb. Angels are exempted from the process (5:3).

2. This entire passage (John 10:3,27–30) deserves to be read as background.

3. This is Richard Bauckham's view, though he holds the contents to be further elaborated in Revelation 10:2,8–10; 11:1–13 (80–84); George Ladd also understands the seals this way but holds the scroll to be the final events of history, including judgment and redemption (*Commentary on the Revelation*, 80). See also Mounce, *Book of Revelation*, 151.

4. Other apocalyptic books from the first century confirm that this Genesis text was understood as messianic prophecy (cf. Testament of Judah 24:5; 2 Esdras 12:31).

5. *Arnion,* the Greek word for "little lamb," is also used once for the second beast, who looks like and is compared to a little "lamb" (13:11).

6. Bauckham calls our attention to the fact that the uses of "Lamb" (a total of twenty-eight) in the book represent a specific pattern: 4 (symbolic of the earth in 7:1 and 20:8 or reality in 5:13 and 14:7) x 7 (the number of completeness) = 28. When John refers to all the people of the earth, he utilizes a fourfold description (tribe, language, people, and nation) found in various orders. Furthermore, he uses this fourfold pattern a total of seven times (5:9; 7:9; 10:11; 11:9; 13:7; 14:6; 17:15). Bauckham concludes, "The 7 x 4 occurrences of 'Lamb' therefore indicate the worldwide scope of his complete victory" (66–67).

7. Of the seventy or more Jewish and Christian apocalypses recovered from the biblical era, only one is not oriented toward pacifistic responses. It is highly characteristic of this type of literature to advocate submissive

faithfulness to God and the acceptance of suffering as the triggers that most surely will bring God into the fray in support of his people.

8. It is difficult, indeed, to see how the word *saints* could possibly be limited to Jews of the tribulation period, as dispensationalists suggest. No clearer description linking saints to the church could be imagined than this text's recognition that these are ransomed "from every tribe and language and people and nation." Ladd's comments are helpful on this much-debated issue (*Commentary on the Revelation*, 89–90).

Chapter 11

THE SEALED FATE
OF A FALLEN WORLD
Rev. 6:1–17

One of the most celebrated sections in John's Revelation, chapter 6 involves the opening of the seals. Everything from renowned cinema, literature, and art to fabled football players have been named after "the four horsemen of the Apocalypse" found in this chapter. The Revelation has just spent two whole chapters preparing us for their arrival. Once we have been adequately assured that "God's in his heaven" and, therefore, no matter what is coming, "All's right with the world" (Robert Browning), Revelation commences the opening of the seals.

The legendary seven seals will reveal appalling images that portray the history of fallen humanity. These are the aftershocks or reverberations set in motion when a world began by eating the forbidden fruit and ended by killing the Lamb. In such a defiant creation, humanity may fantasize all the dreams of perfection known but only find perversion. The dream may be of peace and plenty, but only war attends the best of intentions, and only scarcity is found — not the abundant life. It is death that awaits such a perverse and lost world. This is the true shape of the darkness in which the churches radiate the light of life.

6:1–2 • Again John is using pictographs (i.e., pictorial symbols) derived from the Hebrew Scriptures. In this case, Zechariah 1:7–11 and 6:1–8 are the sources he has appropriated for his own purposes. In Zechariah, the four horsemen patrol the earth and proclaim that the world is at "peace." The character of the horsemen have quite a different purpose in the Revelation, where they have been transmogrified into harbingers of doom.

The first of the seals, the white horseman, immediately exposes some of the chapter's most fundamental questions: What is the "white horse"? Who, or what, is its rider? When does this rider's activity happen? What does it all mean? If these can be answered, then perhaps the significance of all the seals can also be revealed. Happily, there is a wonderful biblical clue upon which John almost certainly expected us to rely. If the profile of the first four seals comes from Zechariah, their structure and content are derived from a different source. The Gospels include a passage known as the "little apocalypse." John surely must have known it, for its order of events is strikingly similar to the progression within the seals (Beasley-Murray, *Book of Revelation,* 130). No doubt, coming from Jesus, it was John's original template for this chapter.

The little apocalypse, a popular passage in the early church, is found in three of the Gospels: in Matthew 24, Mark 13, and Luke 21. In these familiar passages, Jesus is asked by his disciples to elaborate upon the end of the age by explaining the signs of its arrival. In all three texts he gives an order of affairs that is almost identical to the seals. Note Mark's version of the signs of the end:

Mark 13	*Revelation 6*
1. False religious leaders (vv. 5–6, 21–22)	1. White horse rider (?)
2. Rumors of war (vv. 7–8a)	2. Red horse rider (War!)
3. Famine (v. 8b)	3. Black horse rider (Famine!)
4. Death (v. 12)	4. Pale green horse (Death and Hades)
5. Persecuted disciples (vv. 9–20)	5. Martyrs under the altar!
6. The end and the ingathering (vv. 26–27)	6. Cosmic dissolution and judgment!

If the seals are the realities of the end times, an almost unanimous opinion, then it is highly instructive to notice that Jesus once commented on the same issue — the signs of the end times — and gave a very similar answer. But if these are end-time indicators, then the next question will be, When do the end times or last days begin? To this question, the New Testament returns an unexpected and unambiguous response. As Peter begins to deliver his great Pentecost sermon, he preaches concerning an event prophesied by the prophets and now taking place in "the last days" (Acts 2:14–17; cf. 1 Pet. 4:7; Heb. 1:2). Paul agrees, for in 1 Corinthians 10:11 he speaks of his readers as those "on whom the fulfillment of the ages has come." Finally, John himself goes so far as to write that in his day it was already "the last hour" (1 John 2:18). Beyond any doubt, the New Testament clearly declares the end times to have already begun at the death and resurrection of Jesus Christ. From that event onwards, all else takes place in the shadow of this overarching and climactic milestone. After Jesus, the end times have been inaugurated and the messianic age has arrived.

It will not be surprising, then, when we notice another intriguing feature of Jesus' response to his disciples. After he had itemized the several signs of the end, he said, "I tell you the truth, *this generation* will certainly not pass away until all these things have happened" (Mark 13:30, emphasis added). Ten times, in the Gospels, Jesus uses the phrase "this generation" when speaking to his contemporaries. In each instance, he refers to the people of his day; they are solely and exclusively the generation to which he refers (Beasley-Murray, *Jesus and the Future*, 186). Hence, it seems clear, Jesus believed that the events that characterize the end times, that is, the signs he had just listed, would begin during the lifetime of the people to whom he spoke. And so they did (all except Judgment Day, which in some sense is experienced in each individual death), and these events will take place in every generation because each lives in the midst of the end times, at the very least, their own.

Now back to one of the key questions: What is represented by the white horse rider? Does this background from the Gospels help us identify that figure? One popular guess is the conquering Christ,[1] for surely he rides in white, a color of victory associated with the Son of Man and the conquering Messiah (1:14; 19:14). Further, and most significantly, it might seem that the beginning of the race between Christ and the other horsemen is depicted in this chapter, while its conclusion and the announcing of the winner are found in 19:11: "I saw heaven standing open and there before me was a white horse, whose rider is called Faithful and True. With justice he judges and makes war." But this conjecture runs afoul of several symbolic details. For instance, the Lamb does not need to be given a crown, as does the first rider; he innately possesses "many crowns" (19:12) and is already "KING OF KINGS AND LORD OF LORDS" (19:16; cf. 17:14). The only weapon used by the Son of Man and the conqueror of chapter 19 is the sword issuing from his mouth, not the military bow observed in chapter 6. Nor would it be seemly for one of the living creatures, a created being, to issue a summoning command ("Come!") to one who shares the throne of the Creator. But if the warrior of chapter 6 is not Christ, then who or what is this rider on the white horse?

Allowing Mark 13 to guide us, that is, Scripture to interpret Scripture, we would have to conclude that John was referring to the same first element in the list as did Jesus, namely, counterfeit leadership. This explanation clarifies what has led so many to identify the rider with Jesus — the *white* horse. White is indicative of spiritual entities in Revelation, but in this case it is a false and destructive spirituality. It is no accident that John will later, three times, identify one of the Lamb's antagonists as "the false prophet" (16:13; 19:20; 20:10; cf. Mark 13:5–6,21–22), for he is also lamblike in appearance (13:11). Though the rider of chapter 6 may resemble the conquering Christ, he is a quite different reality altogether.

The white horseman stands for those misguided illusions and frightful idols (Rom. 1:21–25) that galvanize humanity into malevolent action. Here is a symbol for all the false ideological banners, religious and secular, under which people have marched, labored, and poured out their lives. Many have served the rider on the white horse in service to political and reverent commitments that are, in fact, opposed to the kingdom of God. And what are the results of such delusional activities?

6:3 – 4 • The second seal suggests a well-known relationship between the idolatry of grandeur, on the one hand, and the bitterness of warfare on the other. When ideology disrupts normative sociopolitical structures and when family and international life are polarized, war between all the families of creation is inevitable. Alienation, human suffering, the misery of war-ravaged lives, even a slaughtered Lamb, are always the disillusioning results of human illusions that "suppress the truth" of God (Rom. 1:18). The sin of unbelief, of revolt against heaven, of calculated deception, always leads to strife, rivalry, discord — WAR. It was once calculated that during the nearly four thousand years of controlled human history we have been able to study, only about 275 were free of war. The history of "man's inhumanity to man" is one of the most enduring themes of our sinful, human heritage.

The first bloodshed in history is represented in the murder of Abel by his brother Cain (Gen. 4). And the eventual outcome of that primeval event is the historical unfolding of Babylon the Great, a city or a way of life, in which is "found the blood . . . of all who have been killed on the earth" (18:24). It is in the city where the seals are the normal social dynamics of life. The red horse's mission would have been quite comprehensible in John's day; during one year alone (A.D. 68–69) four different emperors had ruled Rome.

To this rider is given "a large sword." It is intrinsic to the spirit of false ideologies for worship and service to be coerced in their spheres of influence. Thus, "[the religious beast] exercised all the authority of the first [political] beast on his behalf, and *made* the earth and its inhabitants worship the first beast" (13:12, emphasis added). Unlike the free and joyous adoration at the heavenly throne, coercive control is the modus operandi of false worship. This was the expected norm for life in that time period, for those living in that day experienced unparalleled strife and bloodshed. Joseph Klausner estimates that from 67 B.C. to A.D. 39 no fewer than 200,000 Jews died in wars and civil disorder (167). This is an enormous loss of life, given the size of tiny Palestine, comparable perhaps to forty million Americans dying for similar reasons during the twentieth century. Furthermore, in A.D. 61, a few decades prior to the writing of Revelation, a single revolt in Britain led to 150,000 deaths (Morris, 103). John's day was a supremely somber setting in which life was of little value to the powers that reigned.

John describes the deep background, namely, the spiritual origins, of this slaughter, in a later chapter, where he anchors it in a heavenly battle between supernatural forces (12:7–12). There John describes the revolt of a great dragon against the divine throne; this is the event that ultimately stands behind the beastly reality of war. After the defeat of this monstrous adversary and its angelic cohorts, they were cast out of heaven and came down to the earth. Revelation warns, "Woe to the earth and the sea, / because the devil has gone down to you! / He is filled with fury, / because he knows that his time is short" (12:12)! As Jesus once said, the devil was "a murderer from the beginning" (John 8:44); hence, the second rider continues what has become an age-old drama — "the mystery of lawlessness" (2 Thess. 2:7, NRSV).

6:5 – 6 • Warfare affects not only the immediate combatants, of course, but creates conditions that determine the lives of untold numbers and generations to come who must endure the aftermath of war's destruction. One of the most common is famine. The use of scales indicates a scarcity that will require precise distribution of food (cf. Lev. 26:26; Ezek. 4:16). Conventional wisdom had it that "a quart of wheat" was the daily minimum to maintain one life. If it takes a worker's daily wages to purchase it, then how will his family eat? They will survive only if they abstain from wheat and utilize barley, a less desirable diet. Nevertheless, the price mentioned for the wheat is sixteen times what it actually cost in John's day (Beasley-Murray, *Book of Revelation*, 133). A fearsome competition for food is being projected as the immediate aftermath of the killing fields.

For some interesting and largely unknown reason, "the oil and the wine" come in for special consideration, an occurrence that has long provoked the imaginations of Bible students and led to a wide range of guesses. Is it because these are used in Christian worship (anointing oil and Communion) or to suggest that in the world of the seals the rich will always have their luxuries no matter how severe the outlook? Jewish traditions might indicate that it signals an increase in drunkenness in the days preceding the Messiah's arrival. Still another guess is that it points to the gracious presence of God; even in the midst of famine, God will provide the necessities and even some joy for the poor (Joel 2:19). But given the context of the prostitute's cup (17:2,4; 18:3,6), representing life in Babylon the Great, and the presence of these two commodities among the dainties for which she longs (18:11–14), John's meaning is almost certainly unfavorable. Probably they stand for the ironic evil of self-indulgence in the midst of extreme famine.

And we must not forget that institutionalized regulation of commercial enterprise is foreseen as one of the beast's methods of compelling allegiance. "No one could buy or sell" (13:17) the necessities of life who was not politically reliable and did not serve the beast. Economic oppression and the opportunity for social advancement are not new weapons in the arsenal of evil (Isa. 5:8; Hos. 12:7).

6:7–8 • The final rider, aided by his colleague, is engaged in garnering the results of his prior allies. He is empowered to use the "four deadly acts of judgment" threatened in Ezekiel 14:21 (NRSV). And death is portrayed as the final climax of this train of events because it is, in the final analysis, "the last enemy" (1 Cor. 15:26). The New Testament does not portray human beings as immortal; that belongs to God alone (1 Tim. 6:16). Only in Jesus Christ are life and immortality made possible for us (2 Tim. 1:10; cf. Rom. 2:7; 1 Cor. 15:53). Hence, for those who follow delusional avenues through life, there is only one possible end — eternal darkness. Revelation will speak of this again; it is the fate of those who live their lives in Babylon the Great.

Henry Swete summarizes the first group of four seals in this fashion:

> The first group...describes the condition of the Empire...a vast world-wide power, outwardly victorious and eager for fresh conquests, yet full of the elements of unrest, danger, and misery, war, scarcity, pestilence, mortality in all its forms.... *This series of pictures repeats itself in history.* (87, emphasis added)

At this point a natural division takes place. The first four seals are grouped by a common theme, the four horsemen, while a second group of three deals with other, more transcendental, issues. This is important because we will later discover that both the trumpet judgments (Rev. 8–11) and the bowls (Rev. 15–16) are structured in the same way, that is, four and three.

6:9 • When false political ideologies, religions, and cults run amok, the normative result is fanaticism, hatred, and bigoted persecution, particularly of those aliens on the battlefield whose true homeland and allegiance are elsewhere. Death has already visited many followers of the Lamb, and more are soon to be killed. Among them is one named Antipas, a faithful witness (2:13), and so are others who, as the evidence of their testimony, "did not love their lives so much as to shrink from death" (12:11). Martyrdom is clearly among those approaching realities of which John warns his churches and expects "must soon take place" in their lives (1:1; 22:6).

The sixth seal continues to signify a tragic reality, even today on the eve of the new millennium. One report given at the 1989 Lausanne II conference in Manila, projected that nearly twenty-seven million will have lost their lives in the twentieth century for their confession of faith in Jesus Christ (in Milne, 226).

6:10 – 11 • At this point, Revelation sets in motion a very special cosmic clock. The martyrs under the heavenly altar, as though their tombs were a gateway to the divine presence, cry out, "How long?"[2] It is a question with a long history among God's people (Ps. 6:3; 13:1; 35:17; 74:9–10; 79:5; 80:4; 89:46; 94:3; Isa. 6:11; Hab. 1:2; Zech. 1:12). But these faithful witnesses are not vindictive or crudely lusting for bloody retribution against their persecutors; they are longing for the day when God — the divine presence and justice — will be revealed. Let us not forget, their lives were lost in service to "the word of God" and "the testimony they had maintained." But now, a question as ageless as human grief (cf. Gen. 4:10) — How long? — is finally answered. Until the full number of their fellow servants has joined them, they must rest, and the end must wait. There is, however, a definite, quantifiable limit to divine patience noted (cf. Matt. 23:29–36; 24:22).

The lives of the martyrs become the sand in the hourglass of divine justice. They are the measure and meaning of the future (cf. Luke 18:1–8), for God wants all to come to repentance and for none to perish (2 Pet. 3:9). It is the sacrificial laying down of their lives in that great cause that is paradoxically both delaying and gradually provoking the final outpouring of divine judgment, for their deaths are God's way of winning the victory over great Babylon. Surely some among those under the altar are from Smyrna, Pergamum, and Philadelphia. They might have seemed poor and possessed little social clout; they were persecuted and powerless during life. Nevertheless, their lives are now revealed to be the milestones of history, for they wielded the true power of the universe.

At the turn of the century, A. B. Simpson, founder of the Christian and Missionary Alliance denomination, used to tantalize local news reporters by inviting them to his evangelistic campaigns to hear him predict when the end of the world would come. They, of course, would gladly respond, elated at the prospect of exposing the lunacy of yet another religious charlatan. Finally, at the close of the evening, after preaching the gospel and the challenge of missions, he would reveal the time of the end. And when was it? Simpson simply quoted the following passage from Scripture to conclude his sermon and keep his promise to the reporters: "And this good news of the kingdom will be proclaimed throughout the world, as a testimony to all the nations; and then the end will come" (Matt. 24:14, NRSV).

When will the number of the martyrs be complete and the day of God's justice arrive? The answer is not so mysterious. It will arrive at that moment when a sufficient number of God's servants have sacrificially given their lives, maintaining an effective witness, so that the gospel has finally reached every tongue and tribe, family and nation, for which Jesus died (5:9). Then the end will come! Until then, the heavenly cry of our brothers and sisters must ring disturbingly in our ears (cf. Heb. 12:1–2) so that their day of final justice might also be hastened.

Still, they have been granted white robes in which to rest, robes that have been washed white in the blood of the Lamb (7:13–14). And they rest secure in blessed peace, having received eternal assurances. The situation is considerably different at Sardis and Laodicea (3:4–5,18). John must certainly intend for them "to hear" the message of this scene, even as every Christian who has an ear to hear must be challenged by his vision.

Seals five and six share an antithetical relationship. Seal five shows the effects of the horsemen on the citizens of New Jerusalem, while seal six reveals the end of this process for the denizens of great Babylon.

6:12–14 • Behind these events lurks the evocative language of Joel 2:10,30–32. He too had seen the great and terrible day of Yahweh. It is a day when creation will shudder and dissolve in the presence of its maker. This total disruption of the created universe is but the first of several previews of the final cataclysm (Rev. 18–20). In short, this is a cameo of what John will eventually describe as the coming of "a new heaven and a new earth, for the first heaven and the first earth had passed away, and there was no longer any sea" (21:1). Since the order of events here is about the same as the original creation (Gen. 1–3), through this structuring John seems to be describing nothing less than the systematic decreation of the universe (Ford, 112), for "without [the Word] nothing was made that has been made" (John 1:3).

Furthermore, the underlying symbolism found in this passage is fundamental to biblical theology: when the Creator approaches, the creation is shaken to its foundations because that which once was not cannot much bear the proximity of the One Who Is, Yahweh. The seven elements of the natural order recorded here represent a symbolic way of saying the *whole* universe is involved. These various elements also reflect other Old Testament passages in which the Creator's approach to the creation creates havoc in a fallen and rebellious world (Exod. 19:18; Isa. 2:19; 34:4; Hag. 2:6). We should not turn these theological symbols, however, into scientific photos.

6:15 • As a representative portrayal of all who dwell in great Babylon, seven categories of humanity are involved. The *whole* social register, from top to bottom, will face this Day of Judgment. Here is the society the seven churches are tempted to accommodate and with which they are tempted to compromise. But to do so is to join that which one day will cease to be. All of those who have benefited most and who have been most victimized will participate in this final consummation of history's story. Finally, anticipating their common fate, they will huddle together in the subterranean darkness of the netherworld (cf. John 3:19–21), and there they will croak the music appropriate to their chosen destiny.

6:16–17 • Hiding from the face of God is a theme as old as Adam and Eve in the garden.[3] Those who will not acknowledge God's sovereignty must play ostrich and hide their heads in the dirt, though no hiding place can ever escape those piercing eyes that burn with unquenchable flame. This is a sad scene, one that had already been predicted by Jesus (Luke 23:30; cf. Hos. 10:8).

The phrase "wrath of the Lamb" has often been interpreted as the flip side of the cross, namely, an act of judgmental anger against those who reject the crucified one. This may be, but even more likely, as G. B. Caird suggests, this phrase "has its source not in the true nature of Christ, but in the tragic and paranoiac delusion to which they have surrendered themselves" (92). To those who have so long fled the divine presence, even death seems preferable to encounter.

The sad lament of those who have no standing before God concludes with a wailing cry bereft of hope, "Who is able to stand?" (v. 17, NRSV). When any enter the presence of the one in whom "we live and move and have our being" (Acts 17:28), this is always the ultimate question. It is the cry of the ages (Nah. 1:6; Mal. 3:2), and it will be answered in the next chapter.

Portraying the church age from Pentecost (the coming of the Holy Spirit to form the body of Christ, the church) to the Parousia (the second coming of Christ for that church), the seals represent the general character of the end times as they spiral outward from the System's original rejection of Christ. Here are the essential dynamics of an estranged and alienated world in flight from its Lord, vainly seeking any hope or ideology that holds promise for a new human conquest of history. Four horsemen have ridden across the face of the earth from that day to the present, and they will continue.

The first seal is the prime mover; it is the counterfeit savior whose siren call lures the unsuspecting into futility. A nearly endless roll call of deceiving pretenders has succeeded Rome since John's day: Islam, defunct medieval Christianity, Holy Roman emperors, the age of reason, Hitler, atheistic communism, materialistic capitalism, the many modern cults (including those of Joseph Smith, Charles Taze Russell, Jim Jones, David Koresh, and Marshall Applewhite), etc. Whenever humanity begins to march behind false banners, the remaining seals always follow naturally. And the more things seem to change, the more they remain the same.

Notes

1. For one of the better defenses of this view, see Mulholland, 168–70. George Ladd holds a nuanced version of this approach, taking this rider to represent "the proclamation of the gospel of Christ in all the world" (*Commentary on the Revelation*, 99).

2. Jacques Ellul refers to this prayer of the martyrs as "one of the motor forces of history" and to the martyrs themselves as "the pivot of history" (158–59).

3. Robert Mounce's conclusion is spiritually correct and illuminating: "From the day when Adam and Eve hid themselves from the presence of God (Gen. 3:8), the guilty conscience has made man a fugitive from God" (*Book of Revelation*, 162–63).

Chapter 12

FIRST INTERMISSION

The Sealed Destiny

Rev. 7:1–17

"Who is able to stand?" (NRSV). This question concludes chapter 6 and is the substance of chapter 7. We will now look into one of Revelation's most complete descriptions of the ultimate protection, safety, and standing the church has before its Lord and Master. At the same time and for the first time, this chapter makes use of a structure found elsewhere in the book. Between the sixth and seventh components of the seals, the trumpets, and the bowls, there is a timely intermission or parenthetical theme dealing with some aspect of the seven churches' relationship to that series and its overall theology.

As an interlude separating the sixth and seventh seals, chapter 7 deals with an important issue for the seven churches that was raised in chapter 6 — the martyrs under the heavenly altar. What is their true status, number, and destiny? And what is the answer to their question "How long?" Revelation has painted a grisly picture of the church age through the seal vision. And now, in good pastoral fashion, it is necessary to assure the faithful of their special standing in this present, evil age. They too are carrying out "his purpose ... until God's words are fulfilled" (17:17).

As John proceeds to divulge the destiny of the churches, he gives us a vision in two parts. Verses 1–8 pertain to the famous and much-abused figure of the 144,000, while verses 9–17 discuss the destiny of a great innumerable multitude. These two visions represent a bifocal analysis of the faithful. First, we see the people of the New Jerusalem in their pilgrimage through life (the living body of Christ). Second, the same group is viewed in their second life, beyond the victory of a faithful death (the glorified body of Christ).[1]

7:1 • The four winds are a regular feature of biblical and apocalyptic literature. In a book named after him, Enoch is given a tour of

150

heaven, where he sees the storage place for the winds as well as the repositories of other natural forces. Typical of their symbolic usage is Daniel 7:2–3, where they blow upon the sea and produce four ferocious beasts on a mission of destruction. No doubt, the four winds (four indicating the universality of their effects) are meant to be taken as tornado-like in the devastating power they bring to bear on the inhabitants of earth. Trees, which seem strangely out of place, might be mentioned here because they reveal the presence of wind. In other words, the harnessing of these destructive agents is complete, and their shutdown total. It is good to know that the divine control is absolute and that God always stands with the people of God as the Lord of their pilgrimage and destiny.

It is quite likely that the four winds are another way of speaking of the four horsemen (as is the case in Zech. 6:5) and that this portion of the vision views them just prior to their release, that is, the breaking of the seals. This is G. B. Caird's view. He views the four winds *of* earth blowing *on* the earth as the forces spawned by spiritual rebellion now turning on their creators (94). For the moment, however, they are held back by God (implying their hostile nature) until God's people are first given immunity.

7:2–3 • In a scene vaguely reminiscent of Jesus' prophecy (Matt. 24:31; Mark 13:26–27), John now beholds God's servants being drawn aside for special attention. "Do not harm" again reminds us of what the seals have made clear — the System's ruling elite and its social order stand at cross-purposes with God's creation. But before further damage is inflicted upon the earth and its inhabitants, one special group must be marked with "the seal of the living God" (NRSV).

The objective of this process is to achieve complete sanctuary for the "servants" from the winds (the horsemen),[2] which is explicitly confirmed in 9:4 (those who do not have the seal of God are harmed) and 16:2 (those who do have the mark of the beast are harmed). The same principle probably holds true throughout the seals, trumpets, and bowls. In the midst of all the horror and agony indicated by the signs of the end, the faithful servants of God are to be escorted safely through the lines of battle ("The Lord knows those who are his"; 2 Tim. 2:19). This seal is the official passport of the New Jerusalem. And while it is no guarantee against physical death, it does protect against the second and ultimate death of spiritual annihilation.[3]

But does John have some more specific reality encoded in the word *seal*? After all, it is a word that has an important history in the early church.[4] The Old Testament, the only Bible of the earliest Christians, provides what is probably the origin of the "seal" concept found in the Revelation. There, the prophet Ezekiel beholds an angel who is given a command from God: "Go throughout the city of Jerusalem and put a mark [Heb. *tau*] on the foreheads of those who grieve and lament over all the detestable things that are done in it" (Ezek. 9:4). And though the remainder of those within the city are to be utterly cut off, "do not touch anyone who has the mark" (Ezek. 9:6). Interestingly, the ancient Hebrew letter *tau* was shaped like a T or X similar to a Christian cross. Later, the name of the Lamb and of the Father will be seen impressed on the foreheads of the faithful (14:1; 22:4). This seal shields against the deadly and eternal effects of historical evil.

Another association conjured up by the seal is found in the Pauline letters. In 2 Corinthians 1:21–22, Paul writes, "He anointed us, *set his seal* of ownership on us, and *put his Spirit* in our hearts as a deposit, guaranteeing what is to come" (emphasis added). And again in Ephesians 1:13–14, Paul says that believers in Christ are marked "with a seal, the promised Holy Spirit, who is a deposit guaranteeing our inheritance until the redemption of those who are God's possession." Thus, in Ephesians 4:30, Paul warns, "Do not grieve the Holy Spirit of God, with whom you were sealed for the day of redemption." The church in Ephesus, to which John is also writing, should not have much trouble decoding this symbol; it would have understood the *seal* more readily than any of the other seven churches.

Whether Paul himself fashioned this symbol of the seal as the Holy Spirit or made use of a preexisting Christian concept, the symbol must have been fairly well known. What power can shield the Christian from the judgmental wrath of God and the outrages of fallen Babylon? Paul and John agree — a life renewed and sanctified by the indwelling Holy Spirit. Those who are sealed can face the beast and stand before God, for the Holy Spirit is the umbilical cord of the Kingdom and continuously sustains and nourishes the sealed with every spiritual weapon (Rom. 14:17; Gal. 5:22–23).

7:4–8 • At first glance, "the people of Israel" (NRSV) who are sealed would seem to be the empirical nation of Israel, that is, literal Jewish men and women.[5] However, in a book so highly influenced by symbolism, other considerations need to be calculated before we jump to that conclusion. Who is actually being sealed here?

Apparently, "every tribe" of Israel is being dealt with. Does that not guarantee that physical Israel is being sealed? Perhaps, and perhaps not! In the Hebrew Scriptures, there are twenty separate listings of the twelve tribes. Oddly, only a couple have the same order; in fact, there are eighteen different arrangements (Mounce, *Book of Revelation*, 170). Simply put, there was no agreed-upon, normal way to list the twelve tribes. Revelation's list is different from any other in Scripture.[6] John's ordering is unique because it places Judah first (that is only done in the Old Testament when the tribes are listed geographically from south to north, which is not the case here), eliminates Dan, and doubly includes the family of Manasseh, since his father Joseph is also present. George Ladd, with the majority of commentators, argues that these deliberate irregularities are intended to point away from "literal" and toward "spiritual" Israel, that is, the church (*Commentary on the Revelation,* 115). The placement of Judah first indicates that messianic Israel, the Israel looked forward to in the Hebrew Scriptures, springs from "the Lion of the tribe of Judah, the Root of David" (5:5). Here the followers of the Messiah, twelve divisions strong, are depicted as a messianic army. Note that verses 4–8 are cast in the form of a census of Israel; national census takings in Israel usually functioned as a calculation of potential military strength.

Moreover, the very context of this book does not encourage us to think of twelve tribes of physical Jews. We have heard of them directly only twice, and each time they "say they are Jews and are not, but are a synagogue of Satan" (2:9; cf. 3:9). In fact, when they claim this honor, they "are liars" and will one day come and bow down to the church that is the true object of the Messiah's love (3:9). Later, Revelation will identify the place where the "Lord was crucified," Israel's capital, Jerusalem, with "the great city" — Babylon (11:8). Note that the "tribes of Israel" in 7:4 are the same as the "servants of our God," the general term for Christians in verse 3.[7]

Of particular interest, these specific tribes are also designated by means of a defining number — 144,000. The only other time this symbol is used is in a scene taking place on Mount Zion.[8] While they are being discussed and defined within that vision, they are called those "redeemed from the earth" (14:3) and "purchased from among men" (14:4). Neither designation is linked in any specific way with literal Israel. However, in other texts those of "the earth"[9] who constitute "men"[10] are clearly the whole world of people, Jews and Gentiles. Hence, the second vision of the 144,000 gives no clues in the direction of empirical Israel. It does, however, point to the universal church of Jesus Christ, drawn from both Jewish and Gentile backgrounds (cf. 5:9–10). Given John's propensity to decode important symbols in subsequent passages, there can be little doubt that chapter 14 is decisive to the understanding of this group's identity.

Lastly, and perhaps most importantly, when John wrote this chapter, the church had already achieved a cherished self-understanding. It had come to understand itself as the true descendants of Abraham (Rom. 4:11-12; Gal. 3:6-9,14,26,29); its children as those genuinely circumcised (Eph. 2:11-14; Phil. 3:3; Col. 2:11-13), in other words, as the true Jews (cf. Rom. 2:28-29) or God's own people (Eph. 1:11,14; Titus 2:14). The church can, therefore, even be called "the Israel of God" (Gal. 6:16), a designation probably derived ultimately from Jesus himself (Matt. 19:28; Luke 22:30). Moreover, all the titles appropriate to that status are henceforth bestowed upon the church (James 1:1; 1 Pet. 1:1; 2:9-10, cf. Rev. 1:6; 5:10), for ethnic/racial distinctions wrapped up in the words *Jew* and *Gentile* no longer apply (1 Cor. 12:13; Gal. 3:28; Eph. 2:11-22; Col. 3:11). The true people of God, previously called "Israel," are now the followers of the Messiah, namely, the church.

Concerning this passage, Caird observes that "in the Revelation, John has already applied to the church so many descriptions of the old Israel that it would be perverse to treat the present case as an exception to the general rule" (95). For, if the 144,000 (vv. 1-8) are not the same group as the great multitude to follow (which in vv. 9-17 is clearly the church universal), then we have "a most improbable sequence in John's thought: only the Jewish Christians receive the protective seal, yet it is only the Gentile Christians who, without the seal, survive the great ordeal to enter the presence of God" (95). Thus, we reach the unavoidable conclusion that the two groups — the sealed and the multitude — are one and the same! The distinctions between them reflect a chronological difference (i.e., they are observed at different moments in their pilgrimage) and a theological perspective. In the former, "the Church [is] viewed as the new Israel, a concept which again recurs throughout this book from its earliest paragraphs (1:5f.) to its latest visions (21:10ff.)" (Beasley-Murray, *Book of Revelation*, 140); in the latter, it is the new, eternal humanity that inhabits New Jerusalem.

As for the specific number 144,000, it too represents symbolic realities. First, the number implies that those who are sealed "from" the twelve tribes include a remnant of empirical Israel (cf. Rom. 11:1,5-6). There are many Jews represented here as part of messianic Israel, that is, the body of Christ. And in this "Israel" there are also many who are not Jews. Second, "thousand" was the largest number known in John's day (the cipher *million* had not yet been introduced). Here it is multiplied by twelve, and then again by twelve. Later in Revelation there will be a reference to the twelve tribes and the twelve apostles (21:12–14). If they represent the factors 12 times 12 (equals 144), then when multiplied by 1,000, the final result equals all of the people of God in all time. That, of course, would fit nicely with the description "redeemed from the earth…from among men" (14:3–4). Third, this is the response to the martyrs' question, "How long?" The number is both specific and elusively symbolic, for it stands for the full and ultimately unknown number of those who are yet to spend their lives in the battle with the counterfeit white horse. Therefore, the martyrs' question is not finally answered, except by way of assurance that such a day and number are predetermined.

Let's not forget that the symbol of 144,000, the whole people of God, would be nearly synonymous with "the seven churches" on earth in John's day, for in those (symbolically *seven*) churches was a fellowship that included both Jews (John himself, if he is the apostle) and Gentiles. These churches for whom the book is written are being told that they may face the future valiantly because they are ultimately safe. In fact, the very moment they resist the dragon's System to the utmost, they become fellow conquerors with Jesus Christ (3:21; 12:11). Probably this is the complete yet symbolic *number* of martyrs who must yet join the ranks of those already under the altar (6:11). To the question, "Who can stand?" in the final day when we are all unmasked and our every motive rendered transparent before our Maker, the Revelation returns the answer: the 144,000 can stand, for they are reborn and sealed by the Spirit of Christ (Rom. 8:9,14).

7:9 • Suddenly, John's attention is captured by another vision of a vast and incalculable throng. Robed in white, they are victors who have conquered and won their way to this heavenly shore. They wave "palm branches," as at Jesus' triumphal entry into Jerusalem when the shout of hosanna ("save now") suggested the significance of the palm. From the days of the Maccabees, the palm branch had been the symbol of Hebrew freedom and independence. These have entered into that liberty for which all have longed from the beginning. They are "a great multitude"; they are the descendants of Abraham, who include all the families of the earth and are as innumerable as the sands of the sea or the stars of the sky (Gen. 12:3; 22:17).

7:10 • The rapturous joy of the great multitude is now experienced worshipfully. These words of praise form a part of that "new song" (5:8; 14:3) that only those who have experienced salvation can truly understand and celebrate. The phrase "loud voice" occurs seventeen times in Revelation, and in each occurrence a heavenly source is noted. We are listening to exultant saints whose battles are over and

who are now rejoicing in the experience of eternal bliss as their voices
commingle with the heavenly hosts. The attribution here of salvation
to both God and the Lamb is yet another bold assertion of the New
Testament's Trinitarian theology.

7:11 • All the angels fall down. Many other texts throughout the
Bible depict the angels doing the same: "Let all God's angels worship him" (Heb. 1:6; cf. Job 38:7; Ps. 103:20; 148:2; Matt. 18:10; Heb.
12:22). Jesus once stressed how much "rejoicing" there is "in the presence of the angels of God over one sinner who repents" (Luke 15:10);
now heaven is rip-roaring with boisterous music, for a great multitude of redeemed sinners has arrived home who will further bolster
the heavenly chorus.

7:12 • So rapturous is the mood, the whole heavenly cast joins
in the festivities, praising God for all the wondrous characteristics
(*seven* in number) that emanate from the heavenly throne and create
the unknown future. The new element added to previous ascriptions
of praise is "thanks"; it had not been used in 4:11 or 5:12–13, but
this is a different scene. Think of the most delightful hope one might
possibly have for heaven and know that you have only caught a mere
glimmer of that future and only touched the hem of its garment, for
what that blessedness is actually like has not ever truly entered our
imaginations (1 Cor. 2:9).

7:13–14 • Presented with the mystery of this heavenly multitude, John is puzzled. Still, the elder's query is deliberate, designed
to reveal John's ignorance of eternal realities and his need for
supernatural guidance. Thus, he requests of the heavenly being an
explanation of this mystifying scene: "And he said, 'These are they
who have come out of the great tribulation'"; the Greek word for
"tribulation" (*thlipsis*) is also used in Revelation at 1:9 (the "suffering"
John was currently enduring for his testimony), 2:9 (the "afflictions"
the faithful at Smyrna were already facing), and 2:22 (the intense
"suffering" Jezebel and her followers will experience if they do not
repent). The multitude John beholds is victoriously emerging from
this earthly scene and from all its suffering, distress, and persecution
of the faithful. It would, therefore, have been just as logical for the
translators of the New International Version to use the phrase "the
great suffering/affliction" in this passage or, conversely, to have used
"tribulation" at 1:9 and 2:9,22, as do the King James and Revised
Standard Versions.

To "come out" of this "great tribulation" is to participate in the
grand Exodus, which was merely foreshadowed through Moses; this
is the climactic victory of faith over unbelief. For God's people, the

threat of physical death is not the ultimate peril (Antipas is already dead, and the martyrs are resting; cf. Luke 21:16,18). But triumph over passionless orthodoxy (Ephesus), physical persecution and poverty (Smyrna, Pergamum, Philadelphia), accommodation to the world (Thyatira, Sardis), and the deceptive mirages of wealth and power (Laodicea) — these constitute the great tribulation from which the people of God have escaped or "come out." This theme will at last culminate one final exhortation: "Come out of her [fallen Babylon], my people, / so that you will not share in her sins, / so that you will not receive any of her plagues" (18:4).

From another perspective, "the great tribulation" speaks of the on-going spiritual discord created by the citizens of the New Jerusalem and great Babylon living cheek by jowl (Mulholland, 65, 183). The great multitude has "come out" of "the great tribulation" because they have ears to hear what the Spirit is saying to the churches: "Come out of her, my people!" For John, coming out of great Babylon is tantamount to surviving "the great tribulation." Those whose citizenship is from above are marked aliens within its System. The tribulation they face is the System's persecutions and pressures leveled against those who are not part of its social register.

Steadfast Christians at Smyrna, Pergamum, and Philadelphia are among those who have been "faithful, even to the point of death" (2:10), having maintained a patient endurance (3:10). Hence, "the great tribulation" is to be identified not merely with some future, eschatological period, but rather with the church's whole history — all its past, present, and future.[11] Indeed, tribulation is perennially the lot of those who seek to live the Christian life. Jesus expressly taught that those who follow him will experience *thlipsis* (John 16:33; cf. 2 Tim. 3:12). In fact, this continuing *thlipsis* can be so devastating, it causes some to fall away from the gospel (Matt. 13:21). Jesus further noted something that was to be one of the normal expectations of the Christian life. The faithful should expect that they will deliberately be delivered up to *thlipsis* and even death (Matt. 24:9). In fact, Jesus seems to have categorically promised, not that Christians will avoid facing great persecution or tribulation (*thlipsis*), but that they will endure it all through their lives. Paul and Barnabas strengthened the disciples in Asia Minor by telling them that those who are faithful must be prepared to face many forms of *thlipsis* in order to enter the kingdom of God (Acts 14:22). In this way they replicate the experience of their Master, for Jesus once forewarned them, "If the world hates you, keep in mind that it hated me first," and "'no servant is greater than his master.' If they persecuted me, they will persecute you also" (John 15:18,20). *Thlipsis* is one of the foundational under-pinnings of the faithful life. From it, there is clearly no escape. To seek its avoidance is not only unbiblical but unchristian. These, the many ordeals of life, the persecutions of a hostile system opposed to the Christian counterculture, represent the forces of "the great tribu-lation" that the redeemed multitude escape as they begin to enter into the joy of their Lord.[12]

Since we are told of no other human populations in heaven, be-side the 144,000 who are redeemed from the earth (14:3) and this multitude redeemed from all humankind (7:9), they are undoubtedly the same group, viewed from two different vantage points. In verses 1–8, they are pictured as ready for the ordeal of life, protected and se-cured against every ultimate threat by the seal (of the Spirit); later in verses 9–17, we see them having entered into glorified bliss, beyond the travails of earth. First portrayed as the messianic army prepared for conflict, they are now revealed to be those who have given their lives in that battle. There they are the army of the "Lion of the tribe of Judah, the Root of David" (5:5); here they are the innumerable multitude first promised to the patriarchs (Gen. 13:16; 15:5; 32:12; see Bauckham, 76–78). That they are the same group is virtually guaranteed by the hearing (7:4) and seeing (7:9) motif (cf. 1:10,12–13; 21:1,3). What is *heard* and *seen* is the same reality in both instances, modeled on divergent but complementary presuppositions or viewed from different vantage points.

"They have washed their robes and made them white in the blood of the Lamb," and in so doing, they have participated in the death of the Lamb by entering into that redemption that comes from his blood alone (Heb. 9:13–14; 1 John 1:7). To be washed spotlessly "white" through the ruddy "blood of the Lamb" is another of those holy paradoxes of which John is so fond (cf. 2:9; 3:17; 5:5–6; 7:17). How different the life of redemption is from what great Babylon would expect. It is not just being nice and helpful, enterprising, or even generally successful; it means to enter into and share the life and death of Jesus Christ. And this is why John dedicated his book from the beginning "to him who loves us and has freed [NRSV margin: 'washed'] us from our sins by his blood" (1:6).

7:15–17 • The old country preacher once said that whenever you see a "therefore," you must always ask what it is "there for." Here the reason is really quite simple. Those of the great multitude are sharing in the life of the throne because the one criterion for all generations of Christians has been met. They have walked the val-ley of the shadow of death. They have participated in the testimony and witness to Jesus Christ, shared his fate, and now *they can stand* "before the throne of God"; this is the supreme destiny of God's servants.

Many of the blessings obtained by the great multitude before the throne are derived from the hopes and anticipations of earlier generations whose scriptural heritage had also included wonderful promises (Isa. 49:10; Jer. 2:13; Ezek. 39:23). In the Isaiah passage, the imagery of exodus is fused with a future promise of deliverance from exile and an extraordinary return to the land of Israel thereafter (40:3–4,11).

At the conclusion of Revelation 6, those who have rejected the Lamb cry out in fear at the wrath of one they perceive as an angry lion. Here those who have walked with the Lamb and shared his lot find him to be a shepherd (cf. Isa. 40:11; Ezek. 34:11–16,23; John 10:11–18). What a wonderful paradoxical symbol — a Lamb who is also the Shepherd. His experience allows him to guide his sheep along paths he has first trod. Hence, the Lamb is the pioneer of all the faithful.

Quite possibly, John is experiencing this scene through the gossamer veil of Psalm 23. There the good shepherd is the Lord God who leads the flock to still waters and green pastures, protecting them all the while from evil even while preparing for them a celebratory table. The psalm closes with words that fit the spirit of this vision and its conclusion precisely: "Surely goodness and love will follow me / all the days of my life, / and I will dwell in the house of the LORD forever" (Ps. 23:6). The psalmist did not wholly understand all the images employed, but John fills in the divine intent behind those words:

> Then the angel showed me the river of the water of life, as clear as crystal, flowing from the throne of God and of the Lamb down the middle of the great street of the city ... and his servants will serve him. They will see his face, and his name will be on their foreheads. ... And they will reign for ever and ever. (22:1–5)

Chapter 7 flows out of the structural dynamics of the previous vision in chapter 6. There John had seen the martyrs, apparently overcome and defeated by colossal forces of limitless power (seal five). Then the actual reality of that foe was revealed; in truth, it faces an imminent defeat, a tormented future of utter disaster (seal six). Finally, chapter 7 has revealed the concluding truth about the faithful who have patiently endured. The apparent defeat of martyrdom is their triumph. Their destiny has always been secure, sealed by the

Holy Spirit, and their final destination has now been achieved. They are the ultimate victors; the universe is their laurel crown!

> And God will wipe away every tear from their eyes....There will be no more death or mourning or crying or pain, for the old order of things has passed away...Amen. Come, Lord Jesus. (Rev. 7:17; 21:4; 22:20)

Notes

1. Vernard Eller speaks of this two-part vision as "The Church — Below and Above" and as "The Church of the Living" and "The Church of Those Who Have Died" (94-104).

2. These "servants" who will receive the Revelation (1:1; 22:6) are in the first place Christian prophets (cf. Amos 3:7), but since this is what all God's people are meant to be (19:10), Revelation also uses this term to refer to all believers (7:3; 11:18[?]; 19:5; 22:3). See note 10 below.

3. C. H. Spurgeon once commented: "It is impossible that any ill should happen to the man who is beloved of the Lord. Ill to him is no ill, but only good in a mysterious form. Losses enrich him, sickness is his medicine, reproach is his honour, death is his gain" (in Wilcock, 83).

4. J. Massyngberde Ford lists no fewer than six associations this word would evoke in the minds of John's contemporaries (116-17).

5. This view is still held by M. Robert Mulholland (182). However, to achieve this identification, he must illogically deny that the 144,000 of chapter 7 is the same group similarly identified in chapter 14, even though he correctly understands the latter as the church universal (240-41). Jacques Ellul comes to the same conclusion about the group in chapter 7 but only by completely eliminating any discussion of 14:1-5 (168-69). This is not the prevailing view and, given John's rather consistent use of major symbols, is almost certainly mistaken.

6. The most likely explanation for the formal structure of the twelve names as John gives them was put forward by Austin Farrer (106-8); his analysis is based on the pattern of wives and handmaidens who gave birth to these patriarchs and continues Revelation's interest in the women who give birth to history (cf. 12:1-6; 17:1-2,5).

7. The term *servant(s)* in Revelation seems to be a broad and generic title for Christians (1:1; 2:20; 7:3; 19:5; 22:3-4). In a further subdivision of the church, they can represent a special and zealous group of leaders whom John calls "prophets" (1:1 [cf. 22:9]; 10:7; 11:18[?]; 22:6,9) and even the martyrs (6:11; 19:2). Moses is a "servant" (15:3); angels bear this title as well (19:10; 22:9). Hence, the obvious conclusion is that the term *servant(s)* is a broad-spectrum designation for those whose lives serve God in a variety of meaningful and often specific ways.

8. The rationale for the setting of Mount Zion is also suggested by the number 144,000. Later in the book when John measures the New Jerusalem that descends from heaven, he finds it to be a cube, 12,000 stadia square (21:15–16). Since cubes have a total of twelve edges, the formula 12 [edges] x 12,000 [stadia] yields 144,000 as the number symbolizing this city. In chapter 14, the 144,000, then, stand for the community of the redeemed, or New Jerusalem itself, resident on heavenly Mount Zion (the mountain on which historic Jerusalem was built; cf. Heb. 12:22–24).

9. The same word is found in Revelation 1:7; 6:10,15; 11:10; 13:8,12; 14:6; 17:2,5,8; 19:19.

10. The same word is found in Revelation 9:6; 13:13; 16:21; 21:3.

11. Taking the same tack, Donald Guthrie concludes, "The use of the article denotes the whole series of calamities, not any one specifically. It sums up in a word the entire sequence of harassments to the Christian church which would occur before the coming of Christ" (98). And speaking of "a seven-year period of tribulation" at the end of the church age, Herschel H. Hobbs writes, "I just don't find it.... I think we are in the tribulation now. I think the tribulation began when the Lord went back to heaven or when he rose from the dead" (in George 100–101). Bluntly put, "all Christians are coming out of the great tribulation" (Michelson, 234). Cf. also Wall (120–21).

12. The phrase "great tribulation," far from referring to some specific end-time event, could even be used by early Christians to designate historical events of the past that embodied some type of extreme hardship; note Acts 7:11, where the NIV translates "great suffering," literally "great *thlipsis*," with reference to "a famine" (cf. Rev. 6:5–6). Furthermore, this exact phrase is used to describe the first-century punishment to be visited upon Jezebel and her protégés should they fail to repent ("suffer intensely"; 2:22, NIV). In the early church, this expression had not become the technical term for an eschatological period of suffering as it has for some modern Christians.

Chapter 13

TRUMPETS THAT PROCLAIM
THE DIVINE PURPOSE

Rev. 8:1 – 9:21

The seals come to an end in a most startling and unexpected manner. As the seventh is broken open, we are introduced, not to the end of the drama, but to a whole new series of even more bizarre events. Like a Russian nesting doll, the trumpets are the contents of and emerge from the seventh seal. We will argue that even as the intermission of chapter 7 addressed the church (e.g., the martyrs in seal five) of the end times — protected and on the road to heaven — so now the trumpets take up the nature and destiny of the fallen world. As such, they probably represent additional insights into the nature of the Judgment Day scene observed in seal six. What issues have forged that day? Could the fate of king and commoner alike have been different? How? Whatever their immediate relationship to seal six, the trumpets are indisputably a fresh beginning of new perspectives into the story of "what must soon take place" (1:1). But we must still ask, Why do they come after the seals? What relationship to the seals is intended, and what is their message?

Many answers have been proposed to these questions. The path we are taking is the widely held view that the trumpets cover the same ground the seals; that is, they span the church age, which is also known as the end times. This would mean that different perspectives on the same battlefield are being displayed, and new themes are being highlighted. Like a good teacher, John is retracing his steps, again and again, to review and clarify lessons we dare not miss. The trumpets give us deeper theological understanding — from a different vantage point — of what is also going on in the series of the seals as well as the final judgment.

The seals represent the history of earth as a fallen creation, subject to forces it has given rise to, through which it now lives and by which it is ultimately dominated. Theologically, they represent God's

162

permissive will, for it is only by grace, God's extension of time and opportunity, his tolerance of its wickedness and sustaining presence in all its fallenness, that history is *permitted* to continue and manifest the evil that animates its story. The trumpets, then, explain the rationale for this divine permission. They are the seals in flashback mode, the seals amplified and expanded.

What lies purposively hidden within and beneath the shadows of the seals? History is also God's story, argues John, in which both the arsenal of nature and the evil of humanity are put to divine use to praise and serve God; as the psalmist succinctly puts it, "Human wrath serves only to praise you" (Ps. 76:10, NRSV). This is the message of the trumpets: they proclaim the *purposes* of God and reveal the reason that the seals are permitted to become the human story. To that *purposive will*, the way in which God is working in and through the history of evil and using it against its will, we now turn.

Before doing so, however, in order to understand the trumpets, we must recognize that these visions are not videotapes of reality. They are images or illustrations but not portraits. They certainly do have serious messages to convey, but that does not mean they depict those realities literally or photographically. Apocalyptic conveys its teaching by symbolic language, not the architect's slide rule. Speaking of the first four trumpets, Gordon Fee and Douglas Stuart wisely and specifically warn that "we must not necessarily expect a literal fulfillment of those pictures" (243). The question is, What do they proclaim . . . symbolically?

Chapter 8

8:1 • Despite the many jokes that have attended the "silence" in this passage,[1] it probably indicates a dramatic pause intended to heighten the drama of what follows, a way of saying, "Wake up! Momentous events are about to occur." John may also have been suggesting, however, that silence indicates the presence of a listening God: "Everything we say, every groan, every murmur, every stammering attempt at prayer: all this is listened to" (Peterson, 93). One of the compelling realities, immediately announced in verse 3, is the prayers of the saints. Indeed, the Revelation places a high value on the function of prayer (cf. 5:8). It is a daily sacrifice of time and commitment, offered on heaven's golden altar.

8:2 • These seven may be the angels of the churches John has already noted. He may also be thinking of the seven angels of Jewish tradition often listed and named in apocalyptic literature: Gabriel, Michael, Raphael, Uriel, Raguel, Saraqael, and Remiel.[2] That the end would be accompanied by the sound of the trumpet (cf. the voice of Jesus in 1:10; 4:1) is not new. Prophets had predicted it (Isa. 27:13; Zeph. 1:14–16; Zech. 2:10; 9:14; cf. Joel 2:14); Jesus confirmed it (Matt. 24:31); and Paul described it as "God's trumpet" (1 Thess. 4:16, NRSV), the "last trumpet" (1 Cor. 15:52). "Seven" trumpets can only mean that the essence or depths of the end-time story will now be revealed. The last trumpet does not merely sound once; it is continually and plaintively wailing over this dying age. This will be an important series!

8:3 – 4 • These are the prayers, not of the martyrs alone (6:10), but of the whole church ("all the saints"). The scene is similar to that on Mount Carmel when Elijah prayed for a sign to vindicate his prophecy and reveal God's supremacy over earth's idols. Elijah's ultimate concern was that "it be known today that you are God . . . and that you are turning their [Israel's] hearts back again" (1 Kings 18:36–37). We have been told before that the prayers of the saints are a force to be reckoned with, a force that mingles with the divine will in the accomplishment of the future. As prayers from the seven churches are laid on the altar, they become the kindling that fuels the divine fire.

8:5 – 6 • John could not have said it any more clearly or certainly. The trumpet judgments to follow are a response to the prayers of the saints, which implies some very significant connection between Christian prayer and what are here usually perceived as judgments. We cannot simply equate these prayers with those that came from the martyrs in seal five, but surely theirs are included. They longed for vindication and for the Day of Judgment to come. Nevertheless, they were told of a need to wait, for a more important and yet unfinished process was continuing, namely, the gathering of the people of God. Until the preaching of the gospel to the whole world is completed, the final day is held in abeyance. What they gave their lives for, the preaching of a gospel of repentance, is still in progress. And all prayers, from all the saints, lifted to God for the redemption and repentance of humanity are mingled on this altar and put in play as they are flung to earth. God's will for human salvation will be accomplished paradoxically in the midst of the forces the seals have unleashed.

8:7–12 • The heavily ecological content of these trumpets has not been missed by modern Christians or commentators. Here God is dealing with people who have treated the earth as though it were "their private property" (Michelson, 107). Paul's comment on nature's entanglement in human sin is equally clear:

> For the creation was subjected to frustration...the creation itself will be liberated from its bondage to decay and brought into the glorious freedom of the children of God. We know that the whole creation has been groaning as in the pains of childbirth right up to the present time. (Rom. 8:20–22)

The depredations of human rebellion have reduced the creation to something less than it was intended to be. Moreover, this very series of judgments will end in a telling verdict on those whose crimes against nature have aroused the divine passion: "Your wrath has come. / The time...for destroying those who destroy the earth" (11:18). The first four trumpets easily explain the necessity for the future event described in 21:1, "Then I saw a...new earth."

Probably the most important mistake people tend to make in trying to understand these symbolic/apocalyptic judgments is to turn them into videotapes of literal scientific occurrences.[3] Then they can only be taken as gruesome, catastrophic events pertaining to the extreme limit of history. This is a major mistake! If this series is yet another perspective on the seal judgments, then the trumpets are also analyses of life in the end times, that is, the present church age, not some far-flung future. What is new is the angle of interpretation on this age — *God's purposive will.* The trumpets answer the questions: On what grounds and for what reasons does the gracious Lord of history permit the seals to take place? Why does God allow them (false ideologies and war particularly) to devastate all creation? Why allow any delay in the revelation of the names and future of the redeemed contained in the scroll?

God's purpose is spelled out in precise detail at the conclusion of chapter 9. When the sealed scroll is finally opened and revealed, its ultimate purpose will prove to be redemptive. Trumpets one through four, and others yet to come, are meant to produce what God truly desires of fallen creatures — repentance. Here is the ultimate cause for the divine indulgence of the human story and its forbearance as the seals roll over its history. Hence, concluding the trumpet series, John writes: "The rest of humankind...still did not *repent* of the work of their hands; they did not...*repent* of their murders, their magic arts, their sexual immorality or their thefts" (9:20–21, emphasis added; cf. 16:9). Earlier in history, repentance also had been the intent of the plagues and other events in Egypt, to force Pharaoh to bend to the divine will (Exod. 3:19–20). As in Ezekiel 33:1–16, these trumpet warnings are meant to warn people of imminent danger: "Since he heard the sound of the trumpet but did not take warning, his blood will be on his own head. If he had taken warning, he would have saved himself" (Ezek. 33:5). Let all who have ears hear the trumpets and save their lives.

The Revelation sketches the purposes served by the trumpets in hues derived from the Exodus story because John and the churches are experiencing yet another pharaoh who seeks to enslave their destiny to his own demonic designs. It is quite obvious that trumpet one is more than similar to the seventh plague on Egypt (Exod. 9:24–26); trumpet two, to the first plague (Exod. 7:20–21); trumpet three, to the water of Marah (Exod. 15:23–26); and trumpet four, to the ninth plague (Exod. 10:21–23). So clear is this association between the events in Egypt and the trumpets that, more than once, John even calls them "plagues" (9:18,20; cf. 11:6; 15:1; 16:9; 18:4,8). The Exodus story is once more being lived by those alert to its presence.

Of special importance is John's final decoding of the era during which these plagues function. Their presence is constantly hovering in the background of life, waiting to invade, waken the sleeper, and judge the unrepentant. The God who is the Lord of creation can specifically activate them, making them determinative, for anyone rebelling against the heavenly throne. The Revelation identifies their sphere of action by noting their availability for God's use in *every* generation: "I warn *everyone* who hears the words of the prophecy of this book: If *anyone* adds anything to them, God will add to him *the plagues described in this book*" (22:18, emphasis added). As the messages to the seven churches are for anyone, anywhere and in all generations, who has ears, so the threat of the plagues is omnipresent throughout history. They are available to induce divine justice at any time, not merely at the end of history.

The first four trumpets have sounded forth with terrifying effects on creation and producing untold misery among humankind. Each, except the fourth, has involved the presence of fire, and the fourth produces distress by reducing the light (another aspect of fire) derived from the heavens. Thus, Revelation proclaims that the prayers of the saints, represented as fire cast to earth, are taking their toll (8:4–5). They are petitions for divine justice, including redemption through repentance. Thus, "the judgment of God," explains Eugenio Corsini, "is not only punishment. It is always accompanied by the divine will to draw from it salvation and life for mankind" (173). But now a line is drawn, and John differentiates the last three trumpets by a special designation — the woes.

8:13 • The three remaining judgments of "woe" are directed solely against one group: "the inhabitants of the earth." This is a standard phrase in Revelation for the worshipers of the beast (6:10; 11:10; 13:8,12,14; 17:2,8; cf. 3:10; 14:6). What has preceded has discomfited all; what follows affects most severely the citizens of great Babylon.

Excursus: Seals and Trumpets

Having looked at the first four trumpets, we must now explain why we believe the trumpets are a retake or double exposure of the same era covered by the seals. John has utilized an intentionally contrived structure that reveals an inner harmony and linkage between the two series. First, both are divided into two categories, the first four and the latter three. These two sections consider slightly but genuinely different subjects: the first four deal with external realities pertinent to the objective side of life; the latter three, with truths related to its spiritual and subjective features. The opening seals make this clear by their common image of the horsemen, while the trumpets accomplish this by differentiating the last three as "woes" (v. 13). Second, each series moves toward and finally achieves *the end* of history. This event is found in the sixth seal and the seventh trumpet. Clearly the destination of their contents is the same terminal point. Finally, each series has an intermission or interjected topic between the sixth and seventh members of the series: chapter 7 in the midst of the seals and chapters 10–11 for the trumpets. These intermissions relate the message of the series to the nature and mission of the church. And, of course, it must be noted that the trumpets do emerge out of the seventh seal, surely indicating that they are directly related, the latter unpacking the former.

The structural harmony (or pattern-repeat) is too studied to be accidental; it will even hold true, later in chapter 16, for the bowl judgments. John has correlated their structures into parallel accounts of the same time period — Pentecost (the birth of the church) to Parousia (the second coming of Christ, the conclusion of the church age). The relationship between the seals and trumpets could be called "progressive recapitulation": *recapitulation* because they do cover the same chronological ground, *progressive* because of thematic developments and the increasing grimness with which they affect human life. The latter is revealed by the fractions involved: the seals possess power over one-quarter (6:8) of humankind, whereas the trumpets escalate the level of destruction to a third (8:7-9:18). This broadening volume of devastation seems to say that things must get worse before they will finally get better.

The seals, it would appear, represent the era during which the self-consuming nature of evil is *permitted* to manifest itself and run its course. The trumpets perceive the history of this process from a different vantage point; God has a *purpose* for permitting the history of evil. That is, God will use it as a means of bringing people to redemptive repentance. Hence, the beast's forces have no idea that they help produce the means of their own defeat: "None of the rulers of this age understood it, for if they had, they would not have crucified the Lord of glory" (1 Cor. 2:8). Nor do these evil forces realize that with each additional suppression and persecution of the saints, they advance the clock of their own demise.

Chapter 9

9:1 • The creature who materializes in this scene has been identified in many ways (Morris, 124). He is probably mentioned again in 9:11 as "king" over this abyss. Though certainty eludes us, presumably he is Satan, the beast master himself, who creates and energizes the monster in 11:7 ("the beast that comes up from the Abyss") that "once was, now is not, and will come up out of the Abyss and go to his destruction" (17:8). Furthermore, in John's estimation, it is Satan who constantly stands behind the beast's evil (13:4). And here John's penchant for contrasting opposites surfaces yet again, for this "star" — clearly a dead star or black hole — is a counterfeit; it is Christ who is "the bright Morning Star" (22:16; cf. 2:28). It is he who controls the key of the abyss and who ultimately governs this pit of death (20:1-2). And by virtue of his own conquest of that realm, he retains permanently the "keys of death and Hades" (1:18).

John paints the picture of this fall from heaven to earth with greater detail in 12:7-9 (recapitulation is one of his recurrent artistic formulas) and indicates again that it is the genesis of a great struggle between Satan and those who testify to Jesus (12:13-17). It was a contest in which Paul had taken sides: "For our struggle is not against flesh and blood," wrote the great apostle, "but against the rulers, against the authorities, against the powers of this dark world and against the spiritual forces of evil in the heavenly realms" (Eph. 6:12). Our arms, moreover, are weapons the world knows not of, for they are spiritual in nature (2 Cor. 10:4). John has spent much time writing to the churches concerning these weapons of our warfare, cajoling them into heightened levels of alertness.

In Luke 10:18–20, Jesus reports having seen "Satan fall like lightning from heaven," just at the point when his seventy witnesses returned joyfully from their preaching campaign (cf. John 12:31-32). This downfall precipitates conflict and much grief also for those who are the fellow travelers of this fallen star, for Revelation describes the effect of Christian witness on the followers of the beast as *torment* (11:10; the same Greek word rendered "torture" in 9:5). Part of the torment of life for the unredeemed is the hearing of a gospel that is repeatedly rebuffed and rejected.

9:2–4 • Out of the smokestack of this dark chasm ascend the powers of the netherworld. Nature is no longer the mediating conduit for human suffering (trumpets one through four). Now attention purposefully turns in another direction. The fifth trumpet deals with an anguish and pain inflicted directly upon humanity itself. Whatever the intention of the fallen star, its forces are limited in what they are allowed to do (the key is "given" in v. 1). Whether these powers were originally intended for use against the followers of the Lamb is uncertain but probable. If so, then the intended victims are the only ones spared, for they are sealed (cf. Luke 10:18-19). Thus, "the evil one cannot harm" those who are the brothers or sisters of the Lamb (1 John 5:18). And the locusts end by harming only fellow travelers, journeying toward their own homeland — the abyss of Hades.

G. B. Caird defines this pit as "the cumulative power and virulence of evil, to which all men contribute, and by which all men, whether they choose or not, are affected" (119). Even evil spirits seek to avoid this place (Luke 8:31; cf. 2 Pet. 2:4; Jude 6). In any event, it is solely the allies of the fallen one (unmarked by God) who are unexpectedly afflicted, for the quintessence of evil is its self-consuming nature; the irrationality of this self-destruction remains an age-old theme in the Scriptures (Prov. 4:19; 5:22; 11:5-6; 12:13; 21:7; cf. Rev. 11:18). The wicked are not a "happy band of brothers" (Morris, 206).

The locust symbol comes directly out of Joel 1:4-7; 2:1-11, where an impending judgment of God's people is to be imposed through armies of locusts. There the purifying of Israel is contemplated; here true Israel alone is exempt. But in both places a similar message is proclaimed: repentance not retribution is the true result God desires (Joel 1:13-20; 2:12-17).

9:5–6 • The torturous "agony" is described in terms John has available to him and is partly prescribed by the apocalyptic genre.

Today we would most likely translate this discussion into categories commingling the psychological and spiritual realms of life.[4] They represent the miseries of life lived without meaning, relationships lacking intimacy, material quests that leave the searcher impoverished, hopes that prove hollow, the quest for the transcendent mired in the transitory. These locusts cause such havoc that human life becomes, to use Søren Kierkegaard's phrase, "the sickness unto death" or, as one modern author has put it, a "long day's journey into night."[5] How different from Paul's comment that "to live is Christ and to die is gain" (Phil. 1:21).

But "five months" are not the whole of a year or one's life, just enough to make it perpetually flawed and often wretched.[6] Life that seeks death is a life absorbed in realities that cannot assuage the human hunger, have no sustaining power and no future. These are the forces that, like locusts, are literally "chewing up" people's lives. It is life lived on the edge of the pit.

9:7–10 • Drawn together here are several symbols from the Hebrew Scriptures standing for rapacious and destructive forces in nature and for human wickedness. Here they portray the powers that are decimating life on earth. But all are understood to be under the control of the Almighty. Foremost among these symbols are those that stand for the presence of personal, human evil: "crowns of gold," "human faces," and hair "like women's hair." These are more than hints at the true channels the dark forces use to direct and implement their hateful designs. When John looks into the faces of these demonically inspired legions, he sees the human countenance. For "evil may take many sinister forms," explains Caird, "but in the last analysis it has a human face, for it is caused by the rebellion of human wills against the will of God" (120).

Political forces (the crowns) are represented; a feminine input (remember the great prostitute of chap. 17) is noted; thus, human countenances are the manifestation of these diabolical battalions of locusts. Far from literal locusts, however, these have no interest in a normal diet of grass and green plants. Their unnatural appetites thirst for human pain.[7] The intention of their torture is to detract from that completeness of life that is found in relationship with God alone and that Jesus came to reestablish (John 10:10; Rom. 5:1-5).

9:11 • Noting, as John does, that the name of the monster of the abyss can be recognized and correlated in two different languages might be a cunning clue to yet another name with bilingual potential (13:17-18). The Hebrew ("destruction") and Greek ("destroyer") convey but one meaning: this one is a spiritual Darth Vader, that cosmic counterforce who is the Terminator and whose pit is as deep as heaven is high.

The word *Apollyon* is very similar to the Greek verb *apollumi,* "to destroy," which is itself closely linked to the name *Apollo* (which was considered to be a derivative of the former word by some ancient Greek writers). Furthermore, the locust is also one of the symbols of this same Greek god. Thus, it could well be that John intended to hint at a political reality when he said that the name of the lord of the pit is "Apollyon," for Domitian had dared to claim that he was the living embodiment of the god Apollo. "If John had this in view," G. R. Beasley-Murray comments, "his last word about the fifth trumpet was a master stroke of irony: the destructive host of hell had as its king the emperor of Rome" (*Book of Revelation,* 162–63).[8] If this is the case, then the "star" of 9:1 should be distinguished from this "king."

9:12–15 • The Euphrates River was anciently recognized as the ideal, natural border between Israel and her hostile neighbors (Gen. 15:18; Deut. 11:24; Josh. 1:4). Terrible forces perennially stood at attention on "the great river," ready to attack at any moment. Later, in John's day, this river stood at the far eastern border of the Roman Empire and represented its most feared point of invasion by Parthia, Rome's greatest superpower adversary. This is not to mention the many times in Old Testament history when devastating forces also came from beyond the Euphrates (e.g., Isa. 8:4–8). For John, the Euphrates carried the same emotional freighting as an atomic strike across the Arctic Circle, a tank assault through the Fulda Gap, or a secret ICBM attack once had for America. It is a symbol carefully chosen for its raw shock value. Now that fear is realized; those dreadful forces are loosed.

9:16 • John does not expect, of course, that we will precisely calculate the number involved (RSV: "twice ten thousand times ten thousand"). Thus, he has given us a figure of stupendous, mind-boggling proportions, particularly in his day. Literally, this number might have been more than the entire population of John's world, and it represents the horror's mounted forces, or cavalry, only. In the armies John knew, the cavalry was usually the smaller part of the entire force, with the infantry the predominant group. Just what sort of military organization does John expect us to imagine, where the cavalry alone is so unimaginably gargantuan? He is not inviting a calculation; he summons up a horde of fantastic, incalculable scope.[9] For John, these terror troopers are simply beyond literal description; they are surrealist art.[10] Such a vision declares the ever-present and inescapable demand of divine judgment ("The wrath of God is being revealed from heaven against all the godlessness and wickedness of men"; Rom. 1:18). No one can flee so colossal a foe.

9:17–19 • A collage of the most horrific, abominable, and repulsive scourges ever to terrify humankind is assembled to produce the greatest possible horror. Here is a surrealistic mixing of incongruous elements that creates the theater of the absurd. The hellish horses John sees in his vision are probably inspired by Job's description of Leviathan (a sea monster found in Job 41:19–20) and Habakkuk's portrayal of fierce horses ridden by the Chaldeans (Hab. 1:8). Yet the fraction, "a third," also indicates the divine restraint and mercy in the midst of judicial destruction ("Release the four angels"; v. 14). God's purposive will, John suggests, is driven by a gracious intention.

The bizarre substances emanating from the horses' mouths replicate the same colors found on their breastplates ("fiery red, dark blue, and yellow as sulfur"). This is not the time to begin ranting about modern weapons, "flame-throwers," "tanks," "multi-warhead missiles" (Walvoord, 167). John is writing to the seven churches; if his language does not communicate through understandable phraseology to which they have access, then he has failed to reveal anything that can help them. We ought not to make this language mean what it says; we can only allow it to mean what it means.

What should be noted is that the three colors ("fiery red, dark blue, and yellow") are highly symbolic. They bear the unmistakable signature of the fiery lake of the second death (19:20; 20:10; 21:8; cf. 6:4; 12:3), where "the smoke of their torment rises for ever and ever" (14:11; cf. 19:13) as it burns with sulfur. Hence, John likens the red to fire, the blue to smoke, and the yellow to burning sulfur (v. 18) as he continues his decoding of the message he has seen. And the horses that vomit this hellish breath are ultimately the forces of cosmic evil to be defeated at the return of Christ.[11] They are the escorts that herd fallen humanity toward the gaping maw of death's hellish lake.

9:20–21 • Those not killed have nevertheless been warned that rejection of God leads to inescapable torment (trumpet five) and ultimately to unavoidable, meaningless death (trumpet six). Yet like Israel of old, " 'You have not returned to me [repented],' declares the LORD" (Amos 4:6; cf. 3:6).

One of the chief sources for John's artistry here must have been Amos 4. In this chapter, the great prophet thunders against God's people Israel. Doing so, he enumerates a pattern of seven historical events through which is revealed a complete display of human rebellion and divine judgment. God's purposive will is not merely punitive but also purgative and refining, according to Amos.

The God of Scripture always seeks to awaken his own, even those enthralled by the beast in John's world. And so it is today, "there is nothing new under the sun" (Eccl. 1:9). Humanity goes blindly on its way, hearing of political pork barrels, crack babies, battered wives, industrial mega-pollution, and listening to the agonies of date rape, ethnic cleansing, street people, flying-saucer cults, increasing mental illness and suicide rates, children shooting children, but refusing to hear the trumpets sounding. C. S. Lewis drives this point home when he observes: "God whispers to us in our pleasures, speaks in our conscience, but shouts in our pains: it is His megaphone to rouse a deaf world" (81). Those who do not repent continue doing obeisance to the very forces destroying them. Thus, God's grace and mercy are revealed in the very midst of the age-old mystery of evil!

Notes

1. Some wags have suggested that the half hour of silence proves there are no women in heaven (a dangerous quip in this day and age); others, that there are no children; still others, that all noise (politicians, loquacious salespeople, partygoers, rock-and-roll music, etc.) is indicative of the Fall and human sin; and finally there are those who are convinced that this silence is conclusive concerning the presence of "preachers" in heaven.

2. In the book of Tobit, Raphael represents himself as "one of the seven angels who stand ready and enter before the glory of the Lord" (Tob. 12:15, NRSV; cf. 12:12).

3. "The language of physical change is dramatic and hyperbolic — it is consciously exaggerated. Scientifically, if the sun actually became dark for even a short time, everything would freeze. . . . If the sun, our nearest star, came even slightly closer to us, we would all roast. . . . There is no way to push this language into literal, scientific statements" (Michelson, 185–86). Leon Morris agrees that "it is a great mistake to read this fiery, passionate and poetic spirit as though he were composing a pedantic piece of scientific prose" (120). Bruce Metzger's warning is particularly apt here: "it is important to recognize that the descriptions are *descriptions of symbols, not of the reality conveyed by the symbols*" (14).

4. W. Hendricksen, for example, describes these tortures as "the operation of the powers of darkness in the soul of the wicked during this present age" (147); and M. Robert Mulholland speaks of "the consequences of rebellion in the lives of the rebellious" (194). Ray F. Robbins takes a similar tack but suggests that the trumpets define three avenues through which

divine judgments affect people: natural calamity (trumpets 1–4), internal decay (trumpet 5), and external invasion (trumpet 6; in George 188–91).

5. This is the title of Eugene O'Neill's play, which is widely thought to be autobiographical.

6. Morris draws attention to the use of "five" in a variety of passages (Matt. 14:17; 25:2; Luke 12:52; John 4:18; Acts 20:6; 24:1) where it seems to be used idiomatically for "a few," that is, not the majority but some limited amount (126). It should also be noted that this is approximately the life span of a locust, and John could be alluding to this biological reality for a symbol of "limitedness."

7. "Scholars usually link this diabolic attack to some future moment, but it is better seen as the spiritual attack against mankind which has been going on from all time from the world of the fallen angels, with Satan at their head" (Corsini, 179).

8. Austin Farrer has already called attention to the fact that John should have used the Greek word *Apoleia* to translate the Hebrew word *Abaddon*, a synonym for "Hades" in the Old Testament. That he used "Apollyon" indicates his deliberate desire to employ a "concrete masculine, not a feminine abstract" term (119).

9. To discuss this number as a realistic estimate of the potential strength of military forces in the People's Republic of China is to utterly miss the point. See Robert Mounce's critique of John Walvoord's wooden literalism (*Book of Revelation*, 201) and Michael Wilcock's similar comments in a different context (97 n. 1).

10. Vernard Eller uses Picasso's painting *Guernica* to illustrate the ability of art "to decalendarize" and thus "universalize" such visionary moments. In this way what is being described can never become mere history but remains perpetually open to the present and future (87–89).

11. Wilcock correctly observes that these horsemen are "not only tanks and planes. They are also cancers and road accidents and malnutrition and terrorist bombs and peaceful demises in nursing homes" (99). We should add, they are also the scourge of AIDS and Alzheimer's disease and every chemical addiction.

Chapter 14

SECOND INTERMISSION

The Church's Vocation

Rev. 10:1–11:19

Once again, as with the series of the seals, we now enter an intermission or time-out zone tucked between the sixth and seventh trumpet. John's structure, indicating a more-or-less parallel pattern-repeat to the seals, continues intact. Moreover, in the midst of the horror of the "woe" judgments, we are once more introduced to the specific theme of the people of God and their relationship to these events. This time, however, instead of being shown the safety of God's chosen (as in Rev. 7), we will be introduced to the church's purpose for existing, that is, the church's *vocation*. As the trumpets sound their funereal dirge over the end days, the church has a responsibility to sound its own clarion call of repentance, hope, and redemption. Furthermore, the interlude consists of two scenes (not unlike those of the 144,000 and the great multitude), which are now divided into chapters 10 and 11.

Chapter 10

10:1–4 • This opening scene is based primarily on Daniel 12, where a similar sealing of a divine message takes place. The "mighty angel" ought not to be identified with Jesus Christ, as a few commentators do (Mulholland, 63, 200; Stoffel, 61), not in a book where the Lamb is worshiped (5:13–14) but angels expressly are not (19:9–10; 22:8–9). Jesus is never described as an angel, much less "another" angel. Nevertheless, triumphantly bestriding sea and land, this angel proclaims the all-embracing power of God over the two realms to which the later beasts will also lay claim (13:1,11). In Philadelphia, the church may have but "little strength" (3:8), yet the forces

175

that stand behind her faithful witness span the globe and brook no interference in the eternal designs of heaven's God.

Just as importantly, the mighty angel holds a little scroll, which is later defined as prophecy about many peoples (vv. 9–11). This is not the scroll of chapter 5; it rested in the hand of God and was not described as "little." Likely these designations are meant to differentiate this new document from the scroll to which the Lamb lays claim in chapter 5. But John is again affirming that humanity's fate is determined by forces far beyond its grasp.

Then the "seven thunders" add their voices to the proclamation of the book. Quite unexpectedly, however, we are prevented from receiving their message, and the seven quietly disappear into the background of the Revelation. A good question might be, Why? Why are we not allowed to hear the content of their thunderings? Why does John even bother to mention them? And why does it help us to simply know that they exist?[1]

Perhaps an answer is available! A passage in Leviticus 26 is very important to John's Revelation. In that chapter, Moses warns Israel of dire repercussions should they violate their newly formed relationship with God that was spelled out in the Sinai Covenant. Consequently, *four* threats, each articulated by *seven* elements, are leveled against a potentially disobedient and unrepentant people:

> If after all this you will not listen to me, I will punish you for your sins seven times over. . . .
> If you remain hostile toward me and refuse to listen to me, I will multiply your afflictions seven times over, as your sins deserve. . . .
> If in spite of these things you do not accept my correction but continue to be hostile toward me, I myself will be hostile toward you and will afflict you for your sins seven times over. . . .
> If in spite of this you still do not listen to me but continue to be hostile toward me, then in my anger I will be hostile toward you, and I myself will punish you for your sins seven times over. (Lev. 26:18–28)

Could it be that John notes the presence of a series of judgments called the "seven thunders" simply to complement the number *four* and to alert the reader to the background of these structures as they are found originally in Leviticus? The seals are series one, the trumpets are two, the bowls will be three, but the thunders are the fourth. Though partially suppressed, their message may be represented generally in later chapters. We need not be given an intentional sevenfold outline, however, because it is enough that we know there is a fourth series. This would mean that the four sequences of sevenfold judgments bear the same significant message in the Revelation as in Leviticus: "Repent and return to the holy Covenant" (cf. Rev. 11:19).

10:5 – 7 • However, as John has conceived the contents of the seven thunders, they also transpire before the end. When trumpet seven sounds, after this intermission, that climactic day will occur. "Delay" will no longer permit time for the church to preach its message of repentance. Judgment Day will arrive (11:15–19), and the day of grace will have finally and irretrievably run its course. At that juncture, the third woe will bring forth the final judgment on all the unrepentant, on all opposition to the will of God.

10:8 – 10 • Again the Old Testament is the symbol dictionary through which John conceives his visions, and Ezekiel 3, where a very similar encounter between God and the prophet takes place, is in his mind just now (cf. Jer. 15:15–18). In this scene, John virtually replicates the action of the Lamb in chapter 5. There the Lamb was granted access to the scroll because he had given his life to redeem the people of earth (5:9). Is John also being called to a similar commitment and vocation? Leon Morris imagines the little scroll to be the Word of God, that is, the gospel that must be preached before the end can arrive (Mark 13:10; see Morris, 133). And while it is sweet in the mouth (to preach the gospel is always a joy; cf. Ps. 119:103), when the results — the rejection — of that message have been digested, they will prove full of bile, persecution, and judgment.[2]

10:11 • Once more, as with the mighty angel, we are being reminded that while the people of God often seem weak, ineffective, and powerless, they yet have the duty to speak to the whole world, including mayors, senators, presidents, and even kings. This is John's calling and the church's.

Chapter 11

11:1 – 2 • Here we enter into one of the most intriguing, perplexing, and hotly debated sections of the Revelation. What does this temple have to do with the book's unfolding story? And of what possible significance are its measurements?

In light of the fact that the Jerusalem temple was long destroyed by the time John was writing and that he expressly avers that in the New Jerusalem there is "no temple" (21:22, NRSV), we are forced to ask of what temple he now speaks. Some believe that these two verses might be a preexisting, independent passage (from Jewish or Jewish Christian sources) that John has employed to introduce verses 3–13. Presumably, it would have originally underscored — albeit incorrectly — the inviolability of God's holy temple in Jerusalem (Beasley-Murray, *Book of Revelation,* 177). Even if one grants this possibility, what new meaning did John attach to this recycling of the symbol in its present setting?

Was John thinking of a physical structure to be rebuilt during some future time (not indicated and improbable; cf. 21:22)? What would readers in the seven churches have made of it? Seemingly, it is a well-known first-century Christian symbol, one used elsewhere by Paul and, again, expressly known to the church at Ephesus. In his letter to that congregation, Paul stated that the saints, "built on the foundation of the apostles and prophets, with Christ Jesus himself as the chief cornerstone...[are growing] to become a holy *temple*" (Eph. 2:20–21, emphasis added; cf. Jesus' comment in John 2:19–21). Moreover, the people of God already are "God's *temple*" (1 Cor. 3:16–17, emphasis added). Furthermore, remember that the bride of the Lamb is also known through her measurements (21:9,15–17). And that is the most likely meaning of this passage. Whatever the original context of these verses — if different from the present one — here the temple to be measured (which means *known* and *protected*) is the people of God, that is, the church.[3]

The word John has used for "temple" usually designates the inner temple structure, sitting in the midst of the court of the Gentiles, not the more general word for the entire temple precincts. It is to be measured (i.e., surveyed) and thereby rendered impregnable.[4] Conversely, the outer court of the Gentiles is left unmeasured, and is, therefore, vulnerable to the assaults of a world that is hostile to God and God's redemptive program. The measuring process, which suggests the certitude of divine protection and preservation (cf. 2 Kings 21:13; Isa. 34:1; Amos 7:7; Zech. 2:1–5), is based chiefly on Ezekiel 40–43. There the prophet beholds an angel measuring Jerusalem and its temple, guaranteeing its future as the indisputable and indestructible city of God (Ezek. 43:7). John seems to be saying that the future Ezekiel foresaw, but could not yet identify as the Christian church, has come to reality in the "temple" that is the Christian, or messianic, community.[5] And those who worship in it, the followers of the Lamb, will be protected from ultimate spiritual loss in their ongoing struggle for the truth.

Taking this line of interpretation for the temple permits three major possibilities for "the outer court," which is *not* similarly protected. (1) Since it is the arena of the trampling to come, it could represent those members of the church who have compromised with the System and are only nominal in their faith (e.g., the smugly orthodox, Jezebel and her followers, the rich and self-contented, etc.). Perhaps it is they who are about to be violated and judged for their betrayal of Christ.[6] Their judgment is irremediable. (2) Or the outer court could be even more symbolic and abstract, referring to the outer, physical nature of individual Christians (Caird, 132; Mounce, *Book of Revelation,* 220). While their true life (as part of the temple) is ultimately safe with God, the beast has been granted power to violate their physical, corporeal being (cf. 11:7; 13:7). Hence, the outer court is once again the true church but seen from a different angle where the desecration of the "holy city" is equivalent to Christian martyrdom, like that of Antipas in Pergamum. (3) The last, and least likely, possibility is that the outer court represents the domain of fallen Babylon, the unbelieving world (21:27; 22:15), as distinct from the church (Wall, 143).

Since the Revelation, however, is clear on the self-consuming nature of evil (the third possibility above) and that those who are not completely faithful to Christ are no better than those totally uncommitted (the first), there is little to choose between these two views. Further, Revelation is equally certain that the Christian's eternal redemption is not linked to physical safety now (the second option; cf. 12:11). Perhaps it is sage, therefore, to note the area of overlap. It suggests that the outer court is the arena where the beast savagely rules his System, that faithless Christians have been co-opted by his treachery, but that, here, even the faithful are not spared his raging animosity.

The Revelation speaks a language very much akin to John's Gospel. In both, Jesus is the Lamb (cf. John 1:29); in both, he is the true temple (John 2:21; Rev. 21:22); and by extension, both assert that the church itself shares his status as the temple (John 14:23; Rev. 11:1–2; see Walker, 248).

In verse 2, we hear for the first time of the prominent symbol of the "42 months." Using this cryptic cipher in three different ways, John alternately characterizes the period as "42 months," "1,260 days," and "a time, times and half a time." All identify the same time period — three and a half years. Therefore, when we learn that the nations will "trample on the holy city for 42 months" (11:2), that two witnesses "will prophesy for 1,260 days" (11:3), that a symbolic woman is to be nourished "for 1,260 days" (12:6) or "for a time, times and half a time" (12:14), and finally that the beast is allowed "authority for forty-two months" (13:5), we ought to recognize the same period of time perceived from a variety of vantage points or angles of interpretation. When this period is expressed as "42 months," it depicts an insurgent realm of evil acting out its antipathy to the kingdom of God. The other two expressions, "1,260 days" and "a time, times and half a time," represent the same interval as experienced by redeeming forces engaged in spiritual battle.

The original symbol, three and a half years, derives from a tragic historic period in Israel's past (Dan. 7:25; cf. 9:27 and 12:7). During the reign of Antiochus IV (Epiphanes), 175–163 B.C., there was a period when the temple was utterly desecrated and dedicated to the Greek god Zeus. Antiochus (the Old Testament Hitler) also took steps to annihilate Judaism from the face of the earth through a series of imperial laws that forbade all distinctively Jewish practices. It was the first time in history that the very survival of Judaism as a faith was genuinely in question. From the inception of that tragic ordeal to the final cleansing and rededication of the Jerusalem temple by the victorious Maccabees, producing the feast of Hanukkah, was a period of roughly three and a half years.

The memory of this terrifying spasm in history eventually impressed itself figuratively on other tragic periods (cf. Luke 4:25 and James 5:17 with 1 Kings 18:1: "in the third year"; see Beasley-Murray, *Book of Revelation,* 184 n. 1; Mounce, *Book of Revelation,* 225 n. 21). In short, the phrase "three and a half years" became a conventional stereotyped expression for an era dominated by oppressive evil during which God's people are to expect persecution and potential annihilation. In the apocalyptic genre of literature, it came to stand for "the time of tyranny until the end comes, and also for the period of the earthly glory of the righteous until God draws all to a close" (Court, 116). A further reinforcement of this symbol took place when the Roman siege (and eventual destruction) of Jerusalem, from March of A.D. 67 until September of A.D. 70, lasted exactly forty-two months (Court, 87, 104; Mulholland, 204). This would not have escaped the attention of early Christians or Jews.

Seemingly, John understands the church to be facing a similar epoch, though probably not a literal period of three and a half years. For him, forty-two months is the time of the church's oppression by the beast's System, Great Babylon. He has adapted this historical symbol to his own purposes. It now stands for that time stretching from Pentecost (the birth of the church) to the Parousia (the second coming of Christ): the church age (see Fig. 5).[7] This means, of course, that as part of the church age, we also live during the forty-two months. John has described this time period in terms of the chameleon guise of the beast and its contemporary organization, that is, the System

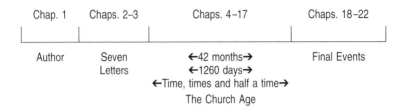

Fig. 5. The Symbolic Epoch of Three-and-a-Half Years

that was Rome. We are meant, however, to also see our own time through the transparency of John's day, for it too is defined by a System that seeks to create us in its own image, to instill its values and ideals within our hearts and make us creatures of its destiny. Like John, we also are prisoners, hemmed in by our own Patmos. We dare not let it define us!

11:3 – 4 • The original witness in Revelation is Jesus himself (1:5; 3:14). He is the primary model who faithfully carried out his testimony (John 18:37) to the point of death. Another witness who has done the same is Antipas (2:13), for great Babylon has already consumed his blood (17:6). John now speaks of "two witnesses" who will prophecy for 1,260 days, and if we are correct, this must mean they carry out their mission during and *throughout* the church age. That is quite an extended period of time for any two humans. Who are they? How is such an extensive mission in time to be accomplished?

The most obvious identifications, noting the actions they are about to carry out (turning water to blood and shutting the sky), would be prophets yet to come who will function like Moses (Deut. 18:15,18) and Elijah (Mal. 4:5). However, if the content of their prophesying is the gospel (which is nearly certain; cf. 19:10), then the two might be interpreted more abstractly as the preaching of the Law (Moses) and the Prophets (Elijah).[8] In this case, they would stand for the biblical twofold proclamation of the Word of God.

Nevertheless, their first identification as "the two olive trees and the two lampstands" leads in another direction. This description is based on Zechariah 4, where the two olive trees and lampstands[9] represent the twin labors of Zerubbabel, the Davidic ruler who with God's aid will complete the rebuilding of the second temple, and Joshua, the high priest who is to purify the people (Zech. 3:9). Through their joint ministries, postexilic Israel is to be revivified. They are the harbingers of the new age that they help create. In this regard, note John's description of the church as a *reigning kingdom* of *priests* (1:6; 5:10), thus combining the functions of Zerubbabel and Joshua.

The description of the prophets as "the two lampstands" is also probably derived from the context of Zechariah 4, though only one is mentioned there. John may be consciously overlaying that original image with his own description of two lampstands, which he conceives as Smyrna and Philadelphia, his ideal exemplars of the church. In any event, this intermingling of symbolic hints — Moses/Elijah with Zerubbabel/Joshua and "two lampstands" — indicates that the two witnesses are a most complex entity, not simply to be identified with two ancient personalities or merely two future figures.

The number *two* is also significant here. A long biblical tradition defines this number as the code cipher for "effective and valid testimony" (see Deut. 17:6; 19:15; cf. Mark 6:7; Luke 10:1). Is it merely accidental that the dragon also has *two* empowered servants (namely, the political and religious beasts) that mimic his appearance in chapter 13 (vv. 1–2,11)? These may be contrasting realities that negatively reflect the labors of the "two witnesses," for John does seem to think in terms of an unholy troika (16:13) and a holy Trinity.

The "sackcloth" worn by the two is indicative of their humility and submission to the purposes of God in their lives. Perhaps John would also have us remember the abject poverty of Smyrna that was shared by many of his early comrades. Also, sackcloth is a fabric frequently connected with repentance (Jer. 4:8; Matt. 11:21) and, therefore, was worn by their prophetic predecessors (Dan. 9:3; Zech. 13:4).

A decisive clue to the identity of the two witnesses, however, is the precise duration of their activities. If the two prophesy for 1,260 days — throughout the church age, that is — then they must represent forces far beyond any two individuals. Almost certainly, Revelation understands them as a dually effective personification of the church itself.[10] The church's vocation and calling in the end times is to proclaim the Word of God (the Law and the Prophets as validly and powerfully as Moses and Elijah had) and establish the Kingdom's work (as effectively as Zerubbabel and Joshua).

John has deliberately withheld the names of these witnesses because they are the names of the saints, but surely one is Antipas. The symbol of the two witnesses is a challenge to the church to walk hand in hand with him and undertake its ministry of prophetic witness (A. Collins, *Crisis and Catharsis,* 151). John will eventually define this sort of witness in the following fashion: "the testimony of Jesus is the spirit of prophecy" (19:10), and Revelation is a book for servant-prophets (22:6).[11]

11:5 • As violent as this response to their oppressors sounds, we must not assume that the witnesses are being encouraged to react cruelly. It is the intent to harm the witnesses that triggers the chain of events to follow, not any inherent animosity against foes. To the contrary, their testimony to Jesus indicates quite the opposite; their intent is to redeem, not harm.

The "fire" that "pours from their mouth" (NRSV) is not napalm spurting from modern flamethrowers or tanks. It is the preached Word of God, and the clue comes first from the Scriptures: "Therefore this is what the LORD God Almighty says: '...I will make my words in your mouth a fire / and these people the wood it consumes" (Jer. 5:14). That this symbolism of the divine word as a devouring fire was appreciated in Israel is confirmed by the second-century B.C. book of Sirach: "Then Elijah arose, a prophet like fire, / and his word burned like a torch" (48:1, NRSV). In subsequent verses, Sirach seemingly interprets these words of fire as the command to shut the heavens, to bring famine, and literally to call down fire.

The point is, those who will not heed the divine word, preached by faithful witnesses, are doomed to the futility of self-destruction. In a similar vein, Paul shared with the Corinthian church this warning: "If anyone destroys God's temple, God will destroy him; for God's temple is sacred, and you are that temple" (1 Cor. 3:17).

11:6 • Powers once belonging to Elijah and Moses are now attributed symbolically to the witnesses, who possess a calling as great as any before them. In fact, their powers exceed even these worthies of the past, for they have access to "every kind" of force, which they can employ "as often as" desired. Let us not forget that the whole series of the trumpets appears to be a response to the prayers of the church (5:8; 8:3–5). Such prayers, seeking salvation for the lost through the bitter circumstances of their rebellion, are no doubt part of the spiritual torment (11:10) experienced by followers of the beast as they reject the testimony of the witnesses. The apocalyptic book known as 2 Esdras has a similar passage in which the Son of God torments the wicked with their very own "evil thoughts" and eventually destroys them, using the law symbolized as "a stream of fire" emanating from his mouth (13:10,38, NRSV). Paul too reminds us that Christian prophecy (the testimony of Jesus) has the effect of disclosing the secrets of unrepentant hearts, reproving and calling unbelievers to account that they might find God (1 Cor. 14:24–25). This is the ministry of the two, the church, a ministry that often is perceived as unrelenting torture by those it is meant to bless.

11:7–8 • John is explicit! As long as the witnesses are carrying out their appointed mission, they cannot be harmed. Not even Antipas had died futilely; his objectives had been met, or he would have been preserved. As part of the "measured" and thus protected people of God — God's temple on earth — they remain invulnerable to the onslaught of the beast and the authority of great Babylon until their work is completed (John 17:4,18). Then and only then may they fall, victims of a spiritual warfare that warps the universe (12:7,17; 13:7). There can be no accident here. The book's first mention of the "beast," in this passage, is linked to the persecution and death of the witnesses.

When the church is truly incarnating the saving presence of Jesus Christ, it too renounces its life for the sake of the lost. But in such moments, a powerful testimony is set free. So it was for Dietrich Bonhoeffer (Germany), Martin Luther King Jr. (United States), Oscar Romero (San Salvador), Oswaldo Mondragón (Nicaragua), and Jerzy Popieluszko (Poland). Another who gave her life but without suffering physical martyrdom was Mother Teresa (India). These and all who quietly, resourcefully, and sacrificially serve the kingdom of God in its war with great Babylon are *the two witnesses.*

In keeping with John's original purpose (1:1), to reveal Jesus Christ as the touchstone of all time and places, the bodies of his witnesses mutely fall in Sodom (legendary for its violent lust and uncharitable attitude toward the poor and needy; see Ezek. 16:49), Egypt (celebrated for its enslavement of God's people; see Hos. 8:13; 9:3,6), and Jerusalem (which did not know the day of its own redemption; Matt. 23:37). But each of these various locales is merely a suburb nestled along the main boulevard that plunges toward the dark heart of the "great city" (16:19; 17:18; 18:10,16,18–19,21), for in great Babylon is to be found "the blood of prophets and of the saints, / and of all who have been killed on the earth" (18:24). John no doubt thought of the dark star of evil as the city of Rome, the unique and illustrious symbol of the empire.[12] Through this historical transparency, we perceive the first representation and greatest example of "the System" or "the world," in which followers of the Lamb, in any age, are called upon to deny themselves and lay down their lives.

11:9–10 • "The world has hated them, for they are not of the world" (John 17:14; cf. Mark 13:13). Such is the bitterness felt toward the witnesses that even in death they are allowed no modicum of dignity or honor. Their ministry has affected people all over the globe (another indicator that they are the church, not merely two individuals). A holiday is celebrated by the citizens of "the great city" (v. 8), who represent all the peoples of earth. They raucously mock and ridicule those who have fallen, contending that their lives had been lost in foolish self-abnegation, for they have faithfully incarnated an alternative and countercultural vision of life centered on the kingdom of the Lamb.

The "three and a half days" of their final humiliation is an unusually precise reckoning for such a process. Once more, these "days" are probably patterned on Daniel, where in chapter 9 the seventy weeks of years are symbolized in terms of single days, each equaling one year. In that case then, this is but another expression of that three-and-a-half-year period that stands for the whole church age. Thus, the great city has existed already for two thousand years. Still it scorns the work of the Kingdom and belittles those who serve it, preferring its own misshapen version of life. As this text says in its apocalyptic fashion, it is always true that the prophetic word afflicts the comfortable and comforts the afflicted.

11:11–12 • At the end of the church's ordeal (the same three and a half days), there will be a day of rejoicing such as this universe has never before experienced. The scene John depicts in condensed and encoded fashion derives from Ezekiel's description of a valley of dry bones, into which the breath of God entered and revived the people's future (Ezek. 37:10). In a wonderful "rebirth of images,"[13] John now sees this prophecy fulfilled in the "first resurrection" (20:5). At the last trumpet, God's end-time people, the church, encounter their Master and his eternal will for them (cf. 1 Cor. 15:50–55; 1 Thess. 4:13–18). At this time, those who have not sought to save their own lives but have willingly laid them down in the service of God (Mark 8:35–36) will hear the heavenly welcome home: "Well done, good and faithful servant!...share your master's happiness" (Matt. 25:21).

11:13 • On the other hand, those who have sought to save their own lives face a far different fate on that day. A devastating earthquake is constantly part and parcel of John's understanding of the last days (cf. v. 19; 6:12; 8:5; 16:18). We should remember, of course, that Jerusalem, indeed all of Israel, was built very near one of earth's major tectonic faults, the Jordan Rift. Beginning far to the north, it continues southward deep into Africa. Both Amos 1:1 and Zechariah 14:5 give evidence of this geological reality (cf. Matt. 27:54; 28:2; Acts 16:26). Nor is it unknown among the prophets that the great day of the Lord would be heralded by a great earthquake (Isa. 29:6; Ezek. 38:19).

Given the estimate of E. P. Sanders that the temple complex occupied one-tenth of the city of Jerusalem (125), it is not impossible that through this reference John is portraying the final death of false religion (the old temple) in contrast with the (new) measured temple. All those who say they worship god, except the followers of the Lamb, are found to be deluded, as their gods fall pell-mell into the abyss. "Seven thousand" might stand for the impending spiritual death of all (7 x 1000) fallen Babylon's citizenry or for a generalized number approximating a tenth (tithe) of the city.[14] Typical of the trumpet series, judgment and natural disaster are meant to produce repentance. Significantly, that is apparently achieved, for here at least some of those who have participated in these events respond to the call of "the eternal gospel" by doing exactly what the angel of 14:6–7 requires — fearing God and giving him glory. This is the alternative, more hopeful response to one noted in 6:15–17 and 9:21.

11:14 • Here is our wake-up call! "Attention!" it says, "The intermission is over; now back to business with the trumpet judgments." Technically, this second woe had already passed at the conclusion of the sixth trumpet in 9:21. John has placed this comment here, however, to indicate the presence of the customary interlude that interrupts items six and seven, presently found in chapters 10 and 11.

11:15 • In light of the unshakable logic of 8:13 (where we are told that three angels are about to sound the three woes), 9:1 (in which angel five sounds the first; cf. v. 12), and 9:13 (the sixth angel sounds the second; cf. 11:14), the seventh angel must represent the third woe. It is the announcement of the end of the age and represents the divine assurance that the human rebellion against the kingdom of God will be put down with finality. Here is the fall of Babylon the Great!

The proclamation of the kingdom of God John gives us here is simply a cameo, a sample miniature of the splendid panoramic vistas seen in chapters 18–22. There he will unpack the full content of these few bold lines in which we savor a foreshadowing of that ultimate future. How very typical of apocalyptic to engage in such regular recapitulation. The story and glory of the end are told and retold in ever greater detail, lest the reader fail to grasp a single particular of that sustaining vision.

11:16–18 • Once more, the medium is the message. Reverent music is the language of eternity, for in the worship of heaven, in which the prayers of the church are mingled, the destiny of the universe is being shaped. What John hears as a paean of praise to God, "the inhabitants of earth" (again, the phrase John uses to characterize the unregenerate, those who worship the beast; see 13:8) experience as the third and final woe. The beast and his devotees have raged (Ps. 2) through all history but to no avail. The heavenly song drowns out their futile discord. Henceforth, John can no longer speak of the Lord God "who is, and who was, and *who is to come*" (1:4,8, emphasis added; cf. 4:8) because the final segment of that title is now outmoded (cf. 16:5). God is no longer "the coming one"; he *has* come. This is the day when all "those who destroy the earth" and "those who reverence God's name" will experience either the wrath or the reward of God's reign. Though appearances have often been deceiving, God has always been in control. Now the Almighty's absolute sovereignty is objectively manifested. Power clearly and publicly changes hands.

11:19 • A new day dawns! Until the death of Jesus and the rending of the temple veil, the ark of the covenant, which stood within the Holy of Holies, was seen only once a year by the high priest. Now, as the book of Hebrews is so fond of demonstrating (chaps. 8–9), the way is clear for all God's people to enter the heavenly sanctuary. For John, the temple of God is virtually a synonym for the New Jerusalem, or that unbridled access to the divine presence enjoyed by all the faithful. Hence, as a physical, historical structure, it never had a future (21:22), for it always represented a communion and fellowship with God, a heavenly experience (11:19) now accessible, throughout the world, to the earthly church (11:1–2).

As John looks homeward, the new covenant, which is the old covenant fulfilled (cf. Lev. 19:18; Matt. 5:17; 22:36–40; Rom. 13:8–10; James 2:8), is seen forever anchored in the will of heaven. And we are given to understand that God will always be faithful to those who keep the eternal covenant. Their future is secure, for those who bear witness to God's covenant are those who hold the testimony of Jesus, which is the spirit of prophecy (19:10). Such prophets, such witnesses, such churches, *we* are meant to be.

Notes

1. The thunders are "indeed a puzzler," as Vernard Eller suggests. "It is difficult to see what significance John intends. . . . John does not tell us enough that we even can begin to guess what the thunders might have said. . . . This is a passage *not* to hang up on" (112).

2. The wonderful symbolic power of "my stomach" as a figure of speech is universal and stands forever enshrined in the *Reader's Digest.*

3. Though not unanimous among commentators, this is the predominant view held by G. R. Beasley-Murray, G. B. Caird, Adela Collins, Vernard

Eller, Elisabeth Fiorenza, Wilfrid Harrington, Leon Morris, Robert Mounce, M. Robert Mulholland, Henry B. Swete, Robert Wall, Michael Wilcock, et al.

4. See Ford (176) for the four basic objectives of "measuring."

5. This conviction was already widely held and taught in the early church (Acts 6:13–14; 7:44–50; 1 Cor. 3:16–17; 2 Cor. 6:16; Eph. 2:11–22; 1 Pet. 2:4–10; cf. Rev. 3:12; 21:22).

6. Hendricksen, 154; Martin Kiddle comments, "People like the adherents of Balaam at Pergamum or of the Jezebel at Thyatira, loveless people like those at Ephesus, formal, insincere people like those at Sardis, smug and self-satisfied people like those at Laodicea — these were no true Christians. Without repentance they could hope for no protection" (189). George Ladd also sees a spiritual differentiation here, but one between a believing remnant of Judaism (the temple) and those who continue "outside" to reject the Messiah (152–53).

7. So H. Boer, G. B. Caird, Elisabeth Fiorenza, George Ladd, M. Robert Mulholland, Mathias Rissi, Ray Robbins, Ernest Stoffel, Michael Wilcock, et al.

8. Cf. Matt. 7:12; 22:40; Luke 16:16; Acts 13:15; Rom. 3:21.

9. Richard Bauckham argues that the reference to "olive trees" means they are two prophets anointed with the oil of the Spirit and to "lampstands" means they project the power and presence of the Spirit (cf. 4:5): "He must mean that they are lampstands bearing the lamps which are the seven Spirits . . . the implication is clear that the seven Spirits are the power of the church's prophetic witness to the world, symbolized by the ministry of the two witnesses" (113).

10. With slight variations (the whole church or only faithful Christian martyrs), this is the very widely held view of G. R. Beasley-Murray, G. B. Caird, Adela Collins, Vernard Eller, Austin Farrer, Martin Kiddle, George Ladd, Leon Morris, Robert Mounce, Robert Wall, et al.

11. Paul's admonitions about God's people and prophecy are appropriate here (cf. 1 Cor. 12:31; 14:1,3–5,24–25,39). Ideally, Paul sees the whole church as engaging in this gift of the Spirit.

12. In the words of Caird, "we take the city to be Rome, for the city limits of Rome extended from the Euphrates to the Pillars of Hercules and from the North Sea to the Sahara Desert" (138).

13. This is the title of a volume on Revelation written by Austin Farrer.

14. The French dramatist and poet Paul Claudel (1868–1955), who combined his devout Catholicism with a profound attraction to the Revelation, once commented that these seven thousand who are slain were probably *biblical scholars* (in Wainwright, 199).

Chapter 15

THE ROSETTA VISION

The Past, the Present, and the Future

Rev. 12:1–14:20

Chapters 12–14 may be the most important ones in the Revelation. For the purpose of understanding the structure and outline of the book, their role cannot be overemphasized. They are nothing less than a miniature portrayal, a cameo presentation, of the chronological (story line) structure of the whole book. Into the framework of these three chapters, the entire contents of Revelation can be arranged and inserted, like cards being shuffled together. Revelation 12–14 is then fittingly described in the title of this chapter as the "Rosetta vision." The Rosetta stone — inscribed in 196 B.C., found in 1799 by French troops near the town of Rosetta in Lower Egypt and deciphered by Jean François Champollion in 1821-22 — was used to decode Egyptian hieroglyphics. In similar fashion, these three chapters decodify fundamental elements in the interpretation of Revelation.

Perhaps the most significant of Revelation's puzzles is *when* the events of chapters 4–17 take place. In that regard, these three chapters reveal the time structure of the book's message. They also function as the basic template, or pattern, of the way history always takes place for the people of God. In brief, these three chapters portray the book's relation to the *past* (chap. 12), *present* (chap. 13), and *future* (chap. 14) in typical models that need to be illustrated anew in every generation.

At midvolume, the end has just been portrayed in chapter 11, but where most authors would be ringing down the curtain, John suddenly and with dramatic flourish raises it again. In fact, he steps way back to the beginning of the tableau as if to make sure we have gotten the point and are still in lockstep with him. In case we are not, these three chapters paint the broad picture of Christian history into

189

which all the rest of the book can be shuffled as the defining details. It is very typical of apocalyptic literature to review major messages over and over, constantly refining and adding details as earlier discussions are clarified by those later and more detailed. As M. Eugene Boring comments, this section of Revelation "is the central axis of the book and the core of its pictorial 'argument'" (*Revelation*, 150).

Chapter 12 begins with the birth of the Messiah, and chapter 14 concludes with his second coming and the Last Judgment. In condensed form, the whole history of the church is summarized in these chapters. Moreover, its greatly compacted form allows us to insert vignettes from other portions of the book into its landscape. In this way, by using the Rosetta vision and coded characteristics of chapters 12–14, chronological issues throughout the Revelation can be resolved.

The Past: Chapter 12

12:1–2 • The vision's first lead character is a woman who, great with child, is clothed with the brilliance and glory of the heavenly spheres.[1] She is not so clearly defined that questions concerning her identity can easily be set aside. Guesses all the way from the original mother, Eve, to God, the ultimate Creator, have been made. And, of course, Jesus' own mother, Mary, clearly figures prominently among the various possibilities. In the context of the total chapter, however, this historical reality wrapped in the symbolic mantle of motherhood is "the messianic community" (Caird, 149; Beasley-Murray, *Book of Revelation*, 198). She stands collectively for all the former people of God ("first for the Jew"; Rom. 1:16) who had long awaited the advent of the Messiah, along with those others ("then for the Gentile"; Rom. 1:16) who, responding to his call, later shape her ideal personality and are persecuted for their faith (vv. 13,17). She and the New Jerusalem stand at opposite ends of the universe from the prostitute and great Babylon. But let us always remember, John is writing "to the seven churches," and they most certainly are included in the symbol of the woman. What follows involves them most particularly.

12:3–4 • John will continue to identify this formidable figure, the great red dragon, but his identity is already beyond doubt. The great enemy of the woman and her child is none other than Satan himself, who briefly animated King Herod the Great (the force active at the very nativity of Jesus; cf. Matt. 2:16) so that he might oppose the birth of the one to come. This child's entrance into life announced the dragon's eventual exit.

12:5–6 • At this point, John is dealing in datable history that can be narrated in terms of known events. We are viewing through the kaleidoscope of apocalyptic vision nothing less than the birth of the Messiah, the keystone of the messianic fellowship. Since Jesus was born some time prior to the death of Herod in 4 B.C., we can rather confidently say that this passage takes place somewhere between 7 and 4 B.C. John must have felt that he was giving his readers an immediate point of chronological reference. Hence, when chapter 14 brings the story to closure, at Judgment Day, these three chapters will have sketched the whole history of the church age, from the first advent (birth) of Messiah to the second. This is the big picture into which nearly all other scenes in the book can be assembled.

The woman's "son," a "male child" destined to "rule" the world, can only be Jesus of Nazareth (cf. Ps. 2:7–9). For a Christian prophet such as John, no other identification is genuinely viable. However, at this point, he is not interested in the story of Jesus' life, which is quickly passed over in favor of his ascension and exaltation to the throne of God, two events that represent Christ's supreme victory and also date the event. The cross and subsequent resurrection, followed by the ascension, can be dated to the year A.D. 30. These two dates — of the Messiah's birth and ascension — then form a time line that must inevitably lead to a structure for dating any further elements of the story. That is, the next aspect of the woman's history follows the last date John has dealt with, namely, A.D. 30.

7–4 B.C. ——————————— A.D. 30 ——→
Messiah's Birth   His Ascension

Fig. 6. The Life of Jesus

In John's continuing portraiture, subsequent to these two critical and datable events, the woman herself (the messianic church) becomes the focus of satanic attention. Why? Since her child has departed the scene, she now personifies his continuing presence in history. As such, she foreshadows "the formation of a counter-community with a counter-consciousness"; the ultimate prophetic function of such a community — the church — is to criticize radically and finally dismantle the dominant consciousness of the prevailing culture (Brueggemann, 28, 80). But recognizing her mission, the dragon forces her, not unlike ancient Israel, to flee to a place of safety —

"into the wilderness" (NRSV). There God, having called her forth from the defilement of great Babylon (18:4), protects and sustains her in the place of his own choosing. This, God will carry out until the day her high calling is fulfilled and the dismantling of the great city is accomplished (cf. 18:20 and 19:14 within the context of these two chapters).

The churches are also implored to hear this calling ("He who has an ear, let him hear what the Spirit says to the churches"), for they are now the communities of the eschatological, messianic redemption. John has been led to write to them that they might discover the nourishing strength of God when the eye of the dragon's attention falls upon them. The wilderness, as it did for ancient Israel, stands for that place of blessing, safety, and peace that passes understanding (cf. John 14:27; 16:33; Phil. 4:7). It is the place where the church stands serenely in the very vortex of the dragon's fury.

Here in the wilderness where God once provided so abundantly for ancient Israel (cf. Hos. 2:14), the continuing people of God will be cared for during the 1,260 days. Since we are in a passage that deals with datable events and, therefore, encourages us to think chronologically, we can only ask, When does this era take place?

7–4 B.C. ————————————— A.D. 30 → (1,260 days)

← ? →

Fig. 7. The Continuing Life of the Church

Is John thinking literally of three and a half years from the last date, A.D. 30? If so, then the period of A.D. 30 to midway through A.D. 33 would be a crucial era. But those years are not noted for strikingly critical events in the church's life. Certainly there is no dramatic intrusion of the dragon during those years. Furthermore, looking for some other explanation of these three and a half years, there is no hint in the passage that John expects us to suddenly leap forward to some far future period of time. Moreover, such a remote time would surely be beyond the vital interests of his struggling congregations. No! We are forced to another solution.

John is once again using the period of "1,260 days" as a symbol standing for the whole life of the church — the time between the two comings of the Lord (Rissi, 39–41). This is at once the more likely explanation and suggests that we are being invited to see ourselves as participating in Revelation's story at this point. We are the people of God — the children of the woman — inhabiting the very significant epoch of the three and a half years. During this period, the church experiences the tribulation of friction with the System, the fury of the beast, and the hatred of the dragon. Yet, as the people of God maintain their witness, there is spiritual nourishment and a place of care that the world knows not of (cf. John 4:31–34). This place is a *wilderness,* which the presence of the Holy Spirit transforms into a garden of spiritual delights, for here the manifold fruit of the Spirit grows abundantly (Gal. 5:22–23).

12:7–9 • Suddenly, John steps back from the tableau he has been presenting, and a minor digression ensues in which he addresses a new issue — the origin of the cosmic conflict in which the church has been caught up. The incarnation of the "son" has led to a powerful confrontation. When the dragon attacked the child, a war in heaven was revealed. Michael, the angel often associated with Israel and its fate,[2] commenced action against those who would harm the woman or her children. This led to the war in which loyal forces expelled those who can no longer participate in the heavenly community.

Unfortunately, the earth has now become the site of a continuing struggle between gargantuan powers contending for a most precious commodity — the commitment and destiny of human worship (cf. 13:4). Yet more than that, it also means that the earth is no longer only the scene of God's creation but, along with the sea, has become the stronghold of dragonish activity (cf. 11:10; 12:12). Now "that ancient serpent" who has deceived "the whole world" walks the earth.

12:10 • Nevertheless, despite the awful activities of the satanic hosts on the earth, their eviction from heaven results in a smashing victory. Forces loyal to the heavenly kingdom are ascendant, and that one who had unleashed ceaseless anguish among the faithful has been decisively dislodged from any position of ultimate authority. Jesus once proclaimed that he had seen Satan "fall like lightning from heaven"; he did so in the context of the mission of the seventy (or seventy-two, NIV), whose commission was to proclaim the gospel. To them he said, "He who listens to you listens to me; he who rejects you rejects me; but he who rejects me rejects him who sent me" (Luke 10:16–18). It is in the preaching of this gospel where the continued battle with Satan and his fall is manifested today.

12:11 • "They" who overcome the dragon are the "brothers" of the previous verse, that is, earthly co-laborers of the faithful heavenly host. They are the ones who have heeded the call of their Lord and defected from the System of great Babylon. Now they spread a new message of hope, having rejected the blandishments of the evil empire that had once captivated their every imagination. They have chosen "to be mistreated along with the people of God rather than to enjoy the pleasures of sin for a short time" (Heb. 11:25). They have maintained the spirit of prophecy by calling attention to a subversive reality, a way of life alternative to the dominant System (19:10).[3]

Verse 11 points to three elements contributing to the co-laborers victory: (1) "the blood of the Lamb" (cf. 7:14); (2) "their testimony" (cf. 19:10); and (3) "they did not love their lives" but spent them daringly (cf. 18:4). Here are the conquerors, members of the churches who were appealed to and designated earlier in the book (2:7; etc.). Chief among them are those who like the martyr of Pergamum are faithful witnesses (2:13) and have dauntlessly carried their valiant testimony to its final validation — death. They are witnesses to the fact that death or social exclusion is not the ultimate horror. In fact, the whole point of verse 11 is that the satanic victory achieved over these conquerors is Pyrrhic, for this apparent defeat is their victory, their conquest of the satanic dominion. There is a fate worse by far than social ostracism or mere death. If one wished to find a "key verse" in the Revelation, 12:11 must be considered a prime choice.

12:12 – 14 • Finally, having surveyed the origin of the church's great ordeal, John returns to the scenario depicted in verses 1–9. Picking up with its concluding theme, conflict between the woman and the dragon, John now continues that story. The gift to the woman of eagle's wings with which to flee her opponent echoes the promises made to God's people earlier in their history (Exod. 19:4; Deut. 32:10–14; Ps. 57:1; 63:7; 91:4). God always makes a way of escape for God's people, even when there appears to be none; this is the perennial promise of the one who ever watches over Israel. Thus, Paul reminds us by word of counsel: "No temptation has seized you except what is common to man. And God is faithful; he will not let you be tempted beyond what you can bear. But when you are tempted, he will also provide a way out so that you can stand up under it" (1 Cor. 10:13). That "way out" may be a steadfast endurance in the midst of poverty and persecution that allows one to remain faithful even in the face of death (Smyrna's way out), or it may be a consuming commitment to the Kingdom's work that overrides every impeding obstacle (Philadelphia's way out). But always there is a way out into the wilderness.

12:15 – 16 • Now the serpent assaults the woman using a new weapon — "water like a river." The flooding waters by which he hopes to destroy the woman are meant to recall the Exodus and the waters that nearly proved a tool of destruction. But they too were dried up as the Creator used his own handiwork to serve him (cf. Judg.

5:20–21). Robert Mounce observes that a flooding torrent is a metaphor often used for rampant evil throughout the Hebrew Scriptures (Ps. 18:4; Isa. 43:2; see *Book of Revelation*, 246). It might also refer to false propaganda and ideology that the lying serpent uses to deceive (cf. Matt. 24:24; 2 Thess. 2:9–12; Rev. 13:14). The latter suggestion is in line with something else that comes from "the mouth of the dragon" (16:13). Three froglike spirits go forth from him to deceive and mislead earth's leaders (16:14). Even those within the church are subjected to this propaganda and are sometimes led astray by the siren calls of secular ideologies that proclaim their self-sufficiency in answering the needs of the human spirit.

But God's earth comes to the aid of the woman, for though occupied by enemy forces, it is never beyond the beck and call of its Master, even as evil is never beyond the control of the Creator. And the river of evil and deceit unleashed against the woman is dried up. There is another river, however, that will satisfy the thirst of the messianic community, the woman's children. New Jerusalem contains a precious gift, a spring producing the "water of life" (21:6); it is also a river but one of living water that flows from the very throne of God and the Lamb. This is the river that heals all the wounds the dragon can ever inflict (22:1; cf. Ezek. 47:12). Again, John has compared and contrasted the waters of death and the waters of life (7:17; 22:17). All are nourished by one wellspring or the other. Nevertheless, the dragon is not yet finished.

12:17 • Who are "the rest of her offspring"? Are they in some sense distinct from the former group that is now safe? Probably not! That they are described as the rest of her children immediately relates them to the woman's firstborn child (cf. 12:5,13), thus characterizing them as brothers and sisters of her eldest son (cf. John 1:12; 11:51–52; Rom. 8:29; Heb. 2:11–13). "The rest" simply means the citizens of the New Jerusalem as distinct from their Lord, who is the firstborn of all creation (Col. 1:15–18). The woman is the collective or symbolic personality that sometimes symbolizes their corporate destiny (the church invisible) and is sometimes viewed separately from the children who live individual lives and face individual challenges (the church visible).

The Present: Chapter 13

A new scene is set. John now describes "the present" as the logical outworking of that past recounted in the previous chapter. Where is the dragon making his presence felt in John's world of the seven churches? And in what arenas does its shape-shifting form presently reveal itself in our day, for now its beastly visage has two faces (13:1,11)? Can the mystery of its cloaked being be penetrated? John tries to respond to such inquiries so his people will be alert to the lurking danger. That peril is found in the challenge posed by two beasts, one from the sea (vv. 1–10) and one from the earth (vv. 11–18).

The Beast from the Sea

13:1 • Boldly standing on the "shore of the sea," continuing to face the woman and her children, is the enemy, and he persists in his evil intent. That he takes his stand in this particular locale (NRSV: "on the sand of the seashore") may indicate once again the collusion of certain allies (cf. Gen. 32:12; Isa. 10:22; Hos. 1:10; Rom. 9:27) whose hostility to the new people of God has previously been noted (cf. 2:9).

Interestingly, creation's story begins with heaven and earth (Gen. 1:1); then the regions under heaven were divided into the dry ground called "land" and water masses called "seas" (Gen. 1:9–10). Thus, by describing two beasts in this chapter, one from the sea and one from the earth, John suggests the extensive nature of the dragon's involvement with creation, but this is only the first level of meaning in these symbols.[4]

"Out of the sea" arises the dragon's next major accomplice. Local authorities (Herod in 12:4) have failed to stem the growing power of the woman and her child. Now empirewide forces are called to the aid of the dragon. "The sea" is closely related and possibly identical to the "many waters" (17:1) of the great prostitute's dominion, where they are defined as "peoples, multitudes, nations and languages" (17:15). In short, "the sea," the cradle of the beast, also represents the roiled masses of earth, the frothing ever-restless citizenry of the beast's monstrous domain, the great city (cf. 11:7–10).

The beast that John sees is virtually a clone of the dragon's own hideous features observed in 12:3. And since it exercises the same malignant powers (13:2,4), the beast, for all practical purposes, is the current surrogate of the dragon. So close is their identification that when the dwellers of earth give the beast their allegiance, they are actually *worshiping* the dragon (v. 4). In other words, secular or state religion is a real spiritual commitment that carries one into relationships far beyond mere political realities.

There is, however, one slight difference in the description of the dragon in 12:3 and the beast in 13:1. Each has seven heads and ten horns, but the dragon possesses "seven crowns" on his *heads,* while the beast has "ten crowns" on his *horns.* These crowns highlight the most important feature of each subject. For the dragon, the "heads" are sources of power that are singled out for attention. They represent the comprehensive sevenfold totality of that hideous strength. On the other hand, the beast's crowned "horns" indicate the practical application of power that has a tenfold ("as far as you can go") ability to extend itself into the future (they "are ten kings who have not yet received a kingdom"; 17:12). Thus, the ten horns perpetuate the life of the beast into the future "until God's words are fulfilled" (17:17).

The beast, then, which John will later describe in even greater detail, is but the first (original) manifestation of a reality that is reincarnated again and again down the (tenfold) corridor of future history. It is truly a chameleon, reinventing itself ever and again to better deceive and delude the inhabitants of earth. Still, it is not entirely new!

13:2 • By appropriating features of three beasts first seen by Daniel in his time (Dan. 7:1–6; they represented various political regimes), John indicates that his contemporary monster has been active in history prior to the first century. It has already had a long career of animosity toward the people of God. The beast of John's day, however, is the irresistible pomp, circumstance, and brute reality of the Roman world. And behind the mask of that mighty System, John sees the hidden smirk of the dragon. That a political system can manifest and be manipulated by unseen forces is not an unexplored concept in the New Testament. Nowhere does this insight receive more powerful exposition than by Paul, who also wrote to the Ephesian church:

> Finally, be strong in the Lord and in his mighty power. Put on the full armor of God so that you can take your stand against the devil's schemes. For our struggle is not against flesh and blood, but against the rulers, against the authorities, against the powers of this dark world and against the spiritual forces of evil in the heavenly realms. (Eph. 6:10–12)

John will shortly add a challenge concerning Rome's "power... throne and great authority"; he will remind his readers of what it means to face such a foe: "This calls for patient endurance and faithfulness on the part of the saints" (13:10).

13:3 • Earlier, in our discussion of chapter 17, we saw John describe the beast as "an eighth king...[who] belongs to the seven"

(17:11). There it was outside the ranks of the seven, yet formed a unity with them. Here the beast is also temporarily beyond the pale of reality but comes back to continue its dreaded presence. Clearly, this is a demonic mockery of Christ's own *death* (cf. "as if... slain" in 5:6 with "seemed to have had a fatal wound") and *resurrection* ("but... healed"). There is probably even more mimicry in the evil symbolism of "once was, now is not, and yet will come" (17:8).

John is likely referring to a bizarre legend in the first century — the myth of *Nero Redivivus*. Nero committed suicide in June of A.D. 68. As death came privately in Nero's own villa, the fiction developed and spread that Nero had actually defected to the East, escaping to Rome's greatest enemy — Parthia. From that enemy kingdom, he was eventually expected to return and seek his maniacal vengeance on Rome. So powerfully did this legend take hold of the Roman imagination and so scarcely could they believe Nero's madness to be finished that during the next two decades, three imperial pretenders arose in Nero's name, claiming to be none other than Nero Redivivus (i.e., Nero revived and come again). John may well be using this widely known story to encode certain delicate political features of his message (Bauckham, 37; Mounce, *Book of Revelation*, 252–53).

If, as suggested in our earlier discussion of chapter 17 (see Chapter 8, pp. 110–15, the lineup of seven kings moves from Augustus toward Domitian, from the emperor at Jesus' birth to the emperor in John's day, then he is understanding Domitian (the eighth king) as a return of the spirit of Nero. Nero was the first to persecute Christians simply for being Christians. Domitian, the second to do so, only revitalized that earlier policy; he was an "eighth" who resurrected the anti-Christian program, which was temporarily interrupted by Nero's death. As G. B. Caird, reflecting on the *Nero Redivivus* legend, so ably puts it: "Nero will indeed return, but reincarnated in a new persecuting emperor" (165; Beasley-Murray, *Book of Revelation*, 210–11).

Apparently, John sees a father (the dragon), son (first beast), and unholy spirit (second beast) leading the forces of cosmic rebellion (cf. 16:13, where the three are seen together and the second beast is called "the false prophet"). There is much interest in the identity of this unholy threesome. But whether John was speaking generally of timeless symbols for those sociopolitical forces that create the cultural idols worshiped by all peoples or was trying to specify who those forces were in his own time, the warning to us and our day is much the same. We, too, face a hostile world awash in the worship of material idolatry and submerged in the competing claims of cultic messiahs.

The whole world is seeking the peace and joy of salvation, but the fate of humanity depends on which triune source of redemption it pins its hopes (cf. 20:10).

13:4 • All of life is a pilgrimage into worship! And only two options exist: we give ourselves to the true God and his service, or we serve the false powers that grow up out of our revolt against heaven. But we all serve something or somebody. For John, the ultimate "somebody" behind the forces of rebellion is the dragon. The beast merely cloaks that hideous and hidden presence; consequently, those living their lives in and for the System were actually serving its ugly designs.

Those who are not awed by the glory and majesty of God's beauty will be mesmerized by the beast's brutish power, the only alternative. That beast was the glory of Rome as far as John was concerned. Its power was apparently the very loom upon which the fabric of history was being woven: "You can't fight the System!" Those who did not fit the warp and woof of Rome's needs were of little consequence.

The boast of its worshipers, "Who is like.... Who can make war against" the beast, is a deliberate imitation of Moses' song after the crossing of the sea. There it is God's invincibility and uniqueness that is intoned (Exod. 15:3–11). Here the beast attempts to usurp that position of divine honor and, in so doing, once again points to one of the main themes of the book, namely, the profound antagonism between the worshipers of the beast and those who worship the true God.

13:5–7 • The phrase "was given" in verse 5 are two little words that simply point to the provisional nature of this activity. It is the will of God to allow this haughty voice to rail at heaven's rule, but the divine toleration of its "proud words and blasphemies" extends only so far and only for so long.

The emperors of Rome had long enjoyed elements of titular divinity embedded in their official titles, but Domitian seemed to take these matters much more seriously than his predecessors. One of the new features of Domitian's reign was the blasphemous title he required when one entered his presence: *Dominus et Deus noster.* "Our Lord and God" was his preferred epithet. Christians, of course, could only take this to be the most flagrant form of pure blasphemy. Nevertheless, this is the way in which every secular ideology and cultish world-view understands itself, namely, as the final arbiter of reality.

The period of "forty-two months" is an overlay, or double exposure, of that time when the witnesses are persecuted for proclaiming the eternal truth of the gospel (11:3) and the woman is being pursued by the dragon (12:6,14). Here these activities of the faithful are described from another angle. They take place at a time when the beast is at war with the saints, killing them as he blasphemes all they stand for.[5] This is the same time period in which the churches are facing their ordeals: John is exiled to Patmos; Antipas is martyred; the saints at Smyrna are being impoverished and persecuted; Ephesian Christians are adopting harsher measures to deal with compromise and are losing compassion; Philadelphia is working harder than ever at missions; but, unhappily, other churches are gradually accommodating to the pressures of the System so they can continue thriving therein. Boasting of having tamed the beast and now enjoying its benefits, Laodicea claims it has become rich and needs nothing. All of this is part of the beast's war against the saints. How ludicrous Laodicea's swaggering pretensions must have seemed to John as he languished on his prison isle. But those who are conquered (killed) by the beast are also the overcomers mentioned in the letters to the churches. And the beast's Pyrrhic victory is exposed when, as promised, Christ places upon them heaven's tripartite name (3:12).

13:8 • Total is the thralldom the beast exercises over all who are unsealed (i.e., unregenerated) by the Lamb. But notice here one of John's significant decoding procedures. Who are the "inhabitants of the earth" in Revelation? Are they simply "people" in general? No! They are those whose names do not appear in the book of life because they serve the beast. The "inhabitants of the earth" are the citizens of great Babylon. Whenever we see this phrase or its abbreviation, we must remember who is being addressed. Conversely, "those who live in heaven" (v. 6), and who are also being blasphemed, are already the citizens of the New Jerusalem that comes "down out of heaven from God" (21:2).

13:9–10 • The opening words of this exhortation remind us that the churches are still being addressed (2:7). The charge itself echoes the words of Jeremiah 15:2; 43:11 and of Jesus in Matthew 26:52. The first couplet ("If ... captivity") suggests the price the System exacts of those who live the Christian life as John did (1:9). Furthermore, it reminds the faithful that their *Dominus et Deus* is still in charge and mysteriously present even in the midst of their persecution. The second couplet ("If ... killed") suggests that Antipas's is not a singular martyrdom; others are also to join with him in carrying a faithful testimony to their graves. On the other hand, if the variant manuscript reading ("If anyone kills ... "; NIV margin) is the better reading, then the point is that the persecutors will receive their recompense in kind. The church is being told that violent resistance is needless and futile, as well as out-of-harmony with the slaughtered Lamb, for those using the power of the sword against the church will ultimately face a time that God has set aside "for destroying those who destroy the earth" (11:18). This is the content of the faith that produces endurance. There is, indeed, great power in a positive eschatology!

The Beast from the Earth

13:11–12 • The second beast, a split personality of the one John just described, is yet another face of the System that seeks to submerge and subvert Christian faith. It emerges from the earth, the other realm that has fallen victim to the satanic rebellion against heaven. In relation to the first beast, this one functions as the "ministry of propaganda." Its function is to lead the earth into submission to the political beast and to institutionalize its control over earth's inhabitants. To achieve this vital objective, the second beast has been given all the power at the disposal of the System.

The appearance and mode of operation of the second beast is benignly religious; it has "two horns like a lamb." This is a clear parody of *the Lamb*. But when it opens its mouth, it has dragon's breath. From now on, beyond this chapter, John will call the propaganda beast "the false prophet" (16:13; 19:20; 20:10), which may help explain why it has "two" horns. Just as God has "two" witnesses who prophesy the truth, this beast gives a twofold (i.e., an effective) witness to the glory of the political beast. Its two forms of witness are its signs (v. 13) and its mark of approval and ownership (13:16). What real-time institution is John characterizing here? Almost certainly, he is thinking of the imperial cult of emperor worship and its provincial council.

In Asia Minor, the "Commune of Asia" was a body of representatives drawn from the major towns of the province; its chief officer was the Asiarch. Among the representatives' administrative duties were the functions of priesthood in their respective imperial shrines. In these temples erected to the glory of Rome, busts and statues of the reigning emperor were venerated as one means of unifying the empire. Here loyal citizens who sought the status and approval that political reliability conferred on the faithful would burn small amounts of incense or swine hair to the godhead of Caesar.[6] Furthermore, the council was also in charge of enforcing this imperial worship throughout the province.

This cult of the emperor was especially popular in Asia Minor.

Hence, the second beast is a supreme propagandist, seeking to promote the acceptance and worship of the first, political beast — the Roman System. It represents those societal forces and agencies that promote the myth of invincibility and absoluteness that engulfs the dominant culture and its institutions.

13:13 – 15 • Whether John truly expected the second beast to perform *miraculous* signs, something not explicitly stated (RSV, NRSV: "great signs"), or *manipulative* events that were cunningly deceptive is far from certain (cf. Acts 13:6 – 8 and the "lawless one" who employs "signs, lying wonders, and every kind of wicked deception" in 2 Thess. 2:9 –10, NRSV). But what is absolutely incontestable is that the world of John's day was often bedazzled by startling incidents *thought to be supernatural.*

Apollonius of Tyana, a friend to Nero, was credited with a miraculous birth, the ability to materialize and dematerialize, to heal the sick and even raise the dead. Many in John's day believed that Simon Magus (cf. Acts 8:9 –24) had the ability to bring statues to life. Trickery and every variety of charlatanism were rampant in the first century. Indeed, they were the stock-in-trade of the religious priesthoods indigenous to Asia. Petroleum-based compounds (similar to napalm) were probably conducted through hidden channels, appearing almost supernaturally to fall on altars and devour offerings; artificial breath emerged from seemingly inert statues; intercom tubes and ventriloquism caused prayers to be answered through the very lips of these idols (Beasley-Murray, *Book of Revelation,* 217; Caird, 172; Kiddle, 253; Ford, 225; Mounce, *Book of Revelation,* 261). John may well be telling us how the priests of the imperial cult induced the worship of the caesars by duplicitous means.

Those who refused to participate in the normal machinations of this secular religion found themselves in an aberrant lifestyle that often led to capital punishment. It must have been exceedingly dangerous to follow Jesus in Pergamum "where Satan has his throne" (2:13). There in the provincial capital, caesar worship would be practiced at maximal intensity. Nor is it any accident that John tells us of a specific execution in this town (2:13), for while some merely wore crosses, martyrs bore the cross. There is always a price to be paid for membership in the Messiah's "countercommunity." The church's "counterconsciousness" was dangerous because it was constantly picking open the flimsy scabs covering the beast's putrefying System.

13:16 – 18 • Probably the most famous cipher in the history of numerical conundrums, "666" has perennially puzzled and delighted the Christian and secular imagination throughout history. John's deliberate invitation to calculate the meaning of the number has been irresistible. Let us remember the warning of G. R. Beasley-Murray and attempt to avoid the ubiquitous "lust for identification" (*Book of Revelation*, 132). Still there is a message here!

Decisively important for understanding this mark is the result it has on the life of its possessor. The ability to "buy or sell" — let us not suddenly adopt literalism here — symbolizes accessibility to the dominant culture. Social mobility, community clout, and the opportunity to participate fully in the lifeblood of the System are the issue. Absolutely no one can afford to be deprived of the beast's cachet. Those without this passport to the prevailing culture are marginalized and condemned to some form of social handicap or even death.

From the vast range of guesses at the identity standing behind this number, two have consistently stood out. The first focuses on the character of the number *six*. By its very nature, *six* is a number signifying that which is incomplete (cf. John 2:6, NRSV: "Jewish rites of purification") or flawed, falling just short of and failing to achieve *seven*, the number of perfection. The triple replication of "sixish imperfection," therefore, might represent any political System seeking the absoluteness of divinity. If this is the correct approach to the number, then the Revelation is saying, "No 'tower of Babel' will ever succeed!" All such undertakings, to set up the kingdom of man on earth, will always fall short (6), be incomplete (6), and fail (6) in their attempts to achieve this illusory goal. Thus, "666" is the number and destiny of a failed beast.

Second, the number might be a gematric identification (see Chapter 1, note 13). Gematria was a widely practiced number game in the first century. In the absence of an Arabic system of numerals, letters functioned in the dual role of sounds and numbers (*A* stood for 1, *B* for 2, *C* for 3, and so on).[7] This meant that every letter, word, and name, indeed every phrase or sentence, could be calculated to represent a numerical by-product. All you had to do was know the value of the letters and calculate their total. Roman numerals (C, I, II, M, V, X) preserve the practice of gematria to this very day.

"It is man's number" (CEV: "it stands for a person"), writes John. Did he mean to identify a specific individual (i.e., it represents a man's or person's name, as in the New English Bible and the New Revised Standard Version)? Comments in 13:17 and in 14:11 suggest that this was his intention. Moreover, there is one such historical identification that has been suggested regularly. When the official title *Caesar Nero* is translated from Greek into Hebrew letters, their total gematric value is exactly 666. And when it is taken from Latin into Hebrew, the resulting letters total 616, the other number attested in some ancient manuscripts (see a study Bible's footnote). If this cryptogram contains the imperial title of Nero, then it satisfies both numbers (666 and 616) found in the Greek manuscripts of Revelation, the only personal identification to do so. That John can think about names across linguistic lines is clearly established in 9:11, where no less a figure than "the angel of the Abyss" is named in both Greek and Hebrew (cf. 16:16).

It is more likely, however, that Caesar Domitian (personified by the sea beast) is the individual of whom John is thinking most directly. How, therefore, would this gematric answer relate to him? Ethelbert Stauffer noticed that Domitian's full imperial title in Greek (*Autokrator Kaisar Dometianos Sebastos Germanikos*) would have the standard abbreviation of *A.KAI.DOMET.SEB.GE;* the total value of the letters in this abbreviation is 666 (in Caird, 175). If they were actively seeking such a linkage to Nero, early Christians might easily have noted the number they shared. And since John has said that the political sea beast is a wounded head now healed, any number that would associate Nero with his spiritual heir, Domitian, would be seen as divinely appointed.

But perhaps we do not need to choose between these competing explanations. Could it be that both yield the answer? Likely there was an early-church tradition that Nero's (and perhaps Domitian's) number was 666. After all, such numbers had been established for other divinities. Jupiter (Zeus to the Greeks) was known by the number 717, and Jesus' code number was 888, the sum of the Greek letters for his name. But what might have moved John most was the providential relationship between the gematric meaning of 666 (Caesar Nero and Domitian) and its more abstract significance, that is, a "triple failure to achieve totalitarian perfection." Where could one find a more perfect code for the beast?

Lastly, and of great significance, why is the mark placed on the "right hand" or the "forehead"? There is nothing casual or unstudied about this element in Revelation's symbolism, for it can only be a deliberate, mocking parody of Jewish phylacteries. There is no other known symbol involving *hand and forehead* in all the ancient world. Those small, leather phylactery boxes, which were required to be bound upon the hand and head (Deut. 6:8), contained a small enscrolled prayer of loyalty to the one true God: "Hear, O Israel: The LORD our God, the LORD is one. Love the LORD your God with all your heart and with all your soul and with all your strength" (Deut.

6:4–5). The beast marks its people in the same places, demanding the same absolute allegiance as that required by the true God. Again John may be hinting at the travesty of Jewish collusion in the war on the church (cf. "synagogue of Satan" in 2:9; 3:9; and "sand of the seashore" in 13:1, NRSV).

The hand-or-forehead quality of the mark also indicates its spiritual nature; it is a mark of religious commitment. As the "seal" received on the forehead from the living God (7:2–3) is spiritual and subjective in essence (the indwelling of the Holy Spirit), so also this counterfeit "mark" of the beast, placed on the forehead or hand (representing the spirit of the world System) is equally hidden and internal by nature. John was not speaking of an obvious and visible bar code or social security number to be emblazoned on people (or even of implanted microchips) in the distant future; he knew men and women living around and within the seven churches who were already so marked. Their hearts beat for the System; their goals and ideals were learned from the great prostitute; their hopes and imaginations were excited by the life of great Babylon. They were branded — owned lock, stock, and barrel — and those countercultures that did not share their vision of reality had no relevance in their world.

The Future: Chapter 14

In this chapter, John completes the chronological survey begun in chapter 12 with the birth, or *first advent,* of the Messiah. Here the *second advent* and the end of history have arrived. In between these bracketing episodes (i.e., chap. 13), all intervening time, and especially the church age, takes place. John's arrangement of these visions, then, suggests that the beast's forty-two-month assault upon the church (13:5; cf. 12:6,14) fills the interim time period between the two advents of the Messiah. Again, the indication is that this three-and-a-half-year era, variously defined in days, months, or times, is the total period from Christ's first coming to his second. In that case, these symbolic forty-two months have already persisted for two thousand years.

14:1–3 • Now one last vision is given of those who refused to worship the beast or to take upon themselves his personality (i.e., number/name). Emblazoned on their *foreheads,* in obvious counterpoint to those just discussed, are God's names, which proclaim their true allegiance. Their safety is assured as they stand with the Lamb on the heavenly mount, for they "have come to Mount Zion, to the heavenly Jerusalem, the city of the living God... to the church of the firstborn, whose names are written in heaven... to Jesus the mediator of a new covenant" (Heb. 12:22–24). Redeemed from the beast's domain, the earth, the 144,000 are the citizens of that heavenly city. Mount Zion, the site on which Jerusalem is built, will remind all those who know the Hebrew Scriptures of that place where God's final victory and deliverance for the people of God is to be celebrated and consummated (Isa. 24:21–23; Joel 2:32; Mic. 4:6–8).

14:4–5 • Frequently in the Hebrew Scriptures, virginity or chastity is a symbol for spiritual faithfulness to God, while its opposite indicates a shocking dereliction of covenant relationship (2 Kings 19:21; Jer. 18:13; Lam. 2:13; Amos 5:2; cf. Jer. 3:6; Ezek. 16; 23; Hos. 2). Paul continues this same imagery when he speaks of his labors among the Corinthians: "I promised you to one husband, to Christ, so that I might present you as a pure virgin to him" (2 Cor. 11:2). In the Revelation, they are already "the bride, the wife of the Lamb" (21:9). On the other hand, in both Pergamum and Thyatira, those who have accommodated themselves to the System are said to have engaged in "fornication" (2:14,20–21, NRSV). The precise infraction these virgins have avoided is, not marriage itself, but an illicit relationship with the great prostitute who is Babylon. Hence, both men and women are numbered among them, for they have not renounced the norm of Genesis 1 and 2 (conjugal unity) but have rejected the debasing defilement of the prostitute's world.

By abstaining from improper entanglements with the great prostitute, the 144,000 have maintained the purity required for spiritual battle against the System. They are prepared for nothing less than a holy war (Deut. 20; 23:9–10; cf. 1 Sam. 21:5; 2 Sam. 11:11) against an unholy world (Caird, 179; Laws, 56–57), for only the pure in heart and commitment will be able to withstand the fury of the beast's assault. It is they who follow the Lamb (Mark 8:34; John 13:36), who are an offering to God, the firstfruits who survive the judgment shortly to arrive (14:15–16). And in their mouths, no lie is found (cf. Rom. 1:18,25; Rev. 2:2; 21:27; 22:15), but like their master, they suffer innocently (Isa. 53:9). Moreover, there is one specific lie they have rejected. They have not taken the phrase *Dominus et Deus* in vain; for them, it refers to their Lord.

John has used the symbol of the 144,000 once again to indicate the destiny of the whole church, the number of the redeemed throughout the long corridor of history. In chapter 7, they were seen being sealed just prior to the ordeal they faced. Here they reveal the serenity of those who have come victoriously through the tribulation of life against the System. Through this symbol, we once again see the "great multitude" now beyond the beast's reach and singing the praises of God (7:9–10; cf. 19:1,6).

14:6 • Immediately preceding the scenes of final judgment, *three* angelic pronouncements are directed toward those who stand outside the sheepfold of the Lamb. It is noteworthy that these three heavenly announcements are not proclamations of wrath but redemptive calls to a dying world; reminding us of the trumpets, they are calls for repentance. This is a message addressed to the four categories of humanity — "nation, tribe, language and people" — (perhaps suggested by the *four* corners of the whole earth; cf. 7:1; 20:8).

14:7 • Those who dwell on the earth are given a final opportunity to recognize the arrival of the terminal hour, to repent and enter the stream of cosmic redemption, before their world recedes once again into the abyss of nothingness out of which it originally came. The call to "fear God" echoes the Hebrew Scriptures:

> Now all has been heard;
>> here is the conclusion of the matter:
> Fear God and keep his commandments,
>> for this is the whole duty of man.
> For God will bring every deed into judgment,
>> including every hidden thing,
>> whether it is good or evil.

> — Eccl. 12:13–14

This ancient counsel is proclaimed to the world one last time.

14:8 • The gospel is also the announcement of the impending doom of the great city and all those who have partaken of its table and shared its Communion cup (chap. 18). It is a cup of adultery because it is a fellowship illicitly alternative to that led by the Lamb. But John notes that there is a camaraderie, a communion, felt and shared by those who do not fear or worship the true God. They share a mark, impressed deeply upon their hearts, that draws them together in an exclusive world-view, one that is insane and unshared by those of the Lamb's sheepfold.[8] The final warning of Babylon's downfall is a call to those who can still hear. They may yet leave the city's precincts (cf. 18:4) and find sanctuary on Mount Zion, the New Jerusalem.

14:9–11 • If the destiny of the redeemed cannot be adequately described, then a similar difficulty must attend the fate of those who lose those indescribable benefits. Note that although John does attempt to describe heaven in chapters 21–22, Paul's comments to the effect that it *cannot* be described (1 Cor. 2:9; 2 Cor. 12:4) warn us not to take John's description literally. It is a metaphorical description of realities for which John had no adequate language. The Bible often uses human and earthly metaphors or symbols to present realities that are totally beyond our range of experience. To take such metaphorical language literally may force it to say too much or too little.

However, John does use the most dreaded and fearsome threats humanity has ever known to depict the fate of those who keep faith with great Babylon. Those who obdurately remain behind in the city, which boasts it shall never fall, will fall with it into an eternal finality from which no recall is possible. John makes that clear! And while the biblical description of hell may well be, as many evangelicals think,[9] described metaphorically rather than literally,[10] still the painfully devastating frustration of those consigned to its torment could not be described in any more ghastly terms. Verses 10–11 represent one of the strongest biblical warrants for those who take the Bible's description of hell to indicate an eternal, conscious, and irremediable punishment.

14:12–13 • In what sense does the patient endurance of the saints derive from the preceding warnings? Very simply! Given the state of the world in which they live and the dire future just enunciated, they must carry on courageously to bring the eternal gospel to the inhabitants of the earth. Martyrdom is not the ultimate danger, for in death they find the blessedness of rest from "their labor,"[11] labor that has brought others into fellowship with "him who loves us and has freed us from our sins by his blood" (1:5). In Daniel, this is the role of "those who are wise" who understand the nature of their high calling (Dan. 12:3).

14:14–16 • In the overview of this three-chapter tableau, John now relates the arrival of the "blessed hope" (Titus 2:13) first proclaimed in the opening verses of the book: "Look, he is coming with the clouds, / and every eye will see him, / even those who pierced him; / and all the peoples of the earth will mourn because of him" (1:7; cf. Dan. 7:13). The return of the Son of Man, described here, is the second advent of the church's resurrected Lord. At that climactic coming, John observes two great harvests (vv. 14–16 and 17–20) that pose yet another problem. Why are *two* described? How do they relate to each other? Are they exactly the same event defined by divergent symbol systems or two sides of one coin, that is, a single judgment experienced differently by two distinct groups?

A simple comparison of the two paragraphs quickly reveals much parallel, almost redundant language, so much so that one is led to wonder, Why does John describe the same scene twice, in much the same terms, and in back-to-back paragraphs with apparently similar results? The best answer is that he is speaking of one event with opposite outcomes for different groups of participants.[12] At this judgment, all depends on how people have reacted to the prior preaching of the eternal gospel (14:6).[13]

This reaping of a grain harvest, in verses 14–16, is already found in the Hebrew Scriptures referring to the final gathering of faithful servants (Isa. 27:12–13; Hos. 6:11; cf. Matt. 3:12; Mark 4:26–28; 13:26–27; Luke 10:2; John 4:35–38), though there are other passages that combine the righteous and unrighteous in the same harvest scene. Strangely, however, an angel coming from the temple instructs the Son of Man when he is to commence his mission. Why would Revelation have an angel instruct the Messiah — Christ — concerning his actions? Let us not forget that Jesus himself had once said that only the Father, not the angels or even the Son, knew the "hour" (Rev. 14:15, NRSV) of the end (Mark 13:32). And the angel has come directly from the temple, the dwelling of God. Who has sent the word — the angel or a much higher authority?

That this is the harvest of the righteous might also be hinted at by the sickle that swings "over [Gk. *epi*] the earth" (v. 16), whereas in the following vision (vv. 17–20), which we believe is the harvest of the ungodly, the angel is putting his sickle "into [Gk. *eis*] the earth" (v. 19).[14] This is only one of many things in Revelation that go "into" the earth. And generally they are divine judgments or have a similar effect (8:5; 9:1; 12:4; 16:1; etc.; cf. 5:6 is the first such event). M. Robert Mulholland suggests, and correctly so, that these "uses of 'into' the earth can be seen as the consequences of the presence of God in the rebellious order" (255). Indeed, the first two trumpet judgments are events that strike into (Gk. *eis*) the earth and the sea. Perhaps these trumpets are meant to be special precursors of the end, presaging the judgment of all the world (earth and sea), that is, episodes of death and ecodisaster in which flashes and foreshadowings of the future are revealed.

However, if we have understood 14:14–16 correctly, then this event is Revelation's description of what Jesus had once pledged:

> Immediately *after the distress* of those days ... the sign of the Son of Man will appear in the sky, and all the nations of the earth will mourn. They will see the Son of Man coming on the clouds of the sky, with power and great glory. And he will send his angels with a loud trumpet

call, and they will gather his elect from the four winds, from one end of the heavens to the other. (Matt. 24:29–31, emphasis added)

This is one of those passages where one can observe that while some biblical texts unmistakably envisage the second coming *after* the tribulation period, there are none that with equal clarity place it *before*.

14:17–20 • The flip side of these final events is less wholesome, for the harvest of the vineyard and the treading of the winepress are a frequent image of God's righteous fury unleashed against the rebellious (Isa. 63:1–6; Lam. 1:15; Joel 3:13; Mal. 4:3; Mark 4:29). It is often asked what the angel "who had charge of the fire" has to do with the scene; he seems rather extraneous. His arrival "from the altar," however, should remind us what is going on there. At the altar, the martyrs and saints are praying for justice (6:9–10; 8:3–5); they too have a vested interest in this harvest. But since this is the harvest of the dark side, this angel's presence is fully apropos, for eventually these clusters of humanity will be consigned to "the fiery lake of burning sulfur" (19:20; 20:14–15). Already, proprietary rights are being asserted.

All this suffering is "*outside* the city." Perhaps this is to remind us which city John is referring to. Weeping and wailing are to be the norm inside great Babylon (18:9,11,19), but there is to be no mourning in the city of God (7:17; 21:4; cf. Isa. 25:8). Nor should we forget that Jesus also suffered "outside the city" (Heb. 13:11–13) or that his cross, too, was a winepress of divine wrath against sin. We all stand outside some city. Either we stand under the cross of Christ, where his life was poured out to wash us from our sins, or we stand in the winepress of divine wrath on our own and pour out our own life's blood for our own sins. All participate in one of these two judgments. Both events take place outside the city (22:15); the first is outside the earthly city; the second, outside the heavenly. Thus, all must choose the city they are willing to stand and forever remain "outside."

The grisly volume of blood John sees running from the winepress would seem to echo, in hyperbolic fashion, Jesus' comment that "wide is the gate and broad is the road that leads to destruction, and many enter through it" (Matt. 7:13). The distance of the flow, literally "1,600 stadia" (about 180 miles), is approximately the length of the Holy Land. Though perhaps more importantly, 1,600 is a square number. It is the square of "four," the earth's number (7:1; 8:1; 20:8), multiplied by the square of "ten," a number of completion

(5:11; 20:6), a fitting symbol for the harvest of the inhabitants of the earth.[15]

The repulsive grotesquerie of unimaginable horror found in these scenes is a vivid and pictorial answer to a familiar question that John must have heard often: "Is it really so terrible to give mere lip service to the emperor and play little games of worship at Caesar's shrine?" These images are the consequences and reverberations of 14:9–11, that is, the "eternal gospel" rejected. Furthermore, they remind that accommodation to the System has serious consequences, indeed.

Just now, these scenes of the consummation are but cameo appearances meant to fill out John's three-chapter synopsis (chaps. 12–14) of the big picture. Both of these harvest scenes will be played out with greater detail in the final panorama of chapters 19–22. John will say, then, that there is something even more awful than death, for death is what Christians were risking as the price of nonparticipation; in fact, there is a death beyond death, the second death that is to be more feared than anything on earth (cf. Matt. 10:28).

Now, in summary, we must comprehend the whole panoramic overview presented in chapters 12–14. It is not too much to say that they represent a boiled-down, encapsulated version of the entire book. Moreover, these three chapters are meant to be transparencies through which every period of church history sees itself playing out the roles depicted. Where is the woman who is seeking to bring Jesus to life *today?* How can the sustaining wilderness of her deliverance be entered? Under what guises do the two beasts go on lumbering through our world? Can their mark be seen among us? In what ways does the angelic announcement of the eternal gospel make itself known in our world? How do the three types of Christian churches (the good, the bad, and the compromised/acculturated) experience these chapters and respond to such questions? Through these issues, chapters 12 (past), 13 (present), and 14 (future) are revealed as the "Rosetta vision" of the Revelation. They are the surveyor's level through which we gain perspective on the lay of this book's difficult but amazing apocalyptic landscape.

Notes

1. "John saw the three women in his visions in the same three roles in which men in virtually every culture perceive the women in their lives — as mother (chap. 12), as prostitute or temptress (chap. 17), and as bride, or wife (chap. 21)" (Michaels, *Interpreting the Book of Revelation*, 137–38).

2. Cf. Dan. 10:13; 12:1; Jude 9; and the apocalyptic literature known as 1 Enoch 90:14; Testament of Daniel 6:2.

3. Walter Brueggemann has aptly defined the essence of prophecy: "The task of prophetic ministry is to nurture, nourish, and evoke a consciousness and perception alternative to the consciousness and perception of the dominant culture around us" (13). I recommend this book as supplemental reading.

4. In other apocalyptic books related beasts are noted. In 1 Enoch, two monsters are described: Leviathan, who dwells in the great ocean abyss, and Behemoth, who is cast into "the dry land of the wilderness" (60:7–8). A similar report is found in 2 Esdras 6:49–52, but it is 2 Baruch 29:4 that traces their origin to the fifth day of creation and their destiny to play a role in the end of history. It was not difficult, then, for John to forge these two well-known mythical creatures into symbols of political and religious functions in his own day (Beasley-Murray, *Book of Revelation*, 215–16).

5. If the three-and-a-half-year time period stands for the church age between Pentecost (the birthday of the church) and the Parousia (the second coming of Christ), then Michael Wilcock has proposed the manner in which it might have been determined: "If it was reckoned that something over three years elapsed between his baptism and his ascension, then 'three and a bit years,' or three and a half years, would be an excellent symbol for the period between the church's 'baptism' at Pentecost and her 'ascension' to meet the Lord when he returns" (130).

6. Certificates were even issued to those who had satisfied this requisite of civic duty. One such certificate is cited by J. Massyngberde Ford, 215.

7. For a larger discussion of this phenomenon, see Ford, 225–27.

8. "It [Babylon the Great] is a symbol for the spirit of godlessness which in every age lures men away from the worship of the Creator. It is the final manifestation of secular humanism in its attempt to destroy the remaining vestiges of true religion. Society set free from God is its own worst enemy" (Mounce, *Book of Revelation*, 274).

9. Among those who hold biblical descriptions of hell to be metaphorical rather than literal are Carl F. H. Henry, Kenneth Kantzer, C. S. Lewis, Leon Morris, J. I. Packer, and Ronald Youngblood.

10. This would seem to be clear from the juxtaposition of two concepts in Jude, where in verse 7 this eternal fate is described as "eternal fire" and in verse 13 it is "deepest darkness" (NRSV). Certainly these two realities are not meant in the normal range of what we would call literal experience. Jesus often refers to hell in the same terms, fire and darkness. Given the wide range of metaphorical uses of both "fire" and "darkness" in first-century Jewish literature, Jesus and Jude are probably using language that is meant to describe an ultimately serious and awful fate for the unrepentant but one that may not involve literal fire or darkness (see Crockett, 43–91).

11. This is the second beatitude of the seven found in Revelation: 1:3; 14:13; 16:15; 19:9; 20:6; 22:7,14. They might themselves, when viewed from

within the context of Revelation, serve as a series of seven challenging devotionals.

12. This is the view of Austin Farrer (167), J. M. Ford (238–39), George Ladd (*Commentary on the Revelation*, 200), M. Robert Mulholland Jr. (251–56), Mathias Rissi (9–10), Henry Barclay Swete (186), and Michael Wilcock (136).

13. An analogous passage in which two harvests affect the godly and ungodly respectively is found in 2 Esdras 4:28–32.

14. The NIV and the NRSV both miss this distinction, translating these two contrasting phrases by the same "swung his sickle over/on the earth" (vv. 16,19).

15. Vernard Eller reports the bizarre calculation of one clever wit who figured the amount of blood that could be recovered from an average human and divided it into a puddle of blood two hundred miles in radius and deep as a horse's bridle: "Even if everyone went through the press of wrath, the cumulative population of the world still has not been nearly enough to provide the juice. It's a bloody shame" (144)!

Chapter 16

THE BOWLS OF
FINAL JUDGMENT

Rev. 15:1–16:21

Now that John has completed the Rosetta panorama that took us from the birth of the Messiah to his climactic return as end-time harvester, John will begin his moving portrayal of history's culmination. The continuation of the divine judgments throughout the church age, previously viewed in the seals and trumpets of chapters 6–7 and 8–11, promptly picks up with the bowl judgments. In this final depiction of the future of the world System, the ancient images of the Exodus from Egypt are again the transparencies through which we are asked to view reality.

An even greater exodus is presently in progress; it will conclude God's grand program for freeing his people from bondage to the fallen world and its evil System. Thus do the bowls pour forth the message, "This world has no future." Resistance to the divine will at the end of history will prove just as futile as was Pharaoh's at the beginning. And just as surely, God will bring that final defiance to its appointed catastrophic end.

A lesson we must never forget in Revelation is to be wary of our tendency toward wooden literalism. This is clearly the case in the bowl series. In these chapters, we cannot force words to mean merely what they say; we must allow them to mean what they mean, not less and certainly not more. John is not snapping 35 mm slides but developing the essence of reality through the liquescent poetry of impressionistic art. The outlines might be colored in by a great many different hues from age to age, yet the outline remains permanently true. The language of the bowls, we cannot overemphasize, is apocalyptic symbolism. Though not real themselves, these symbols really do stand for something. Thus, it is their meaning and application that are of paramount importance.

Chapter 15

15:1–4 • Here begins the concluding denouement, the last opening curtain in the story of creation. From here to the end of the book, terminal realities are being viewed. They are the very last "because with them God's wrath is completed." Thus begins the final era of reality beyond which there are no further historical repercussions.

In good doxologic fashion, an end-time chorus begins the final salvos of judgment. This scene functions similarly to the vision of the heavenly multitude in the intermission between the sixth and seventh seals (7:9–17). Despite the bowls of horror about to be revealed, followers of the Lamb enjoy an ultimate protection and a destiny determined by divine love. Appropriately, those who follow the Lamb are standing beside the sea, as Moses and the people of Israel were when they sang the first great victory song. But, remember, the Hebrews were on the far side, the victorious side, when they lifted their voices in praise of God's victory over Pharaoh. This is the sea, a new spiritual Red Sea of evil, that we must all cross over if we ever hope to sing in that heavenly choir of the redeemed. Those who seek to tread water or merely float on the surface buoyed by its pestilential decay will never find the safety of that far shore, where the redeemed are joyously singing.

Compare this hymn of verses 3–4 with the "Song of Moses." Found in Exodus 15, Moses' song is a magnificent paean of praise to the glorious triumph of God over Pharaoh's army, and it is the original template of the new song that echoes through the corridors of glory, sung by those who are ever freed from the pharaohs of this world and their continuing systems of human bondage.

15:5–8 • Again, as in the beginning with Moses, there is also a new tabernacle, here called "the tabernacle of Testimony." From this place of worship and divine fellowship come the seven angels who possess the final judgments of God on the new pharaoh's System.[1] Remember, however, the purpose of these bowls is to free those who seek political/religious asylum in the heavenly temple. That is the point in chapter 15; chapter 16 will portray this final emancipatory exodus from the viewpoint of the beast's kingdom, for preceding the final entry into the temple, a final cleansing of earth is mandatory. "No one could enter the temple," that is, the eternal heavenly bliss, until the bowls and their plagues are concluded; then will come the new heaven, new earth, and New Jerusalem, eternally cleansed of polluting, sinful rebellion. It is this very process of cleansing that all the power of the great Babylon is resisting.

The "seven golden bowls" are derived largely from the text of Isaiah 51:17, 22:

> Awake, awake!
>   Rise up, O Jerusalem,
> you who have drunk from the hand of the LORD
>   the cup of his wrath,
> you who have drained to its dregs
>   the goblet [NRSV: "bowl"] that makes men stagger.
> . . . .
> This is what your Sovereign LORD says,
>   your God, who defends his people:
> "See, I have taken out of your hand
>   the cup that made you stagger;
> from that cup, the goblet [NRSV: "bowl"] of my wrath,
>   you will never drink again."

In both verses, there is an interplay between the words *cup* and *goblet* (NRSV: "bowl"), indicating their essential identity. *Phialē*, the Greek word John has used, is therefore sometimes translated as "cup," "vial" (KJV), or "bowl" (RSV, NRSV, NIV), but they all evidence a concept of which the Hebrew prophets spoke often, the cup of God's wrath (Jer. 25:15–17; Ezek. 23:31–35; Hab. 2:15–16). John has already noted that similar containers hold the prayers of the saints (5:8), and it might be instructive to remember that "cups" is the word used to designate the wick receptacles on the original menorah described in Exodus 25:31–35. John is clearly hinting that the churches and the prayers of God's people figure mightily in God's execution of final judgment. John will conclude his use of this symbol in Revelation 16:19, where great Babylon is ultimately made to drink and experience the cup of God's righteous fury.

Chapter 16

16:1 • In general, it seems that this rather quick (one-chapter) run-through of the seven bowls is accomplished with less intensity and significance than either the seals (over two chapters) or trumpets (four chapters). However, the bowls do maintain the same structure as the preceding series. They are divided into a group of four plagues and then three more dealing specifically with the beast's kingdom. Moreover, this chapter also maintains an intermission at verse 15, now found ever so briefly between the sixth and seventh components of the series. And the bowls also conclude at the Day of Judgment with the dissolution of the old creation. In these ways, we are told that this group of plagues is yet another description of the church age that comes to an end with the return of Christ. Furthermore, chapter 16 is something of an interpretive expansion of Paul's dire comment: "All this is evidence that God's judgment is right.... God is just: He will pay back trouble to those who trouble you.... They will be punished with everlasting destruction" (2 Thess. 1:5–10).

Nevertheless, even if the bowls do not carry quite as much concise impact as the other series, we must still ask the question, What is their message concerning the battle with the beast and the way in which the age will develop? Let's be looking for that meaning and intent of the bowls as we go through the chapter. What does it add to our understanding of what the church and its enemies face?

16:2 • Quite obviously the first bowl replicates plague six in Egypt by which the Egyptians were afflicted with loathsome boils (Exod. 9:8–12; cf. Deut. 28:35). In other words, just as those who stood with Pharaoh in his manipulation and oppression of the Hebrews suffered physical ailments, so the beast and its cult will also suffer bodily maladies for their idolatrous commitment to the System and abuse of the faithful.

John's technique of apocalyptic writing is revealed here as something akin to "symbolic parables." The "painful sores" may echo or expand on the torturous sting of the demonic locusts and its resultant death wish in 9:4–6. Together they represent the spiritual and physical wounds incurred in rebellious warfare against the King of kings. The law of reciprocity is at work here. Those who have elected to receive one "mark" are now rewarded with its consequence, the corresponding trademarks of "ugly and painful sores." Concerning this bowl, which is similar to trumpet five, Leon Morris wisely observes that "there are some evils that afflict those who give themselves over to wickedness but do not affect other people" (187). This is an insight into Christian life and a spiritual lifestyle that many would gladly "Amen."

16:3 • The first plague in Egypt, the Nile becoming blood (Exod. 7:14–24), is now clearly remembered and will continue to be developed in the third angel's bowl. The term *sea* represents the same word found in 18:17,21, where the commercial base of the beast's domain is judged and this bowl is further defined. Here is the Exodus event "writ large," for this sea stands for the Mediterranean and the other waters of the world known to seafarers. The second bowl announces economic death, for now creation itself, here represented by the waters, fights back against the ravages and depravations of a doomed humanity (cf. Rom. 8:20). Again, reciprocity is involved, for those who would deny the righteous access to buying and selling (13:17) will ultimately be so denied themselves.

16:4 – 7 • Suddenly it becomes clear why the first Egyptian plague has become the basis for two bowl judgments. The concept of "blood" connects the two scenes. Because the kingdom of the beast has spilled the blood of all the righteous dead (cf. 18:24), God now turns the tables and forces that same kingdom to taste the very terror it has been dishing out. Reciprocity is still to the fore, and the response of the altar is meant to remind us that a special group is to be found under its shadow (6:9–10; cf. 8:3–5). Their concern with the events of this tableau is obvious and reminds us of the psalmist's prayer:

> Pay back into the laps of our neighbors seven times
>   the reproach they have hurled at you, O LORD.
> Then we your people, the sheep of your pasture,
>   will praise you forever;
> from generation to generation
>   we will recount your praise.
>
> — Psalm 79:12–13

In light of the common desire to domesticate and tame the divine nature, remaking God in our own image, Robert Mounce's observation is quite appropriate: "All caricatures of God which ignore his intense hatred of sin reveal more about man than about God" (*Book of Revelation*, 295).

Unlike the more distant "sea" mentioned in bowl two, here rivers and springs stand for the daily needs and routines by which people nurture their workaday lives. Hence, given the people's previous actions and failure to repent, the discomfort produced by this plague is amply deserved; it is a judgment fully "true and just": "The nations were angry; / and your wrath has come. / The time has come for... / destroying those who destroy the earth" (11:18). So near is that time that John again (cf. 11:17) drops the third element of his original description of God (i.e., "who is to come"; 1:4,8) when he describes the Holy One ("who are and who were").

Just the opposite, however, is the promised fate of the just: "To him who is thirsty I will give to drink without cost from the spring of the water of life" (21:6), for "the Lamb at the center of the throne will be their shepherd; / he will lead them to springs of living water" (7:17), which emanate from the eternal throne of God and are as "clear as crystal" (22:1). Given the comment in John 7:37–39, the depiction of the throne in Revelation 22:1-2 may well be Trinitarian in nature. If so, the "water of life" is John's shorthand for the spiritually invigorating presence of the Holy Spirit.

16:8 – 9 • Now John utilizes an interesting variation on the theme of the ninth Egyptian plague (Exod. 10:21-23). For Moses, the power of God was reflected in the darkness that fell upon Pharaoh's land (cf. bowl five), but in this final manifestation of the judgment just the reverse takes place, and the beast's realm is scorched by an overabundance of the sun's power. "People" and "they," that is, those who are scorched by this plague, refer back to "the earth" in verse 1, which in turn is further defined by "the people who had the mark of the beast and worshiped his image" in verse 2. For those who are bound for the lake of fire, this scorching is but a prologue to a blistering future (20:14–15; 21:8).

Verse 9 represents the first of two comments indicating that part of the divine intent behind these fearsome disasters is to bring about repentance and redemption (see also v. 11; cf. v. 21). By means of this remark, John assumes a logical relationship between these plagues and an expected, normal response of remorse and resultant contrition. He reminds us that people are not judged by God; they judge themselves when they presume to condemn God. Their curse uttered at heaven comes full circle and ends by condemning themselves.

In this regard, compare the blessedness of those who are expressly sheltered from the scorching sun by God and the Lamb in 7:15-17. Behind this ancient symbolism is the image of God as a "Rock" in the Hebrew Scriptures (Deut. 32:4,15,18; 1 Sam. 2:2; 2 Sam. 22:2-3; Ps. 31:3; 61:2-3; Isa. 32:2). In ancient Israel, rocks were shelters from the oppressive heat of the Middle Eastern sun. In their shadows, tender shoots and sprigs could find just enough protection to maintain life. By extension, the Lord who was the "Rock of his people" provided such sanctuary and similar protection.

Now a change of direction takes place between the first four and last three bowls. The former, though secondarily affecting people, were aimed most directly at nature; the latter strike precisely at the spiritual and political realm of the beast. The ultimate supernatural forces who form the backdrop of the story ("the throne of the beast" in v. 10; "three evil spirits" in v. 13; and "the great city" in v. 19) are now assaulted, and those realities that had enslaved humanity will be overwhelmed and robbed of their own autonomy.

16:10 – 11 • As the bloody plague on the Nile River was given a two-part exposition, so now the darkness "that can be felt" (Exod. 10:21) is similarly treated. God is capable of using light to both singe and scorch or unmask and reveal the abyss of darkness, a darkness of soul so severe that it results in both spiritual ("pains" are subjective) and physical ("sores" are objective) disorders. Is it merely an accident that the smoke from the bottomless pit, noted in trumpet five, also darkens the sun and the air (9:2)? It seems that there are genuine interactions between these series of judgments, indicating their common subject. The darkness engendered by this bowl is very similar in meaning to the torture of the locust hordes viewed in the fifth trumpet. Both are the kinds of torment that afflict only those who do not bear the seal of God.

G. B. Caird suggests that this "darkness" generates a spiritual anguish — "the doubts, suspicions, terrors, and hysteria" — not unlike that which attended the day when "the lights went out all over the empire," and the spiritual misery depicted here is meant to describe the state of mind of "its worshipers, whose deepest agony is to know that they are wholly identified with it in its fall" (205). The eclipse of its power is the demise of their world.

For the second time, John comments on the lack of proper human reaction — *repentance* — to the divine activity. We should not forget that even here there is an interaction with the seven churches. In Thyatira, Jezebel and her followers have been warned to repent on threat of dire consequences (2:20–23). The destiny of that entire church also hangs on its proper response to the darkness spawned by the false prophetess. On the other hand, illumination is one of the ultimate blessings of those who do repent (21:23; 22:5). Those who stand with the Lamb find the truth and the one who said, "I am the light of the world. Whoever follows me will never walk in darkness, but will have the light of life" (John 8:12; cf. John 1:4–5; 3:2; 13:30). No one *must* experience these plagues, and no one's future is beyond hope, not even Jezebel's. The purpose behind the depiction of such awful events is to prod people into changing their ways so they might be exempted from the fate of the anti-God forces. All must choose whether they will stand with the Lamb on Mount Zion, beside the sea of glass, or suffer the overthrow of the kingdom of the beast.

16:12 • Another genuine parallel is forged here between the sixth trumpet (9:14) and the sixth bowl. While there is a clear bond between these two series, a discrete message is also present. The Roman Empire had an almost pathological fear of Parthian hordes descending from the East and devouring Latin civilization. The *Nero Redivivus* legend anticipated that he would vengefully lead those hostile legions against his own people. John is using these anxieties to project a day when all the alarm bells people have ever feared will go off at once, and "the kings from the East" will arrive. However, this is not just for the future. It is also true of every time, as W. Hendricksen understands so well: "Whenever in history the wicked fail to repent in answer to the initial and partial manifestation of God's anger in judgments, the *final* effusion of wrath follows" (in Morris, 181). But where repentance is the response, history can also be changed.

16:13–14 • Foul spirits who go forth to deceive earth's leaders by signs and wonders sound very much like the false messiahs and prophets predicted by Jesus as one of the signs of the end (Matt. 24:4–5,23–26). In this scene, though, John portrays these counterfeit parsons as widemouthed, croaking "frogs" (cf. Exod. 8:3; 1 Kings 22:20–23). Emanating from the unholy trinity of evil, these "Three Stooges of the Apocalypse" seem to represent the propaganda ministry of the beast's System, and their message is a dire one indeed: "Prepare for battle with the Almighty!" Though, of course, they would not agree that God is almighty — that is John's term — for their System would seem to be the only sovereign, self-authenticating System, the dominant context of life that must prevail over all unseen realities.

16:15 • However brief and attenuated, here is the expected parenthesis (most versions, though not the NIV, have literally inserted one) between the sixth and seventh bowls. On behalf of those who are sealed against eternal loss, destined for heaven (first intermission in Rev. 7), and called to the stupendous mission of proclaiming the gospel in the midst of the beast's kingdom (second intermission in Rev. 10–11), John now proclaims the hope, present in every generation of the church's pilgrimage, of the near return of her Lord. This glorious expectation was earlier proclaimed by Paul in 1 Thessalonians 4:16–18:

> For the Lord himself will come down from heaven, with a loud command, with the voice of the archangel and with the trumpet call of God, and the dead in Christ will rise first. After that, we who are still alive and are left will be caught up together with them in the clouds to meet the Lord in the air. And so we will be with the Lord forever. Therefore encourage each other with these words.

Paul described this coming of the Lord as one "like a thief in the night," which necessitated Christians to "be alert" (1 Thess. 5:2,6; cf. Matt. 24:42–44; 2 Pet. 3:10; Rev. 3:3). "Naked" and "exposed" refer to life stripped of the "fine linen, bright and clean" that stands for "the righteous acts of the saints" (19:8). All generations of believers have joyously longed for this blessed hope of the church and been energized by its ever-present prospect. Here is the third of the seven beatitudes in the Revelation.[2]

This passage certainly renders difficult, if not impossible, the attempt to speak of a secret, thief-like rapture of the church at the beginning of chapter 4. Rather, John would seem to be suggesting that this blessed hope of the thief in the night had not yet occurred but now is ever more pressing and imminent. It also indicates that he does not expect all Christians to be martyred at any one time in history (cf. 2:7,10; 3:4,10,20; 11:4; 21:27; see Caird, 32–34, 209).

16:16 • After the intrusion of verse 15, John returns to the croaking frogs of the System ("they gathered"; v. 16). And we can be sure there is more to their "signs" than mere stunts of magic. The effect of their feats is to draw the leaders and people of earth into ever greater and more dramatic confrontation with the King of kings.

Armageddon is the combination of two Hebrew words: *har,* "hill" or "mountain," and *Megiddo,* a town in northern Israel that guarded a vital valley pointing like a dagger into the heart of the nation. The plains of Esdraelon constitute the valley guarded by the ancient town. This valley was a prime invasion route and site of many decisive battles in which the fate of the nation was decided more than once (Judg. 5:19; 2 Kings 9; 23:29; 2 Chron. 35:22). Beyond our focus on Israel, significant conflicts have been fought here from c. 1468 B.C., when Pharaoh Tuthmosis III attacked and besieged Megiddo from the south (often called "the first recorded battle in history"; Davies, 37), to General Allenby's campaigns in the First World War. Throughout history, the name *Megiddo* has been more or less synonymous with the blight of warfare. It is as if John were writing to us and suggesting that there will be one final and climactic Battle of Yorktown, Gettysburg, or the Bulge. However, while there is literally no place on the map that is designated "Armageddon," the fortress city of Megiddo stood high on a tell, or mound, on top of earlier cities built on the same site. This could be the *har,* or "Mount Megiddo," of which John speaks.

One can still go to the site of Megiddo and stand looking to the east at a broad panorama of fertile farmland. Perhaps John, too, had done this at some time. If so, he could have seen the plains around Mount Gilboa, where Saul, Israel's first king, was slain by the Philistines (1 Sam. 31).[3] But the last king of true Israel, John foresees, will reverse the tide of history and emerge triumphant from this valley of death and its last dramatic challenge to the kingdom of God. In such a highly symbolic book, however, we need to hear those commentators who believe that "Armageddon" has chiefly a symbolic meaning. The name may well stand more for an eschatological *event* than a *place*. The event referred to, and appropriately by the reference to Megiddo, is "the last resistance of anti-god forces prior to the kingdom of Christ."[4]

John will dramatize the details of this confrontation more completely in chapter 19, where we will confront a battle that will be initiated by a white-horsed rider called "Faithful and True." In righteousness, he "judges and makes war" (19:11). Then a prior topic will also come to closure. Earlier we were told that no "place" was found for the dragon in heaven (12:8); soon there will also be no place on earth.

16:17–18 • The battle of Armageddon is concluded with the events of the seventh, and final, bowl. Cataclysmic disruption takes place as the throne thunders its final word on the story of history. Using all the most terrifying forces at his disposal, a righteous Creator roars, "It is done!" But are we also meant to remember the comparable phrase in John 19:30 (the only Gospel reporting it), where Jesus on the cross utters the climactic, "It is finished"?[5] There, after all, is where D-day was won and V-day made possible. Here, it is, not "the throne of the beast" (v. 10), but the throne in the temple that has the last word.

16:19–21 • Three zones of destruction are noted; they are, nevertheless, in essence the same hideous reality. The "great city" and its individualized historical manifestations, that is, "the cities of the nations," are "Babylon the Great." The great city comprehends and encapsulates the history of all that stands proudly recalcitrant to the will of God; it is the true eschatological heir of the first city built by the first murderer — Cain (Gen. 4:17).[6]

However, more than just human rebellion is swept away in this great cataclysm. All of nature is affected; everything fixed and seemingly unalterable is suddenly undone. The whole standard frame of reference is fractured. All the time-honored symbols of stability (e.g., bastions of permanence in the seas [islands]) are removed. Similar elements on land (mountains) vanish, and the sky suddenly rains death (a final reference to the original Exodus events; Exod. 9:18–19; cf. Isa. 28:17). All that could be counted on as foundational to a structured existence dramatically dissolves into chaos. Still, the rebellion is not stanched, for the cursing continues. Where all of this ends will be revealed in chapter 20. There, a fitting conclusion to the story of spiritual anarchy is finally put forward. A revealing comment on bowl seven is found in Hebrews 12:26–29:

> "Once more I will shake not only the earth but also the heavens." The words "once more" indicate the removing of what can be shaken — that is, created things — so that what cannot be shaken may remain. Therefore, since we are receiving a kingdom that cannot be shaken,

let us be thankful, and so worship God acceptably with reverence and awe, for our "God is a consuming fire."

The bowls, then, extend the description of the church age toward its outer limits. They focus more clearly on how the seal and trumpet judgments conclude in *total* catastrophe and the absolute breakdown of all that the System has come to think of as unshakable. The Exodus motif stands boldly to the fore because it was a prime example of God's using creational forces to do the divine will. Here, too, nature figures prominently in the bowl scenario, and we are reminded that once before "from the heavens the stars fought, / from their courses they fought against Sisera. / The river Kishon swept them away" (Judg. 5:20–21). And the Jewish book Wisdom of Solomon, picking up on this theme, comments: "The Lord will ... arm all creation to repel his enemies; ... and creation will join with him to fight against his frenzied foes" (5:17,20, NRSV).[7] The bowls highlight the ecological role nature plays in God's continuing struggle with the moral pollution rampant in his universe.

Another feature dramatized in this series is the ever-mounting toll imposed on creation by the ongoing battle for the cosmos. This is illustrated most obviously through the progression of the fractions. Whereas the seals spoke of a destruction extending to one-fourth of humankind (6:8) and the trumpets affected one-third of creation, including people (8:7,9–10,12; 9:18), the bowls involve totality. Their judgments are coextensive with all rebellious existence (16:2–4,8,10,14). Therefore, the *theology of the fractions* suggests that as the conflict moves along and evolves, things will inevitably become worse before they ultimately get better. The end of the age will primarily experience the same spiritual warfare the church always has, but finally at a terminal level.

Notes

1. M. Robert Mulholland concludes that these seven angels are synonymous with the seven angels of the churches. "The angels represent the church," he writes, "that witnesses to the presence of God in the world through its righteous acts" (262).

2. See Chapter 15, note 11.

3. Another theory why Armageddon was chosen as the site for the last confrontation between the people of God and demonic forces is to avenge the death of King Josiah at the hands of Pharaoh Necho (2 Kings 23:29–30; see Davies, 105). Vengeance for the wrong done this second David is required

because "before him there was no king like him, who turned to the LORD with all his heart, with all his soul, and with all his might, according to all the law of Moses; nor did any like him arise after him" (2 Kings 23:25).

4. Beasley-Murray, *Book of Revelation*, 246. For similar views, see also Ladd, *Commentary on the Revelation*, 216; Mounce, *Book of Revelation*, 302; and Wall, 200–201.

5. Eugenio Corsini takes the view that the seventh bowl is an allegory for the death of Jesus and notes several correspondences between the description of events at Calvary and those related here (305–6). Cf. Mulholland, who also suggests that "the seventh bowl is an image of the finality of the slaying of the Lamb as God's response to the rebellious order" (273). He means that the symbolism of the seventh bowl is actually about the definitive and absolutely decisive victory over the world/System/beast won on Golgotha's hill.

6. The great city "stands for civilized man, man in organized community but man ordering his affairs apart from God. It symbolizes the pride of human achievement, the godlessness of those who put their trust in man" (Morris, 195).

7. Caird (202) remarks that the apocryphal Wisdom of Solomon, written only about one century before Revelation, enunciates three principles of divine providence: Wisd. of Sol. 5:17 (the whole creation is God's weapon); 11:5–13 (the means of punishing enemies are blessings to the righteous), and 11:16 (the mode of human sin is also the means of its punishment). Revelation would fully agree!

Chapter 17

THE EXODUS
FROM GREAT BABYLON

Rev. 18:1–24

In Revelation 17, which we considered in chapter 8 so that we would know the identity of the enemy at war with the seven churches, John beheld the face of the chameleon dragon that cloaked itself in the beast and prostitute of his day. As that monster manifested itself through the socioeconomic structures of the first century, it emerged camouflaged in the glory of Rome, the eternal city, and its vast and vaunted empire before which the whole world trembled. Was there ever a grander incarnation of the dragon's true being? Here is John's basic model of the beast. It is Rome, the very transparency through which we are to discern our world.

Unfortunately, this identification of the beast with Rome produces one specific problem for us — an apparent contradiction. What are we to make of Paul's admonition that Christians be subject to the political authorities and not resist the state (Rom. 13:1–6)? Furthermore, writing this to the church at Rome, Paul is certainly advocating this approach to Roman rule itself. In short, what has Romans 13 to do with Revelation 13 (and 17)? The answer is quite simple! When Paul spoke of the Christian's duties to the state, he was speaking under conditions very different from those in the last decade of the first century. In Paul's day, Rome was generally upholding *law and order,* its divinely appointed duty (Rom. 13:3–4), but by John's day, it had forfeited this position as "God's servant" when it began to oppose and oppress God's people, proclaiming its own divinity. Under these changed circumstances, Paul presumably would have agreed with John's assessment in Revelation 13, namely, that the state had become a renegade beast. Interestingly, then, there are two chapter 13s on this subject, Romans and Revelation. In one, the state is "God's servant" (Rom. 13:4), and in the other, it is "a beast" (Rev. 13:1).

Now, in Revelation 18, John moves on to another subject of concern, which is an extension of the bowls. Here we are invited to preview the ultimate overthrow of the beast's System that has oppressed the church throughout the book. This chapter will rip off the mask of glamorous respectability (the whorish exterior) behind which a hideously repulsive visage hides (the beast). John sees only a snarled tangle of illicit illusions once the beast is stripped of its cloak of lying wonders and its luxurious façade, but he also sees its certain future: "Fallen! Fallen" is this foul haunt of demons, destined to be "consumed by fire" (v. 8; cf. vv. 9,18; 19:3). This scene is meant as a great anticipatory hope for those who have felt the dragon's own fiery breath, for they are to be comforted by the knowledge that there is a day when the monster and its multiform incarnations will be destroyed root and branch. But also this chapter begs us to ask, Where does that ancient shape-shifter lurk, shrouded in our world of social and political realities?[1]

The panoramic vision of the great city's destruction found in chapter 18 emanates from a triangulation whose base points of projection rest in chapters 4 and 5. There the eternal rule and holiness of God are the twin peaks from whose juridical perspective this chapter must inevitably emerge. John is also interested, however, in the fate of the seven churches in this titanic collapse of the World System. In keeping with the theme of the bowls, Revelation continues the Exodus motif. The church still plays the ongoing role of ancient Israel and is being liberated by redemptive forces that the great city experiences as world-destroying plagues.

18:1–3 • This dirge over the great city's fall represents a collection of passages drawn out of various taunt songs, laments, and dreary dirges pronounced over many enemy cities that finally had been destroyed (Isa. 13:19–22; 23:1–16; 34:11–15; 47:7–9; Jer. 50:39; 51:37; Zeph. 2:14–15). The great city is merely the last, summary edition of all those insurgent spiritual forces God has been overpowering throughout history.

A proleptic announcement foreshadowing the events of this chapter — "Fallen! Fallen is Babylon the Great!" — hangs forebodingly over its landscape, for as John disrobes her luxuriant beauty, the great prostitute will be exposed, and the truth will be revealed about her economic, political, and religious life.[2] Then we shall see that which animates the core of her rotting carcass, for she represents every fiendish, odious, vile, perverse, and depraved entity ever spawned by the pit (cf. Isa. 13:20–22).

Kings and the enterprises of multinational entities exploiting world commerce have corrupted the human community, writes John, because they have all shared the whore's bed.[3] Her radiance is a sham, a mockery of reality, devoid of any eternal significance; it represents life lived autonomously without reference to and in rebellion against the truth of God. Only one future is imaginable for the prostitute who is the great city (17:18) and also for great Babylon (18:10,21); it is called by Paul "the *wrath* of God . . . revealed from heaven against . . . men who *suppress the truth* by their wickedness" (Rom. 1:18, emphasis added). And she is plainly a supreme truth-suppressor who stifles divine reality and naturally attracts the wrath of the true God. God has revealed the divine truth in the Apocalypse (19:9; 21:5; 22:6), a truth emanating from the "true" one (3:7), that is, the "true witness" (3:14) whose ways are true (15:3), as are God's judgments (16:7; 19:9), and who is always the true avenger of the people of God against this whoring reality (6:10; 19:11).

18:4–5 • It is difficult, if not impossible, to read this passage and not hear the straightforward reference to the Exodus — "Come out of her, my people." It is a phrase that echoes down the long corridor of the divine dealings with God's beloved people (cf. Exod. 3:7–10; 5:1; Isa. 48:20–21; 52:11–12; Jer. 50:8; 51:6–10; 2 Cor. 6:17–18). Appropriately, Revelation invites us to view the eschatological judgment of the world System through the metaphors and ancient experience of the Exodus, for the Exodus of God's people from Egypt was holy history's first and original model of a divine judgment that could at once reprobate (those who reject God's call) or redeem (those who respond). That type of double-edged judgment is exactly what the final day is all about.

"Come out of her, my people" is Revelation's counterpart to Jesus' high priestly prayer:

> For they are not of the world any more than I am of the world. My prayer is not that you take them out of the world but that you protect them from the evil one. They are not of the world, even as I am not of it. (John 17:14–16)

Jesus was deeply concerned that his people maintain a distance from the darkness of the world, lest they become caught up in its demonic machinations and be absorbed by its evil life. But Jesus surely did not mean a total removal from the scenes of everyday reality because he also told his disciples, "As the Father has sent me, I am sending you" (John 20:21). Clearly, he is calling them to be his co-laborers, his "change agents" in this world. And there is always a sense in which Christian people must "come out," remaining apart from the world even as they serve and minister to it. This is a theme as old as Abraham and as recent as our day (cf. Gen. 12:1; Num. 16:23–26; Isa. 48:20; 52:11; Jer. 50:8; 51:6,45). Paul was echoing this tradition when he asked, "For what do righteousness and wickedness have in common? Or what fellowship can light have with darkness? What harmony is there between Christ and Belial? What does a believer have in common with an unbeliever?" (2 Cor. 6:14–15).[4]

In fact, one of the main themes in the Revelation is God's call to the chosen people to remain separate from the beast's kingdom, lest they also become enmeshed in its judgments.[5] All through the book there are constant reminders that the people of the seven churches are involved in the final, the last, eternal Exodus. The "overcomers" in each of the seven churches are God's people who have "come out of her." The following are among the many manifestations of the Exodus motif in the Revelation:

1. "All the sealed" (i.e., the whole church) is defined as 144,000 gathered from "all the tribes of Israel" (7:4–8; i.e., the people of the original Exodus).

2. Jesus is defined most frequently and specifically as "the Lamb" (5:6; etc.), a reference to the Passover lamb of the Exodus (Exod. 12:3–8,21; cf. 1 Cor. 5:7; 1 Pet. 1:18–19).

3. The summons here, "Come out of her, my people," is the counterpoint to the divine invitation through Moses, "Let my people go, so that they may worship me in the desert" (Exod. 7:16; etc.). That ancient theme is also continued in the words of Jeremiah as he prophetically challenged God's people to come out of Babylon at such time when God would eventually judge their oppressor: "*Come out of her, my people! / Run for your lives! / Run from the fierce anger of the LORD*" (Jer. 51:45, emphasis added). This is repeatedly, then, the call to God's Israel to join in the final drama, the last Exodus. Moreover, in Revelation 11:8, "the great city" is unequivocally and metaphorically described as "Egypt," the very place from which God's people were once and now again required to leave.

4. Next, the trumpets and bowls are called "plagues" (9:20; 15:1,8), the same concept as that used to describe the judgments on Egypt (Exod. 8:2; 9:14; 11:1). Furthermore, much of the descriptive substance found in the trumpets and bowls is obviously derived from the contest between Moses and Pharaoh. As in that day, so in a latter day, wonders and mighty acts were meant to inspire and free God's people, even as they forced the hand of God's enemies (cf. Exod. 3:19).[6]

5. When God's people have come out, they will need to cross the Red Sea. John dutifully notes in 15:2–3 that the 144,000 stand by the "sea

of glass" singing the "song of Moses." Since ancient Israel sang that song on the far side of the sea, the side of victory from which they safely watched the destruction of the Egyptian army (Exod. 15), these too must be standing on the distant shore, having crossed over and entered into their purified, redeemed, and eternal future.

6. Once ancient Israel crossed the sea, it entered the desert wilderness, which symbolized safety beyond the reach of Egyptian bondage. Revelation, therefore, continues the pilgrimage of new Israel by announcing her present refuge in the wilderness under God's ever-present protection (12:6,14).

7. The wondrous presence that conducted the Hebrew people through the Sinai desert as a pillar of fire at night and a pillar of cloud by day (Exod. 13:21–22) stands behind the description of a mighty angel "robed in a cloud" with legs "like fiery pillars" (Rev. 10:1).[7] The new Israel is led as graciously and lovingly as was the old; John's churches need to be more aware of this presence standing among the lampstands. That this angel delivers to John a "little scroll" in verse 9 is vaguely reminiscent of that time when God brought the law to Moses at Mount Sinai (cf. Acts 7:53; Gal. 3:19; Heb. 2:2).[8]

8. The church is to become a "kingdom and priests" (Rev. 1:6; 5:10), just as ancient Israel was to be a "kingdom of priests" (Exod. 19:6). Both form the biblical background of the "priesthood of the believer" concept in modern Christendom. Actually, it was already a New Testament commonplace that this was the new identity of the church (1 Pet. 2:9–10).

9. There in the wilderness, the tabernacle, the tent of divine presence, was built for the first time. Within it, the ark of the covenant was kept, and it too originated in the wilderness (Exod. 25:8–10). Once again, John maintains the relationship flawlessly. Accessible and ever-contemporary, the tenting presence of God still overshadows God's people and guides their destiny (Rev. 11:19; 15:5–8).

10. In the Pentateuch, there is a promised land set aside by God for the chosen people as their final resting place. The final destiny of the redeemed in Revelation is "Mount Zion" (14:1), which is also known as "the Holy City, the new Jerusalem" (21:2).

More examples of the Exodus motif in the Revelation could be added to this list; though partial, it serves to demonstrate that the Revelation has gone to great lengths to package its message in a virtual cocoon of Exodus motifs. Its revealing challenge and guidance are directed to a people who are on their journey, on their journey home. Now John will begin the litany of social and spiritual evil from which the churches are called to flee, less the attendant judgments strike them as well.

18:6–8 • The continuing message from heaven makes it abundantly clear why God's people must come out of the belly of the great city: judgment is about to descend upon it, and the law of reciprocity is once again at work. As the city has sown, so shall it reap. Moreover, its evil deeds require a double repayment, and for every luxury it has enjoyed, and deprived others of, a double amount of torment and grief will now be meted out. As a "queen" is how the city vainly imagines itself. Biblical religion, however, was never concerned about one's possessions; the *attitude* toward one's assets was always the issue, for possessions too often end by possessing their possessor (Matt. 6:19–21; Luke 12:32–34).

The city's downfall will be sudden and without warning. In this (its final) day, the Lord of the universe, the Almighty, will try it. The phrase "in one day" is meant to heighten the sense of an astonishingly unanticipated downfall. It will be continued by the repeated chorus of "in one hour."

18:9–10 • Now John begins the indictment of those who suffer the greatest dislocation through the fall of the great city. Chief among those who will lose status and endure formidable losses is the political hierarchy — kings. Their political dalliance with the prostitute will now pay its just wages. Here they are seen mourning the breakup of a System whose *structure of power* gave them their livelihood; indeed, it was the whole of their lives. On this occasion, however, the startling speed of the prostitute's disintegration will deprive them of any opportunity to negotiate their own future. Her fall is their fall, one they fear. Having shared her life as intimates and enjoyed the luxury that connivance and acquiescence afforded, they will now share the doom of her fate as well.

One of the felonies put to their charge is that they "shared her luxury," a reality well documented in Roman literature. We hear of one wealthy lady who with outlandish ostentation appeared at banquets wearing such a quantity of pearls as would be worth tens of millions of current dollars (Charlesworth, 99). Hers was not the only recorded excess:

> At one of Nero's [A.D. 54–68] banquets the Egyptian roses alone cost nearly $100,000. Vitellius [A.D. 69] had a penchant for delicacies like peacocks' brains and nightingales' tongues. In his reign of less than one year he spent $20,000,000, mostly on food. One Roman, after squandering an immense fortune, committed suicide because he could not

live on the pittance which remained — about $300,000. (Mounce, *Book of Revelation*, 329)

Isaiah once spoke of those who "add house to house / and join field to field / till no space is left" except their own interests (Isa. 5:8). He further described the Hebrew rulers as "rebels, / companions of thieves; / they all love bribes / and chase after gifts. / They do not defend the cause of the fatherless; / the widow's case [two conspicuous examples of the helpless, marginalized, and defenseless] does not come before them" (Isa. 1:23). In like manner, there will be none to take up their cause when their patroness, the great prostitute, is called before the court of divine justice.

18:11–17a • Next, with genuine gusto and greater attention to detail, John assails the business and economic interests of the great city — the merchants. Now it is clear that the mourners are not really lamenting the fall of the city but their own losses of position and wealth in a System whose *values* allowed them to manipulate economic realities and to perpetuate their grotesquely destructive commercial enterprises. The alluring commodities of this city are the trappings with which the great prostitute surrounded herself (cf. 17:4). Clearly, John is well aware of the lifestyle led by the rich and famous. Already he has noted the connection between those outside the System and their loss of social or economic opportunity (13:17). These merchants wear the mark of the beast proudly, for they have bought and sold at will.

In this scene, however, the mood on Wall Street in the great city is depression, as they stand aghast, watching the world economy recede into oblivion; here is the ultimate Great Depression. The impressive inventory of merchandise closely approximates that in Ezekiel 27, where the goods and splendor of Tyre are inventoried. It also had been a maritime power and imagined itself to be "a god" of wealth (Ezek. 28:2,5).

Standing at the end of John's list, the "bodies and souls of men" (NRSV: "slaves — and human lives") represent a partial summary, a deeper and more penetrating analysis of the real tolls the System has taken on society. This is intended to remind anyone who knew the facts that as many as sixty million people in the Roman world lived their lives as slaves (Mounce, *Book of Revelation*, 330–31). Henry Swete expressed it this way:

> The world of St. John's day ministered in a thousand ways to the follies and vices of its Babylon, but the climax was reached in the sacrifice of human life which recruited the huge *familiae* [the servants and slaves of

a Roman household] of the rich, filled the *lupanaria* [houses of prostitution], and ministered to the brutal pleasures of the amphitheatre. (231)

There is much more in verses 11–17a than meets the eye. If we listen closely, we will hear that the great city is to be judged for far more than persecution of the church or even its own vigorous immorality. Here we note that *economic corruption* is one of the dominant crimes against which the wrath of God is directed. The commodities listed were not casually or arbitrarily selected as interesting examples of luxuriant living. They were carefully and knowledgeably chosen to illustrate those imports that caused the most devastating human suffering in the countries from which they were extracted. These were the luxury goods required in Rome by the rich and trendy to stay abreast of current fashions.[9] Such goods came into Roman ports from all the known world, including India and China. No wonder her sins are "heaped high as heaven" (v. 5, NRSV). Surely, when John observed that those who do not bear the beast's mark do not have equal access to the marketplace (13:17), these goods are among those they certainly do not enjoy. Wanton and ruinous consumption is specifically singled out as a culpable moral evil against God's creation.[10]

In this damning context, the heavenly voice thunders forth: "Come out of her, my people," for here is the opulence, luxury, exhibition, comfort, and pride of possession that represent the System's standard of values.[11] These are its ultimate commitment for which it is willing to sacrifice "slaves — and human lives" (NRSV),[12] for among the merchandise bartered in great Babylon's streets, John sees human beings. People have become simply another commodity, the most important livestock bought and sold in the marketplace.

There is, of course, an implied angle of perspective or human experience in these words. Revelation views the Roman world, concludes Richard Bauckham, from the "underside of history," that is, the viewpoint of its victims:

> It takes this perspective not because John and his Christian readers necessarily belonged to the classes which suffered rather than shared Rome's power and prosperity. It takes this perspective because, if they are faithful to their witness to the true God, their opposition to Rome's oppression and their dissociation of themselves from Rome's evil will make them victims of Rome. (39)

Perhaps this is always the moral order's choice; we are always *voyeurs* or *victims*.

18:17b–19 • The Dow Jones Transport Index also plummets into depression as commerce and trade go up in the smoke of the System's demise. These men of the sea, captains and sailors alike, are quite blunt and candid about the issue they face: the means by which they "became rich" is being shattered. They lament the loss of a financial power whose *dynamics* produced frenetic trade and a vigorous transit industry. The great prostitute had been the ultimate "mover and shaker"; now she is no more.

Why is the sea the only means of transport mentioned? Rome had an extensive system of land routes that also facilitated commercial enterprise in the empire, but the "sea," remember, holds certain symbolic undertones that are always present in Revelation. We must never forget that within the morning mists, hanging over the sea, is "a beast coming" (13:1). Hence, when at sea, we are in the beast's environment, one of his distinctive domains. And, in John's day, it is the sea that particularly encapsulates the dynamic vigor, rapidity, and vast range of the Roman commercial esprit de corps. The Mediterranean had become a Roman lake wherein goods flowed from one end of the inhabited world to the other as easily as today they go anywhere overnight. Simply put, the seafarer of that day stood for the bold, indomitable spirit of the Roman System.

The kings, merchants, and seafarers of the great city are deeply affected and genuinely mourn what is lost, "for," as Jacques Ellul points out, "from this moment the true judgment upon them is finally having to say: 'All this being abolished, I have then lived for nothing. Of all my works, of all my efforts, nothing remains.' That is the judgment upon the kings and the rich" (201). Reminiscently, in the repeated litany of "one hour," there might be an oblique reference to events as recent as A.D. 79 (some fifteen years before John wrote). In that fateful year, one August night, all the light and life in Pompeii and Herculaneum suddenly flickered out. This suddenly, says John, will be the extinguishing of the great city.

18:20 • Just as the central portion of this chapter is dominated by the command to "come out of her," it ends with the concluding injunction to "rejoice over her."[13] Without the former, however, one does not participate in the latter. Finally, a response has come to those who have "come out," triumphed over the System, and are now gathered in heaven around the altar. We once heard their voices crying out, as did Abel's blood from the ground (Gen. 4:10), "How long, Sovereign Lord, holy and true, until you judge the inhabitants of the earth and avenge our blood?" (Rev. 6:10)? That was the cry of those who had been *slain* for their testimony (6:9; the same word is used of the Lamb in 5:6). This is the city of their death (18:24), for they are among those "bodies and souls of men" (18:13) slaughtered in its stockyards and butchered in the marketplaces, which were so essential to its System.

Rejoicing is called for, of course, but so is something else: a deep sadness, which even the people of God cannot evade. Vernard Eller draws us into this pitiable moment by reminding us of the hidden side of this event — that is, what might have been: "So the tragedy of Babylon is not that anything good is lost but rather the dissipation of all that might have been good, the human investment, the energy and resources that had been poured into Babylon.... 'How sad to realize now how much Babylon has wasted and ruined' " (171)!

18:21–23 • Much of the essential substance in this description of the silencing of great Babylon is drawn from the prophet Jeremiah. In chapters 50–51, he predicted the original downfall of the historical Babylon, and at the conclusion of that prophetic pronouncement, he directed his courier, Seraiah (the one taking his prophecy to Hebrew exiles in Babylonia), to perform a symbolic action. Seraiah was to take the prophetic document he had just read to the captive Hebrews and, tying a stone to it, throw it into the Euphrates River. As this enacted parable was being performed, Seraiah was to announce, "So will Babylon sink to rise no more because of the disaster I will bring upon her" (Jer. 51:64). As it had been with historical Babylon, the classical enemy of God's people, so it shall be for all her spiritual descendants.

Jesus had also once said that "if anyone causes one of these little ones who believe in me to sin, it would be better for him to be thrown into the sea with a large millstone tied around his neck" (Mark 9:42; cf. Matt. 18:6; Luke 17:2). Here Jesus' saying becomes reality. Babylon the Great is demolished and scuttled because it has harmed the "little ones" of whom Jesus spoke; it has killed his prophets and saints (Rev. 18:24).

Noticeable among the enterprises shut down are those that we would ordinarily describe as the vanguard of culture and civilization. The thoughtful reader will be tempted to wonder what is so wrong with music, art, human joy, entrepreneurial enterprise, even the light of an oil lamp. This is very reminiscent of Jesus' comment that when the Son of Man returns he will find life as it was in the day of Noah: "People were eating, drinking, marrying and being given in marriage up to the day ... the flood came and destroyed them all. It was the same in the days of Lot. People were eating and drinking, buying and selling, planting and building" (Luke 17:27–28). What is Jesus' point? Such activities are not typically considered immoral or blame-worthy in Scripture. In the context to which he was speaking, Jesus is illustrating the abruptness of the day of destruction and the un-preparedness of the visionless life adrift from God. The eating and drinking, planting and building, all characterize life lived without a transcendental or divine point of reference. Here there is no North Star giving meaning and direction to life. Many are those for whom these mundane matters are the sum total of existence. As described by John, this is life defined exclusively as human activity turned in upon itself. Here fallen humanity has truly become the measure of its own reality, and all things, even the mundane and normal aspects of life, are "Fallen! Fallen!"

The sea in this picturesque panel is the very one out of which the beast continually arises (13:1) and that is destined to become extinct (21:1); it is home to the dragon-beast's rebellion. Into this sea the great city is cast, never to rise again. The finality of her doom is intrigu-ingly sketched in a sixfold "never...again." This is because her end is the termination of imperfection; she is the city of sixes (perennially short of "sevenish" perfection), but when the eternal city arrives, it will prove itself a city of sevenfold perfection (note the "seven" de-scriptions found in 21:3–4 but the "six" types of people who may not enter it in 22:15). John's apocalyptic fascination with numerical symbols continues to the end and is found in many forms that often go unrecognized.

With the artistry of Hebrew poetics, the last phrases of this pas-sage equate the economics of exploitation, that is, the labors of Roman merchants, the magnates of the earth, with a "magic spell." John is not speaking of crude sorcery or venal witchcraft but the se-ductive and deceitful effects of cultural and spiritual hegemony of the sort Rome had exercised over its empire. Rome had exported its vi-sion of reality and merchandised its wantonness to that world. Thus, John consciously links the fall of this evil city with that of Nineveh, as noted by the prophet Nahum:

> Woe to the city of blood,
>   full of lies,
> full of plunder,
>   never without victims!
> The crack of whips,
>   . . . .
>   piles of dead,
> bodies without number,
>   . . . .

all because of the wanton lust of a harlot,
  alluring, the mistress of sorceries,
who enslaved nations by her prostitution
  and peoples by her witchcraft.
"I am against you," declares the LORD Almighty.
  "I will lift your skirts over your face.
I will show the nations your nakedness
  and the kingdoms your shame."

— Nahum 3:1–5

18:24 • If a day is as a thousand years to God and a thousand years like a day (2 Pet. 3:8), then all the world is like a city, and a city, the world. Nowhere does John more explicitly make this point than when he says that *all* those killed on earth (cf. 17:6) have met their pitiful fate in this *one* city. Great Babylon is John's comprehensive, composite symbol for the entire history of the world's estrangement from its Creator (cf. 17:1,15,18). With his usual incisive skill, Ellul defines the great city as "the world of man, created by him, expressing to the exclusion of every other tendency his will, his intelligence, his purpose — human, exclusively human" (194).

Perhaps the most damning thing that can be said about great Babylon is that the city devours people. They are merely one further commodity, to be bought, sold, or traded. Great Babylon is ultimately the final city of Cain (who committed the first fratricide and built the first city; Gen. 4:17) and the continuing haunt of the beast. "The city of the Antichrist," writes G. R. Beasley-Murray, "fulfills the role of every Babylon of history, and pays the price for every Babylon" (*Book of Revelation, 270).*

The great System, variously called the "prostitute," the "great city," and "Babylon the Great" (for John, these all stand unquestionably for the reality of the Roman Empire), is seen as a manifestation of three interdependent realities: political structure, moral and social values, and the dynamics of commercial life. Those who stand at the center of its reality are the political kingmakers, those who create and merchandise lifestyles, and those who facilitate the supply and demand of the resultant System. Consequently, as it topples, the kings lament the fall of "the city of power" (18:10), the merchants mourn the city's lost "riches [NRSV: "dainties"] and splendor" (v. 14), while the transport industry grieves because "all who had ships on the sea / became rich through her wealth" (v. 19).

The larger context of the book always reminds us that this is where the seven churches are living. In the great city, they are struggling to overcome all these corrosive forces that surround and constantly threaten to submerge them. It is in the light of this continual spiritual warfare that John diagnosed their needs and prescribed for their welfare in the seven letters.

And does that ancient chameleon, shrouded in our world of economic, social, and political realities, still lurk among us today? What does this chapter say to the modern church so often implicated in many of the same dynamics, the same value systems and politics, as those of great Babylon? Do we still identify with the "underside of history"? Jesus was severely criticized for hobnobbing with the outcasts of society; why do these same people now feel so out of place in our churches? These are troubling questions for sensitive spirits; they will lead to further study, much meditative soul searching, and, hopefully, renewed commitment to a "doing" of the word and a "coming out" of the System. This is the continuing challenge "for the seven churches"!

While traveling in Israel, I heard a wonderful (and horrible) description of Christianity: "It began in the Holy Land as a 'relationship'; it went to Rome and became a 'religion'; then to Europe where it was transformed into a 'culture'; finally, it came to America and became an 'enterprise' " (author unknown). "He who has an ear, let him hear what the Spirit says to the churches."

Notes

1. I agree entirely with Paul Minear: "The best procedure is not first to locate Babylon as a particular city, and then to attribute these sins to that city, but first to grasp the character of the sins, and then to infer that where they are found, there is Babylon" (151). Where demons dwell, prostitutes ply their trade, luxury seekers thrive, accommodation and appeasement are rampant, power is the goal of life, and blasphemy is unrestrained, *there is great Babylon.*

2. Robert C. Linthicum finds three causes for the great city's having become the city of Satan. (1) She worships at the throne of a false god (17:1-2; 18:2-3,9-10). Texts speaking of "adultery" are to be understood as suggesting "idolatry" (cf. Jer. 3:8; 29:23; Ezek. 16:32; 23:37). Rome and its emperor are at the center of this false worship of the System. (2) She has victimized the world to indulge her own pointless luxury and economic security (17:4-5; 18:11-19). (3) She misuses her political power to oppress any who seem threatening to her position (17:6; 18:24; see Linthicum, 279-83).

3. D. T. Niles comments, "The harlotry of Jerusalem was apostasy. She left her rightful lord and committed adultery with other lovers. The harlotry of Babylon is rivalry. She set herself up as an alternative to God and caused men and nations to commit adultery with her. Her sin was pride" (86).

4. In an exciting discussion entitled "Attitude toward the Persecutors," Adela Collins explains Revelation's response to the fall of great Babylon. It is, not one of unbridled envy, hatred, or vindictiveness due to its depredations upon the Christian communities (these are unworthy motives for followers of the Lamb), but rather a "social radicalism" that taught Christians to withdraw from its weblike entanglements (particularly the pursuit of wealth). Hence, chapters 17 and 18 represent more a call to social exclusivity, the building of a self-contained community with its own language and value systems, than to genuine mourning or celebrating over the System's downfall (*Crisis and Catharsis*, 116–38).

5. "This call has a rhetorical function similar to the sealing of the 144,000 in chapter 7 and to the measuring of the true worshipers in 11:1–2. In the midst of tribulation, it calls for the eschatological exodus of those who have remained faithful until the great day of judgment" (Fiorenza, *Revelation*, 101).

6. Exodus 3:19 is a decisive text for a proper understanding of the motif of the "hardening of Pharaoh's heart." God's actions, with regard to Ramses II, did not include God's intention of *preventing* him from releasing Israel. Quite the contrary, God was engaged in a process of *compelling* this response, as this text so plainly suggests, not hindering it. I am convinced that no reading of this classic difficulty will do justice to the issues involved without a proper beginning grounded in this programmatic text.

7. The possibility that the angel represents God or Jesus has been suggested more than once. See Mulholland, 200; Ford, 163.

8. In fact, Eugenio Corsini strongly argues that the "little book" is the Old Covenant (i.e., the Old Testament) to which John is invited to add his prophecy, as in "The Law and the Prophets" (188–89).

9. For a critique of liberation theology (which says, in effect, that the United States has also played the role of great Babylon, that it has even been the land of the north (Ezek. 38:2,15; Rev. 20:8), demanding that Latin American nations produce goods and orient themselves for its benefit, see Wainwright, 181–83.

10. I am indebted for the material in this paragraph to Christopher R. Smith, 28–33.

11. By way of counterpoint, G. R. Beasley-Murray notes that "there was nothing sinful in the commodities of the merchants.... The sin of Babylon was its use of these things to seduce mankind to adopt the kind of gross materialism and mammon-worship which is illustrated in the songs of the merchants and seamen" (*Book of Revelation*, 268).

12. As the NRSV footnote indicates, this phrase is literally "human bodies and souls."

13. There are but two commands in this whole chapter, observes M. Eugene Boring, and they are "Come out of her, my people" (v. 4) and "Rejoice over her" (v. 20). The first is as much, or more, spiritual than literal and indicates a solemn and tenacious resistance to the values of this whorish city. The second is a call to enter into the celebration of heaven over the impending arrival of divine justice (*Revelation*, 189).

Chapter 18

THE BRIDE'S BLESSED HOPE
Rev. 19:1–21

Finally, the great day has arrived! It is now time "for rewarding your servants the prophets / and your saints and those who reverence your name, / both small and great — / and for destroying those who destroy the earth" (11:18). Furthermore, "Rejoice over her [Babylon the Fallen], O heaven! / Rejoice, saints and apostles and prophets!" (18:20). And that is exactly what John now reveals to us, for it is the true complement to the doleful lament of the previous chapter. Here is the joy of a positive eschatology — the hope of a blessed future — for when you know that in the end you are on the winning team, you play the game differently.[1] Thus, in the shattering aftermath of the divine judgment on great Babylon, all creation lifts its voice to praise and rejoice in this wondrous work of God. The great revolt has finally been vanquished; the System, subdued and dismantled!

In the midst of its jubilation, the final response is given to Abraham's ancient question: "Will not the Judge of all the earth do right?" (Gen. 18:25). Now justice has come and revealed itself in history, and all those who have ever despaired of such a day, finally, have reason to rejoice. Now is answered that heavenly question that has in fact been playing an important role in the denouement of John's Revelation: "How long, Sovereign Lord,... until you judge the inhabitants of the earth and avenge our blood?" (6:10).

19:1–5 • Once again, Revelation has taken us before the heavenly throne, and just as in chapter 4, we are in the presence of the twenty-four elders, the four creatures, the throne of God, and the great multitude of chapter 7, including the 144,000. In fact, just as then, all heaven is rip-roaring with anthems of musical ecstasy celebrating the downfall of Babylon, the great prostitute.

Chapter 19 has often been called the "Hallelujah Chorus" of the Revelation. In verses 1,3–4,6, John uses the word *Hallelujah,* which is familiar to us from the Psalms, though it is found nowhere else in the New Testament. This Hebrew declaration introduces many Psalms (Ps. 111–13; 117; 135; 146–50) and is also used elsewhere in the Psalter. It means, quite simply, "Praise the Lord." Those who have engaged in such praise in earthly worship, says the Revelation, will one day continue to do so in yet another scene of adoration. "Praise the Lord," say the heavenly celebrants, for the day of redemption and freedom has come, and all that bars the way to eternal truth and love is being set aside. In this moment, everything *Hallelujah* has ever stood for is at hand. All the songs of Hebrew and Christian history are blending together to form one final "Hallelujah Chorus." Martin Kiddle noted that this "hallelujah rings out the old, but it also rings in the new" (378).

The voices of "the four living creatures," lifting as they do the cry of all nature, serve to remind us that this day of victory does not belong alone to God's people but embraces the whole of creation. Their voices call to our attention Paul's "ecological eschatology," in which he argues that all of creation has been blighted by the story of human sin and that even now "the creation waits in eager expectation for the sons of God to be revealed" (Rom. 8:19). In chapter 19, that day is dawning!

19:6–8 • No other book of the Bible so stresses the relation between God and God's people through the images of the "bride" and her "wedding." The origin of these symbols is old; indeed, Jeremiah 2:2 is probably the clearest reference to its original usage and heuristic power in the Hebrew Scriptures: "Go and proclaim in the hearing of Jerusalem: / 'I remember the devotion of your youth, / how as a bride you loved me and followed me through the desert'" (cf. Hos. 2:5,19–20; Isa. 1:21; 54:5–6; Ezek. 16:8; harlotry sometimes symbolizes the opposite of conjugal fidelity). The theme is also picked up in the New Testament by both Jesus (Mark 2:19) and Paul. The latter applies the marital relationship of "Christ and the church" (Eph. 5:32–33) in various ways (cf. Rom. 7:1–4; 2 Cor. 11:2).

The status of this concept in Revelation, while far from novel, nevertheless leads one to wonder about John's own marriage. If Hosea's relationship to his wife, Gomer, was a major channel of God's revelation to him, might John's wife have been the inspiration for his view of what the church is and will be (21:2,9; 22:17)? Does her profile also stand in the shadows behind that of the idyllic woman mentioned in chapter 12? We will have to wait to ask John those questions; however, it cannot on principle be ruled out.

But now in John's vision, the day of the Lord has come, and his bride has made herself ready to receive the "blessed hope" that has sustained her through the millennia (Titus 2:13). Both those who have gone on before and those who are left to behold the event have prepared for this day. By their ceaseless labors, they have been clothing themselves in the righteousness and personality of the kingdom of God. Paul, in his straightforward manner, would have said, "You have taken off your old self with its practices and have put on the new self, which is being renewed in knowledge in the image of its Creator" (Col. 3:9-10). Or to put it more simply, they have engaged in the process of being conformed "to the likeness of his Son" (Rom. 8:29). This practice of spiritual discipline in the living of one's life is what Revelation speaks of through the symbol of being clothed in "fine linen."

John is also on the same wavelength with Paul when he addresses the issue of good works, for John would fully agree that we are redeemed by grace through faith (Eph. 2:8-9). John, however, is quick to add (note "the righteous acts of the saints") that life in Christ Jesus is for the purpose of "good works," which is also a Pauline emphasis (Eph. 2:10). Though Protestants do not often stress the role of "works" in the Christian life, we should recognize the difference between "works of the law" and "works of grace" and be challenged by the Revelation, remembering that good deeds represent the very essence of the life we strive to imitate: "Jesus of Nazareth was a man accredited by God to you by miracles, wonders and signs" and "he went around doing good" (Acts 2:22; 10:38). Righteous acts do not produce redemption, but redemption always produces this legitimating by-product. It is important not to put the cart before the horse; nevertheless, horses are for the pulling of carts.

How would the seven churches have heard this passage? In what ways does the topic of "works" enter into their individual lives? With some, the issue is fairly obvious, for example, Ephesus (2:5-6), Thyatira (2:19,23), Sardis (3:1-2), Philadelphia (3:8), and Laodicea (3:15). But how do you think this theme would fit into the Christian lifestyle of Smyrna and Pergamum? Always remember, John's insights into and his pictures of the future are never meant merely to satisfy spiritual voyeurism. There is always a message for the churches. Prediction of the future is usually, at least partly, a *program* for the present.

19:9-10 • The angelic announcement in this verse represents the fourth beatitude in the book (cf. 1:3; 14:13; 16:15; 19:9; 20:6; 22:7,14). And while no "wedding supper" is later described, we are probably to understand this blessed event as a double exposure of the content of scenes found in chapters 21-22 (cf. 21:2,9). Clearly it is no accident that in John's Gospel the first veiled reference to the Lord's

Supper (in which John begins to interpret its meaning through the miraculous wine) takes place in the midst of a wedding feast at Cana (John 2:1–11). That feast foreshadowed — in the books by John — the future spoken of here. Jesus also indicated that the Lord's Supper would announce the end of history because he was not again to drink the fruit of the vine until the Kingdom had come (Luke 14:15; 22:18). In fact, it had always been the biblical perspective that the end of history would be inaugurated at a great festive banquet:

> On this mountain the LORD Almighty will prepare
> > a feast of rich food for all peoples,
> a banquet of aged wine —
> > the best of meats and the finest of wines.
> . . . .
> > he will swallow up death forever.
> . . . .
> In that day they will say,
> > "Surely this is our God;
> > > we trusted in him, and he saved us."
>
> — Isaiah 25:6, 8–9

The Revelation combines these two great meals — the Lord's Supper and the eschatological banquet of the Lord — in one magnificent "wedding supper of the Lamb." And then the ultimate question — Guess who's coming to dinner? — will finally be answered as the invitations written in the Lamb's book of life are published. That book is the social register of the New Jerusalem, and its citizenry are the chosen guests. To attend this banquet is to enjoy the fulfillment of every biblical hope and promise ever made; it is nothing less than the crowning experience of the Christian life.

John's unsuccessful attempt at angel "worship" is a strange and unexpected intruder in the Revelation. For what purpose is such a topic raised? Perhaps John is responding to local issues. Apparently, some Christians in the Greco-Roman world — where there were cultural precedents — had fallen into the pagan practice of worshiping angels (cf. Col. 2:18), and so a clear criticism is lodged against this unwholesome practice: "Do not do it!"[2] The Christian tradition is one with its spiritual forebear on this matter; Christianity, as Judaism, worships only one divinity, not many. We are left to ask, Did John know that some in the seven churches were specially vulnerable to this aberration? In which church might the problem have been most acute?

The phrase "the testimony of Jesus" is found in only three places in the book prior to this. It is at the heart of what it means to be a Christian, namely, to be about the work of making Jesus known to the world. This is what John expects of those who know God (1:2), and he fully expects that such a lifestyle will inevitably lead to conflict with the dragon (1:9; 12:17; cf. 12:11).

Verse 10 gives us the reason for avoiding angel worship. They too serve God and the Christ by bringing and interpreting the Revelation of Jesus to fellow servants (1:1; 22:16). John here produces what is virtually a definition of the meaning and function of *prophecy* in the Christian church. To prophesy is to testify by means of the spoken word and one's entire life to the renewing presence of Jesus Christ; this is very near to a similar definition given by Paul in 1 Corinthians 14:3–4,24–25. This understanding of prophecy suggests that a significant goal of the Christian life is to model the presence (Rom. 8:29) and proclaim the victory of Jesus Christ (Matt. 28:18–20). John might have said that prophecy is more "profession" than "prediction," but to live a Christlike life is to forecast the realities of heaven. No wonder he is himself deemed a prophet (10:11; 22:9), for what he has written is a powerful testimony to Jesus Christ (cf. 1:2; 22:16,20).[3]

The book of Revelation is a fitting conclusion to the story of the early church at whose inception Peter preached the hope of Hebrew prophecy: " 'In the last days, God says, / I will pour out my Spirit on all people. / Your sons and your daughters will prophesy' " (Acts 2:17). John continues to define the true, sevenfold church as one in which the testimony to Jesus is the continuation of the biblical heritage of prophecy; hence, the comment that they have not denied the name of their Lord is very significant (2:13; 3:8). Consider: What else is notable about the two churches John directly compliments in this regard?

19:11 • In the end, we do not meet an *event* but a *personal savior,* nor do we encounter *something* but rather *someone.* The opening phrase of verse 11, "I saw," is the first of *seven* visions through which the return of Christ and from its consequences for the earth are detailed (cf. 19:11–16,17–18,19–21; 20:1–3,4–10,11–15; 21:1–22:7). Each of the sections begins with the standard formula "then" or "and I saw."[4]

This, the first segment, must be one of the most important scenes in the entire book. Foreshadowing events have preceded it in almost every chapter. From the very beginning ("every eye will see him"; 1:7) and to its ultimate conclusion ("I am coming soon"; 22:20), the matchless hope of Christ's second coming has remained a dominant theme throughout the warp and woof of John's message. But, of course, he has told us from the outset that the whole book truly focuses on "the revelation of Jesus Christ" (1:1). This is the central theme of all prophecy, namely, the revealing testimony that strips away the sham of our make-believe world and unveils the arrival of ultimate reality, the truth in which "we live and move and have our being" (Acts 17:28).

Christ's arrival will not please everyone, however, for it was always destined to cause some to "mourn" (Rev. 1:7); it represents, after all, the divine determination to have the last word with all that has raised the cry of rebellion against God. "The whole world" might believe it impossible to resist or "make war against" the beast, thus allowing it to make "war against the saints" with impunity (13:3–4,7), but now the last battle will reveal that war with God is absolute hell. The forces of evil always believe that the initiative is theirs (16:14); in the final analysis, however, it is God whose action is decisive — "he judges and makes war" (19:11). On the other hand, this event is also a crisis for many within the church because it fulfills the promise that Christ would "fight against them" (2:16) who have counseled compromise from within and weakened the church's will to resist the world. This battle is, then, a vindication of the loyalty and devotion of all those who have stood firm during the agelong conflict with concessionism.

19:12–13 • His eyes have consumed all of history, for nothing is hidden from the piercing insight of divine omniscience. Indeed, "there is nothing concealed that will not be disclosed, or hidden that will not be made known" (Matt. 10:26), said Jesus, which means that "what you have said in the dark will be heard in the daylight, and what you have whispered in the ear in the inner rooms will be proclaimed from the roofs" (Luke 12:3). And so says the whole of Scripture.[5]

Consider, next time you are engaged in some deceitful or shameful venture, just what it will be like when that deed is broadcast in living color to family, friends, and all who have ever trusted you. Can you sense the betrayal felt by those who have bought the bogus product we hawk as ourselves? What will they think when the sham we have put forward as the truth of who we are is shattered? How deep will be the humiliation and damaging the effect? But what a wonderful promise awaits those who have confessed and given all their guilt to him: "You...hurl all our iniquities into the depths of the sea" (Mic. 7:19). Fishing or salvage rights there are granted no one.

Endless are the guesses at the unknown name Jesus secretly bears. Among the more prominent are YHWH (the tetragrammaton, or four letters, that are God's covenant name *Yahweh*); Jesus, "the name that is above every name" (Phil. 2:9); "Faithful and True" (Rev. 19:11);

"the Word of God" (19:13); "the Alpha and the Omega" (22:13; cf. 1:8, where it is God's name). Perhaps it is best to remember that there is always a mystery attached to his person; with him, we must not become blasphemously cozy or outrageously familiar. Jesus is always also *Deus absconditus* (the hidden, unknowable God), the one whose thoughts and ways are higher and not like our own (Isa. 55:8–9). When we add together all the splendid names our creatureliness knows to use, he still presents us with an incomprehensible mystery.

This white-horsed rider has the authority to deal with sin because he wages war in a garment dipped in the blood that once dripped on Calvary. His followers have washed their robes and made them white in this blood (7:14). But, to change the metaphor, those who have not sought shelter under this holy shroud must experience God's last word on sin. No, the blood on his robe does not belong to the defeated enemy; it is Christ's own — the insignia that the faithful follow — for the fighting has not yet even begun. This blood was shed at the first and decisive battle for redemption, and those who do not follow his lead will be responsible for the shedding of their own blood, an event soon to follow. The white-horsed rider wages war, let none forget, by using a "sharp double-edged sword" that issues from his mouth (cf. 1:16; 19:15); that is, he proclaims and executes the judgment against sin that took place on Calvary.[6]

Once again, as is so typical of Revelation, Christ is covered with blood and understood as bearing the marks of slaughter (i.e., the Crucifixion), a reality definitive of the divine Lamb.[7] Yet now we can really see what John meant when he said that this Lamb is actually a lion (5:5–6). The Lamb comes to this battle bearing the marks of his own suffering, a suffering meant to avert this conflict between Creator and creature. He has already engaged in a mighty war against the forces of darkness; now the Lion will end the rebellion, and all hostilities will cease at his roaring.

19:14–16 • The 144,000, who are the legions of the redeemed, are on the march, for they "follow the Lamb wherever he goes" (14:4; cf. those who follow the beast in 13:3–4). This scene clearly connects in a variety of ways with the harvest scene of 14:14–20. The further clarification achieved in this expansion of that vision suggests that the "sickle" used there to reap the earth is actually the sword from the mouth of the one on the white horse. Thus, the earth is harvested by way of its reaction to the word of God. When that word is accepted in humble submission, then much fruit results, but when it meets with stony rejection, only fearful destruction is possible (cf. Matt. 13:18–23).

Those who also follow on white horses come to this final confrontation having already manifested in their lives the "righteous acts of the saints" (v. 8), for they are clothed in "fine linen, white and clean" (cf. the oft-repeated refrain "I know your works" to the seven churches). Is John suggesting that whenever Christians labor, performing such deeds of compassion, service, and self-sacrifice, they are already engaging the enemy in this ultimate battle? Or are the present good works of God's people required "military exercises" in preparation for that final encounter? Perhaps both are true ("To him who overcomes and does my will to the end, I will give authority over the nations"; 2:26), but in either event, John points to the fact that those who ride with the King of kings wear a special and unique style of body armor — "fine linen, white and clean" — for if the Lamb is a lion, then God's workers are God's winners.

To rule with "an iron scepter" is what the Lord's anointed king is set to accomplish: "You will rule them with an iron scepter" (Ps. 2:9). More than merely ironfisted, such a reign is capable of annihilating its enemies. Furthermore, "the winepress" (cf. 14:19), "the fury," and "the wrath" are bleak and somber words that are difficult to hear, but clearly they testify to a final overthrow that is not being conducted by wimpish forces devoid of holy metal. Robert Mounce has it right: "Any view of God which eliminates judgment and his hatred of sin in the interest of an emasculated doctrine of sentimental affection finds no support in the strong and virile realism of the Apocalypse" (*Book of Revelation,* 347).

Only one can carry out the mandates of the preceding paragraph (vv. 11–16). And he is now defined by the name inscribed on his thigh: "KING OF KINGS AND LORD OF LORDS." This authoritative title derives ultimately from Moses' prescription, "For the LORD your God is God of gods and Lord of lords, the great God, mighty and awesome" (Deut. 10:17) and from its reverberations in Daniel 2:47; 1 Timothy 6:15; and Revelation 17:14.

19:17–18 • While the definitive battle has not yet occurred, already heaven is projecting its macabre outcome in this the second of the seven scenes. But what is the point of this proclamation to the birds, which is made even before the opposing forces are assembled? G. R. Beasley-Murray concludes that it underscores "the senselessness and futility of rebellion against God. When man resists God, he can do no more than advance to his judgment" (*Book of Revelation,* 283). This confrontation, therefore, is certain to result in a momentous overthrow of every creature out of conformity with the final manifestation of God's will and kingdom.

The canvas with which we are presently occupied, however, is somewhat different from that found in chapter 6, where apparently the same events are portrayed through the opening of the sixth seal. There the identical individuals (kings, magnates, generals, rich, slave, free — everyone; 6:15) behave quite differently, cowering in the caves and crying to the elements to hide them from the wrath of God. How can we account for this difference? Perhaps it is merely the point in time from which the battle is surveyed. Come early and see the bombast of the earthly armies parading their misguided bravado as they puff up with evil resolve; come later in the program, when they have encountered the Lamb, and see the truth.

Now by all means, do not miss the grisly contrast between "the wedding supper of the Lamb" (v. 9) and this "great supper of God." Christ's presence has radically different effects on the populations of the two cities, New Jerusalem and great Babylon. Two awesome banquets are being thrown, with God providing the means and substance for both. John is clearly suggesting that there is a choice each must make in the banquet of life: "either you can go to the Lamb's supper as *guests,* friends of the bride . . . or you can go to this other supper as part of the *menu,* food for the vultures" (Eller, 177). No matter what, everyone is going to party, each in his or her chosen way.

19:19–21 • Scene three commences with a projected war but ends with a total whipping. In fact, if you blinked, you missed that war! Actually, it was over before it started. Still, what force in this universe can resist the living God? Envisioning a real war between God and some enemy force is to invest that power with abilities and resources no creature controls. Even to imagine a force capable of engaging God in a genuine pitched battle is virtual blasphemy, for it creates another, though lesser, genuine god. John certainly does not mean to do that! He has delighted in describing God as *Pantokratōr* (i.e., the Omnipotent, All-Mighty One; 1:8; 4:8; 11:17; 15:3; 16:7,14; 19:6,15; 21:22).

As a matter of fact, the whole book has built toward this climactic battle, and it must surely be a great surprise to John's expectant readers that none is detailed. Six times John has led us inexorably toward a final conflagration of wills (8:1; 11:15; 14:6–11; 16:17–21; 18:1–8; 19:20–21), but never once has he described the final battle. Each time the beast rolls over, resigns, and is destroyed without a struggle (Ewing, 77). This is one of the major messages of Revelation, in fact. The Lamb is the Lion because the decisive battle, Calvary, is past. The ultimate victory has already been won. D-day is over!

Any future encounter between the Lamb and even a great beast is predetermined, just another V-day.

The legendary and vaunted battle of Armageddon, proleptically introduced in the sixth bowl judgment (16:12–16), has just occurred, but no clash is actually described here. As Paul once observed, when Jesus returns, he will eradicate "the lawless one...with the breath of his mouth and destroy [him] by the splendor of his coming" (2 Thess. 2:8). In other words, as John too has just said, by merely showing up, Jesus ends all opposition and crushes any and all rival forces. No war is pictured, for none can take place. To oppose God is to face a simple and obvious doom.

The rebellious generals, previously captured, are now flung alive to their fiery fate. Their soldiers — later to join them — are first killed by the unique sword from the Lamb's mouth. Here is the scene Isaiah foretold when he spoke of the descendant of Jesse (David's father) who would "with the breath of his lips...slay the wicked" (Isa. 11:4). For the moment, John does not rehearse anew the resultant flood of blood gushing from the winepress of God's wrath (14:20), though this is the same scene. However, the gruesome horror of ghoulish birds glutted with human flesh conveys an even subtler sense of utter doom. The imagery found here is taken from Ezekiel 39:17–20, where the birds are invited to sate themselves on the flesh of Gog and his followers who had participated in an end-time assault on the people of God. Apparently, to attack God's people in any time is, indeed, a discomposing adventure (cf. Isa. 49:26).

By mentioning the sword a second time, John specifies that this weapon of destiny did not come from a military scabbard; it proceeds "out of the mouth" of the one on the white horse. Unlike others, this Messiah has come, not to inflict military defeat upon his foes, but to announce the word and judgment of the Great King upon their rebellion. Rejecting the divine word of redemption is the final judgment, which they themselves have pronounced. "The one who rejects me," said Jesus, "and does not accept my words; that very word which I spoke will condemn him at the last day" (John 12:48). And so it shall be; the last day has come!

Eugene Peterson interprets this chapter under the title "The Last Word on Salvation." His point is that salvation is always governed by two different symbols — Eucharist (the Lord's Table) and Armageddon (the holy war) — for the two defining experiences of redemption are "fellowship" (with God and fellow servants) and "warfare" (with the world) against the System. In Peterson's words, "The moment we walk away from the Eucharist, having received the life of our Lord, we walk into Armageddon, where we exercise the strength of our Lord" (161). In keeping with this theme, there are two fellowships in chapter 19 (i.e., two suppers), and there are two military enterprises (i.e., "the armies of heaven" in v. 14 as well as "the beast and the kings of the earth and their armies" in v. 19). Here are final depictions of the bride and the beast. These are the citizens and fellowships of the two great cities of Revelation and their fates. In other words, those with whom we *fellowship* and what we *fight* for define our world and create the future.

> "Hallelujah!
> Salvation and glory and power belong to our God,
>   for true and just are his judgments."

> — Revelation 19:1–2

Notes

1. Robert Wall's comment at this point is quite helpful: "Sharply put, John's message to the seven churches is this: what has already transpired (5:1–11:19) together with what has not yet taken place (14:1–19:10; 19:11–22:6a) must inform the believing community's response both to God and to its present tribulation (12:1–13:18)" (226). With minor nuancing, I believe this understanding of Revelation's *logical chronology* is correct.

2. "If John discourages angel-worship in these two passages [cf. 22:8], he does so not by abasing angels, but by exalting Christians (cf. Heb. i.-ii.)" (Kiddle, 383).

3. "The 'witness of Jesus' = 'spirit of prophecy' is the Christian community's incarnation of the presence of God in the world by which God is manifest to the life of the world. Such a witness is a disturbing power in a world shaped by rebellion against God. One of the results is seen in 20:4" (Mulholland, 66).

4. I sometimes wonder if behind these stereotyped series of "sevens" there might not have been a succession of messages John had once delivered to his people. Whatever we may think about that, surely there is such a possibility for so using these passages in our day.

5. Ps. 65:5; Eccl. 12:14; Jer. 16:17; Dan. 2:22; Hos. 5:3; Mark 4:22; Luke 8:17; 1 Cor. 4:5; Heb. 4:13.

6. Robert Mounce quite correctly defines the nature of the conquering Messiah's battle sword: "The sharp sword symbolizes the lethal power of his word of judgment. We are not to envision a literal sword but a death-dealing pronouncement which goes forth like a sharp blade from the lips of Christ" (346).

7. John has certainly utilized the symbolism of Isaiah 63:1–6, where God is portrayed as the Divine Warrior slaying his foes in garments stained with

their blood, but that is not the meaning here. John has transformed this symbol of retribution into one of grace. All through the Revelation, it is Christ and his followers who have suffered. Now, the Lamb has taken the penalty of their rebellion upon himself. He bleeds and bears the penalty of their sin. Here the Old Testament is ultimately interpreted by the New.

Chapter 19

THE GREAT WHITE THRONE
Terminus 1
Rev. 20:1–15

Revelation 20 is a chapter of culminations, resolutions, and solutions. As in chapters 21–22 still to come, here ultimate destinies are being fixed, and the Revelation arrives at the climax of its journey. In these three last chapters, the entire human race meets its future either at the great white throne (terminus 1) or in the arrival of the Holy City (terminus 2).

Picking up at the conclusion of the last chapter, where the beast and false prophet were dispatched to the lake of fire, Revelation now consigns the dragon to the pit in which he is imprisoned for one thousand years. Moreover, we are reminded of chapter 9, where the fifth trumpet first conjured the world of this bottomless pit. There a star descended from heaven and opened a shaft to this demonic netherworld, liberating a plague of hellish locusts. Now, for a time, that pestilential domain is to be sealed and put out of commission. No more will it fashion and shape the realities of earth. Nevertheless, even this is not the final milestone in the history of evil.

20:1–3 • At the beginning of John's fourth scene, depicting the consequences of Christ's return (see comment at 19:11), four titles tell us all we need to know about "the dragon" and his real nature. Realizing he has ultimately been defeated (12:7–13), he then invested what power he retained in his surrogate, the System (13:2–4), and vented his wrath upon the church. Known as "Satan" (adversary) and "the devil" (accuser), he is also "that ancient serpent" depicted by a spiritual kaleidoscope in the Hebrew Scriptures (Gen. 3; Job 26:12–13; Isa. 27:1).

Throughout the Revelation, the dragon has been the central symbol for evil and its power. Its origin, however, has remained a mystery, as it is in the rest of the Bible.[1] Where did evil come from? The

Scriptures are puzzlingly silent on this issue. When it is defined as "the dragon" in Revelation, one thing is being said for certain — God is not its author. Evil is serpentine, demonic, and satanic, John writes, and we recognize many backgrounds to these symbols (1 Chron. 21:1; Job 1–2; Zech. 3:1–2; Luke 10:18). Still, with regard to evil's *origin*, not even the symbolic "war in heaven" noted in Revelation 12 gives us any clear or complete answer. Why *war?* What primeval event was its original cradle?

The most widely held theory is that the issue hangs on the Creator's desire to populate the universe with creatures of *free will.* Empowered to make free moral choices, they were coincidentally given the capacity to devise evil and all that is contrary to God's will. Within that "freedom of choice" lies the ultimate origin of evil, whether we are speaking of the angelic ranks or those of earth. This is the background against which Isaiah's famous passage must also be read: "I form the light and create darkness, / I bring prosperity and create disaster; / I, the LORD, do all these things" (Isa. 45:7). This is a Hebraic way of saying that God makes *all* things.[2] Whence comes "disaster"? God is not its direct author, but neither could evil or negativity exist without the provision of free will ordained by the Creator. God does stand behind all things! Ernest Stoffel explains evil's origin in this way: "Man is made free to say Yes or No to God. . . . 'No' is 'the great dragon,' evil, wherever it is found. And 'No' has become a power on earth. The question, then, is whether or not 'No' is strong enough to overcome" (93).

Can "No" overcome? The answer is given in these verses. The ultimate judgment on "No" is quite simply that it is to be bound, cast into the pit, shut out of history, and sealed up. For a thousand years, this primordial power of evil will cease to inflict its sulfurous presence upon the inhabitants of the earth. It is as Isaiah foresaw:

> In that day the LORD will punish
>   the powers in the heavens above,
>   and the kings on the earth below.
> They will be herded together
>   like prisoners bound in a dungeon;
>   they will be shut up in prison
>   and be punished after many days.
>
> — Isaiah 24:21–22

A time will come, agrees Revelation, when the supernatural element in all evil will be voiceless, and what lurks in the heart of humanity, when left to itself, will be revealed. Was Flip Wilson in his quintessential comment correct: Has the devil made us do it? The answer lies in the thousand years to follow.

One of the more mysterious features in this book filled with riddles is the word "must" in verse 3. Just why *must* the dragon be loosed, though briefly, at the end of the millennium? What purpose could possibly be served by once again exposing the human race to the devices of Satan? "Must" tells us that divine purposes are involved but does not completely explain their ultimate rationale.

Biblical scholars and commentators have offered many explanations. Is it meant to reveal that people — with free wills intact — are more than mere by-products of their social environment? Even after a thousand years free of the encroachments of supernatural evil, the human willingness to be seduced is as apparent as ever (rebellion ensues immediately). Does it show that time, the great healer of so many human ills, cannot of itself heal the resilient spiritual infection of sick hearts? Or is it to prove the ultimate powerlessness of the dragon's control over history (his rebellion is immediately quashed, a cameo of his whole career, as it were)? One thing, though, stands out starkly; right to the end, spiritual battle is a constant. Until the white throne gives its ultimate decision, the holy war against evil continues.

20:4 – 6 • Questions immediately arise from this enigmatic passage: Who are the ones about to share the reign of Christ? When does this "first resurrection" and "thousand years" take place? What is the nature and function of their reign? These are the subjects of the fifth scene that follows Christ's return.

As for the first question, those "beheaded because of their testimony" and those who "had not worshiped the beast" have been variously understood as (1) all those who have died as martyrs of Christ throughout history (i.e., one group made up of those who would not worship the beast and were, therefore, martyred — beheaded — is to be distinctively rewarded; cf. 12:11; 13:15) or (2) all genuine Christians who have lived faithful, committed lives (one group manifesting two experiences: some "beheaded" martyrs and some who "had not worshiped" but were not executed).

The latter approach is probably to be preferred because all the seven churches are anticipated to include *overcomers* who have resisted the blandishments of the System and kept faith with Christ (Rev. 2-3). They are those whose names have been recorded in the book of life (3:5; cf. 2:11; 20:6) and who have met the criteria of true discipleship (14:3–5; Wall, 238). These passages do not seem to single out some unique group within the church, but rather speak of all faithful Christians who are equally redeemed and called to service in a variety of ways.

Furthermore, this shared reign of Christ has been anticipated in 2:26 (in a church where martyrdom is not an issue) and 5:10, where it is said, "they will reign on earth." In chapter 5, "they" refers to all the ransomed, from all the peoples on earth, who have been constituted "a kingdom and priests" to serve God (vv. 9–10; cf. 1:5–6). Paul also speaks of a "first" resurrection (1 Thess. 4:16) and later describes that event in a more general scene (1 Cor. 15:51–54), neither of which admits any differentiation among Christians. It is better, therefore, to see those who participate in the "first resurrection" in chapter 20 as all those who have been faithful but through two different life experiences.

Revelation does call our attention to the martyr Antipas (2:13), who was one of those that "did not love their lives so much / as to shrink from death" (12:11), but this same book also refers to a "woman" (who is a symbol for the whole messianic community of believers) who escapes and takes flight from the dragon, seeking protective seclusion from his wrath (12:6,14). Moreover, John himself has experienced the battle differently from Antipas, for John has been banished to Patmos, where he is sharing the social pressures of "the tribulation" (1:9, RSV) but not, as far as we know, martyrdom. Probably, John is thinking of the entire church that has resolutely followed Christ, some through the valley of the shadow of death, others through endless persecutions and deprivations (cf. Luke 18:28–30). These all share equally in the "first resurrection."

Even more debatable is the question, When do this resurrection and the consequent thousand-year reign take place? Three historic interpretations of "the millennium" have been put forward — postmillennial, amillennial, and premillennial.[3]

The *postmillennial* view suggests that the thousand years is symbolic of a still future day of gospel grandeur, achieved as the logical aftermath of the church's evangelistic labors. The term *postmillennial* signifies that the return of Christ is viewed as taking place "after" (from the Latin *post*) the millennium. Held early by such church fathers as Origen and Jerome, this view became the dominant one of American evangelicals during the eighteenth and nineteenth centuries, claiming such luminaries as Jonathan Edwards, A. A. Hodge, and A. H. Strong. Certainly misguided are those who demean this view by suggesting that only fuzzy-minded, utopian liberals have ever espoused it, for it represents a serious attempt to understand

Scripture. In the modern period, it continues to enjoy a degree of popularity among conservative Christians.[4]

What most clearly distinguishes postmillennialism is its *optimistic triumphalism*. It clings to the expectation that the church will one day begin to conquer and overcome the forces of darkness that enslave the world. This victorious breakthrough of the work of the Spirit then produces a magnificent era (the millennium) during which the church's gospel will transform the earth into a spiritual garden of Eden. Earth will finally experience the just society and the reign of peace (genuine *shalom*) for which it was originally created.[5]

From the postmillennial perspective, the "first resurrection" (vv. 4–6) is the event or process that *initiates* the millennial conquest and represents a future extraordinary rebirth of the spirit and power of the martyr's faith, which finally leads to a spiritual conquest of planet Earth. At length, the majestic thousand-year (a symbolic figure) victory produced by this revival of Christian esprit de corps triggers the Kingdom as an earthly reality and leads to the return of Christ. The job of the church — both prior to and during the millennium — is to build the kingdom of God by converting the masses, thus instigating the first resurrection and later compelling Christ's return, so that he might join the party (see Fig. 8).

†_____ / The Millennium / The Return of Christ & Eternity

The   Church   Age

Fig. 8. The Postmillennial View

Amillennialism, which goes back to such early Christians as Justin Martyr and Augustine, remains another important exposition of Revelation 20. It takes a different, nonliteral approach to this major symbol of the thousand-year period. The term *amillennialism* actually means "no millennium," but that is perhaps a misnomer and is clearly not its intent. At least as far back as Augustine, this school has taken the thousand years to be a symbolic, cameo portrayal of the agelong conversion, spiritual reign, and victorious living of believers on earth and/or in heaven after death. Not understanding the thousand years as an intervening period of history betwixt our present and eternal future, amillennialism anticipates no prospective or physical earthly millennium beyond what the Christian is presently experiencing. The thousand years, then, is a totalistic symbol, perhaps a miniature parable, which concisely portrays the spiritual significance of the present age, that is, the entire church age (Pentecost to Parousia).

From the amillennial perspective, the binding of Satan (v. 2) suggests the curbing of his power by the death and resurrection of Jesus at the beginning of the millennium (i.e., the church age). The thrones of those who reign with Christ (v. 4) represent the Christian dead, who enjoy his presence in heaven. From that privileged position, they share in his rule and judgment over those who had martyred them. The first resurrection (vv. 4–6) signifies their *spiritual* conversion and new birth, in this life, which led to their union and eventual presence with the Lord. Taking another direction, some amillennialists feel this resurrection stands for the moment of physical death when the children of God are lifted to the divine fellowship and their mutual reign (the intermediate state) commences. The second resurrection, then, represents the final, *physical* awakening of all the righteous and unrighteous at the Second Coming. Throughout the history of Christianity, the amillennial view has probably remained the predominate opinion in the broader church (see Fig. 9).

†/   The Millennium   / The Return of Christ & Eternity

The   Church   Age

Fig. 9. The Amillennial View

Close on the heels of amillennialism for dominance, however, is *premillennialism*, which has been especially influential among those church traditions known as "evangelical" or "fundamentalist." The term *premillennial* denotes the appearance of the Second Coming "before" (from the Latin *pre*) the millennium. As with its two chief competitors, there are varieties of outlooks espoused by its adherents.[6]

Principally, premillennialism takes a somewhat more literal approach to the subject than the other views, arguing for a real time period, after the Second Coming, when the kingdom of God is objectively manifested on this present earth. Materially, this millennial kingdom is not much different from the postmillennial expectation; however, it is produced, not by the church's labors, but the cataclysmic intervention of the returning Christ. The premillennialist understands the purpose of this time period to be the final vindication of the cause of Jesus Christ within the confines of history. While the beast and the false prophet languish in the lake of fire, those who have given their lives for Christ enjoy all the delights at his command. Indeed, it represents both their terminal and tangible triumph over evil and the final realization "of what we hope for . . . of what we do not see" (Heb. 11:1).[7]

According to the premillennial view, the "first resurrection" is that discussed in 1 Thessalonians 4:13–18, where the people of God are physically raised from the dead to meet and greet their Lord in the air.[8] The "reign" of the saints is the resultant period of time (not necessarily a literal thousand years) during which the redeemed share in the rule of Christ over an idyllic period of earthly splendor. The period when "the rest of the dead . . . come to life" then indicates the general resurrection of all humanity at the end of the epoch (see Fig. 10).

† _____ / Tribulation Period / Return of Christ & Millennium / Judgment & Eternity

The   Church   Age

Fig. 10. The Premillennial View

There are admirable characteristics associated with each view, and each has had notable Christian proponents. The postmillennialist constantly reminds us that the Kingdom is among us, ever struggling to transform humanity through the church's labors. Further, it encourages us to avoid pessimism and the deadly chill of defeatist fatalism. To the contrary, it embodies the empowering call to "stand firm. Let nothing move you. Always give yourselves fully to the work of the Lord, because you know that your labor in the Lord is not in vain" (1 Cor. 15:58). Amillennialism stresses the symbolic nature of Revelation. Thus, when it suggests that the thousand years is a figurative or parabolic representation of the whole of Christian experience, it seeks a simple fidelity to the core of this book of symbols. And, finally, premillennialism makes its contribution by cautioning us against unrealistic utopianism. Our efforts do not ultimately cause the Kingdom's arrival; in the last analysis, only the Sovereign Lord can so change the world. Such a dose of reality is important as we contemplate the church's future, but it also suggests that when God has accomplished his purposes, this earth will see the Kingdom it was made to manifest.[9]

The answer to the question, What is the nature of the reign they share with Christ? depends on one's approach to the whole issue. For the amillennialist, the reign must be coextensive with observed realities characteristic of the church age; it is essentially a religious reign governed by spiritual dynamics. This would mean that the church is engaged in a process of producing and imposing those forces that are the opposite of the principalities and powers, namely, "love, joy, peace, patience, kindness, goodness, faithfulness, gentleness and self-control" (Gal. 5:22–23). Moreover, the reign would take into account Jesus' command that "all authority in heaven and on earth has been given to me ... go and make disciples of all nations. ... And surely I am with you always, to the very end of the age" (Matt. 28:18–20). Thus, does the church exercise "the keys of the kingdom" (Matt. 16:19; cf. John 20:22–23).

For the postmillennialist as for the premillennialist, it is an epoch that is future, idealistic, and focused on this earth. "Reigning" signifies much the same thing as it does for the amillennialist — instituting the Kingdom — though the context would be a future age conceived as a totally different or transformed environment. These views differ, however, on the nature of its inauguration. The postmillennialist usually expects a smooth, perhaps even gradual, transition into the millennial period; it emerges out of and essentially expands the qualities of the church age. The premillennialist, on the other hand, sees it beginning in a cataclysmic inbreaking of Christ that ends the tribulation period and commences a quite new reality — a renewed age upon this earth.

Though it is not precisely spelled out in Scripture, the premillennialist could come to a rather startling conclusion concerning the nature of the reign and the millennium in general. It is more than possible that the heavenly city described in 21:9–22:5 encompasses both the millennial epoch as well as the new heaven and earth. Several similarities point in this direction. In 21:9, the city of God, the bride city, is introduced in nearly the identical terms used to announce the prostitute city in 17:1 ("One of the seven angels who had the seven bowls came and said to me, 'Come, I will show you'"). These two cities, then, are deliberately contrasted with each other, for *both stand on the earth* (cf. 21:10, where coming down out of heaven must mean to the earth). Hence, once the prostitute city is destroyed (chap. 18), what reality rules on earth prior to the bride city (chap. 21)? In Revelation 19:6–9, a series of hallelujahs greet the overthrow of the prostitute city, and the last of these proclaims:

> "Hallelujah!
>   For our Lord God Almighty reigns.
> Let us rejoice and be glad
>   and give him glory!

> For the wedding of the Lamb has come,
> and his bride has made herself ready."

. . . .

"Write: 'Blessed are those who are invited to the wedding supper of the Lamb!' "

Since 21:2,9–10 equates the New Jerusalem with the bride and 19:6–9 announces both the inauguration of the reign of God and the advent of the Lamb's marriage to the bride, it would seem natural (or at least possible) that the bride city begins its history at this point (the same time as the millennium of chapter 20 is being established), namely, during the death throws of the prostitute's city.

It is, then, this bride city that is defined in 20:9 as "the camp of God's people, the city he loves." Furthermore, Gog and Magog — the final assault force — no longer represent forces to the north of Palestine, as they did in Ezekiel 38–39, but now personify "the nations in the four corners of the earth" (v. 8). And when this battle is over, we are never told the *beloved city* passes away. On the contrary, it has been defended and preserved. This means that there is good reason to believe that John thought of "the city he [God] loves" as the foreshadowing or the prefinalized form of the ultimate city of God.

If this interpretation is correct, then we have the explanation for the frequent observation that many features of the New Jerusalem (in chaps. 21–22) are equally appropriate to life on this earth. For example, note that while "the nations will walk by its light, and the kings of the earth will bring their splendor into it . . . nothing impure will ever enter it, nor will anyone who does what is shameful or deceitful, but only those whose names are written in the Lamb's book of life" (21:24–27). Further, the tree of life within it is "for the healing of the nations" (22:2), but "the dogs, those who practice magic arts, the sexually immoral, the murderers, the idolaters," are to be excluded (22:15). Strange language, indeed, in an environment where "the first heaven and the first earth had passed away, and there was no longer any sea" (21:1). Whence come the kings or nations in need of healing, impure things, and even unclean people? Such realities sound like forces upon *this* rather than the *new* earth. In fact, reading the description of the New Jerusalem in 21:9–22:5, one finds a constant commingling of realities appropriate to the old age as well as the new. But that is, perhaps, exactly what the new city of God is: it is the kingdom of God, both millennial (finally consummated on this earth as the Lord's Prayer predicts) and eternal (not of this earth) — the bride city of Christ.[10]

20:7–9 • Regardless of the view one holds concerning the millennium, the event in these verses is understood much the same. At the extreme limit of old earth's history, there is to be one final convulsion of catastrophic evil. Once again, as in the garden, Satan goes forth to seduce the nations with his malevolent "no-to-God" propaganda. Intriguingly, his role is portrayed, not so much as the author of evil, but rather as the orchestrator of that which is latent and awaiting his call, just beneath the surface of the human heart.

In describing this scene, Revelation draws upon prophecies derived from Ezekiel 38–39, concerning Gog and Magog. Originally they spoke of a final, end-time attack on Israel, but now Revelation reapplies them to describe the final assault against "God's people, the city he loves" (Rev. 20:9). What had been perceived as an attack from the "north" (Ezek. 38:6,15; 39:2), the conventional route of invasion into Palestine, is now inclusive of all four points on the compass. The onslaught is worldwide and suggests something similar — that it is vast — about "the camp of God's people." Nevertheless, this battle is as ill-fated for the foes of God as Ezekiel had foreseen: "I will summon a sword against Gog.... I will pour down torrents of rain, hailstones and burning sulfur on him and on his troops.... And so I will show my greatness and my holiness, and I will make myself known in the sight of many nations. Then they will know that I am the LORD" (Ezek. 38:21–23; cf. 39:6; 2 Kings 1:9–16). One might also hear an echo of the brothers James and John when they wished to call down fire to consume a Samaritan village that had been unreceptive to Jesus' ministry (Luke 9:52–54).

20:10 • The devil, as he is known to us in Scripture, is always, and never more than, God's devil. He never functions independently nor strays beyond the control or permission of the Almighty. Just so, having played his role — revealing the rebellion quietly lurking within the human heart — the devil is immediately dispatched to his eternal destiny, forever inconsequential, never to be heard from again. Here the ancient story of Job comes to its ultimate conclusion. The tormentor will be eternally tormented. Finally, humiliatingly, he shares the same wretched fate as his underlings. Not Satan bound but Satan and all his minions *destroyed* is Scripture's ultimate promise.

20:11–12 • Now, in his sixth scene, John is brought face-to-face with the ultimate terminus of time, where everything has vanished except God's throne. Here John gives voice to the conviction that every knee shall bend and every tongue be silenced before that throne, "for we will all stand before God's judgment seat" (Rom. 14:10). And on that day, the Lord "will bring to light what is hidden in darkness and will expose the motives of men's hearts" (1 Cor. 4:5). John does not take this opportunity to describe the scenery, for that has been done previously in chapters 4 and 5. There the "cockpit of history," towering above the trifling tyrants of time, was shown to be overpoweringly in charge of creation's destiny. This is that destiny. Time is bracketed by two thrones. In the beginning stands the throne of the Creator; at the end, the throne of the Judge. All will stand before that bar of divine justice, and all will answer for the use of life, opportunity, talent, and time God has graciously given.

A small detail, often overlooked as we read this passage, is the very marrow of the matter. At the ultimate moment, a startling process of "dual bookkeeping" is revealed. Two sets of books are lying on the heavenly bar of justice. One proclaims what we have done with all that has been given to us, and one reveals all that has been done for us. Behind one lies a smoldering omniscience; behind the other, an unquenchable love. Which is the primary text? On this, John is *unambiguous.*

The rocky relationship between "faith and works," "law and grace," is not a new dilemma in Scripture and clearly not in the Revelation. Of his own heavenly vision, Daniel commented, "As I looked, / "thrones were set in place, / and the Ancient of Days took his seat... / The court was seated, / and the books were opened" (Dan. 7:9–10; cf. 12:1). Similarly, Jeremiah wrote, "I the LORD search the heart / and examine the mind, / to reward a man according to his conduct, / according to what his deeds deserve" (17:10; cf. Rom. 2:6; 1 Pet. 1:17).[11] That the actions of every individual are observed and noted is the clear counsel of Scripture. Furthermore, it is apparent that individual accounts are constantly tallied and balances credited or debited. Thus, Jesus warned, "From everyone who has been given much, much will be demanded; and from the one who has been entrusted with much, much more will be asked" (Luke 12:48; cf. Matt. 25:14–30). From this, Paul took his cue when he argued that we have been redeemed by faith for the very purpose of "good works, which God prepared in advance for us to do" (Eph. 2:10; cf. 1 Cor. 3:10–15). Further, we have already noted how regularly Revelation comments on the decisive role played by our accomplishments (cf. 2:2,5,19,22,26; 3:1,8,15; 14:13; 18:6); indeed, it even concludes with the promise (or threat?), "Behold, I am coming soon! My reward is with me, and I will give to everyone according to what he has done" (22:12). This stream of doctrine represents one of the important tributaries to Revelation's central current of theology.

Nevertheless, no one finds salvation on the sliding scale of achievement. The psalmist already knew that: "If you, O LORD, kept a record of sins, / O Lord, who could stand?" (Ps. 130:3). Thus, Paul concludes, in one of his most famous comments: "We hold that a person is justified by faith apart from works prescribed by the law" (Rom. 3:28, NRSV; cf. Gal. 3:10–14). The point is, when it comes to avoiding a destiny in "the lake of fire," the text of only one book matters. In the last analysis, it is never what *we* have done that earns the right to redemption but solely what *Jesus* has done for us. "The book of life" mentioned here is elsewhere called "the Lamb's book of life" (21:27; cf. 13:8). It is the prime and only text of decisive importance for entrance into the city of God. For that city, it is the registry of citizenship. It belongs to the Lamb because he was "slaughtered and by ... [his] blood ... ransomed for God / saints from every tribe and language and people and nation; ... / and they will reign on earth" (5:9–10, NRSV).

20:13 • Should it appear strange that "the sea" is set apart from "death and Hades" (the general realm of the dead), though not the deserts or mountains, let us remember the structure of Hebrew parallelism (Mulholland, 312). "Sea" in the first line parallels "death and Hades" in the second, which suggests that the sea (soon to be described in 21:1 as "no longer") stands for the entire realm of sin and death; that is, the "sea" equals "death and Hades" — not literal oceans. In Revelation, "the sea" is a quite comprehensive symbol that seems to stand for the repository of all that is disfigured in God's creation.

The judgment according to what had been accomplished is apparently not unlike that mentioned by Paul where the "Day" and "the fire will test the quality of each man's work" (1 Cor. 3:13). John, too, expresses the conviction that each and every deed is of ultimate consequence and will be taken into account. But how such a tallying of "what he had done" might affect the fate of one whose name is not written in the book of life is not commented on and is not clear. Are there gradations of punishment for the damned as there seem to be varieties of rewards for the righteous? John seems to imply as much but leaves off commenting just where we would have wished for more insight.

20:14–15 • Ultimately, death and Hades are just as powerless as all the other forces of evil. These ghoulish wanderers, rambling through history on the back of the fourth horse (6:8), will meet the fate common to all who resist the will of God. John is allowed to glimpse that joyous day when "the last enemy to be destroyed is death" (1 Cor. 15:26; an event anticipated as early as Isa. 25:7). Death is one of those distortions of creation that reside in the sea, which is shortly to be eternally destroyed.

Which book is preeminent? Plainly, all the good works imaginable are inadequate if one is not inscribed in the book of life. "Only those who are not written in the Book of Life (and not those who have produced bad works)," notes Jacques Ellul, "are thrown into the second death" (212). Jesus taught this to his disciples when he said that there would be, one day, some who will plead the quantity and quality of their works as the basis for their acceptance into the final Kingdom. "Lord, Lord, did we not prophesy in your name, and in your name drive out demons and perform many miracles?" (Matt. 7:22), they will contend. "Then I will tell them plainly, 'I never knew you. Away from me, you evildoers!'" (7:23). What a rude awakening to believe your accomplishments were adequate, only to discover that all was in vain. That is certainly a sobering thought! What is the motivation of our deeds (cf. Luke 17:7–10)? Are our works the reverberations of a living relationship with Jesus or the by-products of our own egos? His words, "I never knew you," are the key.

When Revelation speaks of a "first resurrection" and a "second death," it implies the actuality of a "second resurrection" and a "first death." Of these interrelated destinies, Henry Alford remarked, "As there is a second and higher life, so there is also a second and deeper death. And as after that life there is no more death . . . so after that death there is no more life."[12]

No one and no thing escapes! As Robert Mounce observes, everything associated with sin is henceforth consigned to eternal destruction, namely,

> Satan, who first rebelled against God (20:10); the beast and false prophet, who carried out his evil designs in history (20:10); the men of the world, who chose to worship Satan (20:15); death, his last weapon (20:14); and Hades, Satan's appropriate domain (20:14). The victory of God is complete! (*What Are We Waiting For?* 108)

Their destiny definitive and impotence irreversible, they are everlastingly condemned to the second and ultimate death.[13] This brings the story of history, of "No!" and its futile, unproductive rebellion, to its terminus. But what of those whose names are written in the book of life? What awaits them? This will be fully disclosed in the *seventh* scene, which reveals the full significance of Christ's return as his bride's blessed hope; it is detailed in chapters 21–22.

Notes

1. Some will point to Isaiah 14 and Ezekiel 28 for solutions to this mystery. However, since their authors specifically identify the subjects they speak of as the king of Babylon (Isa. 14:4) and the prince or king of Tyre (Ezek. 28:2,12), by far the majority of evangelical biblical scholars reject the identification of these chapters with the origin of Satan.

2. The technical term for this literary device is *merismus,* a word that identifies the mention of two representative but opposite components of an entity to stand for the whole. So "both young and old" means the entire range of ages from young to old. "Light and darkness," "prosperity and disaster," mean the entire range of options entailed in these concepts.

3. For a brief, yet wide-ranging, introduction to the subject, I recommend Stanley J. Grenz's *The Millennial Maze.* For a more detailed approach to the same issues, see Robert G. Clouse's *The Meaning of the Millennium.* One of the most engagingly written accounts of the history of these views is found in part 1 of Arthur Wainwright's *Mysterious Apocalypse.*

4. See the writings of John J. Davis of Gordon-Conwell Seminary.

5. For a catalog of the hopes, visions, poetry, and aspirations of those who hold this view, see "The Transformation of Society" in Wainwright, 177–87.

6. For a digest of the special views held by dispensationalists, deriving from J. N. Darby, an Irish Anglican leader among the early nineteenth-century Plymouth Brethren, see Grenz, 91–125.

7. Robert Mounce agrees but also sees in the millennium "a special reward for those who have paid with their lives the price of faithful opposition to the idolatrous claims of Antichrist" (359). He sees this period of time as a response to the prayer of those at the altar in 6:9–11.

8. Insightfully, George Ladd deemed the first resurrection to be the crux of the entire passage concerning the millennium: "Now, John again sees the souls of the martyrs; but he immediately adds, 'they came to life again.' This is the most important word in the entire passage. The exegete must decide whether or not it means resurrection; and upon this decision will be determined how he interprets the entire passage" (Ladd, *Commentary on the Revelation,* 265). The verb used here, "they came to life," is used elsewhere in Revelation only in 2:8 and 13:14 (where the beast mimics Christ), which almost certainly refer to resurrection. Henry Alford's famous rejoinder is still astute: "If, in a passage where *two resurrections* are mentioned...the first resurrection may be understood to mean *spiritual* rising with Christ, while the second means *literal* rising from the grave [as in both post- and amillennial positions]; — then there is an end of all significance in language, and Scripture is wiped out as a definite testimony to anything" (in Mounce, *Book of Revelation,* 356).

9. On the other hand, if one wishes to avoid the acrimony and strife that have often accompanied these competing schools of thought and to

inject a little humor into the discussion, I commend "pan-millennialism." *Pan-millennialism* seeks to avoid the rancor of historical debates by simply affirming that in the end everything will *pan* out all right, the very way God wishes. Sometimes it is useful to inject a little whimsy when discussing debatable issues many hold dear. In such a context, I enjoy relating a charmingly naive statement by John Calvin (who did not attempt a commentary on Revelation, perhaps for this very reason). Commenting on Daniel 7:25, Calvin cleverly observed: "Interpreters differ widely about these words, and I will not bring forward all their opinions, otherwise it would be necessary to refute them, but I will follow my own custom of shortly expressing the genuine sense of the prophet, and thus all difficulty will be removed" (in Richardson, 7).

10. For an expansion of these arguments, see the discussion by G. R. Beasley-Murray (in George, 63–66).

11. As the old proverb recognizes, Sow a thought and reap a deed; sow a deed and reap a habit; sow a habit and reap a character; sow a character and reap a destiny. The same point is made in Dante's *Divine Comedy* where "men are seen permanently fastened to the central meaning which they have given to their lives" (in Mounce, *Book of Revelation*, 365, n. 35).

12. In Mounce, *Book of Revelation*, 367. Austin Farrer makes the interesting observation: "A man might die ... to this world, and not die for the world to come; the incurable sinner might die to both.... The 'first death' is virtually universal ...; the second death is selective.... The first resurrection, on the contrary, is highly selective ... the second absolutely universal" (206).

13. A very readable and stimulating, but brief, account of the main views on the fate of the unredeemed will be found in Crockett.

Chapter 20

THE CITY OF GOD, THE NEW JERUSALEM

Terminus 2

Rev. 21:1–22:21

Chapters 21–22 are not only the conclusion of Revelation but also of the whole of Scripture. To transmogrify the unforgettable words of Winston Churchill, the biblical story of God and God's people is not coming to an end, not even the beginning of the end, but now Revelation's climactic chapters introduce us to what is certainly the end of the beginning.

The return of the garden of Eden, the original home lovingly shared with the Creator, is at hand. It had always represented the original purposes of God and the greatest hopes of the people of God: "How lovely is your dwelling place, / O LORD Almighty! My soul yearns, even faints, / for the courts of the LORD; / my heart and my flesh cry out / for the living God" (Ps. 84:1–2). In response to the psalmist, Jesus promised, "In my Father's house are many rooms.... I am going there to prepare a place for you" (John 14:2). The hope forged through all of Scripture and for which all God's people have longingly yearned finally arrives — "I will dwell in the house of the LORD / forever" (Ps. 23:6). Ultimately, says Revelation, there will be a time when all of God's intentions for humanity will be achieved. Then God's everlasting love for the elect will be the Alpha and Omega of their reality. That future John will now survey from his own Mount Pisgah, as Moses once scanned the Holy Land.

What we are about to read is exquisite art painted in the hues of holy poetry, where earthly symbols describe that which is beyond all human experience. When we read of "golden streets" and "pearly gates," such poetic art is not to be taken factually any more than Jesus' descriptions of himself as a "gate" (John 10:9) or "vine" (John

15:1) are to be taken literally. This is a world of spiritual symbolism, not the stuff of videotapes.[1]

John's inspiring images remind one of the unfortunate Jewish women living out their last days in the Nazi concentration camps. One of the numerous ways in which they coped with their terminal situation was to produce, of all things, *cookbooks.* They knew that they would never again be able to prepare the wondrous dishes they disclosed to others; nevertheless, these culinary visions represented hopes for a day beyond the horrors of the Nazi period when, as their recipes proclaimed, a new beginning would allow these books to nourish a brighter future. Such books were the food of their spirits commended to another day where their children and others could be nurtured by their faith. So it is with these chapters; they speak of a time when all the hopes of biblical faith will have become sight (2 Cor. 5:7). And, at long last, those churches struggling to maintain their spiritual identity and balance in the cities of Ephesus, Smyrna, Pergamum, Thyatira, Sardis, Philadelphia, and Laodicea will inherit the Holy City.[2] The blessings of this wondrous place are envisioned through the categories of *place, people,* and the *presence* of God (Bauckham, 132). These three commingle to create the New Jerusalem.

Chapter 21

21:1–2 • This opening passage of the final two chapters reveals one of the most important functions of the Revelation: it is meant to refurbish and revitalize our Christian imaginations, to help us perceive the world in a way alternative to the dominant culture. From this infusion of holy poetics, restoring our vision and stimulating our imagination, we derive the strength to resist the blandishments of the System. The Holy City is John's most extensive and extravagant eschatological picture, but he is far from the first New Testament author to use this image (cf. Gal. 4:25–26; Heb. 11:10; 12:22–24; 13:14).

At a much earlier time, in one of his concluding passages, Isaiah once heard the Lord revealing the future in similar fashion:

> "Behold, I will create
>   new heavens and a new earth.
> The former things will not be remembered,
>   nor will they come to mind.

> But be glad and rejoice...
> for I will create Jerusalem to be a delight
> and its people a joy."
>
> — Isaiah 65:17–18, 25

But the common teaching of the Scriptures is that the eternal future of humanity is already encoded in the foundational story of Eden, the earthly garden. Hence, in many ways, the future is a return to its original model, the past. Biblical perspectives on that distant future consistently speak of a redeemed and regenerated earth. Humankind's future, therefore, is always an *earthy* hope, not a disembodied, spiritual flight into the heavens.[3] Eventually, all that the garden of Eden stood for, namely, the creational purposes of God for God's children, will be reconstituted. That means, of course, that the future is dynamically purposeful.

The boring, clichéd cartoon of a winged human floating on a cloud, strumming a harp, is as tiresome as it is biblically irrelevant. In the garden, there was work before the curse of sin appeared (Gen. 2:15), and so there will be once again, but of what sort we can only speculate. In the Bible, work is not the result of sin; slackness is. Work is where we invest the gifts God has bestowed in the future of his universe.

Of course, "there was no longer any sea"! All that separated John from his beloved congregations on the mainland will be part of the past. But more than simple physical separation is addressed here. John is thinking of a renewed world where the forces of the dragon have been swept away (the sea is the home of the beast; 13:1,6–8). When all the effects of fallen history on the earth, its subjection to "frustration" and its "bondage to decay," will be eradicated, then will be revealed the "glorious freedom of the children of God" (Rom. 8:20–21). What is being constructed is nothing less than the home of God, in which all the ruinous consequences of human sin are extinguished. No longer will the misery of creation's brokenness mar the earthly scene. The seething cauldron of evil, known as the "sea," will vanish into nothingness, as though it had never existed.

Center stage, then, is immediately taken by the Holy City, which comes down out of heaven and is described as "a bride beautifully dressed for her husband." Having this reality arrive from heaven is another way of saying that the future is not the by-product of human enterprise but is available only from the Creator — it descends from above. On the other hand, what John means by saying that the city is like a *bride* is about to be clarified.

21:3 – 4 • The sea dispensed with, John straightway reveals the ultimate hope of human destiny: an eternal fellowship with God. From the very outset, this theme of human/divine fellowship has been a core motif in biblical theology. In the beginning, Genesis locates "God … walking in the garden in the cool of the day" (Gen. 3:8); apparently, Adam and Eve were accustomed to sharing that part of the evening with their Maker. Later at Sinai, after the Fall, God promised eventually to repair the disruption: "I will put my dwelling place among you, and I will not abhor you. I will walk among you and be your God, and you will be my people" (Lev. 26:11–12; cf. Jer. 7:23; 11:4). The prayers of the temple also echoed this hope: "Lord, you have been our dwelling place / throughout all generations" (Ps. 90:1). Moreover, the prophets continue the theme by predicting a time when "my dwelling place will be with them; I will be their God, and they will be my people" (Ezek. 37:27; cf. Jer. 30:22; Ezek. 36:28; Hos. 1:23; Zech. 8:8). And finally, that dwelling of God with humanity reached a new level when "the Word became flesh and made his dwelling [literally 'tabernacled'] among us" (John 1:14; cf. Rom. 9:24–25; 1 Pet. 2:9–10). Now, says Revelation, God's people will truly be at home, "and God himself will be with them," for the curse of the Fall and humanity's alienation from God are utterly reversed.

21:5 – 8 • Indeed, "It is done"! The identical words are found at the conclusion of the bowls in 16:17. Expressing an eschatological, climactic statement from God, 21:5–8 brings us to the central denouement of the book, where redemption is completed and the eternal story of *Immanuel* (which means "God with us") begins. The title "the Alpha and the Omega" was first used of God in 1:8, as it is here, but in 22:13 it is Christ's title. This deliberate use of the title for both God and Christ indicates that the Father and Son, jointly, control the whole history of the universe.

All of humankind is divided into two camps, the overcomers, who are for the first time "my son(s)" ("children," NRSV), and those who fall into a variety of other disqualifying categories. Intriguingly to this point only Jesus has specifically been called God's "Son" (2:18), though this relationship to his "Father" has been implied several times (1:6; 2:27; 3:5,21; 14:1). Not until 21:7, as part of the New Jerusalem, however, does this status expand to include all believers. Is it only an accident that this passage represents the seventh and final appearance of this motif in the book? Those who conquer (i.e., who remain true to the Lamb and the testimony of their faith, which is the oft-repeated challenge to the churches) will inherit "all this," that is, the new heaven, the new earth, and the status of God's own "children" (NRSV). However, for the remainder, there is only a fearful judgment that is known as the "second death."

The Greek language possesses two words signifying "new": *neos* indicates something unique, never seen before, or "brand-new," while *kainos* points to something previously existent that is now in a fresh, "renewed" form. In 21:1 and 21:5, John uses the word *kainos.* What is coming is new in character or restored but not something unique or never before experienced. Hence, there is a new name (2:17), a new song (5:9), as well as the new heaven and earth (21:1). They each represent various continuities with the old and that which is passing away (Thompson, 84). Leonard Thompson suggests that the proclamation "It is done" should be translated, "All has been transformed" (85). Seemingly, the future is not one made of all new things but of all things made new.[4] This is the foundation for Revelation's later assertion that into this New Jerusalem will be brought all the best of human culture, while excluding all that is unworthy (21:26–27).

But why does this future sketch continue to speak to the cowardly, faithless, and so on? The last we heard of them, they were consigned to the lake of fire. By resurrecting their presence, as it were, John assures that this vision of the coming world functions not only as a comfort to those inside but also as a foreboding challenge to those outside the church. Revelation 21:8,27 and 22:15 assure that no simple universalism can be manufactured from these scenes of extraordinary beauty. The unrepentant have no place in this city! Still, biblical prophecy is never provided simply to satisfy the lunatic curiosity of spiritual voyeurs. Prediction is often a program for penitence in the present!

When we know the heading, goals, and outcomes of God's future, then we are obliged to begin marching in that direction. When those reading and hearing this book survey those who are denied access to the Holy City, it represents a call for repentance within the church and a challenge to renewed evangelistic outreach beyond its doors. If we read biblical prophecy and assume the posture of self-satisfaction as an enlightened one, as one "in the know," we engage in spiritual sin, Laodicea's sin, for prediction is always a demand for action. We are to be facilitators of the future!

21:9–14 • The two phrases "I will show you the bride" and "he...showed me the Holy City" indicate that this city, the New Jerusalem, is something much more than a mere geographical place; it is in reality nothing less than the people of God themselves (21:2), namely, "the bride, the wife of the Lamb" (cf. 19:7–9). When John describes the Holy City, then, he is not so much picturing a *physical site* of great attraction, though that certainly is involved. More precisely, he is defining a *spiritual state of being* and its sublime loveliness. Symbolically, John is depicting the beauty of a *people* more than a *place* and a people luxuriating in the perfect presence of God. In this vision, as Michael Wilcock so nicely puts it, there is a message for the seven churches of John's day and our own: "all of us are looking into a mirror in these verses. We are not merely spectators — we are ourselves the spectacle: it is we who are 'God's building' (1 Cor. 3:9). The city shown to us here is what we shall be in the age to come, what in a sense we already are" (207).

The two main cities of Revelation, great Babylon and the New Jerusalem, stand for alternate and opposite grids of human experience, two ways of inhabiting and relating to life. Hence, the people of God (the bride city = New Jerusalem) are not a gemstone ("jasper"; v. 11), though they have been made clean as crystal by the blood of the Lamb (7:14–17) and, therefore, have been clothed in bright linen (19:8). Nor do they consist of gates and foundations, though these symbols make serious statements about them.[5]

The gates of the New Jerusalem, named after the twelve tribes of Israel, were first mentioned in Ezekiel's visionary city named "THE LORD IS THERE" (Ezek. 48:30–35). Throughout biblical history, city and sanctuary gates have been recurring symbols of protection against aggression (Deut. 3:5; 1 Sam. 23:7; Isa. 24:12; Ezek. 21:22; Nah. 3:13), barriers to uncleanness (1 Chron. 9:23–24; 2 Chron. 23:19; Rev. 22:14) and Sabbath impurity (Neh. 13:22; Jer. 17:24–25), and entryways of thanksgiving and praise (Ps. 100:4; Isa. 60:18), with unrestricted gates indicating an absolute safety sustained by measureless power and wealth (Isa. 60:11; cf. Jer. 49:31). The latter image is directly associated with the Holy City, "On no day will its gates ever be shut, for there will be no night there" (Rev. 21:25). The bride city is a lively fellowship totally sheltered, enlightened, and carefree.

The twelve foundations on which the city is built are the twelve apostles. John seems to be saying that this fellowship is safeguarded and made festive by its Hebrew heritage but stands on the essentials established by the apostolic community. Biblically, a foundation represents that which is fundamental, stable, and lends support to all that stands thereon (1 Kings 5:17; 7:9–10; Isa. 28:16). On the other hand, a place of waste and devastation no longer stands on its proper foundations (Ps. 11:3; Lam. 4:11; Ezek. 30:4). And we, whose essential nature (foundation) is dust, face a precarious future, indeed (Job 4:19–21; 22:16). There is good reason, then, for Paul to argue that only one foundation holds everlastingly firm, "for no one can lay any foundation other than the one already laid, which is Jesus Christ" (1 Cor. 3:11; cf. Heb. 11:10).

"Architectural motifs" have been used more than once in the New Testament community to symbolize the Christian fellowship. Peter advised Christians to "let yourselves be built into a spiritual house" (1 Pet. 2:5, NRSV). And Paul voiced the same perspective, writing that we are "members of God's household, built on the foundation of the apostles and prophets, with Christ Jesus himself as the chief cornerstone. In him the whole building is joined together and rises to become a holy temple in the Lord...a dwelling in which God lives by his Spirit" (Eph. 2:19–22). Elsewhere, he observed that "you yourselves are God's temple" (1 Cor. 3:16). John concludes this theme with the two phrases, "I will show you the bride" and "he...showed me the Holy City."

21:15–21 • Now come the bridal measurements. This nuptial city, the eternal communion of God with the people of God, is glorified in every way possible to indicate the exquisite beauty and immaculate holiness of its connubial bliss. Surely its size is meant to stupefy. Converted into modern equivalents, 12,000 stadia would represent about 1,500 miles, but such conversions tend to obscure what John specifically intended his reader to note: every feature of the city is defined in terms of twelves. In Revelation, "twelve" always means the people of God, comprehended as either the twelve tribes or twelve apostles. With regard to community and fellowship, this is the number of totality. Thus, the city is 12,000 stadia (1,500 miles) square; such a city would represent an area more than filling the entire western half of America from the Mississippi to the coast; that would be the entirety of the Holy Land many times over.

Since its length, width, and height are equal, this city has the shape of a gigantic cube. And once again, we are faced with a symbol taken from our Hebrew heritage. The only other biblical structure so shaped is the inner sanctum of the temple known as the Holy of Holies. In Solomon's temple, it was 20 cubits long, wide, and high — a perfect cube — and the very locale of God's dwelling (1 Kings 6:20). But Solomon's Holy of Holies is now in the New Jerusalem extravagantly enlarged; instead of 2,700 cubic feet (converted from cubits), it has become 3,225,000 cubic miles (Peterson, 177). So, argues the Revelation, God's dwelling place is no longer in the temple's most recessed and inaccessible cubicle. Now the Holy City is itself the Holy of Holies, the very place where God lives and dwells with God's children. Instead of only "once a year," now the elect have permanent access to the divine presence (cf. Exod. 30:10; Lev. 16:34).

Such immediate entrée to God is already presaged in the Christian's current access to that fellowship (cf. Heb. 10:19–22). Moreover, this vision of heaven is meant to affirm the direct correspondence between what God's people have already begun to experience and what yet lies ahead as the *kainos*. The future is not some bizarre mysticism totally dissociated from the present; it is the present relationship already being enjoyed but completed and consummated, multiplied to the highest power.

One more curious fact about a cube is that it has *twelve* edges. Hence, by means of the simple equation 12 (edges) times 12,000 (stadia), we again reach the number of God's true Israel — 144,000 (Farrer, 217). On every hand, the city is defined in terms of twelves because it is the bride, the community of the faithful (twelve patriarchs and twelve apostles) in direct communion with God. Simply put, it is *people* as well as a *place* basking in the *presence* of God.

Continuing the theme of twelves, John describes the city wall as being "144 cubits" (one cubit is the length of the forearm, which is approximately eighteen inches), whether height or width is not specifically mentioned, though the New International Version has assumed the latter due to the greater difficulty of the former. But either way, a little more than 200 feet is patently ludicrous when the city being protected is 1,500 miles wide and high. Compared with so imposing a city, such a paper-thin wall would be vastly disproportionate. But it is neither width nor height that John describes, for the wall symbolically "defines" the city. In other words, that which envelops and sets the bounds of its reality is 144 (12 x 12), fraternity's formula for the dynamic relationship between Israel and the church. Nothing and no one else may enter through these walls. Only the people of God are included; all others are excluded. Symbolic dimensions aside, it is, in fact, "a great, high wall" (v. 12).

There is no need to ask whether pure gold, too soft even for jewelry, would be suitable for such vast architectural purposes or how it could possibly be transparent as glass. Nor are the wall's dimensions a difficulty, because this is poetic symbolism for that which cannot be described: "What God has planned for people who love him is more than eyes have seen or ears have heard"; no, beyond our wildest imagination, "it has never even entered our minds" (1 Cor. 2:9, CEV)! The enumeration of stunning jewels is calculated to touch the hem of poetic imagination, where reality shades into apocalyptic symbolism. Had the Jewish world known of diamonds or platinum, then surely they too would have been used to elaborate on the splendor of this city. The very fact, however, that they are not used indicates once again that this description is not meant to be taken literally since only those realities that were known are candidates for symbolic usage.

Though described by partially variant names, the stones are derived from the ancient breastplate worn by the Aaronic priest. On it, twelve stones were individually engraved with the names of the twelve tribes of Israel (Exod. 28:15–21). This is yet another indication that the bride of Christ is a vast combination of all those saints from the past, present, and future, all contributing to the glory that is the bride city. These radiant, natural gemstones also remind us that *creation* itself has a divinely appointed goal — to build and reflect the majesty of God. The divine glory is always manifested in the magnificence of natural beauty. This was always the prophetic vision of nature: "Holy, holy, holy is the LORD Almighty; / the whole earth is full of his glory" (Isa. 6:3). The New Testament theologian would agree with Isaiah, "for since the creation of the world," writes Paul, "God's invisible qualities — his eternal power and divine nature — have been clearly seen, being understood from what has been made" (Rom. 1:20). And so the Holy City reveals God's beauty through elements of creation and through God's people.

21:22–27 • The city itself is a vast cathedral, a place of direct and intimate interaction between God and God's loved ones, all of whom are priests and kings (cf. Rev. 1:6; 5:10; 20:6); hence, no temple is found within its precincts.[6] As in the Gospel of John, the true temple is Jesus (John 2:13–14,16–19,21–22) and his Father. Thus, there will be no need for a locale of mediated worship (i.e., a temple), for the Almighty will once again walk intimately among the people. One of the most wonderful aspects of this city is noted in the simple words, "they will see his face" (22:4). This is the city of which Ezekiel once spoke: "And the name of the city from that time on will be: THE LORD IS THERE" (Ezek. 48:35). It is a blessed city, where the distinction between sacred and secular has been erased and all aspects of life take place in the presence of the Creator.

The gates are always open, an invitation to all, because the one reason ancient cities had for closing gates — the need for protection — is no longer of concern. Unlike fallen Babylon, this is a city that has nothing to fear "because all crime is gone, justice for all prevails, and economic security is so accorded to all the people that none need fear robbery from anyone else" (Linthicum, 288). In other words, the requirements for a covenant-keeping society, a just society, spoken of so powerfully and consistently by the prophets, are here the substance of daily life. Here is the fulfilled promise made through Isaiah: "The LORD will be your everlasting light" (Isa. 60:19–20). Therefore, this city of "no night" never dwells under the haunting shadow of darkness, never pauses or closes, and never ceases throbbing with vigorous life and purposeful work.

A *walled* city (21:12) with *no shut gates* (21:25) is nearly a contradiction in terms but is also a perfect illustration of John's use of tensive symbols that are, not contradictory, but crosscurrents in the stream of truth. As a "great, high wall" indicates the presence of insiders and outsiders (inclusion and exclusion), gates that will not "ever be shut" indicate effortless access to the divine presence as well as freedom from danger. Those who inhabit this city are insiders. While there are outsiders (22:15) who have been excluded, no longer do they represent aspects of human grief or any barrier to God's unobstructed presence, nor do they threaten the freedom of God's people.[7]

This is the Holy City, the homeland of those whose names are written in "the Lamb's book of life," first glimpsed in chapter 5. Nothing, not even the judgment of the unholy city or the demise of Satan, is as compelling as the contents of this book. For it, the universe was set in motion; for it, the triune Godhead has endured the vicious and excruciating cycle of history; for it, the Son of God gave his life (cf. Ps. 87). When one asks, If God knew in advance what human history was to be like, why did God create us? the only answer is that as the Omega, God always knew that the end result, the Holy City, would justify the appalling agonies a rebellious creation would first cause.

John's continued discussion of nations and kings "of the earth" bringing glory into the city, while noting that nothing unclean is granted entrance, is noteworthy (vv. 24–27). It is either a further clue to the city's dual nature — the millennial camp of the saints and the eternal abode of the righteous — or a continuation of the "prediction is a program for the present" theme. If the latter, then Revelation is not suggesting that rival kings will continue to dot the landscape of God's eternal city, but the book is counseling patience and endurance for the present because the pomp and circumstance of the world will one day be inherited by the meek; that is, God's people. These two possibilities, of course, are not mutually exclusive. And we must also remember that to some legitimate extent John is forced to use the imagery of the present to describe the future. We must know when to allow imagery to be just that and not force it to say more than intended. So perhaps this motif means to do no more than contrast the self-indulgent exploitation of wealth, so characteristic of great Babylon, and the joy with which God's people, the new kings of the earth, bring their abundance into the Holy City.

There is, however, a possible hint at something fairly staggering. Does humanity contribute to this city? Do the labors of our
spirits, the fruition of our civilization and intellectual exploits, continue within the New Jerusalem? It would seem in this passage that
the Holy City is the consummation of all human history and even
embraces aspects of human culture, at least to the extent they are
compatible with the ultimate design of God (Bauckham, 135). Is the
music of Mozart and Beethoven, the art of Rembrandt and Monet,
the works of Michelangelo and Rodin, the poetry of Shelley and
Keats, the writing of Shakespeare, and much more that has enno-
bled the life of humanity simply to perish and be no more? Do
the labors of these who were made in the image of God and whose
works stem from that image mean nothing? Or has something of genuinely eternal value been a part of our collective earthly journey?
Should this be the case, and John may have foreseen such (vv. 24,26),
then the whole of human history, our work and highest endeav-
ors, are more directed toward the eternal future then ever we had
imagined.

Chapter 22

22:1–5 • There is a stream flowing through Scripture from one
end to the other; it is "the river of the water of life." Just as rivers
of water once radiated outward from Eden to nourish the earth and
bring it to life (Gen. 2:6,10), surging continuously through the lives
of God's people (Ps. 1:1–3; Jer. 17:7), so now, in the renewed universe,
"the throne of God and of the Lamb" is the hub of this current's radiant presence (cf. the prophetic hope; Joel 3:18; Ezek. 47:1–12; Zech.
14:8). Again, we return to a central theme of the entire book — the
transcendent throne. Here the "water" and "tree of life," which only
God's throne can make possible, represent the sustenance of eternal
life. Note the easy unity of God and the Lamb on the throne that is
so consistently presumed, and if the river proceeding from them alludes to the Holy Spirit (cf. John 4:14; 7:37–39), then once again the
complete Trinity is present.

Yes, the frustrated dreams of all generations will eventually be realized, for there is a fountain of youth — where all is fresh, renewed,
and vibrant — flowing from the throne of God. God's people will not
merely rest for eternity but dynamically participate in the business
of the universe, sharing what was their predestined position from the
beginning, namely, dominion, rule, and reign (Gen. 1:28; Ps. 8:5–8).

Paradoxically, it is only in this holy service that we find our perfect freedom. "Because God's will is the moral truth of our own being as his creatures," comments Richard Bauckham, "we shall find our fulfillment only when, through our free obedience, his will becomes also the spontaneous desire of our hearts" (142–43). This is the essence of heaven and life lived in the shadow of the throne.

The theme of eternal life is highlighted by the divine river, the Edenic tree, and the very presence of the Almighty. God is the one, as Paul once discerned of the King of kings and Lord of lords, "who alone is immortal" (1 Tim. 6:15–16). Such is not the inherent condition of humanity. Biblically speaking, only God possesses eternal life, and God is its solitary source for those who share in that life (cf. 1 Cor. 15:53; 2 Tim. 1:10). Thus, on the banks of this eternal river, flowing from the throne, the tree of life flourishes as never before, bringing forth twelve kinds of fruit, one for every portion of the year. Though once forbidden to Eden's renegades (Gen. 3:22–24), it flowers again for those who find shelter beneath its boughs. Here, there is no more curse, for God has redeemed God's people from all that the Fall had wrought. In the shadow of this throne is found the tenth and final fruit of the Spirit (Gal. 5:22–23), the fruit whose seed springs up to life everlasting.

One of the priceless blessings of this city that is a temple and a throne room is noted in the simple words, "They will see his face." It is the face that no mortal could see and survive that they are to behold (Exod. 33:20–23). To look upon the face of God is to know and experience what is in God's own self. This *beatific vision* is the supreme joy of heaven.

22:6 • From beginning (1:1) to end, Revelation concerns what "must soon take place." What is soon to be is the wonderful appearing of the Lord Jesus and those events that perennially presage that glorious day, that is, the signs of the end times or church age. When a book or portion thereof begins and concludes with the same theme, an inclusio structure is in place. Everything between these twin outposts is tethered to their precincts (e.g., Ps. 146–50; Eccl. 1:2; 12:8). Thus, the entire message of Revelation is about those events that precede and signal the second advent of Jesus Christ. They are the enduring cycle of rebellion and retribution that will finally be terminated by the returning, victorious Lord.

22:7 • The beatitude of the one who keeps the message of this book is the sixth of seven and indicates that this prophecy is not meant to lead to subtle calculation but Christian commitment. The *practice* of godly living, not prediction, is the core program of prophecy. Indeed, laboring to advance "the testimony of Jesus is the spirit of prophecy" (19:10).

The yet unrelieved tension between the promise "I am coming soon!" and the passage of two millennia is one the careful Bible student must face. The authors of the New Testament would certainly have been shocked to be told that history was to continue at least two thousand years beyond their day. Already at that time some were saying, "Where is this 'coming' he promised? Ever since our fathers died, everything goes on as it has since the beginning of creation" (2 Pet. 3:4). Correspondingly, we must never be discouraged by the unexpected passing of time but must plan and build for the next two thousand years, if such be the Lord's will. The Creator takes a very different view of time than we do, for "with the Lord a day is like a thousand years, and a thousand years are like a day" (2 Pet. 3:8). There may be many *days* yet to come, because our Lord has given us a very large universe in which to manifest the dominion of the image of God!

Those who try to use the Revelation as a Ouija board to inquire of the future are not only doing the book a very great disservice but are also deliberately rejecting the express injunction of the book's real author. He said, "It is not for you to know the times or dates the Father has set by his own authority. But you...will be my witnesses" (Acts 1:7–8). In the words of the Contemporary English Version, "You don't need to know the time of those events that only the Father controls." The future is on a need-to-know basis. What the church needs to do is to witness to the truth; that is "the spirit of prophecy." The attempt to domesticate the future through mastery of its mysteries is a spiritual lust.

22:8–11 • When prophecy achieves its goal, people serve and worship God. Always, the objective of the Revelation is to lead us to worshipful service, not speculation. One wonders if the main incentive motivating those who constantly speculate and set dates is reverence for their superior, exotic knowledge. This the angel rejects as improper!

The inclusio framework continues, adding further elements for consideration. The first element is another confirmation of the author's role. John is not the inventor or initiator but only the recipient of this prophecy (v. 8; cf. 1:1-2), which is a genuine revelation. The second element restates the critical emphasis on *keeping* what is revealed in this book (v. 9; cf. 1:3; 22:7). And the third, another component of the initial inclusio in verse 6 ("things that must soon take place"), is now modified to "the time is near" (v. 10; cf. 1:3).

The inclusio structure is very clear in what it wishes to teach. The seven churches are facing the events revealed in this book. To cope with such immediate realities, they must keep (or obey) the spiritual guidelines laid down by the Spirit and communicated through John.

John has been genuinely unnerved by the Revelation he has received ("I fell down"; cf. Dan. 10:7–9), which perhaps partly explains the continued temptation of angel worship (cf. 19:10). But also, he senses that the challenge of this message and its claims on his and his people's lives demand action, not complacency. To keep Revelation's message means to become involved, to be the church by implementing the purposes of God. The goal of the book is, not a mind crammed with facts and speculations, but a life galvanized into action. This is its challenge for the seven churches, and its message must be kept *now!*

In contradistinction to Revelation, the Old Testament's single apocalyptic book, Daniel, is admonished to keep its message *sealed* until the end (Dan. 12:4,9; cf. Isa. 8:16), which is seemingly somewhat distant. No such admonishment appears in the Revelation, for the time is near at hand. Surely, John's time assessment was correct; his generation engaged the same realities and dynamics of spiritual warfare that have continued since the death of Jesus: "For our struggle is...against the powers of this dark world and against the spiritual forces of evil in the heavenly realms.... *Stand firm then*" (Eph. 6:12–14, emphasis added). This is the battle that every generation of Christians faces no matter when they live or what face of the beast is bared in their day.

22:12–14 • The coming of the Lord should be a spur to holiness of life, not date setting, and is meant to motivate the keeping of this book and its call to a completely committed lifestyle. This great hope of the church does not produce a calendar for sophomoric voyeurs; it intends to change us and the way we engage our world. John elsewhere explains that "everyone who has this hope in him purifies himself, just as he is pure" (1 John 3:3). No doubt, John would also agree with Paul's counsel: "Therefore, my dear brothers, stand firm. Let nothing move you. Always give yourselves fully to the work of the Lord...your labor in the Lord is not in vain" (1 Cor. 15:58). Not in vain, indeed, is your work because rewards for life lived here are reserved for the faithful in the Holy City (cf. Dan. 12:13; Luke 6:23; 1 Cor. 3:14; 9:17). Here, John agrees fully: "Watch out that you do not lose what you have worked for, but that you may be rewarded fully" (2 John 8).

The "reward" the Lord returns bringing is eternal life, life in the

Holy City; this is the redemption to which all God's people have looked forward since the beginning of time. The final beatitude, number seven, is a tribute to all those who will receive this reward. Because they have "washed their robes" in the blood of the Lamb (cf. 7:14), they will now be granted eternal life, that is, access "through the gates into the city" to the "tree of life." If the NRSV margin reading at 1:5 is correct ("*washed* us from our sins by his blood," emphasis added), then this may be one more inclusio, distinguishing the dual nature of redemption. What redemption requires of us is ultimately only made possible by and in reaction to what Christ has first done. He has made a motion; we must second it! So much for those who are now "insiders."

22:15 • As for the "outsiders," John now gives us the second of two vice lists in Revelation (cf. 21:8). They bear a marked similarity to Paul's (1 Cor. 6:9–10; 1 Tim. 1:10). Jointly, they remind us that there are very definite exclusionary lines drawn around this city, over which some may not pass. But let no one imagine that God has willingly purposed their eternal expulsion from this, their originally intended home. Scripture is unequivocal on this matter. God does not send people away into outer darkness; God has never desired that. Quite the contrary, Jesus explicitly proclaimed that through his crucifixion, he would draw *all* to himself (John 12:32), while Paul further observed that God "wants all men to be saved and to come to a knowledge of the truth" (1 Tim. 2:4). Peter adds that the Lord is "not wanting anyone to perish, but everyone to come to repentance" (2 Pet. 3:9).

Hell is a memorial to the gravity and significance of free moral agency. God seeks to spend eternity, not with redeemed robots, but with companions who have chosen the divine presence freely. The real truth is that people send themselves to hell, against the expressed wishes of the Creator. But that is the nature of hell; it is where God treats all creatures as adults. There God respects, takes seriously, and accepts the free moral choices they have made, for the one thing love never engages in is coercion. As C. S. Lewis once remarked, in the end there will be just two kinds of people, those who say to God, "Thy will be done," and enter into the joy of their Lord, and those to whom God says, with tears in his eyes, "Thy will be done" as they walk away into outer darkness, where there is weeping and wailing and gnashing of teeth (*The Great Divorce*, 72).

Most of the classes of persons denied access to the Holy City are obvious choices for exclusion. But what of "dogs"? Some of us are more or less certain that dogs would have to be included in any blissful future. The New International Version suggests that the categories in the remainder of verse 15 define the term *dogs*. Most versions, however, take this term to be a separate designation of some aberrant lifestyle. If the latter is accurate, John might have thought the word to contain a quite special connotation. Because of its use in Deuteronomy 23:17–18 (see NRSV) to designate male prostitutes who worked in the Canaanite shrines, the rabbis often used the term *dog* to refer to homosexuals (Metzger, 106).[8] In an even broader sense, it could also mean (impure) "Gentiles" (Matt. 15:22–27; cf. Matt. 7:6). For Paul, dogs are part of a group that includes Judaizers (Phil. 3:2; cf. Gal. 5:12).[9] It is not clear in this passage which background John had in mind, conceivably all, though Gentiles and overly conservative Judaizers are not the likely candidates.

John observes, however, that all of these groupings practice "falsehood." This is a way of saying that their lives are closely aligned with their father, "that ancient serpent . . . who leads the whole world astray (12:9; NRSV: "the deceiver of the whole world"; cf. 13:14). Their being represents the essence of falsity because their wickedness suppresses and distorts the essential nature of God's truth concerning creation and God's will for all creatures (Rom. 1:18). The divine image no longer shines through them, only the dark, spiny shadows of the beast, and their lives cloak the presence of the supreme liar (John 8:44).

22:16–17 • The entire revelation to John has been, from beginning to end, "for the churches." Never forget that this book was meant for church people, not quacks or cults, not even theologians, but plainly for all the people of the seven churches. We must do all that we can to once again make it available to them: "Blessed is the one who" (1:3) *teaches* this book to those who live among the seven churches (1:4).

The one who has revealed this message for the churches is not only the descendant ("offspring") of David, heretofore Israel's most illustrious king, but also David's own ancestor ("root"), for as Jesus also claimed, "Before Abraham was born, I am!" (John 8:58). Indeed, "he is before all things, and in him all things hold together" (Col. 1:17). Thus, he is both David's forebear and his offspring, progenitor and progeny, as only the Son of God could possibly be. He is also the "bright Morning Star" of eternity's yet untold story (a title falsely claimed by other kings; cf. Isa. 14:12; Rev. 9:1), for he is the only dawning of true life. "Come!" is the only reasonable response when what is coming is an "Omega" that is also "Alpha," a "last" that has been foreordained from the "first" and an "ending" that is the genuine "beginning" of a bright and brilliant future (22:13).

Are the churches and those outside thirsty for what God offers? Do they have ears to listen to the Spirit's voice? Those who wish to share in the continuing story of the universe are invited, for the final time, to come and take the "water of life." It is their invitation to merge with the stream of reality surging into the future's yet unknown channels; they too may partake of all that is yet to be.

To drink of those waters suggests, minimally, that one will have access to the seven blessings mentioned throughout this book. What does it mean to enjoy and manifest these beatitudes? They stand for (1) a life that proclaims and manifests this Revelation from Jesus (1:3); (2) purposeful labor aimed at the achievement of a final rest enshrined and sanctified by many accomplishments (14:13); (3) an expectant lifestyle, alert and ever-vigilant for the Bridegroom's approach (16:15); (4) an open invitation to join the festivities of the Lamb's wedding (19:9); (5) a part in the first resurrection so that the second death is no longer a threat (20:6); (6) a faithful obedience to the "words" of this prophecy (22:7); (7) and a life washed in the blood of the Lamb so that one might enjoy the eternal fruit of the tree of life (22:14). This is what life in the new garden of Eden, already inaugurated in the church but not yet fully finalized, is meant to be.

22:18–19 • The final warning not to increase or diminish the substance of this volume is an echo of a similar charge given to Israel by Moses. The passage in Deuteronomy, however, explains through parallel statements what these processes of increasing or diminishing the book really stand for: "Do not add to what I command you and do not subtract from it, but keep the commands of the LORD your God that I give you" (Deut. 4:2). What does it mean not to add or subtract? Quite simply, it is to *do all I command you; do not add to it or take away from it*" (Deut. 12:32, emphasis added). This concept has little to do with expanding or diminishing the canon of Scripture, nor is it pronounced primarily against cultic tinkering with the Bible. It is plainly addressed to the seven churches, to Christians. As Moses spoke to Israel of old, so now its descendants are similarly warned: Do not fail to comply, conform to, and heed the teaching of this book. Here is an injunction from the Lord, and while originally intended to apply to this book, it surely includes all of Scripture.

The penalty attached is, indeed, dire. To fail to live up to the prophetic message of the Revelation is to endure the "plagues" and lose forever the tree of life in the Holy City. This, of course, indicates that those plagues described in the Revelation must be operative and available in every generation, even as those who are potentially the violators of these injunctions are. The plagues (trumpets and bowls) are not merely descriptions of events to take place eventually as futurists suggest; they are forever our contemporaries.

Nothing can be added and nothing ought to be deleted, because this book is a survival manual *for the seven churches.* It was never meant to be abused in the fashion of the cults (to distort Christian doctrine), the millennial maniacs (to promote date setting), or the escapists (to flee involvement in a troubled world). No! Its first readers and John himself fought earnestly for the right to enter into its hope by heroic involvement in the pain and pleasure, the agony and ecstasy, of the here and now. They struggled long and hard, maintaining the faith that we too might enter into the fruit of their labors. Now, like the endless succession of waves that fall on the shore, it is our turn; we are the generation, the churches, surging toward the coastline of the future.

22:20 • Finally, the last inclusio element arrives, hearkening back to the opening of the book: "Look, he is coming with the clouds, / and every eye will see him, / even those who pierced him; / and all the peoples of the earth will mourn because of him. / So shall it be! Amen" (1:7). The inclusio pattern of themes serves to remind us of those issues we were meant to take note of throughout the book. And the expectation of Christ's soon appearing is one of these core themes. Revelation is not a completely new set of doctrines or unique, esoteric knowledge concerning God; it is a grand summary of the whole counsel of Scripture, now revolving around Jesus Christ and his revelation. It is given as a "sacrament of the imagination" (Wilcock, 222), a work of pure art to round out the biblical doctrine of the Messiah; this is the Revelation of Jesus Christ.

In John's final plea, "Come, Lord Jesus," there echoes one of the first prayers shared among the earliest churches. What the "Doxology" is in many modern congregations, a regular staple of our liturgy, this simple prayer was to the first Christians. It is found in 1 Corinthians 16:22, where the Aramaic phrase *Marana tha* is translated as "Come, O Lord!" For Christians of all times, and for those who have grasped the message of this book, the urgent issue is no longer a question of dates but preparing for the Groom's arrival. This is where life according to the beast is so deficient. It *was,* and it is *to come,* but it is never really *present* (17:8). Yes, it plays with and distorts our understanding of the past, it promises its own fraudulent version of the future, but it never keeps faith in the present. There is a sense of emptiness where the past is concerned, and while there may be twisted hopes for what is coming, the present is never fulfilling, never genuine contentment. It deals, not with things that *are* — that genuinely exist — but with what is not. It is the great *"No,"* the quest for illusions that always ends in emptiness. There is only one who lives in and masters all the time periods, all the seasons of reality — "For in him we live and move and have our being" (Acts 17:28).

Christians had frequently prayed this prayer, *Marana tha,* as they celebrated the Lord's Supper. For there at the table Jesus had continuously made himself *present,* by way of *remembrance,* and each successive celebration also pointed to *a future* banquet that would again be shared immediately with the Lord himself (Matt. 26:29; Luke 14:15; 22:18,30; Rev. 19:9). The Revelation began on "the Lord's day" (1:10), and now it concludes by anticipating the ultimate day of the Lord, that is, the endless banquet of messianic joy yet to come.

22:21 • "The grace of the Lord Jesus be with God's people. Amen."

Notes

1. Gordon Fee similarly suggests, "We need to learn that pictures of the future are just that — pictures. The pictures express a reality but they are not themselves to be confused with the reality, nor are the details of every picture necessarily to be 'fulfilled' in some specific way" (Fee and Stuart, 243).

2. And let us never forget those seven cities include Evanston, Savannah, Poughkeepsie, Tucson, Seattle, Palm Beach, and Los Angeles, as well as many others around the world, wherever God's people are contending with Satan's System.

3. George Ladd's comment catches the biblical and Hebraic thrust of these words: "Throughout the entire Bible, the ultimate destiny of God's people is an earthly destiny. In typical dualistic Greek thought, the universe was divided into two realms: the earthly or transitory, and the eternal spiritual world. Salvation consisted of the flight of the soul from the sphere of the transitory and ephemeral to the realm of eternal reality" (*Commentary on the Revelation,* 275).

4. "What is spoken of here is not in opposition to the creation of Genesis, or the destruction of it to replace it with something quite different; it is rather the continuation, the perfection of that first creation" (Corsini, 392).

5. Among the many who take the eternal city as a metaphor for the everlasting people of God are Robert Gundry ("The New Jerusalem," 254–64), Robert Mounce (*What Are We Waiting For?* 111), and Robert Wall (243–45).

6. If we consider the whole city to be one massive temple, a place where God is served, this may alleviate a perceived tension between this text and John's description of the saints emerging from the tribulation who are said to "serve him day and night in his temple" (7:15). Furthermore, "day and

night" would mean "all the time" and would thus not contradict the "no night" of 21:25. In any event, John means to say, not that in the renewal of creation half of each day (night) ceases to exist, but rather that it no longer suffers from the impediment of darkness.

7. Notice that John continues to link the Lamb with the Almighty (one temple and one light). The prominence of Trinitarian thought, that absolute equality among the Father, Son, and Holy Spirit, continues to reveal itself as a hallmark of the Revelation (cf. 1:4–5).

8. This is the view of R. H. Charles (2:178). For a more recent appraisal of this connection between the word *dogs* and homosexuality, see the work of Thomas E. Schmidt (97–98), which is one of the premier available volumes, stressing traditional views on this controversial subject.

9. The term *Judaizers* describes very conservative Jewish Christians who opposed Paul's bringing Gentiles into what had been a purely Jewish Christian community. They would have viewed him as a destructive liberal force in the early church's life.

WORKS CITED

Anderson, Robert A. *Signs and Wonders: A Commentary on the Book of Daniel.* International Theological Commentary. Grand Rapids: Eerdmans, 1984.

Armerding, Carl E., and W. Ward Gasque, eds. *Dreams, Visions & Oracles: The Layman's Guide to Biblical Prophecy.* Grand Rapids: Baker, 1977.

Aune, David E. "Revelation." In *Harper's Bible Commentary,* ed. James L. Mays. San Francisco: Harper & Row, 1988, 1300–1319.

Baker, Wesley C. *Hope in This World.* Philadelphia: Westminster, 1970.

Barclay, William. *Letters to the Seven Churches.* Living Church Books. London: SCM Press, 1964.

———. *The Revelation of John.* 2 vols. 2d ed. Philadelphia: Westminster, 1960.

Bauckham, Richard. *The Theology of the Book of Revelation.* Cambridge: Cambridge University Press, 1993.

Beale, G. K. "Interpretive Problem of Revelation 1:19." *Novum Testamentum* 34 (1992): 360–87.

Beasley-Murray, G. R. *The Book of Revelation.* New Century Bible Commentary. Grand Rapids: Eerdmans, 1981.

———. *Jesus and the Future.* London: Macmillan, 1954.

Berdyaev, Nicholas. *Dream and Reality.* New York: Macmillan, 1951.

Blevins, James L. *Revelation as Drama.* Nashville: Broadman Press, 1984.

Boring, M. Eugene. *Revelation.* Interpretation: A Bible Commentary for Teaching and Preaching. Louisville: John Knox, 1989.

———. "Revelation 19–21: End without Closure." *Princeton Seminary Bulletin* 3 (1994): 83–84.

Bowman, John W. "Revelation, Book of." *The Interpreter's Dictionary of the Bible,* ed. George Arthur Buttrick. New York: Abingdon, 1962, 4:58–71.

Bruce, F. F. *Israel and the Nations.* Grand Rapids: Eerdmans, 1969.

Brueggemann, Walter. *The Prophetic Imagination.* Philadelphia: Fortress, 1978.

Caird, G. B. *A Commentary on the Revelation of St. John the Divine.* Harper's New Testament Commentaries. New York: Harper & Row, 1966.

Carrington, Philip. *The Meaning of the Revelation.* London: SPCK, 1931.

Charles, R. H. *A Critical and Exegetical Commentary on the Revelation of St. John.* 2 vols. International Critical Commentary. Edinburgh: T. & T. Clark, 1920.

Charlesworth, Martin P. *Trade Routes and Commerce of the Roman Empire.* 2d ed. New York: Cooper Square, 1970.

Chesterton, G. K. *Orthodoxy.* New York: John Lane, 1908.

289

Clouse, Robert G., ed. *The Meaning of the Millennium: Four Views.* Downers Grove, Ill.: InterVarsity Press, 1977.

Collins, Adela Yarbro. *The Apocalypse.* New Testament Message 22. Wilmington, Del.: Michael Glazier, 1982.

———. *Crisis and Catharsis: The Power of the Apocalypse.* Philadelphia: Westminster, 1984.

Collins, John J., ed. *Apocalypse: The Morphology of a Genre.* Semeia 14. Missoula, Mont.: Society of Biblical Literature, 1979.

———. *The Apocalyptic Imagination.* New York: Crossroad, 1984.

Cornfeld, Gaalyah, and David Noel Freedman. *Archaeology of the Bible: Book by Book.* San Francisco: Harper & Row, 1976.

Corsini, Eugenio. *The Apocalypse: The Perennial Revelation of Jesus Christ.* Good News Studies 5. Trans. Francis J. Moloney. Wilmington, Del.: Michael Glazier, 1983.

Court, John M. *Myth and History in the Book of Revelation.* Atlanta: John Knox, 1979.

Crockett, William, ed. *Four Views on Hell.* Grand Rapids: Zondervan, 1992.

Davies, Graham I. *Megiddo.* Cities of the Biblical World. Cambridge: Lutterworth Press, 1986.

Dodd, C. H. *The Apostolic Preaching and Its Development.* 3d ed. New York: Harper & Row, 1963.

Eller, Vernard. *The Most Revealing Book of the Bible: Making Sense out of Revelation.* Grand Rapids: Eerdmans, 1974.

Ellul, Jacques. *Apocalypse: The Book of Revelation.* Crossroad Book. Trans. George W. Schreiner. New York: Seabury Press, 1977.

Ewing, Ward. *The Power of the Lamb: Revelation's Theology of Liberation for You.* Cambridge, Mass.: Cowley Publications, 1990.

Farrer, Austin. *The Revelation of St. John the Divine.* Oxford: Clarendon Press, 1964.

Fee, Gordon D., and Douglas Stuart. *How to Read the Bible for All Its Worth.* 2d ed. Grand Rapids: Zondervan, 1993.

Finegan, Jack. *The Archeology of the New Testament: The Life of Jesus and the Beginning of the Early Church.* Rev. ed. Princeton: Princeton University Press, 1992.

Fiorenza, Elisabeth Schüssler. *The Book of Revelation: Justice and Judgment.* Philadelphia: Fortress, 1985.

———. *Revelation: Vision of a Just World.* Proclamation Commentaries. Minneapolis: Fortress, 1991.

Ford, Josephine Massyngberde. *Revelation.* Anchor Bible. Garden City, N.Y.: Doubleday, 1975.

Gammie, John G. *Daniel.* Knox Preaching Guides. Atlanta: John Knox, 1983.

George, David C., ed. *Revelation: Three Viewpoints.* Nashville: Broadman Press, 1977.

Goldingay, John E. *Daniel.* Word Biblical Commentary. Dallas: Word, 1989.

———. *Daniel.* Word Biblical Themes. Dallas: Word, 1989.

Green, Joel B. *How to Read Prophecy*. Downers Grove, Ill.: InterVarsity Press, 1984.

Grenz, Stanley J. *The Millennial Maze: Sorting Out Evangelical Options*. Downers Grove, Ill.: InterVarsity Press, 1992.

Gundry, Robert H. *The Church and the Tribulation*. Grand Rapids: Zondervan, 1973.

———. "The New Jerusalem: People as Place, Not Place for People." *Novum Testamentum* 29 (1987): 254–64.

Guthrie, Donald. *New Testament Introduction: Hebrews to Revelation*. Chicago: InterVarsity Press, 1962.

———. *The Relevance of John's Apocalypse*. Grand Rapids: Eerdmans, 1987.

Hanson, Paul D., ed. *Visionaries and Their Apocalypses*. Issues in Religion and Theology 2. Philadelphia: Fortress, 1983.

Harrington, Wilfrid J. *Understanding the Apocalypse*. Washington, D.C.: Corpus Books, 1969.

Harrison, Everett F. *Introduction to the New Testament*. Grand Rapids: Eerdmans, 1964.

Hayes, John H. *Introduction to the Bible*. Philadelphia: Westminster, 1971.

Hemer, Colin J. *The Letters to the Seven Churches of Asia in Their Local Setting*. Journal for the Study of the New Testament — Supplement Series 11. Sheffield, U.K.: JSOT Press, 1986.

Hendricksen, W. *More Than Conquerors: An Interpretation of the Book of Revelation*. Grand Rapids: Baker, 1940.

Hughes, Philip Edgcumbe. *Interpreting Prophecy*. Grand Rapids: Eerdmans, 1976.

Kaiser, Walter C., Jr. *Back toward the Future: Hints for Interpreting Biblical Prophecy*. Grand Rapids: Baker, 1989.

Kiddle, Martin. *The Revelation of St. John*. Moffatt New Testament Commentary. New York: Harper & Row, 1941.

Klausner, Joseph. *Jesus of Nazareth: His Life, Times, and Teaching*. Trans. Herbert Danby. Boston: Beacon Press, 1964.

Koch, Klaus. *The Rediscovery of Apocalyptic*. Studies in Biblical Theology, 2d ser., 22. London: SCM Press, 1972.

Ladd, George E. *A Commentary on the Revelation of John*. Grand Rapids: Eerdmans, 1972.

———. "Why Not Prophetic-Apocalyptic?" *Journal of Biblical Literature* 76 (1957): 192–200.

Lawrence, D. H. *Apocalypse*. Harmondsworth, U.K.: Penguin, 1960.

Laws, Sophie. *In the Light of the Lamb: Imagery, Parody, and Theology in the Apocalypse of John*. Good News Studies 31. Wilmington, Del.: Michael Glazier, 1988.

Lederach, Paul M. *Daniel*. Believer's Church Bible Commentary. Scottdale, Pa.: Herald Press, 1994.

Levy, Steven. "Will the Bug Bite the Bull?" *Newsweek*, 4 May 1998, 62.

Lewis, C. S. *The Great Divorce.* A Touchstone Book. New York: Simon & Schuster, 1946.

———. *The Problem of Pain.* Fontana Books. London: Collins, 1967.

Lindsey, Hal, with C. C. Carlson. *The Late Great Planet Earth.* Grand Rapids: Zondervan, 1970.

Linthicum, Robert C. *City of God, City of Satan: A Biblical Theology of the Urban Church.* Grand Rapids: Zondervan, 1991.

Love, Julian P. *The Revelation to John.* Layman's Bible Commentary. Richmond: John Knox, 1960.

Metzger, Bruce. *Breaking the Code: Understanding the Book of Revelation.* Nashville: Abingdon, 1993.

Michaels, J. Ramsey. *Interpreting the Book of Revelation.* Guides to New Testament Exegesis. Grand Rapids: Baker, 1992.

———. "Revelation 1:19 and the Narrative Voices of the Apocalypse." *New Testament Studies* 37 (1991): 604–20.

Michelson, A. Berkeley. *Daniel & Revelation: Riddles or Realities?* Nashville: Thomas Nelson, 1984.

Miladin, George C. *Is This Really the End? A Reformed Analysis of* The Late Great Planet Earth. Cherry Hill, N.J.: Mack Publishing, 1972.

Milne, Bruce. "The Message of John: Here Is Your King!" in *The Bible Speaks Today* [NT ed. John R. W. Stott]. Leicester, U.K.: Inter-Varsity Press, 1993.

Minear, Paul S. *I Saw a New Earth: An Introduction to the Visions of the Apocalypse.* Washington, D.C.: Corpus Books, 1968.

Morris, Leon. *The Book of Revelation: An Introduction and Commentary.* Rev. ed. Tyndale New Testament Commentaries. Grand Rapids: Eerdmans, 1987.

Mounce, Robert H. *The Book of Revelation.* New International Commentary on the New Testament 17. Grand Rapids: Eerdmans, 1977.

———. *What Are We Waiting For? A Commentary on Revelation.* Grand Rapids: Eerdmans, 1992.

Mulholland, M. Robert, Jr. *Revelation: Holy Living in an Unholy World.* Francis Asbury Press Commentary. Grand Rapids: Zondervan, 1990.

Niles, D. T. *As Seeing the Invisible: A Study of the Book of Revelation.* London: SCM Press, 1964.

Peterson, Eugene H. *Reversed Thunder: The Revelation of John and the Praying Imagination.* San Francisco: Harper & Row, 1988.

Preston, Ronald H., and Anthony T. Hanson. *The Revelation of Saint John the Divine: The Book of Glory.* Torch Bible Commentaries. London: SCM Press, 1968.

Reznick, Leibel. *The Holy Temple Revisited.* Northvale, N.J.: Jason Aronson, 1993.

Richardson, Donald W. *The Revelation of Jesus Christ.* Atlanta: John Knox, 1976.

Rissi, Mathias. *Time and History: A Study on the Revelation.* Trans. Gordon C. Winsor. Richmond: John Knox, 1965.

Robbins, Ray Frank. *The Revelation of Jesus Christ.* Nashville: Broadman Press, 1975.

Rowley, H. H. *The Relevance of Apocalyptic.* 2d. ed. London: Lutterworth Press, 1947.

Rudwick, M. J. S., and E. M. B. Green. "The Laodicean Lukewarmness." *Expository Times* 69 (1957–58): 176–78.

Russell, D. S. *Daniel.* Daily Study Bible Series. Philadelphia: Westminster, 1981.

———. *The Method and Message of Jewish Apocalyptic.* Philadelphia: Westminster, 1964.

Sanders, E. P. *Judaism: Practice & Belief, 63 BCE-66 CE.* London: SCM Press, 1992.

Schmidt, Thomas E. *Straight & Narrow? Compassion & Clarity in the Homosexuality Debate.* Downers Grove, Ill.: InterVarsity Press, 1995.

Scofield, C. I., ed. *The Scofield Reference Bible.* New York: Oxford University Press, 1945.

Shepherd, Massey H., Jr. *The Paschal Liturgy and the Apocalypse.* Ecumenical Studies in Worship 6. Richmond: John Knox, 1960.

Smith, Christopher R. "Reclaiming the Social Justice Message of Revelation: Materialism, Imperialism, and Divine Judgement in Revelation 18." *Transformation* 7 (1990): 28–33.

Sternau, Cynthia, and Martin H. Greenberg, eds. *The Secret Prophecies of Nostradamus.* New York: MJF Books, 1995.

Stoffel, Ernest Lee. *The Dragon Bound: The Revelation Speaks to Our Time.* Atlanta: John Knox, 1981.

Swete, Henry Barclay. *The Apocalypse of St. John.* 3d ed. London: Macmillan, 1922.

Thompson, Leonard L. *The Book of Revelation: Apocalypse and Empire.* New York: Oxford University Press, 1990.

Wainwright, Arthur W. *Mysterious Apocalypse: Interpreting the Book of Revelation.* Nashville: Abingdon, 1993.

Walker, Peter W. L. *Jesus and the Holy City: New Testament Perspectives on Jerusalem.* Grand Rapids: Eerdmans, 1995.

Wall, Robert W. *Revelation.* New International Biblical Commentary. Peabody, Mass.: Hendrickson, 1991.

Walters, Stanley D. "Hal Lindsey: Recalculating the Second Coming." *Christian Century,* 12 September 1979, 839–40.

Walvoord, John F. *The Revelation of Jesus Christ.* Chicago: Moody, 1966.

Wilcock, Michael. *I Saw Heaven Opened: The Message of Revelation.* The Bible Speaks Today. Downers Grove, Ill.: InterVarsity Press, 1975.

SCRIPTURE INDEX

SUBJECT INDEX